RURAL LIFE AND URBANIZED SOCIETY

Rural Life
and Urbanized Society

LEE TAYLOR

ARTHUR R. JONES, Jr.

LOUISIANA STATE UNIVERSITY

NEW YORK

OXFORD UNIVERSITY PRESS 1964

Copyright © 1964 by Oxford University Press, Inc.
Library of Congress Catalogue Card Number: 64-11239
Printed in the United States of America

For Jackie and Donna

PREFACE

Changes in rural-urban life have been widespread in America. A profusion of rural sociology research has reported many of these significant changes. A new orientation in light of these changes is necessary if the student is to obtain a comprehensive understanding of human relations in rural America.

The purpose of this book is to present a new interpretation of rural life in America. This interpretation may be summarized by the concept *urbanized social organization*. The concept refers to the situation in which both rural and urban citizens live in relation to the same pattern of social organization. Conversely, it does not refer to an urban place of residence or to an urban way of life distinct from rural. The following examples illustrate this principle. The agricultural sector of this country faces governmental policies which affect food and fiber production, much as any other category of industry faces governmental policies which affect its functioning. A farmer may or may not feel the necessity to support an agricultural lobby or participate in a farm union movement, much as any other businessman may or may not support a lobby appropriate to his interests, or a city laborer participate in a trade union. In urbanized society the normative structure of lobbies, governmental policies for business enterprise, unions, and management-union bargaining is the same for the people regardless of whether they live in rural or urban places.

According to this thesis an entire population becomes subject to a common pattern of social organization. But the entire population does not respond to the dominant system of social organization in the same way. Behavioral differences among social classes and groups are readily observable, and an individual's behavior in urbanized society will reflect his age, sex, position in social groups, and social class background. Differences in the behavior patterns of rural and urban people will be apparent, as will differences between professionals and laborers in the city and between commercial business farmers and nonfarm laborers in rural areas. These differences, however, are the result of different characteristics of the respective social groups and not of separate systems of social organization operating for the city and for the country.

Although the primary concept, urbanized social organization, has been derived from the analysis of contemporary research data, a historical perspective is evident throughout the work. Such a perspective provides an adequate background against which to view contemporary change in rural life and the developing social structures of urbanized society. In Part I the concept is laid out in some detail. In order to place the concept in relief a brief analysis is presented of a society characterized by ruralized social organization. Such a society is seen to be in sharp contrast to contemporary life. To illustrate ruralized social organization, the middle period of the Middle Ages in West-Central Europe and England is briefly described. During that period the social organization in those areas was completely rural. From the Middle Ages through the seventeenth century and part of the eighteenth, Western society was characterized by dynamic rural-urban differences. These differences marked the period of transition from ruralized social organization to urbanized social organization.

North America was colonized during this period of dynamic rural-urban differentiation in Western Europe. Colonial America appeared to be characterized by ruralized social organization during the seventeenth century more because of its physical wilderness than ideology. The position is taken in this book that in order to understand the rapid transition from rural to urban life in the United States, one must first understand the earlier shift from ruralized social organization to rural-urban differentiation in Europe. The American scene was a continuation of that period and not an ideological reversion to ruralized social organization. Consequently, it was possible for American society to move quickly toward urbanized social organization, that is, for an entire national life to be dominated by urban-derived social structures. The subject of this book concerns, therefore, all of the contemporary human relations in open-country America. The subject is broader than farmers, or even the food and fiber industry as a whole.

In Part II special attention is given to all populations in rural areas— rural farm, nonfarm, and suburban—and their social interaction. No longer is it correct to associate rurality with agriculture, as though agriculture were the only activity in rural areas. The proportion of nonfarm people in rural areas is greater now than the proportion of farm people. In the rural labor force the number of persons who are employed in operative and laboring types of work is greater than the number of farmers. Locating industry in rural areas has resulted in the expansion of the rural labor market and, consequently, in the absorption of many workers who have not been able to enter farming as an occupation.

Many rural-nonfarm people have maintained residence in open-country places, while many others have moved to the rural-urban fringe to live among exurbanites. This merging population phenomenon has had the effect of greatly reducing the sharp contrast between rural and urban ways of life. The rural-urban fringe fades into both the city and the country and provides a continuous pattern of socially interrelated populations living under one dominant system of organization. As the national population has increased, the physical boundaries of cities have moved deeper into rural areas, and small country towns have grown into small urban places. Children from farm families have moved to cities and many have maintained close family ties with relatives in rural areas. The growing value of outdoor recreation has brought a large number of vacationing itinerants into wilderness areas and into the open country. Improvements in transportation and increased utilization of the mass media, along with the above factors, have brought urbanized social organization into rural areas.

The importance of urbanized social organization for rural life is reflected in the developing social structure of food and fiber production. In Part III vertical integration and agribusiness are discussed as contemporary developments in which there is an interdependent relationship between agricultural suppliers, farmers, and agricultural product distributors and processors. Within this structure the application of modern science and technology to agriculture by professionals and specialists has resulted in spectacular progress in food and fiber production. With the aid of specialists and technical experts, trained mostly in the nation's land-grant college system, farm workers (6 per cent of the labor force in 1960) have been able to overproduce for the national food and fiber needs. Part IV treats family life, schools, religion, politics, health and welfare, and the artistic expressions of rural people as each of these have been influenced by the dominant social values and national goals of urbanized society. Special consideration is given to the inclusion of research data from all regions of the United States.

This volume may be regarded from two different aspects. Its descriptive treatment of research data is comprehensive and can stand by itself for the person who wants only a description of rural life. On the other hand, the authors have organized the research data into a systematic treatment of the concept of urbanized social organization. This systematic treatment is important for the professional student of human behavior.

Specific acknowledgment is made for encouragement and intellectual stimulation given to the authors by Don Martindale and Alvin L. Bertrand. Special recognition is also accorded to those teachers, colleagues, and friends who have directly and indirectly furthered the preparation of this book—namely, Gordon Bultena, Roy G. Francis, Rudolf Heberle, Homer L. Hitt, A. Dean McKenzie, Lowry Nelson, Vernon J. Parenton, Roland J. Pellegrin, and George B. Vold. To earlier teachers who showed us a depth in the meaning of life and a way of scholarship, Ralph Lynn, Lowell C. Pratt, and Ruth Tiedeman, special appreciation is due.

Special acknowledgment is also extended to the Farm Campus Library staff of the University of Minnesota and to the many Louisiana State University librarians who contributed professionally and enthusiastically to our research. The preparation of the manuscript was greatly facilitated by the environment in the Louisiana State University Department of Sociology and Rural Sociology and by the Louisiana State University Graduate School.

The compilation of this manuscript represents a joint effort on the part of both authors. The initial formulation of the thesis and the major task of the first draft were the responsibility of Lee Taylor. The collaborative effort grew out of a period of joint study and research. The final form of this book reflects the thinking and research of both authors.

The entire manuscript was proofread by Mrs. Ruth S. Kugel and Dr. Audrey F. Borenstein, an invaluable service which the authors greatly appreciate. Mrs. Jacquelin Taylor typed much of the first draft of the manuscript and read the entire work during its many stages. It is with deepest appreciation that we recognize the understanding and encouragement of our wives, Jackie and Donna, throughout the preparation of this manuscript.

Baton Rouge, Louisiana   LEE TAYLOR
January 1964   ARTHUR R. JONES, JR.

ACKNOWLEDGMENTS

Acknowledgment is made to the following authors, publishers, and agents who have granted permission to reprint excerpts from copyrighted publications.

American Academy of Political and Social Science for excerpts from: Lauren K. Soth, "Farm Policy, Foreign Policy, and Farm Opinion," *Annals of the American Academy of Political and Social Science,* 331 (Sept., 1960).

American Farm Economics Association for excerpts from: Stefan H. Robock, "Rural Industries and Agricultural Development," *Journal of Farm Economics,* 34 (Aug., 1952).

Appleton-Century-Crofts for excerpts from: Richard G. Boone, *Education in the United States* (New York: Appleton-Century-Crofts, Inc., 1903).

Association of American Geographers for excerpts from: Wilber Zelinsky, "An Approach to the Religious Geography of the United States," *Annals of the Association of American Geographers,* 51 (June, 1961).

Beacon Press for excerpts from: Arnold Toynbee, *The Industrial Revolution* (Boston: Beacon Press, 1956).

Columbia University Press for excerpts from: Ralph Foster Weld, *Brooklyn Village, 1816-1834* (New York: Columbia University Press, 1938), and James West, *Plainville, U.S.A.* (New York: Columbia University Press, 1945).

Drew Theological Seminary for excerpts from: Ralph A. Felton, *New Ministers* (Madison, N.J.: Drew Theological Seminary, 1949).

The Free Press of Glencoe, Inc., for excerpts from: Walter Goldschmidt, *As You Sow* (New York: Harcourt, Brace and Co., Inc., 1947), and Anselm L. Strauss, *Images of the American City* (New York: The Free Press of Glencoe, Inc., 1961).

Harper and Row, Publishers, for excerpts from: E. B. White, *Here Is New York* (New York: Harper and Brothers, Inc., 1949).

Harvard Business School for excerpts from: John H. Davis and Ray A. Goldberg, *A Concept of Agribusiness* (Boston: Harvard Business School, Division of Research, 1957).

Harvard University Press for excerpts from: John Sirjamaki, *The American Family in the Twentieth Century* (Cambridge: Harvard University Press, 1953).

Houghton Mifflin Company for a figure titled "A Typical Manor": Wallace K. Ferguson and Geoffery Brunn, *A Survey of European Civilization* (2nd ed., Boston: Houghton Mifflin Co., 1947).

Iowa State University Press for excerpts from: Don F. Hadwiger, "Political Aspects of Changes in Farm Labor Force," in *Labor Mobility and Population in Agriculture* (Ames: Iowa State University Press, 1961).

Johnson Reprint Corporation for excerpts from: Charles Lively, Introduction, *Rural Sociology,* 18 (June, 1953).

Alfred A. Knopf for excerpts from: Sidney Painter, *A History of the Middle Ages, 284–1500* (New York: Alfred A. Knopf, Inc., 1953).

McGraw-Hill Book Company, Inc. for excerpts from: Ronald Freedman, *et al., Family Planning, Sterility, and Population Growth* (New York: McGraw-Hill Book Co., 1959).

Methuen and Co. Ltd., Publishers, for excerpts from: Eileen Power, *Medieval People* (New York: Doubleday Anchor Books, 1954).

The New Scientist for excerpts from: L. Dudley Stamp, "Planning the Use of Land," *The New Scientist,* 8 (Aug. 25, 1960).

The New York Times for excerpts from: "Country Dining in Manhattan," *New York Times Magazine* (July 14, 1957), and Kenneth S. Davis, "The Challenge of the Country Church," *New York Times Magazine* (May 22, 1955).

Princeton University Press for excerpts from: Henri Pirenne, *Medieval Cities* (New York: Doubleday Anchor Books, 1956).

Resources for the Future, Inc., for excerpts from: Marion Clawson, *Statistics on Outdoor Recreation* (Washington, Resources for the Future, 1958).

Routledge and Kegan Paul, Ltd., for excerpts from: John Saville, *Rural Depopulation in England and Wales, 1851–1951* (London: Routledge and Kegan Paul, Ltd., 1957).

Charles Scribner's Sons for excerpts from: Jesse Lynch Williams, "Back to the Town," *Scribner Magazine,* 58 (1915).

Stanford University Press for excerpts from: William Carol Bark, *Origins of the Medieval World* (New York: Doubleday Anchor Books, 1960).

Twentieth Century Fund for excerpts from: Murray R. Benedict, *Farm Policies of the United States, 1790–1950: A Study of Their Origins and Development* (New York: The Twentieth Century Fund, 1953).

University of California Press for excerpts from: John C. Bollens, *Special District Governments in the United States* (Berkeley: University of California Press, 1957).

University of Illinois Press for excerpts from: Wayne D. Rasmussen, (ed.), *Readings in the History of American Agriculture* (Urbana: University of Illinois Press, 1960), and Marion Clawson, "Land Use and the Demand for Land in the United States," in *Modern Land Policy* (Urbana: University of Illinois Press, 1960).

University of Michigan for excerpts from: Don J. Bogne, *The Structure of the Metropolitan Community* (Ann Arbor: University of Michigan Press, 1949).

University of Minnesota for excerpts from: Pitirim A. Sorokin *et al., A Systematic Source Book in Rural Sociology,* Vol. I (Minneapolis: University of Minnesota Press, 1930).

University of North Carolina Press for excerpts from: Edward Jerome Dies, *Titans of the Soil* (Chapel Hill: University of North Carolina Press, 1949).

C. A. Watts and Co., Ltd., for excerpts from: Raymond Firth, *Elements of Social Organization* (London: C. A. Watts and Co., Ltd., 1952).

John Wiley and Sons, Inc., for excerpts from: Otis D. Duncan and Albert J. Reiss, Jr., *Social Characteristics of Urban and Rural Communities, 1950* (New York: John Wiley and Sons, Inc., 1956).

CONTENTS

IV SOCIAL INSTITUTIONS IN URBANIZED SOCIETY

I SOCIAL ORGANIZATION AND RURAL–URBAN DIFFERENCES

1 MEDIEVAL LIFE:
RURALIZED SOCIAL ORGANIZATION

The history of human society has been largely the history of rural life. Indeed, it has been estimated that in the population of the world today, four out of every five people still live in rural areas. The dominance of rural life is clearly apparent in China, India, Africa, South America, and Central America. Although there are mammoth cities [1] in all these areas, the great masses of population have little contact with them.

The historical predominance of rural life is emphasized for two reasons. In the first place, the contemporary American is likely to be immersed in urban life. Unless he is equipped with an adequate knowledge of history, he is prone to overlook the historic, massive rural nature of the world. In the second place, an awareness of the dominance of rural life provides the necessary perspective for a study of urbanized social organization. Any understanding of contemporary American life is grossly incomplete until it is placed within the context of historic rural life.

HISTORICAL PERSPECTIVE: THE MIDDLE AGES

One of the most completely rural eras of which we have a reasonable record is that of the Middle Ages in Western Europe. The social structures and human relations characteristic of the part of the Middle Ages between the ninth and eleventh centuries, in the area known today as England, France, and Germany, most clearly exemplify complete rural life. The total period of the Middle Ages is considered by scholars to extend from

3

approximately A.D. 200 to 1500. It covered all areas around the Mediterranean and north to the Norse Viking land. The ninth century was a period of transition from Roman to medieval civilization. The tenth and eleventh centuries constituted the heart of the medieval period. The fourteenth and fifteenth centuries have been treated as the period of transition to modern times by way of the Renaissance.[2]

Feudal social organization. The Middle Ages were not completely static, but nearly so. Feudalism dominated a social order which was not noted for change. The primary characteristic of feudal social structure was a relatively fixed social hierarchy in which a dozen or more social ranks were specified. The Domesday Survey of 34 English counties (1086) revealed the following social ranks.[3]

Social Ranks	Number	Per Cent
Villeins	108,456	38.4
Bordars	82,624	29.2
Servi	25,156	8.9
Sokemen	23,090	8.2
Liberi homines	12,384	4.4
Burgesses	7,968	2.8
Mesne lords	7,871	2.8
Cotters	6,818	2.4
Tenants-in-chief	1,400	0.5
Homines	1,287	0.4
Others	5,638	2.0
Total	282,692	100.0

There were many social ranks, but most people were represented in the categories *villeins, bordars, servi,* and *sokemen.* In some localities distinctions were not even made between *villeins* and *bordars.* In effect, they were all tenants with different amounts of land, animals, rights, and duties. They could make some decisions for themselves, but they were bound to the land. To this extent they were not free in terms of geographical mobility. *Servi* were personally unfree, and hence even lower in the hierarchy than villeins. *Sokemen* and *liberi homines* were occasionally treated as a higher class. They were a part of a superior tenancy category comprising *tenants-in-chief, mesne lords, liberi homines, radknights,* and others. *Tenants-in-chief* held land in direct charge from the king. *Mesne lords* held land from *tenants-in-chief* or other vassals in direct line to the king. *Porcarii* and *bovarii* cared for the herds, swine and oxen.[4]

Other distinctions of social rank were more spurious than real. Eileen Power indicated that the rank distinctions meant very little in daily living; moreover, they were merged into a large class of *villeins* in a few centuries' time.[5] It is nevertheless important to keep in mind that feudal society was stratified, that is, it was founded on the superordination and subordination of classes.

The second major characteristic of feudal society was the method of organization of the land for production. Villages were centered around a manor house in fertile farming areas. In poor agricultural areas, hamlets were developed in the absence of the manorial system.[6] In hamlet areas, land was exploited until exhausted and then a new plot was cultivated. In manorial village areas a three-field rotation system was used on the arable land. This manorial land division and social organization were most characteristic of the time.

Operation of a large manor was a major enterprise. It involved a labyrinth of details related to status, fees, and services. An agent or manager was in charge of the total operation and accountable to the lord. His title was *villein* or *major* on the Continent, and *steward* or *bailiff* in England. Originally the steward was appointed by the lord and was subject to dismissal, but in time his position became hereditary.

Produce was distributed among the tenants, barons, knights, bishops, abbots, and others. Allotments were based upon social rank. For every right to use land there was an established fee: for the use of arable land, a portion of one's oats and hay went to the lord; to fish, part of the catch went to the manor house; to run pigs in the woods, a portion of the pork, and so on. Such a system of food and fiber production was characteristically local and self-sufficing. No commerce or trade was needed, and very little existed.

Absence of trade and commerce. Urban life had proliferated during the height of the Roman Empire, but by the ninth century it had become virtually extinct. The civil wars of the third century led to a decline of commerce, and the ensuing Germanic invasions wrought destruction on cities. The Germanic tribes had no particular interest in cities, certainly no desire to live in them.

By the ninth century there was no question of the dominance of agricultural social organization, yet the physical presence of burgs and towns was never completely obliterated. The presence or absence of cities is in part a matter of definition. In his essay entitled *Medieval Cities,* Pirenne reported:

If by city is meant a locality the population of which, instead of living by cultivating the soil, devotes itself to commercial activity, the answer will have to be 'no.' The answer will also be negative if we understand by 'city' a community endowed with legal entity and possessing laws and institutions peculiar to itself. On the other hand, if we think of a city as a center of administration and as a fortress, it is clear that the Carolingian period knew nearly as many cities as the centuries which followed it must have known. That is merely another way of saying that the cities which were then to be found were without two of the fundamental attributes of the cities of . . . modern times—a middle class population and a communal organization.[7]

Towns in the ninth century had a far greater physical existence than social existence. For purposes of the study of human relations as contrasted, say, with the study of architecture, the ninth-century city was of no real importance. Indeed, the modern English word *town* originally meant an enclosure rather than a specific populace. In times of peace the ninth-century town was essentially void of inhabitants. People congregated there only for religious, civil, and social ceremonies. Commercial organization did not exist. Separate government for rural and urban areas was essentially meaningless. In time of attack or war the town enclosure served as a place of refuge and protection.

Lay people in medieval society typically did not live in cities; only bishops and other higher clergy took residence in them. The little prestige that cities possessed accrued from the importance of their clergy. Merchants who once plied the streets with their trade were absent and with them went the urban way of life. Even church organization was not urban. It was concerned with saving souls on either side of the city wall. Kingdoms or political areas were constituted on an agrarian basis. Cities were of little importance as governmental centers. The line of authority was from king to lord to vassal, and it bypassed cities completely. Pirenne concludes:

. . . the period which opened with the Carolingian era knew cities neither in the social sense, nor in the economic sense, nor in the legal sense of that word. The towns and the burgs were merely fortified places and headquarters of administration. Their inhabitants enjoyed neither special laws nor institutions of their own, and their manner of living did not distinguish them in any way from the rest of society.

Commercial and industrial activity were completely foreign to them. In no respect were they out of key with the agricultural civilization of their times.

The groups they formed were, after all, of trifling importance. It is not possible, in the lack of reliable information, to give an exact figure, but everything indicates that the population of the burgs never consisted of more than a few hundred men and that that of the towns probably did not pass the figure of two to three thousand souls.[8]

The ninth through eleventh centuries were rural. The urban way of life had vanished. The essentials of commerce and trade were totally lost. Arteries of transportation, roads and bridges, had fallen into decay. There was an acute shortage of money, although it never completely disappeared. Life was rural and agricultural, and men lived directly from the land. This is best illustrated by reconstructing an image of the social institutions of the time. Situations related to family life, economic production, religious manifestations, educational experiences, political order, literature, music, and art all expressed a rural idiom.

AGRICULTURAL ORGANIZATION IN THE MIDDLE AGES

Cultivation practices were primitive, particularly in the hamlet areas. Plots of land were small. Fertilizer was scarce, and was usually obtained from the dung of one's cattle. After a year or two the land was exhausted, and a new plot was selected. This farming system was called "in-field" and "out-field" exploitation.

In prosperous agricultural districts the large manorial village system prevailed. Two to five hundred people usually lived on a manorial estate. The people lived in houses grouped around the parish church and the manor. The manorial village was located on a large tract of land, divided into hundreds of smaller parcels separated by foot paths (see Fig. 1). The separate parcels were individual villagers' holdings, units of property as well as units for production. A peasant's holdings were scattered and were typically separated by the land of several others. A *villein* or freeman might hold a number of strips of land. Thirty strips constituted the typical holding. Although the freeman's property holdings were several in number, land tenure was not free but involved obligation to the lord of the manor. The majority of land holders were *villeins* and were often called *peasants* or *serfs,* although the categories are not strictly synonymous. These were bound to the land with duties, fees, and services to be rendered to the lord. Land could not be transferred but was a permanent part of the particular village system. However, acknowledging these duties, the land was the peasant's property while it was allotted to him,

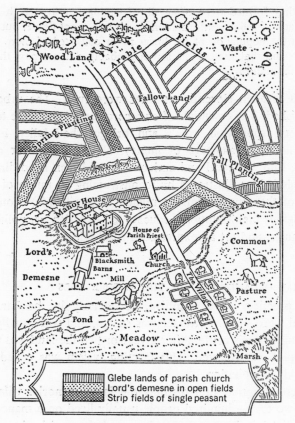

FIGURE 1. A TYPICAL MANOR

Source: Wallace K. Ferguson and Geoffrey Bruun, *A Survey of European Civilization* (second edition, Boston: Houghton Mifflin Co., 1947), p. 191.

and he was free to make certain entrepreneurial decisions concerning its operation.

All categories of villagers—lord, freeman, and serf—were bound by village policy to cultivate the common fields in accordance with the general community plan. Village lands were divided into three large, separate fields, within which each man was allotted a smaller plot. A rotation system of planting was used, so that each year one field lay fallow. Cattle were grazed on the fallow field; wheat and rye were planted on the second field, and barley and oats were planted on the third field.

Technical agricultural improvements were nearly impossible with this system of small, separated land parcels. Improvements were needed since yields were low. Painter reported that, by the thirteenth century, utilization of the most improved farming practices made it possible for the best farmers to obtain only ten bushels of wheat per acre after planting it with two bushels of seed.[10] This low yield was serious, since grain was used not only for food but for ale. It was necessary, therefore, to put every available acre into grain. Hay was also needed to feed oxen, and, unfortunately, it grew best only on land as fertile as that used for grain.

The horse collar was the major agricultural innovation introduced into Western Europe in the eleventh century. The horse was a far more efficient draft animal than the ox. The horse was faster than the ox and could plow more land in a given time, but the added speed and energy were costly in that the horse required greater quantities of food. Only a few areas, generally in France, had high enough production rates to make utilization of the horse feasible.

Low yields were also partly the result of sowing by broadcast. This ancient method left the seeds exposed to be eaten by birds. No matter how one views it, life was a hand-to-mouth existence in the Middle Ages.

Peasants typically had fruit trees, vegetable gardens, honey bees, and other small operations adjacent to their homes. They had the right to graze their flocks on the common pasture. Village woods were used for running pigs, and one finds in the Domesday Survey that the size of a woods was reported in terms of the number of pigs it could support. The villager's wood was also cut from the timber plot, where rights and usage were strictly specified. If a stream passed through the village, peasants could fish in it. The price for this privilege was that part of the catch had to go to the manor house. There was a division of labor involving specialists. Herdsmen, swinemen, and other specialists cared for their animals and those of their neighbors. For this service they were provided a portion of the field produce or other commodities. In this agricultural system there was common property and personal-use property. One's means of sustenance came from both, with use and quantity being clearly stipulated. Some authorities have suggested this was not communal but agricultural partnership.

The whole social organization was centered in the agricultural manor village or hamlet. Most of the people were in some category of peasant tenancy, subject to the authority of a lord or clergymen in turn for which they received protection from the manor house. In the hamlets, people worked their own fields for their own gain, as shown by parts of Germany and the Danish settlements in England in the tenth century. But, regardless of location, village or hamlet, free or manorial, the way of life and the economy were agrarian.

POLITICAL ORDER AND LEGAL STATUS

Political organization and legal status varied in detail from area to area and from village to village, but medieval social organization was fundamentally a universal system in its major aspects. In fact, one of the merits of the manorial system was its encouragement of stability, tranquility, and law among people who had been accustomed to violence.[11] It was a system of superordinate-subordinate reciprocity wherein both lord and peasant knew what was expected of the other. Individual rights for all people were few. There was no ideology of individualism. The system was such that a peasant could not migrate; but he had security, for neither could he be evicted. Rents and services were not to be increased, once established by custom. In actuality, stories of many injustices were heard, but this was a system of social order which continued through several centuries.

The state itself, to the extent that it existed, was constituted on an agrarian basis. Characteristically, the Carolingian palaces were not located in towns but on the countryside. Similarly, the Germanic tribes avoided cities and thereby contributed to the state's rural character.

Political districts were without real seats of authority. Persons to whom power was entrusted did not necessarly settle in a given location. Centers of judicial administration were not geographically established but depended upon the location of the administrator at any given time. In other words, cities lost their function as centers of civil administration and retained only that of centers for religious administration.

FAMILY SOCIAL PATTERNS

Family life was centered in the agricultural manorial village or hamlet. People had few contacts with the world beyond their village limits. Local priests administered the religious rites for birth, marriage, and death. Amusements were provided by the occasional fairs, the weekly market place, and other local gatherings. Religious holidays were often devoted more to leisure than to piety. Life was exceedingly simple and often routine. The work day lasted from sunup to sunset. Tenants were required to work for the lord. The amount of work duties varied greatly with local customs, but three days' work per week for the lord was not uncommon.

Eileen Power describes the life of a ninth-century peasant family.[12] The family lived under the jurisdiction of the St. Germain monks in the time of Charlemagne. Their residence was located on a small plot of arable land, which was used to raise some of their own food and some for the steward. The peasant was required to work for the steward on the monks' land. The steward was given a bribe of eggs and fruit to assure his good temper. Work began early and lasted until dusk and was accomplished with the assistance of the peasant's ox and boy. Duties were usually plowing, fence building, and wood cutting. Work activities for women were also highly specific.

Food, clothing, and shelter—such as they were—came from the village. The peasant abode was a hovel, a hut of wattle and daub with a thatched roof. The art of baking bricks had been lost with the Romans. The dwelling lacked the conveniences of either chimney or window, and the only opening for smoke, debris, animals, or man was a single door. The lord's dwelling, whether abbey, castle, or manor house, was well constructed by comparison to the surrounding buildings. It was often of stone but seldom pretentious. Variation in size and type of building material was generally an index of the wealth of the lord.

Food was scarce and the type consumed was determined by one's place in the social hierarchy. Beef and mutton, when available, figured in the bill of fare for the manor house. Peasants, with a little luck, had a few chickens, but pork was the only meat regularly available. Pigs could fend for themselves in the woods, and although thin and tough, they were edible. The meat diet was also supplemented by eels and waterfowl if the village was near the water front. Fruits, vegetables, nuts, and berries were supplied, in season, from village gardens and woods. The chief food was bread, and all fare was accompanied by ale or wine. With low yields and population increases there was a continual pressure to provide enough food for all the people.[13]

The lord of the land had considerable control over the personal life of his tenants. The great mass of agricultural workers had few rights. During the tenth and eleventh centuries there was a power struggle between the church and the lords concerning the claim to rights by the *villein*. The church agitated for individual rights, and it is reported that the church was victorious in this fight for human dignity. But the victory was hardly recognized, even by the twelfth century.

The lords wanted to deprive the serfs of all rights of human beings, to say they had no souls and to refuse to call their unions marriages. Although the church won the contest, the lords continued to refer to the family of a serf as his *sequela,* or brood.[14]

Servi could marry but not outside the village except with the lord's approval. The lords of the land considered marriage and family life as of little importance for tenants. Customs of dignity and refinement were not subjects of proper tenant concern. The *servi* were bound to the land, and their labor was bound with them.

Family relationships for the lord were more discernible, although probably not more refined. Marriage of a daughter was an important political and economic event.

When the daughter of a vassal married, she carried to her husband as her marriage portion some part of her father's fief, and thus gave him an interest and a foothold in the lord's lands. No lord could be expected to permit an enemy to secure such a position. Hence the vassal was bound to secure the lord's approval of his son-in-law to be. If a vassal died leaving a son too young to fight or an unmarried daughter, there was no one to perform the services of the fief. The lord then had the right to demand that some male have custody of the fief and perform the service. Sometimes it was customary to have this function filled by a relative of the heir or heiress. Usually this duty fell on the eldest brother of the heir's mother, who could never inherit the fief and thus had no reason to want to remove the heir. If an uncle on the father's side were given custody, he might be tempted to get rid of the heir to secure his own succession.[15]

Often it was the custom for the lord himself to take custody of an heir and to hold his land in trust. If the heir was female, the lord had to find her a mate. This was an opportunity for a lord to give a fief plus a wife to an aspiring young knight. In any case, marriage had two different functions in this ruralized society. The church fathers viewed it as the rightful avenue of procreation; the feudal lords viewed it as a mechanism controlling land, forming alliances, and providing labor.

Courtly love added a third dimension to the marriage situation in the twelfth century. Its principal effect was confusion. Romantic love appeared to have had no meaningful role in the social order except to embellish extramarital relationships. Some evidence suggests that the lower classes usually entered marriage when pregnancy occurred, but the records are not conclusive.[16]

LEISURE ACTIVITIES

Leisure was seldom categorically distinct from toil, yet often the workaday life went along with a song. Peasants sang when at work. Even the names of the months indicated the toil and delights: Winter-month, January; Mud-month, February; Spring-month, March; Easter-month, April; Joy-month, May; Plow-month, June; Hay-month, July; Harvest-month, August; Wind-month, September; Vintage-month, October; Autumn-month, November; Holy-month, December.[17] During Holy-month one heard in England the wassail carol ("Here's Good Health to You"):

> Wassail, Wassail, all over the town,
> Our bread it is white and our ale it is brown,
> Our bowl is made of the green maple tree,
> In the wassail bowl we'll drink unto thee.
>
> Here's health to the ox and to his right eye,
> Pray God send our master a good Christmas pie,
> A good Christmas pie as e'er I did see,
> In the wassail bowl we'll drink unto thee.
>
> Here's health to the ox and to his right horn,
> Pray God send our master a good crop of corn,
> A good crop of corn as e'er I did see,
> In the wassail bowl we'll drink unto thee.

There were also holidays, Sundays, and saints' days. On all of these days the church disapproved of servile work.

Neither shall men perform their rustic labors, tending vines, ploughing fields, reaping corn and mowing hay, setting up hedges or fencing woods, cutting trees, or working in quarries or building houses; nor shall they work in the garden, nor come to the law courts, nor follow the chase. But three carrying services it is lawful to do on Sunday, to wit carrying for the army, carrying food, or carrying (if need be) the body of a lord to its grave. Items, women shall not do their textile works, nor cut out clothes, nor stitch them together with the needle, nor card wool, nor be at help, nor wash clothes in public, nor shear sheep; so that there may be rest on the Lord's day. But let them come together from all sides to Mass in the Church and praise God for all the good things He did for us on that day.[18]

The situation developed so that the institutions of religion and of leisure were difficult to distinguish at some points. Serfs were not prepared to go quietly to church, contemplate the saints, and go solemnly home again. Quite the contrary; they spent their holidays in singing, dancing, and buffoonery—which has been characteristic of plain folk until this contemporary self-conscious age.[19] They chose for their place of merriment and unrefined jesting nothing less than the churchyard. Many of their songs and much of their merriment expressed the idiom of their pagan forefathers—much of which the church wisely overlooked, but of which it nonetheless disapproved. Bishops forbade the singing of "wicked" songs and the pleasures of dancing women. Nevertheless, such pastimes persisted and were tenaciously supported by the people, and sometimes by the local priest as well. There were also wandering minstrels who entertained by singing profane and secular songs. They were popular with the nobles and disdained by the clergy.

BELLES-LETTRES

Arts were limited during these times, and few examples have been preserved. Latin was the language of the scholars; and the only scholars, few as they were, were among the clergy. Accordingly, theology, philosophy, and official documents were in Latin, but none of these was particularly significant. The most notable of the secular songs in Latin were the Goliardic songs. Those were the utterances of wanderers, presumably university students. Most of these were gay poems about drinking, love making, and escapades.[20] These poems stimulated some revival of interest in Latin literature in the twelfth century.

Medieval literature of greatest importance, from the viewpoint of quantity and enjoyment by the people, was in the vernacular languages. German works were among the earliest that still survive. They were epic poems concerned with the heroic deeds of warriors. The Anglo-Saxon epic poem *Beowulf* was the most important of the early works. Beowulf was a hero who had slain two savage monsters and a dragon, and was ultimately killed himself.

In the eleventh and twelfth centuries, literature came to have a more established role in society. For entertaining feudal men there were stories of fighting and politics, while lyric poems were written for women. From the nobles and their courts came the call for entertainment. Wandering minstrels filled the long evenings with good tales.

Most education during the early Middle Ages was characteristically practical. Scholars who loved learning were exceptions, not the rule. The ideology of education was for the individual to have only that knowledge or skill suitable for his particular occupation; more education was considered dangerous. Accordingly, daughters of the nobles were taught to read so that they could better perform their devotions, but they were denied training in penmanship to deter their writing love letters.[21] Learning for noblemen took place in the baronial household. There the baron trained the sons of vassals and of relatives to be good knights. Young ladies were prepared for marriage by the baron's wife. Apprenticeship in the master's house served many guilds, but for the mass of serfs there was no education at all. Clerics in monasteries and cathedrals controlled practically all schools from the sixth to the twelfth century. They trained clerks and members of their orders to read their devotionals. Even the secular education of clerks was under the direction of bishops. Universities ultimately came to be the most important educational institutions in the Middle Ages. They were academic guilds, formed to protect their members. The oldest of the universities were located in Bologna and Paris. Dates of their establishment are uncertain, but there are reports of their activities in the eleventh and twelfth centuries.[22] In any event, the arts and education were a specialized form of human expression, little-known in the ruralized society of the ninth and tenth centuries.

RELIGIOUS BEHAVIOR

Christianity was the nominal religion in Western Europe in the Middle Ages, as it had been for several centuries before. Nevertheless, superstitions were rampant, and the peasants clung tenaciously to old, often pagan, beliefs. Abbot Irminon's records indicated that peasants chanted incantations over newly planted fields, such as:

> Earth, Earth, Earth! O Earth, our mother!
> May the All-Wieder, Ever-Lord grant thee
> Acres a-waxing, upwards a-growing,
> Pregnant with corn and plenteous in strength!
> Host of grain shafts and of glittering plants!
> Of broad barley the blossoms,
> And of white wheat ears waxing,
> Of the whole land the harvest. . . .[23]

Or, when planting, they might sing this verse:

> Acre, full-fed bring forth fodder for men!
> Blossoming brightly, blessed become!
> And the God who wrought with earth grant us gift of growing
> That each of all the corns may come unto our need.[24]

And the women, in their duties about the house and yard, would also recite verses in behalf of the gods. A peasant's wife might say, when hearing the bees swarming:

> Christ, there is a swarm of bees outside,
> Fly hither, my little cattle,
> In blest peace, in God's protection,
> Come home safe and sound,
> Sit down, sit down, bee,
> St. Mary commanded thee.
> Thou shalt not have leave
> Thou shalt not fly to the wood.
> Thou shalt not escape me,
> Nor go away from me.
> Sit very still,
> Wait God's will! [25]

But the church was stern, or tried to be. When peasants went to confession, the priests asked if they had contacted magicians, made vows to trees, or drunk magic potions.[26] When the answer was yes, the priest was severe yet kind. The penance was less than that for a noble who might commit the same offenses.

The church was one of the pioneering movements of the times. With an insufficient clergy its task was to reach the masses of people who were widely scattered in isolated rural villages.

Pioneer monks lived with the peasants and shared their labors in plowing and planting, in reclaiming land and in clearing away forests. . . . The missionaries were seen to be more than preachers of a new religion; they were teachers, builders, physicians, metal-workers—above all, perhaps, they were farmers, like the people among whom they lived.[27]

Christianity was a break with the old pagan ways. At the same time it achieved a remarkable integration with the past as the people were allowed to accept it gradually. From one point of view, the clergy constituted an occupational specialty; from another point of view, it was perfectly integrated into the ruralized social organization of the times.

CONCEPT OF RURALIZED SOCIAL ORGANIZATION

Utilizing the example of the Middle Ages, we can now understand that ruralized social organization is a form of societal integration whereby all the major social institutions have an agrarian basis. There are no significant social structures in which the folkways and mores are urban. Farming organization, political order, family life, leisure pursuits, religious expression, and the arts are all characterized by a bucolic idiom in societies dominated by ruralized social organization.

Ruralized social organization is not synonymous with farm organization. It is a total way of life, with cultural universals ideally binding on all persons in the society. It is one type of social organization, the central features of which are primary interaction, village living, localization, isolation, primary production and distribution of goods, and reciprocal provision of services. Ruralized social organization is not correctly understood as one end of a rural-urban continuum.

The social structure of the ninth to the eleventh century was characterized by ruralized social organization. Indeed, there was a conspicuous absence of an urban way of life. Life was generally simple and hard. Social experiences were limited and isolated. There was a great homogeneity within areas, and the division of labor was not complex. The greatest variations in social organization occurred between areas rather than within them. Put another way, the social distance between the lord and the serf was often less within a given village than the difference between the manor's and the hamlet's agricultural systems. Social distance between the priest and peasant was often not great; frequently, they were both farmers. Specialists and social hierarchies were few, and were based typically on the agrarian system.

There were customs and patterns of behavior, but institutions were far from well formulated. Family life, economic production, religious activities, political justice, educational and literary activities were all identifiable patterns of behavior, but each was dominated by the agricultural way of life. Sanctity of the family was often not observed. At one point the family life of peasants reached such a low level of importance that the lords in conflict with the clergy wanted to avoid any recognition of peasant marriage. Most of the social importance of vassal and lord marriages was of an economic or political nature, and the subject of land transfer. Education was minimal; at best, it was apprenticeship for one's station in life. Religious poems and songs expressed a rural idiom. Patterns of behavior related to the major functions of social life could be discerned, but the universal characteristics of the society were related to things rural.

Social life in the Middle Ages involved far more than farming. In the strictest sense, all people were not farmers, but the abiding character of all life, farm or nonfarm, was an ethos of rurality. Villages existed from an earlier period, but they were seldom inhabited permanently in the

Middle Ages. When they were filled with people, their residents were primarily from the demesne. The totality of life was rural, regardless of occupation and regardless of place of residence. Intellectual conceptions were few, and when formed were local and limited in character. There were no grandiose notions of large societies or empires to which masses of people would give allegiance. It is this isolated, nearly static existence which we call ruralized social organization. Under such social conditions the proper study of rural human relations necessarily includes all human relations, because they are all rural. The study of farm organization, or the manorial system, is too specific; it is only a part of rural life. One could study the social interaction and ideology of the *villeins,* but even this would involve analysis of their complicated reciprocal relations with practically all others in the small village. In a village of two or three hundred people, there was a high degree of social interaction between the inhabitants and practically none outside. Village life in the ninth century did not involve interrelations with the larger society that are characteristic of a mass society in the mid-twentieth century.[28]

SUMMARY

In order to understand more completely the meaning of urbanization in the United States, one must examine ruralized society in some detail. The Middle Ages—specifically the period from the ninth through the eleventh centuries—provides an outstanding example of ruralized social organization. During that time in the areas now know as England, France, and Germany, there were no significant rural-urban differences. Cities did not exist in a social sense; they were merely walled enclosures, which were relatively unpopulated except by a few of the clergy. People came to the cities for fairs, celebrations, or, in times of siege, for protection.

There were no special patterns of behavior or folkways and mores which differentiated life in cities from life on the manor. Indeed, there were no craft and trade people who lived regularly in cities. Trade and commerce were conspicuously absent.

All life was isolated, localized, and bucolic during those times. Feudalistic order dominated the society. What division of labor or social stratification there was existed as a part of feudal society. Status was determined by one's relation to the land. Most *peasants* and *serfs* were bound to the land. *Tenants-in-chief* or lords of the manor directed the production of food and fiber and other activities of the manor. Rights, duties, and obligations of people were all reciprocally provided for in the feudal order. The notions of rights and individualism were, however, hardly known. The peasant family was in jeopardy for its very existence for a period of time. The lords tended to consider all peasants as simple property of the manor. The clergy was ultimately able to defend the right of individual families.

Political organization was not centered in the cities. Justice, when there was any, was meted out wherever the lord might be at a given time and in terms of the social position of the parties involved. There was little or no notion of centralized government. Religion was a relatively strong institution. Christianity was expanding, but often the parish priest tilled the fields, teaching his parishioners by example. Songs and religious rites combined rural idiom, paganism, and Christian teaching. Leisure was hardly ever enjoyed, except during religious holidays. The church specified that people should not toil at plowing, sewing, and a great variety of daily domestic tasks on the Sabbath Day. Such holidays were often occasions for singing, drinking, and merrymaking. The idiom again was typically rural—songs and verses set to the simple way of life of a rural people.

The concept *ruralized social organization* connotes that all of social life is dominated by man's relation to the land. Ruralization of society means far more than farm domination. All aspects of living—domestic, economic, political, religious, artistic—are given a rural character. Division of labor is minimized, spatial localization is maximized, and social interaction is limited. Such a way of life stands in sharp contrast to contemporary American society.

NOTES

1. "The World's Great Cities," *Population Bulletin,* 16 (Sept., 1960), 109–30.

2. Sidney Painter, *A History of the Middle Ages, 284–1500* (New York: Alfred A. Knopf, 1953), pp. v–vi.

3. A. H. Inman, *Domesday and Feudal Statistics with a Chapter on Agricultural Statistics* (London: Elliot Stock, 1900), pp. 1–2.

4. *Ibid.,* pp. 13 ff.

5. Eileen Power, *Medieval People* (New York: Doubleday Anchor Books, 1954), p. 18.

6. Painter, *op. cit.,* pp. 95–6.

7. Henri Pierenne, *Medieval Cities* (New York: Doubleday Anchor Books, 1956), p. 39.

8. *Ibid.*, p. 53.

9. Painter, *op. cit.*, p. 95.

10. *Ibid.*, p. 97.

11. G. M. Trevelyan, *History of England* (New York: Doubleday Anchor Books, n.d.), I, p. 201.

12. Power, *op. cit.*, pp. 20 ff.

13. *Loc. cit.*

14. *Ibid.*, p. 22.

15. Painter, *op. cit.*, pp. 97–8.

16. *Ibid.*, p. 100.

17. *Ibid.*, p. 111.

18. *Ibid.*, p. 441.

19. Power, *op. cit.*, p. 25.

20. *Ibid.*, pp. 27–8.

21. Power, *op. cit.*, p. 28.

22. Painter, *op. cit.*, p. 447.

23. *Ibid.*, p. 465.

24. Trevelyan, *op. cit.*, pp. 240–45; and Charles Homer Haskins, *The Rise of Universities* (Ithaca: Cornell University Press, 1957).

25. Power, *op. cit.*, p. 25.

26. *Ibid.*, p. 26.

27. *Loc. cit.*

28. *Ibid.*, p. 27.

29. William Carol Bark, *Origins of the Medieval World* (New York: Doubleday Anchor Books, 1960), pp. 112–13.

30. Arthur J. Vidich and Joseph Bensmen, *Small Town in Mass Society* (New York: Doubleday Anchor Books, 1960).

SELECTED READINGS

Artz, B. Frederick. *The Mind of the Middle Ages.* New York: Alfred A. Knopf, 1953.
    A historical survey of the interests of the intellectual classes in medieval times.

Bark, William Carol. *Origins of the Medieval World.* New York: Doubleday Anchor Books, 1960.

In this monograph the author presents a critical interpretation of how and in what circumstances the ancient world came to an end in Western Europe and how the medieval world began.

Martindale, Don. *American Social Structure.* New York: Appleton-Century-Crofts, 1960. Chapter 8.
A brief statement of recent attempts to study rural communities within the framework of a taxonomic schema developed from Toennies's concepts, *Gemeinschaft* and *Gesellschaft.*

————. *American Society.* New York: D. Van Nostrand Co., Inc., 1960. Chapter 6.
A concise treatment of the roles of the factory system, science, and governmental policies in the transformation of the unique form of rural community and agriculture during the nineteenth and twentieth centuries.

Painter, Sidney. *A History of the Middle Ages, 284–1500.* New York: Alfred A. Knopf, 1953.
An effort by a noted historian to present the essential elements of medieval civilization as it developed after the unification of Western Christendom.

Pirenne, Henri. *Economics and Social History of Medieval Europe.* London: Kegan Paul, Trench, Trubner and Co., 1936.
A study of the general movement of the economic and social evolution of Western Europe from the end of the Roman Empire to the middle of the fifteenth century.

————. *Medieval Cities.* New York: Doubleday Anchor Books, 1956.
A general treatise on the economic awakening and the birth of urban civilization in Western Europe during the Middle Ages.

Power, Eileen. *Medieval People.* New York: Doubleday Anchor Books, 1954.
A social historical treatment of peasant and domestic life, monastic life, trade and early industry in the Middle Ages.

Trevelyan, G. M., *History of England.* Vol. I. New York: Doubleday Anchor Books, n.d.
A comprehensive analysis of the social development, economic conditions, political institutions, and overseas activities of England from the earliest times to the Reformation.

2 CONTEMPORARY AMERICA: URBANIZED SOCIAL ORGANIZATION

The people of the United States live in an urbanized society. Urbanization is taking place throughout much of the world but nowhere more rapidly or dramatically than in the United States.[1] Urbanization is advancing at such a rapid rate that its full character is not yet clearly understood; indeed, the structure is not yet completely established. Cities appear to be engulfing their surrounding lands. At the same time, human relations in the countryside bring frustrations to exurbanites and farmers alike. The interplay of human relations between the populations of cities and the open country indicates in part the developing structures of urbanization. There are complaints from exurbanites about the work practices of farming. For example, those caught in the suburban sprawl of California's Santa Clara Valley have expressed objection to being awakened in the mornings by tractors, smudge pots, and the use of various sprays.[2] There is also the probability of greatly increased taxes to support the demand for city-type services desired by the new open-country residents. These costs are a burden on farm and nonfarm people alike. Zoning, or the absence of zoning, constitutes another serious problem. Land is often so unsystematically used that its economic, political, and aesthetic values are not fully realized. Farmers are lured by the exceedingly high prices offered for parcels of their land. They frequently sell it in such unusually shaped patterns that commercial farming is no longer profitable. The result for agriculture is that part-time farming becomes the prevailing practice in suburban fringe locations.

INTRODUCTION TO THE CONCEPT OF URBANIZED SOCIAL ORGANIZATION

Urbanized social organization is a concept applied to human relations inside and outside the corporate political limits of cities. It applies to social structures which originated in cities but which have now been accepted by people outside cities as well. In the process of being accepted in open country areas the social organization characteristic of cities has often been modified, but qualities reflecting urban origin still dominate. Urbanized social organization is a system of human life tending toward universal social institutions for all members of the society. There are no precise distinctions between the way of life in the cities and on the farms. The ways of life are so intertwined that whatever institutional structures obtain in the society will be constraining in approximately the same way on all people, regardless of their rural or urban residential location. This, in short, is the essence of the concept *urbanized social organization.* It is an ideal type, and, therefore, not to be observed in a concrete situation. In addition, it must be reiterated that urbanized social organization is still in the process of becoming established. It cannot be illustrated by examining an earlier society, as was the concept of ruralized social organization by an analysis of the Middle Ages. Yet contemporary American society stands among those at the vanguard of urbanized social organization.

HISTORICAL SETTING OF URBANIZED SOCIAL ORGANIZATION

Colonial period. The United States was settled by Europeans most of whom were moving away from conditions of feudal society. While there was some effort to establish a feudal manorial system of social organization in the American colonies, the attempt was abortive. Europe was still essentially rural during the period of colonialism in America, but its rurality was disintegrating. Enclosures were more and more apparent in the England of the seventeenth and eighteenth centuries. During this same time, experimentation in animal breeding and in crop rotation was advanced.[3] There had already emerged a new scientific technique of food and fiber production. These conditions of systematic and scientific inquiry, no matter how primitive, were germane in the Europe that gave birth to colonial America. The new ideas were available to the early colonists, and there continued to be a flow of people and ideas from Europe to the colonies, and later to the new nation. European ruralized social organization as it was known in the Middle Ages was disintegrating at the time of the founding of Jamestown. Yet, advances were being made in the Old World and, although scientific development was slow in the early years of frontier America, colonists shared continually in it. The infant science of agriculture was an important part of the cognitive system within which colonial America was founded and grew.

National period. The establishment of the United States as a nation coincided with the Industrial Revolution in England.[4] Ideas of industrialization were generated in the same cultural stream which guided the development of the new nation. The notions of both systematic agriculture and industrialism were a part of the new nation's culture from its very inception. Only by recognizing the European origin of systematic ideas can one understand the early and rapid scientific development of American agriculture and industry. The American orientation has been toward urbanized social organization from the time of national origin.

The impact of industrialism on every phase of human life, Samuel Hayes asserted, has been the story of America.[5] He suggested that the great change in social organization took place for the most part prior to 1914. It was a metamorphosis from a frontier nation to one in which farmers, laborers, merchants, and manufacturers—persons in all walks of life—saw a transition from local business affairs to nationwide markets, industrialism, and a complex division of labor.[6]

The nation was in the process of developing urbanized social organization even prior to the time when the majority of people lived in cities. The mass migration from farms to urban areas was simultaneous with the expansion of the new urban culture into the countryside. The concomitant movement of people and of ideas must not be overlooked. Such interaction brought about an urbanized social organization rather than a dichotomous city-farm society.

Expanding industrialization was one of the major facilitating factors in the development of urbanized social organization. Nationwide transportation networks supplanted the systems of local firms and eventually brought all areas of the United States into close geographical or physical interdependence. Agriculture became only one part of a nationwide industrial system. The role of agriculture was coming to be more precisely defined. As the nation was responding to industrialism, agriculture was also responding to urbanized social organization. Farms were becoming production centers of food and fiber for a whole nation's population.

Their operations became more scientific as they endeavored to meet demands of the mass market.

Industrialism, as one of several dimensions of urbanized social organization, provided a vast opportunity for Americans to achieve higher levels of living.[7] Most of the human relations in farming have become adjusted to industrial success mechanisms. In a society oriented to success and prestige, the values of the bucolic way of life are destined to reduced importance. Belief in man's ability to mold and perfect his environment is pervasive. Yet any society which defines success and establishes mechanisms for achieving it must inevitably contend with failure. Consequently, there is a nostalgia and at times a calling for the less perplexing, more tranquil way of life. Hence, industrial social organization does not characterize the total society. There remain rural cultural islands and some forms of human relations that are still relatively more rural than urbanized. Cultural islands are part of the story of human adjustment to a new type of social organization rather than evidence of a dichotomous social organization existing in society.

There is some evidence for the tendency of agriculture to become adjusted to a market-oriented social structure even during the colonial period. Martindale, for example, has identified market-oriented agriculture even prior to the Revolution.[8] Although not typical of colonial agriculture, the sale of wheat and grains from New England farms to the mother country has been recorded. The Revolution stimulated excess agricultural production. Men were taken off farms to fight in the Revolutionary Army, and there was a need to provide food for them. Thus the need for surplus was created. After the Revolution some measure of market-oriented agriculture continued, particularly in the plantation South. Agriculture in this area was typically a business enterprise, not a way of life.

The Civil War provided another great opportunity for agriculture to develop on a business basis. Like the Revolutionary War, it created a market for agricultural products while taking men from the agricultural labor force to serve in the respective armies. If there had been considerable reversion to subsistence agriculture after the Revolution, there was far less after the Civil War. The Civil War armies were much larger, also the degree of mechanization prior to the war and the stimulation of markets during the war were of such great magnitude that American agriculture was never again based upon a subsistence level. From the point of view of differential social organization, the Civil War was a power struggle between ruralized and urbanized social organization, the latter being the victor. Henceforth agriculture was to be a specialty, one of the elements of urbanized society. The possibility for a rural way of life to dominate the social structure had passed. The precise details and the exact dimensions of this new role had not yet been carved out. But there was no question, regardless of the character of the details, that the major purpose of agriculture was clear. It was to be a special industry to provide the necessary food and fiber to feed an enormous labor force and a great number of people who could not be employed in the enterprise of providing their own sustenance.

These were the historical developments which set the human stage for the advancement of an urbanized social organization. We turn now to some of the measures of urbanization which came to be characteristic of the entire national way of life.

SOME MEASURES OF URBANIZATION

Population trends. The 1920 Census of Population was the first to report more Americans living in cities than in rural areas. A city in recent years has been defined as a population center having 2,500 people or more. From the point of view of residential location, the United States has been dominated by urbanization since the 1920's. City residents have increased rapidly in number and proportion since 1920. Now well over two-thirds of the nation's people reside in cities, and over half of the people reside in 213 urbanized areas. Urbanized areas contain at least one city of 50,000 inhabitants or more, plus the surrounding closely settled areas that meet certain density and related requirements.[9] By contrast to these recent trends it was reported in the first census of the United States (1790) that only 5 per cent of the population resided in cities and 95 per cent in rural areas.

Accompanying the rapid urbanization of the nation, there was developed at the time of the 1920 Census a new residential concept which identified rural nonfarm people. Therefore, since 1920 it has become customary to analyze the characteristics of the population according to three standard categories, namely, urban, rural nonfarm, and rural farm. In more recent years, a growing proportion of the rural nonfarm people have come to live more closely to the nation's major cities and urbanized areas than to rural farm areas both in physical distance and in social ideology. Many of the rural nonfarm people reside in small hamlets and villages of less than 2,500 population. Many of these smaller population centers are in the suburban and fringe areas adjacent to sizable cities or urbanized areas where the social characteristics of life are more city-oriented than farm-oriented. Sociologically, there is a far greater proportion of the population in the urbanized category than the population statistics customarily reveal.

The 1950 Census reported the rural farm population as 23,048,350; the rural nonfarm population as 31,181,325 and the urban population as 96,467,686. By 1960 the number of people in these three categories was reported as 13,444,898, 40,596,990, and 125,283,783, respectively.

Duncan and Reiss studied the characteristics of rural and urban populations reported in the 1950 Census.[10] They analyzed the characteristics of people in eleven different sizes of place locations:

1. Urbanized areas of 3,000,000 or more,
2. Urbanized areas of 1,000,000 to 3,000,000,
3. Urbanized areas of 250,000 to 1,000,000,
4. Urbanized areas of less than 250,000,
5. Urban places outside urbanized areas of 25,000 or more,
6. Urban places outside urbanized areas of 10,000 to 25,000,
7. Urban places outside urbanized areas of 2,500 to 10,000,
8. Villages (incorporated and unincorporated) of 1,000 to 2,500,
9. Villages (incorporated only) of less than 1,000,
10. Other rural, nonfarm,
11. Other rural, farm.

This analysis revealed greater insight into the characteristics of urbanized society than was possible by using the three traditional categories of urban, rural nonfarm, and rural farm. The findings of the study were complex, but even a summary statement revealed that villages resemble small towns more than farm or other rural populations. Greater differences in demographic characteristics were observed among people in the core of large central cities and those in small cities of approximately 2,500 than between all urban people and all farm people. When Duncan and Reiss studied the characteristics of people in communities between 1,000 and 2,500 and compared them with those in larger cities and rural farm areas, they discovered that people in the smaller villages and hamlets frequently exhibit characteristics more similar to those in the cities between 2,500 and 25,000 than to those of their rural farm neighbors.

Levels of living. Farm level of living studies [11] have revealed that, in an urbanized society, farmers in close proximity to large urban areas have consumption patterns that aprpoximate those of urban people to a greater extent than those of farmers in the relatively more rural states. The highest farm level of living indexes have been reported for the states of California, New Jersey, and Connecticut, followed by Iowa, a classic farm state. Among all the counties, Kern in Southern California had the highest level of living index. This county is in the hinterland of one of the nation's most urbanized states.

Statistics of this type support the position that urbanized society, as a way of life, tends to be commonplace for all people, regardless of their residential location. With the breakdown of physical and social isolation, rural-urban differences in the patterns of living of the nation's families are minimized. This situation is highly similar to that observed by Pirenne for the Middle Ages when cities in the social sense ceased to exist. While they were a physical part of the landscape, the patterns of life, social interaction, thought, and ideology were not essentially different for those few people who lived in the cities and those who lived in the surrounding rural hamlets and manorial areas. One now observes that, as contemporary American society becomes more urbanized, there is essentially a common way of life—including patterns of social interaction, of consumption, of ideology, and of thought—for all the people. Where they can be identified at all, differences between rural and urban people in contemporary American society are more a matter of degree than a matter of kind.

Trends in the labor force. The differential growth of the labor force in the United States has changed greatly over the years due to a dramatic increase in the population and to a shift from agricultural to nonagricultural employment. Between 1820 and 1960, farm workers in the nation's labor force decreased from 72 to 6 per cent.[12] Nonfarm workers increased from 28 per cent in 1820 to 94 per cent in 1960. Nonfarm occupations have grown more rapidly than farm occupations in each decade since 1820. The nineteenth century was a time when the frontier was being settled and a time around which much romantic history has been written. The frontier has been glorified as a great American tradition to such an extent that it has perhaps overshadowed the fact that the number of people involved in nonagricultural development far exceeded the number in frontier and agricultural development. This is another way of saying that urbanization of social organization in these United States has been developing over a long period, but only recently has urbanization come to pervade national behavioral patterns. There has not been a decade in the past 140 years when nonfarm occupations failed to grow at least 25 per cent faster than agricultural occupations.[13] In most decades they grew twice as fast.

Statistical reports of differential growth of agricultural and nonagricultural elements of the labor force most often imply an oversimplified distinction between farm and nonfarm occupations. In a later chapter the difficulties of distinguishing between farm and nonfarm occupations are considered. At this point, however, labor force statistics are valid for illustrating that a few farmers are increasingly capable of filling their specialized roles of providing food and fiber for great proportions of people not engaged in that basic enterprise. Distinctions between farm and nonfarm work are tenuous, yet the specialized role of agriculture and its impressive accomplishments in record outputs are readily apparent.

Increased participation of women in the labor force has been another dramatic change related to urbanized social organization. Bancroft has indicated that, as urbanization of the population has advanced, employment opportunities for women have multiplied. Also there has been a reduction in labor force participation on the part of younger and older men.[14] In the past fifty years the typical American woman's role has changed from that of a farm housewife to a city or suburban dweller. At the turn of the century the only women who could expect to be employed were the unmarried or widowed.[15] By the midpoint of the twentieth century, American women were well trained for many specialized occupations. They often seek employment during the period of time between graduation from high school or college and marriage. The number of women employed subsequent to marriage or the arrival of children has declined, although there has been a tendency for women to re-enter the labor force at the termination of the child-rearing period for a few years prior to their retirement.

Transportation and communication. In the early days of the new nation, men envisioned interstate highways and other major arteries of transportation. The very fact that such men could conceive of an interstate highway system is important, because it reveals in their thinking a departure from the isolationism of the earlier ruralized social organization of Europe. Such a concept of ruralized social organization was not part of the thinking of the leaders of the new American nation. Transportation was needed; the only real question was how it should be provided. The alternatives appeared to be private investment, state construction, or federal development.[16] Construction of roads and waterways involved excessive long-term investments, and the founders of the new nation had limited cash resources. There were many short toll roads and toll bridges, but such operations were never successful on a large scale. States had insufficient revenue, just as their inhabitants had insufficient incomes. The development of a state highway system which might be coordinated and linked with another state system involved cumbersome agreements to which the parties were seldom willing to submit. The federal government's constitutional authority to undertake highway building was not clearly defined. The several states did not trust the growing power of the federal government. And, the federal government, like the several states, had an insufficient amount of money.

Madison proposed, apparently in 1796, that a surplus of post office revenues be used for building post roads. Jefferson wrote Madison, in March of 1796, that he did not favor the idea, that in his opinion "it would be a source of boundless patronage to the executive, jobbing to members of congress and their friends and a bottomless abyss of public money." He also raised the question whether the constitutional power to 'establish' postal roads was specific enough. A Constitutional amendment might be necessary. Hamilton, in a memorandum to Representative Drayton, had expressed the view that an amendment to the Constitution would be necessary to authorize the general government to open canals through the territory of two or more states. He also said, however, that such an amendment would be advisable partly because the making of these improvements by the federal government would be "a useful source of influence." (The quote from Hamilton came from a memorandum found in Van Buren's papers, is undated; it may or may not be authentic.) [17]

A nationwide system of transportation was achieved between the period 1820–1915 despite early differences concerning the proper method for construction.[18] In 1802, the Ohio Act provided for the Cumberland Road from Cumberland, Maryland, to Ohio. This was followed by the Gallatin and Jefferson Plan, in 1808, for a national system of highways and canals. This master plan was aggressive for its time. It provided: one, a canal system, two, improvement of rivers flowing eastward or westward, three, highways to run north and northwest connecting the Hudson to the western area, and four, the improvement of local connecting highways. The plan never materialized, probably because of the imminence of war.

Efforts toward improving transportation systems continued. In 1825, John Quincy Adams assumed the presidency. The new President was a prominent supporter of a great national road and canal system which transcended local interests. Such a transportation system, he contended, was to serve the whole nation. This again provides a concrete example of the power struggle between two ways of life—one based on localism or ruralized social organization and another on nationalism or an emerging nationwide urbanized social organization.

Railroad construction started in the 1830's, following the extensive road and canal building in the 1820's. Railroads quickly surpassed canals in importance. Canals were too expensive, transportation on rivers and through canals was too slow, and canals did not connect all the nation's production centers. Farmers were quick to develop an interest in railroads. Many of them based their future plans on the possibility of railroads coming through their area. Nevertheless, actual construction of railroads was somewhat slow. By 1850 there were less than 10,000 miles of railroad. During the next decade rail lines doubled in length. The value of the railroad was apparent to farmers and nonfarmers alike. By 1850, rail lines reached Chicago opening an important outlet for the products of the fertile lands of Illinois, Wisconsin, and Iowa, and the processed goods of the East.

Farmers were often anxious to participate in financing new railway construction. They, of course, were small entrepreneurs, and the capital resources they invested were much too meager. The major capital resources for this undertaking came from federal, state, and foreign governments. This was a period of speculation and "get-rich-quick" promotion techniques. Many farmers lost the small investments which they had made in railroads. Moreover, high freight rates soon caused considerable friction between farm people and railroad developers.

Prior to the Civil War most railroad construction had been in the East. Between 1868 and 1893 there was an acceleration of railroad construction. This was the period of expansion to the Pacific coast. From this time forth, railroad mileage grew rapidly. Connecting East and West ultimately had the effect of bringing all areas and all segments of the economy into close interaction. The efficiency of rail transportation stimulated the development of national markets. The dominance of the local market had ended as mass production and mass consumption became dominant social patterns.[19]

Important developments in communication paralleled advances in transportation. Samuel Morse invented the first successful telegraph in 1844, and its practical utility was established beyond all doubt during the Civil War. Similarly, Alexander Graham Bell's telephone proved successful in 1876 and soon replaced the human messenger system in the expanding urban centers. The rotary press, invented in 1875, was a communications tool the importance of which has often been overlooked. It increased the output and lowered the cost of newspaper publication. Nationwide advertising resulted, first in religious journals because they were the most widely circulated publications of the time.[20]

As transportation and communication complemented each other, new nationwide marketing and selling practices were developed. In the 1890's, companies no longer operated on the basis of existing markets. Instead, they developed advertising schemes and created new markets; supply anticipated demand.[21] Jobbers or middlemen between the manufacturers and the retail stores were often bypassed. Producers and wholesalers were able to sell directly to regional retail firms. With increased advertising, firms registered the brand names of their mass-produced products with the patent office so that their commodities might be distinguished from similar items. Rural Free Delivery (1896) and Parcel Post (1913) were two other striking developments in the expansion of urbanized social organization. These innovations further enabled manufacturers and retailers to sell directly to people in remote locations. By utilizing these mail services, such mass retailing stores as Sears Roebuck and Montgomery Ward became big businesses, catering to rural and urban residents alike.

In this social environment, farmers became major consumers as well as major producers. The self-sufficient farm family which had provided its own food, clothing, furniture, and equipment no longer existed on the social landscape. National markets destroyed local craft production and consumption practices. Household sewing and clothes-making met the competition of mass producers of manufactured clothing. Home gardening and food preservation met the competition of mass production and mass processing of food products.[22] These were some of the means by which farm people came to participate in the complex industrial system of the urbanized society.

Rural electrification. Electrification of farms has become an accomplished fact. In 1959, the Rural Electrification Administration reported that 96 per cent of the nation's farms were receiving electricity.[23] States with the greatest proportion of electric service were the most heavily populated and most urbanized. States with the least service, such as Nevada and North Dakota and South Dakota, were sparsely populated. Most of the new customers of rural electric service have been rural nonfarm users.

New R.E.A. loans have continually been made. Generally, the purposes of such loans have been for the extension of existing service. Energy sales continue to increase. Rural nonfarm electric consumption has surpassed farm electric consumption. In 1959, about 54 per cent of electricity sales were to nonfarm consumers. Average kilowatt-hour usage for farm families per month was 319. This average monthly farm usage increased by about 10 per cent annually from 1948 to 1958. Since electric service has become widely available, attention has shifted from provision of service to specific patterns of utilization. For example, electric heating of rural homes has been promoted.

Electrification has been desired by rural people and its availability and utilization have served to minimize rural-urban differences. Although differences in consumption patterns on the part of farm and rural nonfarm people still obtain, they too are destined to vanish.

The Rural Electrification Administration's program was extended by Congress in 1949 to provide for loans to telephone companies, both of the private and cooperative type.[24] By 1959, R.E.A. had nearly 700 telephone company borrowers, two-thirds of whom were private companies and one-third, cooperatives. Loans have been made to companies located in nearly all of the states. During the decade 1949–1959, telephone service to farmers increased from 38 to 60 per cent. R.E.A. has helped provide new telephone service, improved existing service, and promoted new telephone uses. In promoting new telephone use, companies have suggested that rural people install telephones in homes, barns, and cars. R.E.A. telephone service has become another tangible connecting link between open country and cities. Its contribution to closing the rural-urban gap is manifold.

Social institutions. Domestic, educational, religious, political, and economic institutions in the United States have been studied traditionally to illustrate rural-urban differences. Historically, distinctions were made, for example, between the rural church and the urban church, the rural school and the urban school, the rural family and the urban family. Rural-urban differences in institutions have suggested a distinct way of life in the city and the country. Many of the various measures or indexes which have been used in the studies of organization in colonial-frontier

America and in urbanized America are valid. Yet, the differences were not due to ideology of ruralized social organization versus urbanized social organization. Rather, they pertained to the age of the society. The rural family and the rural school, with characteristics which have so often been extolled, reflected frontier conditions and a spatial separation of the population in a new and expanding area. The development of transportation, the consumption of electricity, and the level of living indexes all indicate that, with the exception of some cultural islands, rural people have been motivated to strive for those goals which have been common to the total nation. Proverbs such as "hard work and diligence make one a good American" are given lip service by many rural people, but scientific commercial farmers go about daily activities in a manner similar to people in nonrural areas.

The social landscape in which institutions have been differentiated on a rural-urban basis is succumbing to mass urbanized society. For example, the nation has one school system, with teachers trained in colleges and certified by the states. Differential educational attainment for the nation's farm, rural nonfarm, and urban school children has been reduced in recent years.

A movement toward the consolidation of small rural churches has also been observed. Graded Sunday schools have become the accepted pattern in American churches, regardless of their location. Large congregations are needed in order to grade Sunday school classes effectively. This has stimulated consolidation, although a movement toward church consolidation has been slower than school consolidation.

All differences in the rural-urban experience have not been dispelled, and, in a technical sense, there is little reason to expect that they ever will be. But differences in the institutional patterns of behavior within various urban areas are more significant than those between the rural and urban areas. Today in the United States, however, there is essentially a common institutional pattern of behavior.

AGRICULTURE IN URBANIZED SOCIAL ORGANIZATION

Springdale.[25] There are a number of studies which reveal the typical integration of agriculture and rural people into the greater society. Vidich and Bensman studied the daily life of people in a small rural community in New York. They reported in detail the roles which politics, religion, social class, and education played in the experience of Springdale's 2,500 inhabitants. They were particularly concerned with the impact of the larger mass society on Springdale's inhabitants. Springdale was settled in 1793. Its history, therefore, was substantial enough for it to have experienced the transition from rural to urban life.

Springdalers had a self-image, which they thought differentiated them from outsiders. They were "just plain folks." There were "town folk," "country folk," "good folk," "bad folk," and the like in Springdale. Metropolitan dwellers were referred to as "city people," thereby implying that they were considerably different from Springdale people. The term "plain folks" involved a whole set of social values, namely, honesty, fair play, trustworthiness, good neighborliness, helpfulness, sobriety, and clean living.[26] In contrast, the conception of the city was that of a place that breeds corruption; hence it was thought to constitute an unwholesome environment for children. Washington was described as a place overridden with bureaucrats. Big universities and churches were thought to be centers of atheism and secularism.[27] But these expressions are abstract sentiments which idealize some particular location. They do not express the actual social organization or way of life. In spite of localized abstract sentiments, Springdalers had succumbed to the mass society. They were proud Americans—proud of the productive capacity of these United States and proud of the military might of their nation.[28]

In addition to espousing its abstract sentiments, Springdalers were related to the mass society in a variety of ways. Some of these relationships were exceedingly tangible. There were organizers and experts in the community, most of whom migrated there. These persons were typically college trained and their skills and information could not adequately be evaluated by the indigenous population. For example, the county and home agents represented the state's land-grant college extension program. These were persons concerned with progress, and their goals were to improve farm and homemaking practices. They constituted a direct contact for the Springdaler with the larger society. Experts who were concerned with civil defense, charity drives, and recreational programs also contributed outside ideas to new developments in the local community.

Businessmen had contacts with the larger society, often of a highly tangible nature. Store keepers, service station operators, appliance dealers, car and farm implement dealers, and other merchants all depended on the external world for supplies and commodities which they sold. The over-all conditions of the national economy placed real limitations on their potential business and earnings, and ultimately on their style of life. Many businessmen were connected to larger firms by franchises or contracts; some were even managers for absentee-owner firms. But whether businesses were absentee or locally owned, they were influenced in their operations by manufacturing, production, and other economic developments outside of the community. Locally owned businesses might be free of executive directives from a home office, but they were inevitably influenced by the system of competition which included the larger chain firms.

Professionals and specialists constituted another type of connecting link between local areas and the larger society. These persons had a status in the community that was largely determined by their own associational culture and over which the local people had a minimum of control. Professionals belonged to organizations outside the community, they were trained outside the community, and they were licensed or certified by organizations or agencies outside the community. Their specialized knowledge was greater than that of the typical resident. This placed the local person at a disadvantage in evaluating the competence of the specialist.

Professionals and specialists were the college-trained people of the community. They included ministers, teachers, lawyers, engineers, and medical specialists. The various specialists who represented the state and federal governmental agencies were also a part of this group. In the case of Springdale, all but two of the professional-specialists had migrated into the community after their adult training, a pattern found in many other similar communities. These persons had prestige because of their education, their specialized knowledge, and their ability to represent the community to the outside world and, in turn, to manipulate the outside world for the local community's interest. As a result of their contacts, they could accomplish various things which were impossible for other persons in the community. The social status of the professional-specialist group was relatively high. Nevertheless, they did not fit clearly into the stratification system of the indigenous community. They were prized for their styles of taste and cultural consumption which were beyond those of the local people. Often their "alien" or "exotic" tastes corresponded to those of the larger urban world more than to the local community. The professional-specialists who did become established in the local community became numbered among the community's elite and among the other pacesetters for the area.

In addition to people who moved in from outside the community, there were organizations in Springdale such as 4-H Clubs, Future Farmers of America, Masons, Odd Fellows, American Legion, Grange, and several other branches of national organizations and their auxiliaries. All of these had the effect of relating the Springdaler to the larger society. In these various organizations, programs, rituals, and national offices all had their influence on the local chapter or division. They promoted social interaction with people from outside the local community through regional meetings, national conventions, and other occasions when people from the various local units interacted with one another.

The impact of mass media was forceful. Motion pictures brought the "four corners of the world" to Springdale. Television offered coverage as extensive as that of the movies. Daily papers brought news from the world over, and most Springdalers were not satisfied with only a local newspaper. Typically, they subscribed to one of the major metropolitan papers.[29] National magazines reached the people in Springdale with great regularity. Issues of *Life* and *Time,* and perhaps a dozen others, contributed to the Springdaler's inevitable existence as a real part of the nation and the world.

As the nation experienced a suburban movement and an increase in the rural nonfarm population, a sizable number of residents in Springdale who were industrial workers were employed in out-of-town plants. These people were for the most part migrants who had come from two directions, namely, from the large central cities and from the open country. Some moved to the smaller rural towns to avoid the congestion of the city; others had been forced out of agricultural pursuits. These industrially employed people did not fit into any clear niche in Springdale society. Their work outside of the community was sufficient to orient them toward the larger society. Their jobs often depended upon the prosperity of national markets. They commuted several hours a day to and from their place of employment and, thus, spent a great proportion of their time outside the local community. These workers had a minimum of social and economic interaction within the community, though some of them made an effort to become a part of it. Often they maintained an affiliation with a local church. But, to the time of the study, even though the migrant stream to the smaller community was increasing, it was not sufficiently large or persistent to allow these people to be fitted into the social class hierarchy.

Springdale farmers were of two distinct types, rational and traditional. Rational farmers were oriented toward scientific agriculture, mass production, and mass marketing. Traditional farmers were oriented to local situations, if not in some cases to subsistence and part-time operations.[30] Those who were concerned with the mass markets were also concerned with price subsidies, regulations on quality standards, and types of items that could be marketed, as well as with the relation of large-scale government to farming. Rational farmers typically had large investments, and they were interested in expanding their operations. Indeed, they were operating businesses according to a success orientation. Traditional farmers were typically older men, and many of them had experienced the depression years of the 1930's. Rational farmers were active members of the rural middle class, while traditional farmers often ranked lower in the social hierarchy.

Class structure in Springdale revealed in still another way the interaction of the local community with the larger society. People in occupational groups that were linked to the larger society were in a position to be socially, economically, and politically powerful people in the community. The dynamics of social organization resulted in the awarding of high social class status to persons who were newcomers to Springdale. The boundary which had in the past served to insulate the local community was now necessarily broken. The local area could be physically identified, but in terms of social behavior, residents regularly interacted both within and outside the local community. Inevitably, therefore, to be a recluse in the local community was to abandon one's high position in the class hierarchy.

Politically, the local community had surrendered to the mass society. There were, of course, the usual local political organizations, the most powerful of which was town government. This local government was elected by the people. It was concerned with such matters as water supply, street lights, fire protection, roads, parks, and sewage disposal. In many of these matters, the local community had to accept standards, regulations, and laws which were promulgated by county, state, and federal governments. In a complex way the local political organization relied upon specialists; for example, engineers, attorneys, and a host of others provided services which were indispensable to the ongoing life of the community. The local tax structure, likewise, was oriented to equalization formulas which were essentially determined at a state level. Highway construction was largely directed at a state level. Health and welfare boards had to meet directives and regulations from outside the local community. In short, many important political decisions for a community like Springdale were made outside its local domain.

The school board was faced with outside regulations of a similar nature. While it was elected locally, it depended to a great extent on advice by specialists, such as the superintendent, principal, and teachers, to interpret the needs of the school in accordance with state education standards. The school board might attempt to control the operation of the school, yet Springdalers did not want their children to receive a second-rate education or have their education jeopardized. Consequently, the school system had to be "as good as any other," and the final judgment of this, in most cases, rested with persons outside the local community.

Springdalers differentiated their community from the larger society, but an examination of the social structure indicated that it was highly interrelated with the larger society. Ideologically, the people supported the general goals of their society and were aware of the contribution of their community to the nation.

Wasco. In a study of Wasco, Southern California, an industrialized agricultural community of some 4,000 people, Goldschmidt reported that "from industrialized sowing of the soil was reaped an urbanized rural society." [31] The community came into existence in the 1920's. In terms of the census definition, Wasco was a city because it had over 2,500 people. But at the time of the study it was not incorporated (as it has since become) due to the desire of the people to remain free from the complications of government. In Wasco there was an absence of community loyalty of the type so prevalent in Springdale.

Goldschmidt did not find the traditional rural characteristics of face-to-face contacts, individualism, and low education in Wasco. People were more interested in progress than in traditionalism. They wanted to be an ongoing part of the larger society, not a remote unit separate from it. [32]

Wasco was a young community and one which has been highly mechanized almost from its time of origin. Its location in an area requiring expensive irrigation necessitated a systematic and mechanized system of agriculture. A local farmer made the point clear to Goldschmidt by asserting, "There is one thing I want you to put down in your book. Farming in this country is a business, it is not a way of life." [33] Such a statement was made by a man who was operating a 200-acre farm, not a large factory farm.

The main characteristics of mechanized or industrialized farming in Wasco were intensive production, large investments, impersonal hiring of laborers, complete commercialization, and a high degree of specialization and efficiency.[34] The goals were cash cropping and high yields per acre.

An important development of urbanized agriculture was the virtual disappearance of the barnyard. It was unusual for Wasco farmers to keep a cow for their own milk, to have some chickens for their own eggs and meat, or to have a garden to provide their own fresh vegetables. It meant more prestige to buy such commodities at a local supermarket. This had the effect of emancipating the farm housewife from her historic duties of barnyard chores, garden raising, and food preserving. The old saying "but a woman's work is never done" no longer applied to the urbanized farming area. Families were smaller, and electric labor-saving devices were extensively used. Hence the rural farm wife in Wasco, like the town housewife, had time to devote to various social activities. This change broke another barrier or boundary-maintenance mechanism between rural and urban people.

In an urbanized rural community of the Wasco type even the meaning of machinery was complex. Its first meaning was, of course, utility. Farming was a business, and the tractor and other equipment had an important cost-accounting relationship for that business. A second meaning of machinery was luxury. Goldschmidt found the tractor to be a source of pride for many farmers—a way in which they could display affluency. One implement dealer reported farmers in the area manifested as much pride and joy in their new farm equipment as a boy with a new car. Many of them purchased farm equipment beyond their needs and were prone to follow new styles in machinery design.[35]

Urbanized agriculture also affected the townspeople. Wasco was the smallest population center in its area, yet it was large enough to meet the regular needs of the people in terms of groceries, clothing, lumber, furniture, cars, farm equipment, and seed. From this point of view, Wasco was a self-sufficient economic unit. But, like Springdale, Wasco was almost completely dependent upon the outside world for its source of goods, indeed for its very existence. Big business had its interests in the local community. Electricity to pump water was provided by an outside firm, and gas was also piped in from outside. The local bank was a branch of one of the nation's largest banking firms. Chain firms and franchise-type operations were also found in Wasco. There were many absentee-owner businesses. Smaller, locally owned businesses were influenced by the absentee operations in the areas of competition and supply of commodities. Wasco had one large local corporation, but its major interests and activities were directed from outside the community. It was necessarily concerned with other large corporations, union-management relationships, and government controls of production.

Wasco, like other rural communities in the nation, was experiencing an increasing amount of governmental control from county, state, and national agencies—all outside the local domain. On the surface there was considerable autonomy in the local school. The school board was elected by local people and had considerable jurisdiction over salaries. It could hire and dismiss the staff at the local level. Nevertheless, the curriculum, form of classroom instruction, training of teachers, provision of textbooks, utilization of supervisory personnel, along with many other activities and services involved in the operation of the school, were either controlled or much influenced by agencies and laws outside the local community.

The tendency for local control and autonomy to be usurped by state and federal forms of government has become characteristic throughout the whole of America. This process has been accelerated in rural communities caught up in the vortex of industrialization. If, in addition, there are the various mass media of outside advertising, metropolitan newspapers with their syndicated columns, mass production and mass marketing, then there is little basis for integrating the small community around a core of local traditions. Significant life situations come to be found more and more outside the residential location. Local communities exist in a residential sense but hardly in a social sense. There is little ethnocentrism on the part of their members. The major types of identification which a resident has are with the state, the nation, the larger areas of society. Localism and traditionalism have little place in such urbanized social organization.

Plainville, U.S.A.[36] Plainville, U.S.A., was first studied in 1939 and 1940. It was a Midwestern community of less than 1,000 inhabitants, which existed as a small trading and social center for farmers living in the surrounding area. Plainville was settled in the 1830's as a part of the general westward migration. Transportation and communication in Plainville were oriented toward the conventional patterns of the national society. In the late 1890's a railroad from the nearest metropolitan area came to a nearby town, and a profitable stagecoach line connected Plainville to the rail center. At the time of the study, highways were the most important arteries of transportation. Plainville had a paved road over which trucks carried most of the produce and livestock sold from the community and, in return, over which deliveries of merchandise were made. Other local roads were not surfaced and often muddy and impassable at various times of the year. Electricity had not yet come to all homes. One high line served the town, but service was often suspended for as much as several hours during storms. Consequently, two-thirds of the houses had relatively unreliable electric service. Other village houses and most of the farm houses were lighted by kerosene lamps. Rural mail, telegraph, and telephones had been available for some forty years.[37] A county newspaper and some ten or twelve copies of a metropolitan newspaper were brought daily to Plainville. Many farmers subscribed to magazines such as *The State Farmer, Country Gentleman,* and *Pictorial Review.* A local liquor dealer had installed a magazine stand from which he made considerable profit. The greatest proportion of the magazine consumers were townspeople to whom he regularly sold copies of *Life, Collier's, Liberty,* and *The Saturday Evening Post.* Radio was introduced to Plainville in 1920. By the 1940's, radios were widespread; indeed, they were considered a virtual necessity.

In this remote rural community, Plainvillers—like Springdalers and Wasco people—were linked to the outside world by roads, cars, rural free delivery, press, mail-order catalogues, telephones, and telegraph. They were also linked to the larger society by the migration of nearly half of their children for employment outside the local community. From these migratory youth there were letters describing conditions in other areas of the nation. Plainville folks "subscribe in main to the American credo of vertical mobility and believe that a man (though hardly a woman) can become anything he wants to 'if he'll just work at it.' " [38]

Regardless of the many avenues of transportation and communication which connected Plainvillers with the outside world, this was a community which impressed the city person as being "isolated" and "backward." Plainvillers themselves sensed this isolation of their community and of its being "behind the times." Yet, older people indicated that in their youth they had been unaware of any better place. With the communication growth of the outside, the young people complained "there's nothin' to do, away off back here away from ever' place!" [39]

Plainville had only a few professional-specialists and only a few outside-owned businesses. The county agent lived in Plainville, but his office was in the county seat. Only half a dozen of the town's businesses were considered to be operating on a paying basis.[40] Even operators of these businesses were oriented to the local farm community. For example, the doctor and the produce man each raised rather large gardens and generally kept a cow and a hog to supply their milk and meat.

Plainville had a number of organizations such as Odd Fellows, Woodmen, and Masons. While these organizations had the usual relationship to outside areas, their importance and esteem in the local community had become traditional within the Plainville area. They were valued for their contribution to health insurance, burial benefits, male solidarity, horseplay, and practical joking at initiations. The importance of these organizations was locally recognized in another way when one respondent indicated, "A man that knew the Masonic handshake used to could cash a check anywhere." [41] But lodges were of declining importance in Plainville. Reasons given for their decline were increased cost, large-city orientation, and secular interests. In addition, they had to compete with new attractions such as movies and radio.

Plainville, like the other communities cited, was faced with change. The high school was consolidated and vocational agriculture courses were making their impact. The automobile provided employment opportunities for mechanics and a means for people to move out of the community to other employment sites. Prospects for more rationalized and scientific farming suggested still greater change for the future. Plainville, like Springdale and Wasco, was confronted with the alternatives of either changing or losing population and continuing to decline.

CONCEPT OF URBANIZED SOCIAL ORGANIZATION

Urbanized social organization is initially generated out of city life. In its mature form its cultural universals dominate an entire society. It involves some assimilation, so that urbanized cultural universals are ultimately built on patterns of behavior from both city and country life. It is an integrative type of organization which tends to break down boundaries between socially differentiated areas. Rural and urban differences eventually disappear as behavioral systems and people in both ecological areas embrace common cultural goals and expectations.

Urbanized social organization is a complete way of life to which practically all people in a given society give allegiance and by which their activities are directed. It is characterized by extensive division of labor and specialization. Experts and professionals abound, and people everywhere are dependent on them. They, in turn, are dependent on the social system of which they are a part to continually develop situations requiring their services. Transportation and communication are unifying forces in urbanized society. Secondary, rather than primary, social interaction is widespread. Significant others are not necessarily in geographical proximity to residents. Awareness of these social patterns is no longer confined to specific areas.

Institutional patterns support urbanized cultural norms. High levels of educational attainment are required for all people if they are to be contributing citizens. Consequently, the rural and urban school systems become fused into one. During the elementary years, practically every child attends school and is exposed to a universal socialization experience. Economic situations are national in scope. Minimum wage laws structure the earning circumstances for an ever expanding number of people, and there are national income taxes. Government is increasingly an urbanized universal pattern. Rules of social order, rights, duties, privileges, and expectancies must be essentially the same throughout all of the land. Without such a system of universal order, there would be normlessness. Indeed, social integration would be impossible if members of a society were forced to learn a different system of order for each locality. Townships and often county governments are, therefore, coming to be less important.

Family patterns support the norms of materialism, success, and accomplishment. Horatio Alger stories, tales of office boy to president, and many other myths are part of cultural patterns which have given inspiration to many an American family, whether rural or urban. Birth rates, both rural and urban, contract and expand according to the condition of the national economy.

No area of life escapes the influence of urbanized normative patterns. Urbanized social organization is an abstract type and not expected to be identified in any concrete situation. Like ruralized social organization, it involves the domination of society by a way of life common to all people. Its focus is universality, specialization, division of labor, and accomplishment.

SUMMARY

Americans currently live in one of the world's most urbanized societies. The experience of urbanization is new. In fact, it is still going on, and it

is now impossible to know how completely urbanized a society can become. In America, urbanization is taking the form of mass society. All
people everywhere are reached by such mass media as radio, television,
and the press. Ideas and standards of behavior which guide men in their
daily life are essentially the same, regardless of place of residence in a city
or the open country. Cultural universals reach most of the nation's more
than 179,000,000 (1960) people. Rural-urban differences are rapidly
diminishing as the nation adopts a common, mass way of life.

Colonial America was founded at a time when feudalism and ruralized
social organization were rapidly declining in Europe. In England land
was being enclosed in the form of private property. Notions of centralized
government, indeed the very experience of colonial expansion, signified
the termination of rurality. The American colonies were dominated by
physical rurality but never by ideological rurality. Attempts to establish
feudal society in the colonies failed.

The Revolution and the founding of the United States of America took
place at the time of the Industrial Revolution in England. The new nation
had continual contact with the developments in Europe. Immigrants continued to bring knowledge of the changing social order in Europe. Accordingly, American history records the experiences of industrialization,
market-oriented urban development, and rapid change from rural to urban
society, but never the experience of ruralized social organization. Both
the Revolutionary and Civil Wars provided markets for agricultural
products. Technology and science, from colonial times to the present, have
been utilized by farmers to increase production and provide excess food
and fiber for nonfarm peoples.

Urbanization has been rapid. It can be illustrated by a number of
measures or indexes of change. Only 5 per cent of the population lived in
cities in 1790. By 1920, more than half of all Americans were urban
residents. By 1960, over two-thirds of the nation's people resided in cities.
Rural nonfarm people outnumber rural farm people. Farm people
number less than 20,000,000, and each census in recent years has reported their decline.

Levels of living are increasing for all farm people. Farm families in
close proximity to large population centers and in the most urbanized
states have the highest level of living. Farm operators now constitute less
than 10 per cent of the labor force. Transportation and communication
are both largely national in scope. Rural isolation is virtually nonexistent.
Production and distribution of goods are required to fill the needs of a

national market. Public utility consumption is similar in both rural and urban areas.

Social institutions are now less bifurcated into rural and urban types. The family life of the business farmer is very similar to that of his city cousin. The rural school is being consolidated, and so are the rural churches. One now observes that America has only one school system and also only one church system, rather than the historically differentiated rural and urban types. In the cases where fusion is not yet complete it is more a matter of a time-lag than of divergent ideologies. The social institutions of government, welfare, recreation, and leisure are experiencing similar rural-urban fusion.

Farm and small-town life are now becoming irrevocably intertwined with national life. Farming is one element or part among the many parts of a large ongoing urbanized society. Farming is neither a matter of subsistence nor a way of life. It is a business, the role of which is to provide basic food and fiber needs for the masses of nonfarm people.

Classic case studies of communities like Plainville, U.S.A., Wasco, and Springdale reveal that rural life is directly and indirectly influenced by pressures and forces outside of the local community. Local people often express an abstract and sentimental preference for the quiet simple life but, in fact, contradict themselves by their overt behavior. They are proud of their nation, its accomplishments, progress, and strength. Certainly, they want to be, and are, loyal citizens.

Urbanized social organization is an integrated way of life subscribed to by all people in a given society. Rural-urban differences diminish. The division of labor is complex, specialization is widespread, and isolation is minimized. The way of life is neither urban nor rural; these are fused into one common way.

NOTES

1. *The Exploding Metropolis* (New York: Doubleday Anchor Books, 1957).

2. *Ibid.,* p. 120.

3. H. E. Bracey, *English Rural Life: Village Activities; Organizations and Institutions* (London: Routledge and Kegan Paul, 1959), pp. 1–15; and L. Dudley Stamp, *Man and the Land* (London: Collins, 1955), pp. 127 ff.

4. Arnold Toynbee, *The Industrial Revolution* (Boston: The Beacon Press, 1956).

5. Samuel P. Hayes, *The Response to Industrialism, 1885–1914* (Chicago: The University of Chicago Press, 1957).

6. *Ibid.*, p. 1.

7. *Ibid.*, p. 2.

8. Don Martindale, *American Society* (New York: D. Van Nostrand, 1960), pp. 122 ff.

9. For a complete definition of urbanized areas, see U.S. Bureau of the Census, *U.S. Census of Population: 1960, Number of Inhabitants,* State Final Reports, PC (Washington: U.S. Government Printing Office, 1960).

10. Otis Dudley Duncan and Albert J. Reiss, Jr., *Social Characteristics of Urban and Rural Communities, 1950* (New York: John Wiley and Sons, 1956).

11. Margaret Jarman Hagood, *et al., Farm-Operator Family Level-of-Living Indexes for Counties of the United States 1945, 1950, and 1954* (Washington: U.S. Department of Agriculture, Agriculture Marketing Service, 1957); Alvin L. Bertrand, *Trends and Patterns in Levels-of-Living of Farm Families in the U.S.* (Washington: U.S. Department of Agriculture, Agriculture Information Bulletin 181, 1958).

12. Donald J. Bogue, *The Population of the United States* (Glencoe: Free Press, 1959).

13. *Ibid.*, p. 478.

14. Gertrude Bancroft, *The American Labor Force: Its Growth and Changing Composition* (New York: John Wiley and Sons, 1958), pp. 28–9.

15. *Ibid.*, p. 39.

16. Murray R. Benedict, *Farm Policies of the United States, 1790–1950: A Study of Their Origins and Development* (New York: The Twentieth Century Fund, 1953), p. 61.

17. *Ibid.*

18. Hayes, *op. cit.*, p. 5.

19. *Ibid.*, p. 7.

20. *Ibid.*, p. 8.

21. *Ibid.*, p. 12.

22. *Ibid.*, p. 13.

23. *Report of the Administration of the Rural Electrification Administration, 1959* (Washington: U.S. Government Printing Office, 1959), pp. 16–17 ff.

24. *Rural Telephone Service—U.S.A.* (Rural Electrification Administration, U.S. D.A. Miscellaneous Publication No. 823, May, 1960).

25. Arthur J. Vidich and Joseph Bensman, *Small Town in Mass Society* (New York: Doubleday Anchor Books, 1960).

26. *Ibid.*, p. 31.

27. *Ibid.*, p. 33.

28. *Ibid.*, p. 80.

29. *Ibid.*, p. 85.

30. *Ibid.*, p. 96.

31. Walter Goldschmidt, *As You Sow* (New York: Harcourt, Brace and Co., 1947), p. vii.

32. *Ibid.*

33. *Ibid.*, p. 23.

34. *Ibid.*, p. 24.

35. *Ibid.*, p. 33.

36. James West, *Plainville, U.S.A.* (New York: Columbia University Press, 1945); and Art Gallaher, Jr., *Plainville Fifteen Years Later* (New York: Columbia University Press, 1961).

37. West, *op. cit.*, pp. 13–14.

38. *Ibid.*, pp. 18–19.

39. *Ibid.*, p. 54.

40. *Ibid.*, p. 22.

41. *Ibid.*, p. 82.

SELECTED READINGS

Gallaher, Art. *Plainville Fifteen Years Later.* New York: Columbia University Press, 1961.

A restudy of a low-income farm community, focusing on the forces, impact, and effects of cultural and social change as well as leadership and adjustment processes emerging in changing sociocultural conditions.

Goldschmidt, Walter. *As You Sow.* New York: Harcourt, Brace and Co., 1947.

A report on the impact being made by industrialization and technology on business agriculture.

Hayes, Samuel P. *The Response to Industrialism, 1885–1914.* Chicago: University of Chicago Press, 1957.

A sociohistorical analysis of the impact of industrialization on different groups of Americans between the Civil War and World War I, and their responses to the drastic innovations.

Vidich, Arthur and Joseph Bensman. *Small Town in Mass Society.* New York: Doubleday Anchor Books, 1960.

The report of a study of social integration in a small community which lacks the power to control the institutions that regulate and direct its existence.

West, James. *Plainville, U.S.A.* New York: Columbia University Press, 1945.

A case study of the responses of a relatively isolated agricultural community to the influx of outside cultural influences.

3 RURAL–URBAN DIFFERENCES

There is an ancient worldwide tradition of differentiating rural and urban people.[1] In the United States there is a specific history of the so-called rural-urban dichotomy. In America the transition from dominant ruralized social organization to a dominant urbanized social organization has been rapid. A society characterized by pronounced rural-urban differences is transitional, shifting either from rural to urban or from urban to rural. Following a brief historical introduction, the body of this chapter is devoted to a consideration of the rural-urban dichotomy in the United States.

HISTORICAL DEVELOPMENT

Students of history generally have agreed that nomadic life and tribal organization preceded the establishment of cities. In times of nomadic life, rural-urban differences were few, but they increased as cities were founded. Ancient cities in Syria, Egypt, and Babylonia were characterized by many rural traits. Their populations were consumption-oriented. They relied heavily on the production of the land around them, and they in turn produced very little. Later, cities were characterized as places of refuge for clans and rural people. Like consumption cities, refuge cities were closely related to the rural hinterland, but they were also seats of rulers and officials. They provided some service to the local rural people in the form of protection.

49

Rural-urban differences increased as Renaissance cities came to be the abode of artisans and craftsmen rather than of land owners and cultivators. Renaissance city craftsmen traded primarily with the inhabitants of the immediate hinterland. Rural people marketed at the nearest city. Development from the Renaissance city to the modern metropolis further increased rural-urban differences.

The modern metropolis became more than a center of mercantilism. It was a center which combined manufacturing, government, education, and culture. It has been oriented to mass markets, international markets, and national markets, and served its own local hinterland only as a matter of course. As the metropolis extended its sphere of influence beyond the local hinterland, major changes have been wrought in social organization. Cultural universals became dominated by urban ideologies, and rural-urban differences were reduced. In a milieu of urbanized social organization, some differences continue to exist but they are more of degree than of kind.

INDEXES OF RURAL-URBAN DIFFERENTIATION

Some major rural-urban differences that have been enumerated are occupation, environment, size of community, density of population, heterogeneity, social differentiation, mobility, and system of social interaction. The character and importance of these indexes of rural-urban differences are indicated in the following outline.

	Rural World	*Urban World*
Occupation	Totality of cultivators and their families. In the community there are usually a few representatives of several nonagricultural pursuits. They, however, do not compose the proper subject of rural sociology.	Totality of people engaged principally in manufacturing, mechanical pursuits, trade, commerce, professions, governing, and other nonagricultural occupations.
Environment	Predominance of nature over anthro-social environment. Direct human relationship to nature.	Greater isolation from nature. Predominance of manmade environment over natural. Poorer air. Stone and iron.

	Rural World	*Urban World*
Size of Community	Open farms or small communities, "agrarianism" and size of community are negatively correlated.	As a rule in the same country and at the same period, the size of the urban community is much larger than that of the rural community. In other words, urbanization and size of community are positively correlated.
Density of Population	In the same country and at the same period the density is lower than in the urban community. Generally, density and rurality are negatively correlated.	Greater than in rural communities. Urbanity and density are positively correlated.
Heterogeneity and Homogeneity of the Population	Compared with urban populations, the populations of rural communities are more homogeneous in racial and psychosocial traits. (Negative correlation with heterogeneity.)	More heterogeneous than rural communities (at the same time.) Urbanity and density are positively correlated.
Social Differentiation and Stratification	Rural differentiation and stratification are less than urban ones.	Differentiation and stratification show positive correlation with urbanity.
Mobility	Territorial, occupational, and other forms of social mobility of the population are comparatively less intensive. Normally, the migration current carries more individuals from the country to the city.	More intensive. Urbanity and mobility are positively correlated. Only in periods of social catastrophe is the migration from the city to the country greater than that from the country to the city.

	Rural World	*Urban World*
System of Interaction	Less numerous contacts per man. Narrower area of the interaction system of its members and the whole aggregate. More prominent part is occupied by primary contacts. Predominance of personal and relatively durable relations. Comparative simplicity and sincerity of relations. "Man is interacted with as a human person."	More numerous contacts. Wider area of interaction system per man and per aggregate. Predominance of impersonal, casual, and short-lived relations. Greater complexity, manifoldness, superficiality, and standardized formality of relations. Man is interacted with as a "number" and "address." [2]

As urbanized social organization has continued to dominate American society in recent years, even these major rural-urban differences have diminished in validity.[3]

Farming is still the classic rural occupation, but the scientific farmer operates a large urbanized business. His work experience and career pattern are becoming more and more similar to those of his urban counterparts. Moreover, as agribusiness advances, much of the farm-related work in open-country America is that of specialists who supply farm equipment and process farm products. Hence farmers constitute one of the smaller occupational categories in the nation. Agribusiness workers, however, constitute a larger proportion of the labor force. The net result of changes in the work patterns of farmers and the expansion of agribusiness careers has been a reduction in the importance of occupations for differentiating rural-urban behavior.[4]

The physical environments of rural and urban life are less differentiated in an urbanized than in a ruralized society. Business farmers now operate large mechanized enterprises through which they are able to modify their physical work environment. For example, tractor lights enable the farmer to extend his work hours. Electricity in barns and shops allow him to work longer periods in a manner similar to city businessmen and industrial workers.

Size of communities is also changing.[5] Small country towns are less able to supply the materials needed by mechanized farmers than they were in the past. Consequently, farm people are drawn into more direct social interaction with the populations of larger urban places. Moreover, the population itself is shifting in an exodus from farms to nonfarm places. The latter are variously referred to as suburbs, satellite cities, and fringe areas. These population shifts also contribute to the heterogeneity of the open-country population. By the second half of the twentieth century, most people living in the open country are not engaged in farming.

Both social mobility and complex social interaction have been extended into rural areas, particularly into fringe areas.[6] Rural residents in the fringe are a mobile people, more like those of the city than the traditional farm. As city residents move into the fringe areas, they interact with their new farm neighbors as well as with their former city acquaintances.

These indexes of rural-urban differences were valid for the United States during the nineteenth and early twentieth centuries. By the second half of the twentieth century, urbanized social organization was dominant throughout the length and breadth of the land, for all people, whether farm or city. Vertical integration and agribusiness were specific social structures which facilitated the incorporation of the food and fiber industry into the total national economy.

Census rural-urban differentiation. The most persuasive rural-urban differentiation in the United States has been exercised by the Bureau of the Census both through its manner of collecting data and through its dichotomous classification: [7]

The general distinction between urban and rural, as opposing concepts, runs far back into the history of civilization. . . . The rural concept sometimes specifically included the small villages, especially in those countries where most of the agricultural workers lived in villages.

Against this common background, different countries have followed different procedures in setting up census classifications under which their population could be classified in statistical terms as urban and rural, putting varying emphasis on size of place, density of settlement, type of political organization, or prevalence of agricultural occupations, and sometimes making provision for an intermediate semi-urban or semi-rural classification.[8]

In the United States, census rural-urban differentiation has been based primarily on size of place as measured by number of people. Historically, the urban population included only those people in the incorporated limits of municipalities of a designated minimum size. The first direct reference to the need for a rural-urban classification appeared in the Seventh Census

(1850). It was stated with regret that the census did not differentiate between urban and rural population. The censuses of 1860 and 1870 contained no references to rural-urban classifications.

The first official analysis of the urban population of the nation appeared in the *Statistical Atlas of the United States of 1874*.[9] The statistical atlas was not primarily designed to analyze the urban population. Indeed, it appeared only as a byproduct of maps showing the density of population. In the chapter entitled "Progress of the Nation," there were maps showing the urban population (for places of 8,000 or more) from each census dating from 1790 onward. Unfortunately, the maps showed the population per square mile throughout the country and did not distinguish the corresponding rural population.

In the 1880 Census, the statistical maps were brought up to date. Again they showed the urban population using the minimum size of 8,000. Urbanization had already reached such a point of complexity that identifying cities of 8,000 people or more presented several problems. Concerning this situation Walker wrote in the *Statistical Atlas:*

Several difficulties, not a little annoying, arise during the reduction of these results to a form for comparison. For instance, what constitutes a city? In some states, the laws relating to the incorporation of villages and boroughs are so liberal, and the people are so well disposed towards this form of civil organization, that there is no danger of any considerable town failing to be distinguished from the mass of settlement. The liability to mistake is here rather in the chance that a "city" of 8,000 inhabitants may not imply a strictly urban population of those members, the municipal limits being sometimes so extended as to include considerable rural districts.[10]

In addition for the 1880 Census the urban population was also computed for all places of 4,000 or more persons. This change in definition added another 294 places to the urban category, bringing the total of urban places to 580. Between 1880 and 1910, urban definitions vacillated between minimums of 8,000 and 4,000. In 1910, the census reduced the minimum number of people for cities to 2,500. Since 1910 the definition of 2,500 or more has continued to serve as the basis of rural-urban differentiation. The minimum figure was also accompanied by many qualifications to make the definition more appropriate to specific situations.

In 1920 a major addition was made to the census classificatory system. This was the threefold classification of the population into farm, rural-nonfarm (village), and urban. This distinction was made in a special census monograph entitled *Farm Population of the United States, 1920*.[11]

From 1930 to 1960 selected census data have been reported in the categories urban, rural nonfarm, and rural farm.

RURALISMS WIDESPREAD IN THE EIGHTEENTH AND NINETEENTH CENTURIES

Cities of the colonial and early national period were small and so pervaded with ruralisms that they were often difficult to distinguish from the country environs.[12] Early American cities were in physical proximity to the countryside. They were virtually undistinguishable from the hinterland on a sociopsychological basis. Through most of the first half of the nineteenth century, agricultural sights and sounds were a familiar part of life on the city streets. Horse-drawn farm wagons and horse-drawn city streetcars had much in common. Trees, grass, and gardens formed the landscape of the city dwellers. Land use in the city often allowed ample space for vegetable gardens and fruit tree cultivation.[13]

Rural people went into the towns for commercial purposes and other reasons of social interaction, and urban dwellers went out into the countryside. Many townspeople lived close enough to walk or ride through the country. Moreover, as Bridenbaugh has indicated, the newly rich gentry of the colonial cities desired to acquire a country estate as soon as possible. Country towns attracted some of the new wealthy city families as soon as carriage travel made it possible for them to travel between their place of residence and their city businesses.[14]

RURAL-URBAN DIFFERENCES MOST PRONOUNCED IN THE NINETEENTH CENTURY

During the first half of the nineteenth century, ruralisms in city life grew to vast proportions. They originated, through cultural diffusion, with the movement of indigenous rural people from farms to cities, and with the migration of rural Europeans to American cities. Many migrants to the cities were forced to find housing in the crowded tenements, but as quickly as they were capable of accumulating sufficient wealth, they moved to more spacious locations on the periphery of the cities. Even second- and third-generation city people placed high value on a variety of ruralisms. For example, the values for gardening and for home cooking were sustained as signs of prestige after they were no longer materially functional. In residential areas around the peripheries of many cities, street nomenclature retained a highly rural flavor. This is reflected in names like Shady Lane, Garden Lane, Buena Vista Drive, Creek Side Drive, and Walnut Creek Road. Lane, road, and drive all came to imply more prestige than street, boulevard, or avenue.

Throughout the first half of the nineteenth century, the city and country landscapes grew farther apart, each acquiring its own distinct character. In the prevailing value system, urban areas were thought to be less desirable places for rearing children than open country and fringe areas. Many of those who desired most to live in the central city also had the means for a sojourn to the country in the summer. Such individuals established the pattern of alternating residence between city and small town or open country.

The countryside was stereotyped for its virtues as a counterbalance to the evils of the cities. It was suggested that a person who did not leave the cities for the country in the summer was denying himself a revitalization of life. In short, it was asserted that urban life had to be revitalized at the pure source, namely, country life. To appreciate the higher value of the country was one's personal duty. These were the values of vanishing agrarianism, which were being extolled just prior to the Civil War.

Cities, nevertheless, became strong. To some they were sinful and coarse, while to others they were the zenith of culture and civilization. But regardless of the value judgments about urban and country life, cities were firmly established. The perpetuation of judgments, charges, and countercharges are illustrated by books such as *Cities Are Abnormal* and *Exploding Metropolis*.

The contest to determine whether urban or rural values would prevail throughout the length and breadth of the nation was an integral aspect of the Civil War. The interests of ruralized social organization lost in that strife. From the Civil War to the present, society has become continually more characterized by urbanized social organization. The shift in value orientation from ruralized to urbanized social organization took most of the nineteenth century.

During the middle of the nineteenth century, major indexes of rural-urban differentiation reached their highest point of prominence. Occupational differentiation between farm and industrial work was never greater. Scientific experimentation in agriculture was well-known, but scientific agriculture was not yet typically practiced. Vertical integration of agriculture was unknown, and agribusiness was not yet conceived. Some mechanization was widespread in farming, and farming for market sales was established. Both rapidly accelerated after the Civil War. Prior to the Civil War, family farming was still both the dominant way of life and the agrarian principle, but factory work was soon to be characterized by scientific management and unionism. With factory development came job proliferation. All of these developments contributed to marked differences between urban and rural ways of life.

Physical environmental differences were never greater than in the nineteenth century. Many inventions which greatly changed human relations were incorporated into urban life. These were exemplified by the telegraph (1844), the incandescent lamp (1841), and the telephone (1876). They quickened the pace of business and extended the day into the night. The popularity of certain expressions such as "city slicker" and "country hick" accompanied these changing norms. But these distinctions were ephemeral. Rural free delivery mail service was established in 1896. This was followed in the early part of the twentieth century by parcel post (1913). The result of these developments along with accelerated rail transportation was that urbanites invaded the open country. More important, rural people came into social contact with the city people. Communication with the cities for supplies both for farm and household were further promoted by the establishment of mail-order houses. These were supplemented by the construction of farm-to-market roads, many of which still existed by the middle of the twentieth century.

Urbanisms were much sought by farm people. Hence, rural electrification programs and telephone service were established. Thus, as soon as material developments reached a point of major differentiation between rural and urban environments, there was a concomitant movement to eliminate these differences. In this way, the levels of living of rural and urban people came to approximate each other.

The importance of differential community size continued into the early twentieth century, after which it declined abruptly. Streams of migration were primarily from rural to urban areas. However, by the end of the nineteenth century there were notable compensating currents of migration in the movement of people from cities to rural areas. Country and suburban living for nonfarm people developed in the 1880's. It became an "ism" (suburbanism), however, only after World War II. Differences in community size diminished with the shifts and growth of the nation's population in the twentieth century. By 1920 the declining importance of the farm population was apparent in the introduction of the concept rural nonfarm into the census. Farm people in rural America continued to live typically in a dispersed pattern, but most noncity people were rural nonfarm rather than farm residents. With the ever increasing presence of mass communication and mass transportation, the size of community became a minor factor in differentiating rural from urban populations.

Social stratification became more pronounced with the urbanization of society. Social class distinctions were most amenable to the consumption-oriented development of the society. These distinctions proliferated most rapidly in urban areas. But social stratification became more pronounced in rural areas as their populations obtained more education, wider social participation, more scientific orientations, and more technological advantages. Social stratification in rural areas was also furthered by migration of people into rural nonfarm areas.

A specific city culture was fully developed by the middle of the nineteenth century, and its growth accelerated for decades thereafter. Patterns of urban culture included the theater, symphony, opera, art museum, and spectator sports like baseball, football, and basketball. Also in the complex of urban culture were the city clubs, the country clubs, and night clubs.

Even these major developments in city culture were soon to have their counterparts in small towns and rural areas. The rural theater was established by the end of the nineteenth century and enjoyed considerable popularity. Rural music programs were soon to develop along the lines of the operetta in place of the opera. The nearest equivalent to the urban area's symphony was the rural area's marching band, of which there were many in the 1880's and 1890's. Rural arts and crafts have been identified since colonial days. While there were few rural arts programs during the latter part of the nineteenth century, art programs for rural people had become quite commonplace by the middle of the twentieth century. Other recreational developments in the urban areas that had a widespread popularity in rural places were fairs and circuses.

There were important differences in the manifest organization of these patterns of behavior in rural and urban areas, but they were more of a diffuse qualitative nature, more of degree than of kind. Differentiation between rural music and urban music, rural art and urban art, a rural theater and an urban theater, was a subject at least as problematical as that between rural life and urban life in general. As the condition of urbanized social organization advanced, the most pronounced differences between rural and urban life were reduced in quantity and relegated to matters of degree. Nevertheless, such differences have certainly not totally disappeared.

METROPOLITAN LIFE OF THE TWENTIETH CENTURY: DIMINISHED RURAL-URBAN DIFFERENCES

By the twentieth century, city life began to dominate all American life. Although urban behavior patterns prevailed, many survivals of the earlier rural culture remained. The process of urbanization was, in fact, a new assimilation, through which ruralisms permeated the city life. Cities were vigorously defended by their new inhabitants, and often rural virtues were unwittingly extolled in this defense of urban life. Even New Yorkers assert that friendly neighborhood social life is widespread in their city. Indeed, they hold that their city is a composite of many little neighborhoods. Loyalty to the home area is great, and many New Yorkers live out their life primarily in the locale of a few blocks, often smaller than a country town.[15] Big-city values and their integration with ruralisms are to be found in Jesse Lynch Williams's satire, "Back to the Town." [16] In this work, Williams described the virtues of bucolic city living. The contrast between city noise and rural quietness of life is so well-known as to be a platitude. Williams had this to say on the subject:

But to be tucked away in a snug little flat near the towering top of a tall apartment house on a quiet street, looking serenely down upon the teeming town with its towers, steeples, domes, and bridges melting in the distant haze, its noise and turmoil reaching your eerie retreat only as a muffled hum . . . this is to know the joys of true privacy and the luxury of deep sleep. Out in the country, one is usually awakened at dawn by one's bird neighbors saying "Cheap, cheap," though it is not, or by the bark of our four-footed friends devouring the morning paper.[17]

Sorokin observed, in contrasting the physical environment of country with city living, that there was nature in the open landscape and only artificiality in the city. His very argument, nevertheless, revealed the existence of ruralism in the city, namely, the provision for plants and trees.

It has been asserted that even with seven million neighbors, in New York City, a spirit of neighborliness still prevails.[18] Migrants from small towns and rural areas to the city also have reinforced themes of ruralisms, in many cases by observing that one often meets many people just like oneself. Unfriendliness and an impersonal atmosphere are more presumed than real.[19]

Ruralisms in the city are evident in the flower pots and the roof gardens, and other attempts to bring nature to the population centers. One writer observes:

that even New Yorkers do not dispense with rural amenities when dining in the city. The criticism that there is a certain artificiality about much of this urban rurality is simply beside the point. This rurality (in its physical aspects) derives much of its particular flavor and impact from its very conjunction with the physical city. There is more subtlety here than meets the eye. Beyond the measure of escape and relief that country-like sights may give to the city dweller are those aspects of rurality that please his very urbanity. It is, for instance, the contrast of "rural" with "urban" that lends occasional piquancy to being an urban man; and to such showing interest stories as those about the wild ducks that landed in the city lagoon and stayed some weeks, or the mallard who (in Milwaukee) built her nest and raised her ducklings on a piling close to a bridge only a few feet from the busiest thoroughfare in town.[20]

Ruralisms entered the *New Yorker* magazine, too. They are the subject of many cartoons as well as many items in "Talk of the Town" illustrating the interplay between rural and urban culture. One such theme depicted a lady walking a bored pet hen in Central Park. Ruralisms appear on the cover of the *New Yorker* in the form of drawings of men raking autumn leaves, shoveling snow, and attending to other unsophisticated chores.[21] The farmers' market or the advertisement of country fresh eggs were rural prestige symbols in the city. Rural imagery in the metropolis is further apparent in children's parks and playgrounds, many of which include an area for the keeping of barnyard animals. In the hymns and songs and plays of the people, one finds ruralisms again and again recorded. "Home, Sweet Home," "My Old Kentucky Home," "America the Beautiful," and "The Good Shepherd" are all illustrations.

Suburbia: One dimension in the development of urbanized social organization. With the rise of suburbia the era of rural-urban differentiation had come to a point of diminishing returns. Suburbia in its most distinct phases has been but one of the processes of the expanding urbanized social organization. In 1905, Zueblin charged that the future belongs to the suburbs, not the city.[22] The suburb gradually emerged in the early nineteenth century, but its major impact was felt only in the twentieth century. Interest in comparing the advantages of country with city living were illustrated in the real estate advertisements of the time. For example the following appeared in the 1820's in New York:

Situated directly opposite the S-W part of the city, and being the nearest country retreat, and easiest of access from the center of business that now remains unoccupied; the distance not exceeding an average of fifteen minutes to twenty-five minutes walk, including the passage of the river; the ground elevated and perfectly healthy at all seasons; views of water and landscape both extensive and beautiful; as a place of residence all the advantages of the country with most of the conveniences of the city.[23]

Original inhabitants of the suburbs were typically townspeople. By the middle of the twentieth century, new suburban residents migrated both from farms and towns. Migration to suburbia had a near compulsory character by the middle of the twentieth century.[24] In England, migration to suburbia has been reported with concern. Gordon Cullen and Ian Nairn have viewed with trepidation the vanishing of both urban and rural Britain into what they consider a dreary, spreading "subtopia." Judgments considering the suburban development were colorful, but not value free. For example, one lecturer has suggested that our greatest material improvements recently have been made in urban fringes, while the heart of the city has been left to deteriorate. Yet if the urban fringe represents the greatness of our civilization the accomplishment is antiseptic, dull, garish, and inhuman.[25]

Several specific structures of social organization have been proposed in an effort to provide for an orderly development of suburban growth. Most notable among these were the concepts for "Garden City" and "green belt." The notion of Garden City was specifically formulated by the English reformer Sir Ebenezer Howard in the 1890's.[26] The Garden City concept was based on the principle of self-sufficient communities. The new towns were to have their own central core, residential districts, factories, and—most important of all—a permanent area of agricultural land from which produce could be supplied to the townspeople. The name "green belt" was applied to this strip of agricultural land. It was to have been owned by the city and to have remained a permanently green area. In 1903, the first Garden City of Lechworth was founded near London. It was followed in a little more than a decade by Welwyn Garden City. They were far from the dormitory or parasite types of suburban developments that have followed more numerously in recent years.

In America, Howard's Garden City concept was implemented, but in a greatly amended form. Examples of American green belt cities, begun in the 1920's, are Radburn in New Jersey, TVA's Nolis, Tennessee; Maremount, Ohio, and Kingsport, Tennessee.[27] These are residential towns, planned to include recreation areas and to exclude through-traffic. The green belt conceived by Howard to be both aesthetic and economic was modified in America to serve as a protective wall, as it were, keeping out commerce and vulgarity and insulating the grace of suburban life within. In 1936, President Roosevelt, visiting a green belt area, observed that it would protect the town from undesirable commercial or industrial developments.[28] And so it was that from the outset, in the United States, green belt suburbia was not a self-sufficient city but a residential home-stead area where each man should have his own garden—parks, if you will—but where residents were bound to the larger city for economic employment by the umbilical cord of commuter facilities. The green belts in America lacked an independent character; at best, they were satellites of the larger urban areas.

The social class of persons who migrate to the suburbs has changed through the years. Originally, suburban movement in the United States was predominantly an upper-class phenomenon. By the second quarter of the twentieth century, the suburban movement was characterized to a greater extent by middle-class people. The middle class needed the space of the suburbs because they were unable to sustain the status symbols of affluency in the central city.

They use space to differentiate themselves—space was equipped with accompanying symbols of a house, a garden, a place with a fancy name. They often have a veritable separation-complex, and their course can sometimes be plotted from point to point within the city proper until they break through the symbolic zone of suburbs. Once there, they may remain immovable for many years, improving the lawn, adding shrubbery, and watching it grow over the years with evident satisfaction, rearing their children far from the dangerous streets of the city. For those who have come up the hard way, from the slums themselves, the suburban haven is even more poignantly enjoyable, no doubt.[29]

Poor men historically had few choices for a place of residence. Usually they accepted the cheapest lodging close to factories, or lean-to shacks in rural slums. In the past there have been experimental working class suburbs,[30] but with mass suburbia, the "blue collar" suburb has become a widespread phenomenon.

Suburbs have continued to develop in abundant proportion, whether measured by increase in population, increase in land utilization, or impact on the total social organization of the society. It has been written that in a crowded world man must be either suburban or savage.[31] Such an observation poignantly implies the vanishing significance of the nineteenth-century rural-urban dichotomy.

Whether or not a suburb is to be considered a *species sui generis* is a question that is still debated. In the introduction to the 1953 issue of *Rural Sociology,* Charles Lively suggested three hypotheses:

One, the rural-urban fringe represents a position on a continuum within a single rural-urban distribution. Two, the rural-urban fringe represents an overlapping of two distinct distributions—the rural and the urban—providing a scrambled confusion within the area of overlap. Three, the rural-urban fringe represents a third distribution with some characteristics of both the rural and the urban, but with some new ones found only in the fringe.[32]

Queen and Carpenter concluded that their data negated the hypothesis that the fringe is a type of social organization more urban than rural. They found the suburban residents to be more aligned with urban residents in terms of employment, but more aligned with the rural way of life in other values.[33] A study of the rural-urban fringe of Baton Rouge, Louisiana, in the 1950's revealed an overwhelming merging of the behavioral traits of people on the periphery.[34] It was found that farmers were virtually un-differentiated from city people in most of their behavioral patterns, institutional orientations, and value notions.

SUMMARY

Men have observed rural-urban differences from antiquity to the present time. The comparative analysis of these differences has always revealed societies in transition. Societies tend to be dominated by either rural or urban social structures. Therefore, when rural-urban differences are most pronounced, the societies are experiencing the greatest dynamics of social change.

The specific history of rural-urban differences in the United States in the past three hundred years has been particularly dynamic. Social life in America has rapidly changed from a nearly completely ruralized social organization to a pattern that is approaching urbanized social organization.

Much of the history of America is concerned with rural-urban differences. Specific indexes of rural-urban differences have been enumerated. The most important are occupation, size of community, mobility, social stratification, and population density. For many years, census data have been presented in such a way as specifically to identify the urban population. By 1920, the important concepts of urban, rural nonfarm, and rural farm were used by the census.

Most of the indexes and definitions used for differentiating rural and urban populations have been of limited value to the social sciences. What is more meaningful is that the earliest American cities were characterized by many ruralisms in their inhabitants' patterns of social interaction. And by the second half of the twentieth century, the patterns of behavior in cities and metropolitan areas dominated the whole of American life, although there were survivals of rural culture. Put another way, there have always been rural-urban differences, but they were less important in the colonial period and in the twentieth century than in the nineteenth century.

The vast suburban growth, particularly of the twentieth century, is primarily a dimension of urbanized social organization which is encompassing the entire nation. People move out of the cities and away from farms into suburbs. But, regardless of the place of origin of suburbanites, most studies reveal that, once in the suburbs, their way of life is most dominated by urbanized patterns of behavior. Rural-urban differences in America are rapidly diminishing in the second half of the twentieth century in the face of advancing urbanized social organization.

NOTES

1. Pitirim A. Sorokin *et al., A Systematic Sourcebook in Rural Sociology* (3 vols., Minneapolis: University of Minnesota Press, 1930).

2. *Ibid.,* Vol. I, pp. 239–41.

3. Richard Dewey, "The Rural-Urban Continuum: Real but Relatively Unimportant," *American Journal of Sociology,* 66 (July, 1960), 60–66; Thomas Cochran and William Miller, *The Age of Enterprise* (New York: The Macmillan Co., 1942); Richard A. Kurtz and Joanne B. Eicher, "Fringe and Suburb: A Confusion of Concepts," *Social Forces,* 37 (Oct., 1958), 32–4; J. A. Kolb and R. A. Polson, *Trends in Town-Country Relations* (Wisconsin Agricultural Experiment Station Research Bulletin 117, 1933); and Charles T. Stewart, Jr., "The Urban-Rural Dichotomy: Concepts and Uses," *American Journal of Sociology,* 64 (Sept., 1958), 152–8.

4. Lee Taylor and Arthur R. Jones, *Louisiana's Human Resources,* Part II: *Agribusiness and the Labor Force* (Louisiana Agricultural Experiment Station Bulletin 562, 1962); E. Gartly Jaco and Ivan Belkamp, "Is a New Family Form Emerging in the Urban Fringe?" *American Sociological Review,* 18 (Oct., 1953), 551–7; and

Sylvania Fleis Fava, "Suburbanism as a Way of Life," *American Sociological Review,* 21 (Feb., 1956), 34–7.

5. Otis Dudley Duncan, "Community Size and the Rural-Urban Continuum," in Paul Hatt and Albert J. Reiss, Jr. (eds.), *Cities and Society* (Glencoe: Free Press, 1957), pp. 35–45; Lewis W. Jones, "The Hinterland Reconsidered," *American Sociological Review,* 20 (Feb., 1955), 40–44; Walter T. Martin, *The Rural-Urban Fringe: A Study of Adjustment to Residence Location* (Eugene, Ore.: University of Oregon Monograph Studies in Sociology, No. I, Nov., 1953).

6. J. Allan Beegle and Widick Schroeder, *Social Organization in the North Lansing Fringe* (Michigan Agricultural Experiment Station Technical Bulletin 251, 1955); Noel P. Gist, "Ecological Decentralization and Rural-Urban Relationships," *Rural Sociology,* 17 (Dec., 1952), 328–35; Solon T. Kimball, *The New Social Frontier: The Fringe* (Michigan Agricultural Experiment Station Special Bulletin 360, 1949); Robert E. Dickinson, "The Geography of Commuting: The Netherlands and Belgium," *Geographical Review,* 47 (Oct., 1957), 521–38; J. A. Kolb, *Interdependence in Town and Country Relations in Rural Society* (Wisconsin Agricultural Experiment Station Research Bulletin, 172, 1950); and Paul H. Price and George A. Hillery, Jr., *The Rural-Urban Fringe and Louisiana's Agriculture* (Louisiana Agricultural Experiment Station Bulletin 526, 1959).

7. Leon E. Truesdell, *The Development of the Urban-Rural Classification in the United States: 1874–1949* (Washington: Bureau of the Census, Series P-23, No. 1, 1949).

8. *Ibid.,* p. 1.

9. Francis A. Walker, *Statistical Atlas of the United States* (Washington, 1874).

10. *Loc. cit.*

11. Leon E. Truesdell, *Farm Population of the United States,* 1920 (Washington: Bureau of the Census, 1926). See especially pp. 51 ff.

12. Carl Bridenbaugh, *Cities in Revolt* (New York: Alfred A. Knopf, 1955); Truesdell, *Development of Urban Rural Classification;* and M. Curti *et al., An American History* (New York: Harper and Brothers, 1950), see especially p. 249.

13. Anselm L. Strauss, *Images of the American City* (New York: The Free Press of Glencoe, 1961), pp. 216 ff.

14. Bridenbaugh, *op. cit.*

15. E. B. White, *Here Is New York* (New York: Harper and Brothers, 1949), pp. 27–30.

16. Jesse Lynch Williams, *Scribner's,* 58 (1915), 534–44.

17. *Loc. cit.*

18. Al Smith, *American Magazine,* 116 (Aug., 1933), 36–8.

19. Robert Benchley, "The Typical New Yorker," in Alexander Klein (ed.), *The Empire City* (New York: Rinehart and Co., 1955), pp. 338–42.

20. *New York Times Magazine,* July 14, 1957, p. 32, "Country Dining in Manhattan."

21. Strauss, *op. cit.,* pp. 228–9.

22. Charles Zueblin, *A Decade of Civic Development* (Chicago: University of Chicago Press, 1905), p. 169.

23. Ralph Foster Weld, *Brooklyn Village, 1816–1834* (New York: Columbia University Press, 1938), p. 28.

24. Grady Clay, "Metropolis Regained," *Horizon,* I (July, 1959), pp. 5–15.

25. *Ibid.,* p. 7.

26. Ebenezer, Howard, *Garden Cities of Tomorrow* (London: Faber and Faber, 1951).

27. Clay, *op. cit.,* p. 11.

28. *Ibid.,* pp. 1–12.

29. Strauss, *op. cit.,* p. 237.

30. Graham Romeyn Taylor, *Satellite Cities: A Study of Industrial Suburbs* (New York: D. Appleton and Co., 1915).

31. Harlan Paul Douglas, *The Suburban Trend* (New York: The Century Co., 1925), pp. 312, 326 ff.

32. *Rural Sociology,* 18 (June, 1953), 101.

33. *Ibid.,* pp. 102–8.

34. Price and Hillery, *op. cit.*

SELECTED READINGS

Clay, Grady. "Metropolis Regained," *Horizon,* I (July, 1959), pp. 5–15.
    This article provides an illustrative discussion of green belt areas and related plans to integrate rural elements with city living.

Dewey, Richard. "The Rural-Urban Continuum: Real but Relatively Unimportant," *American Journal of Sociology,* 66 (July, 1960), 60–66.
    A critical review of the concepts of rural and urban that reports gross lack of agreement on their use in current publications.

Howard, Ebenezer. *Garden Cities of Tomorrow.* London: Faber and Faber, 1951.
    An original statement of the Garden City concept. It also provides a detailed description of the first garden cities in England.

Rural Sociology, 18 (June, 1953).
    A special feature issue concerning the rural-urban fringe development.

Sorokin, Pitirim A., *et al. A Systematic Sourcebook in Rural Sociology.* Minneapolis: University of Minnesota Press, 1930.

A classic review of rural-urban literature, offering a descriptive synthesis of major sources from ancient times through the first quarter of the twentieth century.

Strauss, Anselm L. *Images of the American City*. New York: Free Press of Glencoe, 1961.

The author illustrates the meaning of the city image by contrasting it with rural conditions. Important rural-urban comparisons are made in the chapters titled "Era and Geography in Urban Symbolism" and "Rural Aspects of Metropolitan Living."

Truesdell, Leon E. *The Development of the Urban-Rural Classification in the United States: 1874–1949* (Washington: Bureau of the Census, Series P-23, No. 1, 1949).

A comprehensive history of the rural-urban concept as used by the Census Bureau.

II POPULATIONS AND SOCIAL INTERACTION IN RURAL AREAS

4 FARM PEOPLE

Farm people constitute a minority of America's total population. In 1790, 95 per cent of the nation's people were rural and most of them were farm people. By 1960, 70 per cent of the nation's people were urban and few of the remaining 30 per cent were farmers. However, in light of the fact that today's smaller farm force has vastly increased its agricultural production, this drastic reduction in the farm population has not threatened the nation's supplies of food and fiber. Productivity itself is related to certain population shifts. A significant proportion of the rural-urban shift has been made possible by the growth and expansion of farm supply and food processing businesses, most of which are located in cities. This has released people from farm work, making them available for agribusiness work and other jobs in cities. In effect, the reduction of the farm population has been largely a byproduct of the shift from subsistence agriculture to agribusiness.

These changes in the social structure have made the task of identifying and defining the farm people a difficult one. Many people who work in agribusiness supply and processing jobs are fulfilling essential agricultural roles, but they are not farmers. They may or may not live in the country, but they are rarely included with the total farm population.

In this chapter the historical development of the farm population is briefly traced and, since its recent history involves changing definitions, these are also reviewed. The major focus of the chapter is on the characteristics of the farm population.

71

HISTORICAL TRENDS

The urban population has grown more rapidly than the rural population each decade since 1790, with the one exception of 1810 to 1820 (see Table I and Fig. 2). During most decades the urban population has grown twice as fast as the rural population.[1]

The farm population reached a peak of 32,076,960 in 1910. It declined to less than half that number by 1960. This precipitous decline was not steady. In 1940 the farm population was slightly larger than in 1930. Moreover, in recent years some of the decline has been a function of changing definitions. Yet, in spite of these qualifications, the downward trend has been clear.

Viewed in terms of the labor force, over 70 per cent (2,068,958) of the nation's workers in 1820 were engaged in agricultural pursuits (see Table II). By 1910 the agricultural labor force had reached the numerical high point of 11,591,767, or 31 per cent of the labor force. In 1960 the Population Census reported only 2,505,684 farmers, or 3.9 per cent of the national labor force, and 1,444,807 farm laborers, or 2.2 per cent of the national labor force. Farmers have become one of the smallest occupational categories in the nation's labor force in the twentieth century.

RURAL-URBAN MIGRATION

The farm population historically has supplied more migrants to the cities than the cities have returned to farms, although streams of migrants have moved in both directions. More rural people left farms for cities each year between 1920 and 1960, except for 1931–1932 and 1945.[2] In 1931 and 1932 the farm population experienced a net migration increase of 763,000, which was largely caused by the depression. High unemployment constituted a push factor forcing individuals out of cities into country areas. During these years poor farming areas, like the cut-over land in the lake states (primarily in Michigan, Wisconsin, and Minnesota) and much of the mountain country in Kentucky and Tennessee and in the Missouri-Arkansas Ozarks, became more densely populated. These areas have from time to time fulfilled a shock absorber function during abrupt shifts in the social structure. Business farming enterprises could seldom be maintained in these cut-over and mountainous areas, but by traditionalistic farming methods, individuals could provide a subsistence level of living for themselves. Therefore these areas were used for subsistence

TABLE I. URBAN AND RURAL POPULATION OF THE UNITED STATES: 1790 TO 1960

Census Date	Urban Population	Urban Increase over Preceding Census Number	Urban Increase over Preceding Census Per Cent	Rural Population	Rural Increase over Preceding Census Number	Rural Increase over Preceding Census Per Cent	Per Cent of Total Urban	Per Cent of Total Rural
Current Urban Definition								
1960	124,699,022	28,231,336	29.3	53,765,214	−464,461	−0.9	69.0	30.1
1950	96,467,686			54,229,675			64.0	36.0
Previous Urban Definition								
1960	112,531,941	22,782,878	25.4	65,932,295	4,983,997	8.2	63.1	36.9
1950	189,749,063	15,325,361	20.6	160,948,298	3,702,725	6.5	59.6	40.4
1940	74,423,702	5,468,879	7.9	57,245,573	3,425,350	6.4	56.5	43.5
1930	68,954,823	14,796,859	27.3	53,820,223	2,267,576	4.4	56.2	43.8
1920	54,157,973	12,159,041	29.0	51,522,647	1,579,313	3.2	51.2	48.8
1910	41,998,932	11,839,011	39.3	49,973,334	4,138,680	9.0	45.7	54.3
1900	30,159,921	8,053,656	36.4	45,834,654	4,993,205	12.2	39.7	60.3
1890	22,106,265	7,976,530	56.5	40,841,449	4,815,401	13.4	35.1	64.9
1880	14,129,735	4,227,374	42.7	36,026,048	7,370,038	25.7	28.2	71.8
1870	9,902,361	3,685,843	59.3	28,656,010	3,429,207	13.6	25.7	74.3
1860	6,216,518	2,672,802	75.4	25,226,803	5,578,643	28.4	19.8	80.2
1850	3,543,716	1,698,661	92.1	19,648,160	4,423,762	29.1	15.3	84.7
1840	1,845,055	717,808	63.7	15,224,398	3,485,625	29.7	10.8	89.2
1830	1,127,247	433,992	62.6	11,738,773	2,793,575	31.2	8.8	91.2
1820	693,255	167,796	31.9	8,945,198	2,230,776	33.2	7.2	92.8
1810	525,459	203,088	63.0	6,714,422	1,728,310	34.7	7.3	92.7
1800	322,371	120,716	59.9	4,986,112	1,258,553	33.8	6.1	93.9
1790	201,655			3,727,559			5.1	94.9

Source: U.S. Bureau of the Census, *U.S. Census of Population: 1960*, Number of Inhabitants, U.S. Summary, Final Report PC(1)-1A, p. 4.

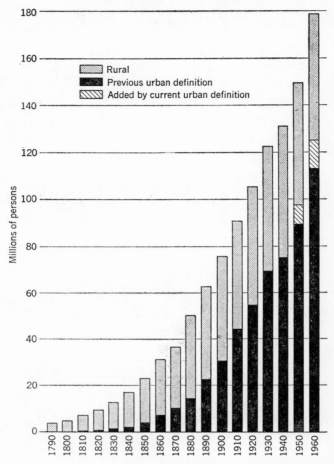

FIGURE 2. URBAN AND RURAL POPULATION, 1790 TO 1960

Source: U.S. Bureau of the Census, *U.S. Census of Population: 1960. Number of Inhabitants, United States Summary, Final Report* PC(1)—1A. U.S. Government Printing Office, Washington, D.C., 1961.

farming during the depression years. By 1933–1934 the dominant stream of migration from farms to cities resumed.

The farm population dropped sharply during World War II from 30,500,000 in 1940, to 25,500,000 by 1944–1945. After 1945 the farm population experienced a net migration increase of a scant 161,000.[3] From 1945 on, the historic downward trend of the farm population has continued to the present. During the war period a great number of people left farms, even though farm manpower shortages enabled many to be

TABLE II. THE LABOR FORCE OF THE UNITED STATES, IN TWO LARGE OCCUPATIONAL CLASSES, AGRICULTURAL PURSUITS AND NONAGRICULTURAL PURSUITS: 1820 TO 1960

Census Year	All Occupations	Agricultural Pursuits		Nonagricultural Pursuits	
		Number	Per Cent	Number	Per Cent
1820	2,881,000	2,068,958	71.8	812,042	28.2
1830	3,931,537	2,772,453	70.5	1,159,084	29.5
1840	5,420,000	3,719,951	68.6	1,700,049	31.4
1850	7,697,196	4,901,882	63.7	2,795,314	36.3
1860	10,532,750	6,207,634	58.9	4,325,116	41.1
1870	12,924,951	6,849,772	53.0	6,075,179	47.0
1880	17,392,099	8,584,810	49.4	8,807,289	50.6
1890	23,938,373	9,938,373	42.6	13,379,810	57.4
1900	29,073,233	10,911,998	37.5	18,161,235	62.5
1910	37,370,794	11,591,767	31.0	25,779,027	69.0
1920	42,433,535	11,448,770	27.0	30,984,765	73.0
1930	48,829,920	10,471,998	21.4	38,357,922	78.6
1940	52,148,251	9,162,547	17.6	42,985,704	82.4
1950*	59,915,464	6,837,652	11.5	52,177,812	88.4
1960†	67,990,069	4,034,869	5.9	63,955,200	94.1

Source: U.S. Department of Commerce, Bureau of the Census, Series P-9, No. 11, *Trends in Proportion of the Nation's Labor Force Engaged in Agriculture: 1820–1940.*

* U.S. Bureau of the Census, *U.S. Census of Population: 1950, Vol. II, Characteristics of the Population,* Part I, U.S. Summary, Chapter B, U.S. Government Printing Office, Washington, 1952.

† U.S. Bureau of the Census, *U.S. Census of Population: 1960, General Social and Economic Characteristics,* U.S. Summary, Final Report PC(1), U.S. Government Printing Office, Washington, 1962.

granted deferments. In most cases, the impact of the war on the farm labor force met responses like farm consolidation, farm mechanization, and more scientific farming.

CHANGING DEFINITIONS OF THE FARM POPULATION

Definitions of farm population, farm residence, and agricultural work have become tenuous. Moreover, they have been changed greatly in recent decades. Prior to 1960, the number of farmers reported in the Census of Population was the result of subjective inquiry, while those reported in the Census of Agriculture were the result of objective inquiry. Population census enumerators were instructed to ask the respondent if his house was on a farm or a ranch. The respondent's opinion was accepted as valid.

Enumerators for the Census of Agriculture, by contrast, were instructed to determine the number of acres, amount of sales, and other factors. The agricultural census directors determined on the basis of these data whether the respondent resided on a farm or not [4] (see Fig. 3).

FIGURE 3.   DEFINITIONS OF FARMS USED IN THE CURRENT POPULATION SURVEYS AND THE POPULATION AND AGRICULTURE CENSUSES: 1950–1960

Current Population Surveys and Population Census	Agriculture Census
1959 and 1960	**1959**
Respondents were asked: "Is this house on a place of less than ten acres or on a place of ten or more acres?"	Detailed questions on acreage of the unit and on products sold were asked. Place is a farm if it had ten or more acres and $50 or more of products sold in the year, or if it had less than ten acres, but $250 or more of products sold.
If *less than ten acres:* "Last year (date), did sales of crops, livestock, and other farm products from this place amount to $250 or more?"	
If *ten acres or more:* "Last year (date), did sales of crops, livestock, and other farm products from this place amount to $50 or more?" For renters: "Does your rent include any land used for farming (or ranching)?" *	
1950 to 1959	**1950 and 1954**
Respondents were asked: "Is this house on a farm (or ranch)?"	Detailed questions on acreage of the unit and on production and sale of products were asked. Place was a farm if it had three or more acres and $150 worth of production (excluding home garden products), or if it had less than three acres but $150 or more of products sold.
If respondent raised question, enumerator was instructed to classify as nonfarm places consisting of house and yard only for which cash rent was paid.	

* Additional question not asked of renters in the April 1960 Current Population Survey. Source: Calvin L. Beale and Gladys K. Bowles, "The 1960 Definition of Farm Residence and Its Marked Effect on Farm Population Data," Paper presented at the Association of Southern Agricultural Workers meeting, Jackson, Miss., 1961.

Changes in definition were prompted largely by a national survey in 1957 which showed that, although a great number of people reported they were residing on farms, their operations did not qualify them as farmers according to the Census of Agriculture. Some of the survey respondents were originally engaged in farming but had discontinued it and accepted nonfarm employment while continuing to live on their farm land or in the farmstead. Many others were city persons who had moved into the open country by occupying farmsteads that had become vacant due to consolidation of farm lands.[5] The earlier definition of a farm was also found too broad and unworkable by major users of census data.

The result was a new and more restricted definition of farm to be utilized in the Census of Agriculture. This new definition was employed in an abbreviated form by the Census of Population. The subjective technique of determining farm residence used by the census was abandoned. The 1960 definition was designed to exclude from the farm population those individuals who lived on places they considered to be farms but from which no agricultural products were sold or from which the sales were below a specified minimum. Conversely, the 1960 definition included a small number of people as farmers who previously had not considered themselves as such.

The net result of this definitional change was to exclude more than 4,000,000 persons from the rural farm population of 1960, who according to their subjective response by the 1950 definition were living on farms. These people were subsequently recorded as part of the rural nonfarm population. The farm population, by the new definition, totaled only 9 per cent of the national population and only 25 per cent of the rural population. The farm population had become not only a minority in the nation but also a minority in open-country rural America. Some three-quarters of the open-country rural population was reported to be rural nonfarm. The new definition reduced the farm population by nearly 20 per cent in the nation and by approximately 25 per cent in the West, South, and Northeast regions. It was reduced by only 9 per cent in the North-Central region.[6]

The people who, under the new definition, were not counted in the farm category were essentially nonagricultural. Their sex ratio of 103 males to each 100 females was in sharp contrast to the sex ratio for the farm population, which was 109 males for each 100 females. In terms of age structure, the persons shifted to the rural nonfarm population had a disproportionate number of persons 65 years and over. Approximately 80 per cent of the males who were excluded from the farm population worked entirely or primarily in nonagricultural jobs. By contrast, only 27 per cent of the remaining farm males were engaged in nonagricultural employment. This change in definition contributed greatly toward establishing homogeneity in the farm residence population.

DEMOGRAPHIC CHARACTERISTICS OF FARM PEOPLE

The major demographic characteristics of the farm population discussed in this chapter are sex, age, education, occupation, and geographical location. They illustrate the similarities and differences of farm people in respect to other major population categories.

Sex composition. There are typically more men than women in the farm population. The farm population sex ratio (males to 100 females) was 109 in 1960. The corresponding sex ratios were 103 for rural nonfarm areas and 94 for urban areas. There are many factors contributing to the maintenance of high rural sex ratios. One of the most prominent characteristics of urbanized society is the declining opportunity for employment of women in the farm areas. Furthermore, until recently, human physical energy was more in demand in farm work than in much manufacturing and office work. The normative belief that women should not engage in hard physical labor has long prevailed in the United States. Women have worked on farms and do work on farms, but their employment has been greatly restricted, often seasonal, and rarely in demand.

Cities, in contrast to farms, have been characterized by low sex ratios. Urban women have had the greatest opportunity for freedom and equality in the labor force. In some cases they have experienced preferential treatment over males.

Age composition. The farm population has been characterized by a disproportionately large number of young people under age twenty, and by a slightly disproportionate number of persons over sixty years of age. The farm population has experienced an out-migration loss of people between the years twenty and sixty, or those in the productive period of life. The rural nonfarm population has a slight excess of young people, particularly under age ten. The urban population has a sharp contraction in the group under age twenty, but a slight expansion under age five, due to the higher birth rates after World War II. An essential feature of the urban population structure is that it expands precipitously after ages twenty to twenty-five through age sixty. The increase in population during these productive years is even greater for females than males. This structure reflects not only a migration of people from farms to cities but the differential migration of men and women, with women predominant in the urban population.

The social significance of these age differences has been great. For example, the farm population has borne a disproportionately large share of the burden of providing the cost and care for rearing children and educating them. Yet, when these children reach the productive age, they typically migrate to the cities, thus contributing their productivity and resources to the urban society rather than to the rural society which generated them. Indirectly, this heavy burden placed on the farm people for rearing and educating children has been a major factor in justifying the argument for statewide systems of education, which often led to consolidation, standardized educational programs, and central distribution of school funds. No comparable concession has been made to farm people for the other costs of rearing their children. The United States has long had an undeclared population policy favoring large families. This is indicated by tax exemptions for families with children under specified ages. It is further illustrated by subsidized school lunch programs. Programs such as these, which favor families with children, have shown little if any preference for the rural family over families in other ecological areas.

The demand for standardized education has been greatly supported by the migration of the farm population to urban areas upon completion of elementary and secondary school. In urbanized society, there has been much justification for the pressures brought by urban people to elevate the standards of rural schools and to exercise jurisdiction over the curriculum of the rural schools. This trend has been functional for the entire nation, although inconsistent with the value of local control. Ideally, it facilitates the training of young people in rural areas to assume their labor force responsibilities in urban areas.

In the past, farm children have been an economic asset as members of the family farm's labor force. Now child labor has been displaced both in urban and rural areas, and there has been an almost simultaneous requirement for more education, supported by compulsory school attendance laws and extensive mechanization of farm operations. School attendance requirements have removed the children from the farm and exempted them from many of their traditional chores. Mechanization has required that they achieve greater knowledge to be successful either as farmers or as members of the industrial labor force. The need for children on the farm now barely surpasses the need for children in the city. The historic justification for the large farm family, therefore, is declining.

The differential proportions of the aged people in the urban, rural nonfarm, and farm populations were reduced by the 1960's. Historically there has been a current of migration from the city of older rural-born people who went back to the farm in their declining years. This "back-to-the-farm" movement has lost its advantages, in terms of contemporary welfare policies. There is now less difference in the distribution of the aged population between rural and urban areas than between major regions of the nation.

Educational characteristics of the farm population. Farm people continue to have less education than city people, as measured by the number of school years completed. It was reported in the 1960 Census, for the population age 25 and over, that the median number of school years completed for the farm population was 8.8, for the rural nonfarm population 9.5, and for the urban population 11.1. Differential educational attainments for males and females also continued to prevail. Farm women completed more years of school than farm men; in 1960 the figures were 9.2 and 8.6, respectively.

When rural people were more bucolic and more oriented to subsistence farming, there was less need for educational attainment among them than among the city people. There was even a considerable opposition to formal education manifested by many rural people as late as the first quarter of the twentieth century. Emotional arguments suggesting that "Too much education would take the farm out of the boy" often were heard. From the point of view of rural values, this expression was frequently accurate. However, from the standpoint of national goals, "taking the farm out of the boy" was to be recommended, in view of the diminishing opportunities to enter farming.

One of the most important characteristics of America's farm people, contrary to their alleged provincialism, has been their willingness to learn practical new ideas. Vocational education, short courses, agricultural extension, correspondence courses, lectures, lyceums, conferences, farm and home weeks—all illustrate the social mechanisms by which farm people have learned new ideas. Among the outstanding characteristics of American agriculture is the pride which rural farm people have taken in the acceptance of new ideas. Agricultural extension and other adult education programs are advanced among farm people. It cannot be over-emphasized that education in its various forms among farm people has contributed to their vast technical competence. Much of the nation's abundance of food and fiber is the result of American farm educational mechanisms.

Occupations of farm people. Farming has been the classic rural occupation. But by 1960, nearly 40 per cent of the farm population was engaged in nonfarm employment (see Table III). Of all the farm workers, 44 per cent were owner-operators or managers and 15 per cent farm laborers. Among the nonfarm occupations, operatives formed the largest single category (11 per cent). Craftsmen constituted nearly 5.8 per cent of the farm nonagricultural labor force. All other occupational categories represented in the farm population constituted less than 5 per cent each.

TABLE III. OCCUPATION OF EMPLOYED PERSONS BY RURAL-URBAN RESIDENCE, FOR THE UNITED STATES: 1960

Occupation	Urban Per Cent	Rural Total Per Cent	Rural Nonfarm Per Cent	Rural Farm Per Cent
Farm occupation	0.7	20.9	6.7	59.1
Farmers and farm managers	0.3	13.8	2.6	43.9
Farm laborers and foremen	0.5	7.1	4.1	15.2
Nonfarm occupations	93.9	75.5	89.3	38.3
Professional	12.4	7.7	9.2	3.9
Manager	9.0	6.6	8.1	2.6
Clerical	16.6	8.2	9.7	4.5
Sales	8.0	5.0	5.9	2.4
Craftsmen	13.6	13.3	16.1	5.8
Operative	17.9	19.8	23.0	11.1
Private household work	2.7	2.7	2.9	1.9
Service work	9.2	6.4	7.7	3.0
Laborer	4.5	5.8	6.7	3.1
Not reported	5.4	3.6	4.0	2.5
Total	100.0	100.0	100.0	100.0

Source: U.S. Bureau of the Census, *U.S. Census of Population, General and Social Economic Characteristics,* U.S. Summary, Final Report, PC(1), 1962, p. 216.

Between 1940 and 1960, blue collar workers (craftsmen and operatives) replaced farmers as the largest rural occupational category [7] (see Fig. 4). About half of the employed rural people in 1940 were either farm operators, managers, or laborers. Twenty years later, only one-fifth of the employed rural workers were listed in those categories. In 1960, more rural persons were employed in blue collar and white collar occupations than in agricultural occupations.

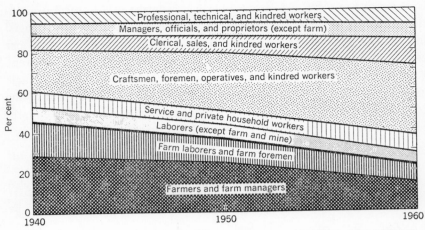

FIGURE 4. BLUE–COLLAR WORKERS REPLACE FARMERS AS LARGEST
RURAL OCCUPATIONAL GROUP

Source: Louis J. Ducoff, "Changing Occupations and Level-of-Living of Rural People,"
talk presented at the 40th Annual Agricultural Outlook Conference, Washington, D.C.,
1962, p. 11.

Nonfarm employment of farm women had become commonplace by
1960. Beale and Bowles reported that over half of the farm women who
were regularly employed worked in nonfarm jobs.[8] This was accurate
despite the number of unpaid women who worked on farms.

Geographic location of farm people. The South continued to have the
greatest proportion of the nation's farm people. It was reported in the
1960 Census that 7,500,000 farm people were located in the South. This
was 47 per cent of the nation's farm people. The North-Central region
had the second largest number of farm people, 5,700,000, or 36 per cent.
The West had nearly 1,500,000 farm people, and the Northeast about
1,200,000, or 9 and 8 per cent, respectively.

The major proportion of the nation's large business farmers, those in
economic class III and above (with sales of $10,000 or more), were
located in the North-Central region (see Fig. 5). That region was still
justifiably called the bread basket of the nation. Viewed another way,
there were 20,000 class I farms, producing one-fifth of all farm products
sold in 1959. These constituted only one-half of one per cent of the total
number of farms in the nation. Economic classes II to IV farms, also
disproportionately located in the North-Central region, accounted for
nearly three-fifths of all farm products sold.[9]

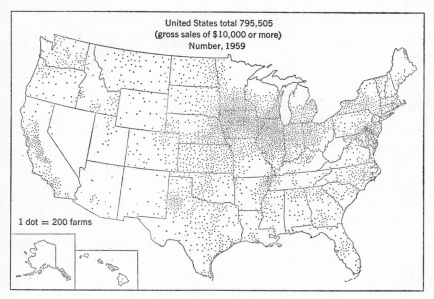

United States total 795,505
(gross sales of $10,000 or more)
Number, 1959

1 dot = 200 farms

FIGURE 5. CLASS I, II, AND III FARMS

Source: U.S. Bureau of the Census, *U.S. Census of Agriculture: 1959.* Vol. II, General Report Statistics by Subjects, Chapter XI (Washington, D.C.: U.S. Government Printing Office, 1962), p. 1201.

There was a disproportionate number of subsistence operators as well as small farm operators (economic classes IV to VI and all other noncommercial farms with sales of $9,999 or less) in the South.

HIRED FARM LABOR FORCE

Hired farm workers constitute a significant segment of the farm population.[10] By current definition, farm laborers are divided into four categories: year-round workers, those who work 250 days or more; regular workers, working 150 to 249 days; seasonal workers, working 25 to 149 days; and casual workers, working less than 25 days.

Hired workers who worked 150 days or more constitute a regular part of the total farm labor force. They exceeded a million workers in 1947 and 1948, and in more recent years have fluctuated between approximately 650,000 and 830,000 (see Table IV). Many of the short-term farm workers have not been an integral part of the farm labor force. A large proportion represent housewives and students and, therefore, are not in the labor force at all during much of the year. The number of

TABLE IV. NUMBER OF HIRED FARM WORKERS EMPLOYED 150 DAYS AND OVER

Year	Number of Workers	Year	Number of Workers
1945	801,000	1952	720,000
1946	864,000	1954	834,000
1947	1,033,000	1956	748,000
1948	1,001,000	1957	655,000
1949	967,000	1959	800,000
1951	852,000	1960	829,000

Source: Reed E. Friend and Robert R. Stansberry, Jr., *The Hired Farm Working Force of 1960* (Washington: U.S.D.A., Economic Research Service, Agriculture Information Bulletin 266, 1961), p. 30.

migratory workers has fluctuated. In 1960 they were estimated at 409,000. Since the midpoint of the century they have reached a low of 352,000 in 1952 and a high of 477,000 in 1959.

SOCIAL PARTICIPATION PATTERNS

Historically, social participation of farm people has been family-centered. It has been oriented toward group solidarity more than toward individual aggrandizement. The dispersed farm settlement pattern, which has characterized most of rural America, has offered distinct advantages in the technical operation of the farm. It has distinct disadvantages in terms of social participation. By contrast, village settlement patterns, which prevailed throughout most rural areas of the world, offered social advantages and technological disadvantages. In rural farm America, prior to the day of all-weather roads and mass communication, rural people had little time and opportunity for social gatherings except in the form of quilting bees, corn husking bees, barn or house raisings, and church suppers. There is, in fact, much reason to believe that those so-called early forms of rural mutual aid and cooperation were more significant for providing opportunities for social interaction than for accomplishing the task at hand.

For many years social participation among farm people was sharply structured by the character of farm life. Now mechanization, scientific farming, and agribusiness have combined to reduce the dependence for social participation among rural people on the previous traditional structure of farming. Nevertheless, some dependence continues to exist. Dairy-

ing operations require daily attendance, and the work load in many
farming occupations still varies with planting and harvesting seasons.
Yet, as changes in technology continue, there is reason to believe that
these participation patterns are less an index of differential ideology than
of differential technology.

Participation patterns among farm people have been reported to vary
among owners, tenants, and laborers. Owners report the greatest participation and laborers the least. Similarly, participation patterns were more
intense among scientific than among subsistence farmers. Differential
participation patterns among business farmers and the nonfarm population have been sharply diminishing.

Informal social participation. There are two major forms of social participation, formal and informal ones. Formal participation has become widespread in urbanized America among both farm and nonfarm people. By
definition, it involves social interaction of people on a voluntary basis in
situations where roles are defined in categories such as member, officer,
committeeman, and chairman. Informal social participation has become
even more prevalent. It involves voluntary participation in activities where
role specification is not precise, where there is a conspicuous absence of
social patterns, defined obligations and hierarchical ranks.

Studies have shown that informal participation is particularly extensive
among farm families. Anderson [11] found that eight out of ten rural families in New York associated informally with at least three other families.
Typically, those rural families that had a minimum of informal social
participation consisted of aged individuals. Similarly, the older families
participated less in formal organizations. The most characteristic forms
of informal participation were visiting, taking of meals with friends, going
for auto rides, attending shows or community plays, borrowing, cooperative shopping, and picnicking.

Informal participation activities were often carried out within kinship
groups. It is probable that informal social interaction between relatives
was more widespread among farm than among urban families. Rural
families were less migratory and tended to remain in their home communities. Urban people, by contrast, migrated widely and were often
separated from their relatives by great distances.

The geographical areas within which informal associations take place
are small. In New York State it was discovered that most families asso-

ciated informally with others who were within three miles of their place of residence. Traveling more than ten miles to visit friends was infrequent. It was found that rural people traveled farther for informal visits with relatives than with nonrelatives. Seen another way, family relationships tend to strengthen informal participation throughout larger geographical areas.

Informal relationships in which farm people participated generally persisted over several decades. Such friendships were of long-standing duration. This was consistent with the finding that much of the informal participation was with relatives. Informal participation among nonrelated families was found to be of shorter duration. Friendship due to proximity was less typical of farm than of suburban families. Participants in informal farm family social relationships, both relatives and nonrelatives, were generally individuals who had known one another over a longer period of years than had informal participants in small towns and suburban areas.

About half of the open-country families formed informal social relationships with other families who were in the same occupational class. In his New York studies, Anderson found that 53 per cent of the informal participants who were not related were in the same occupational category. Only 44 per cent of the related families were in the same occupational categories.[12] As in other cases, occupational homogeneity was often found in association patterns of nonrelatives. Work associations in and of themselves often generate a way of life which embraces whole families. Farmers, professionals, and skilled workers, according to Table V, were most homogeneous in terms of associating with their fellow occupational types.

Formal social participation. Since the middle of the twentieth century it has been recognized widely that rural organizations have been conditioned by factors in both rural and urban life. A study of rural organizational life in Oneida County, New York, illustrated the character of farm peoples' participation.[13] Rural people participated more in school and church groups than in other types of organizations. These other types include farmers' economic associations, civic patriotic organizations, general farm organizations, fraternal organizations, recreational associations, and youth organizations.

Farmer economic organizations are exemplified by cooperatives. There are cooperatives for the marketing of products, specialized production work, dairy herd improvement, and artificial insemination. Hay and Polson wrote,

The stated objectives of one cooperative, the Dairymen's League Cooperative Association, are: to build and maintain a strong organization, owned and operated by farmers, with a well-informed membership; to create for the dairy industry a better understanding of dairy farmers' problems; and to build an assured market for dairy products at a fair living price.[14]

These associations have developed women's auxiliaries and special children's programs. Formal participation in them could have been a simple family affair but, stratified into age and sex groups, it becomes typical of urbanized social organization. The long list of farmer cooperatives had, to a greater or lesser degree, similar participation characteristics. Many of

TABLE V. THE PROPORTIONS OF THE MALE HEADS OF ONTARIO COUNTY, OTSEGO COUNTY, AND TRUMANSBURG VILLAGE FAMILIES IN DIFFERENT OCCUPATIONAL CLASSES WHO ASSOCIATE WITH FAMILIES WORKING IN THE SAME TYPE OF OCCUPATION

Occupational Class	Trumansburg Village		Ontario County		Otsego County		Total	
	Relatives	Non-relatives	Relatives	Non-relatives	Relatives	Non-relatives	Relatives	Non-relatives
Professional	14	51	50	0	0	33	31	49
Farming	79	54	41	45	61	80	51	62
Proprietor, manager, official	29	36	0	37	0	0	12	36
Clerical and kindred worker	16	17	20	7	0	0	20	18
Skilled worker	31	46	25	25	16	66	27	42
Semi-skilled worker	8	18	0	14	0	25	4	18
Unskilled worker	69	45	44	17	66	44	61	38
Farm laborer	0	0	0	0	11	10	13	8
Retired	50	21	31	27	0	33	28	24
Students	0	25	0	0	0	0	0	25
Total	34	35	39	42	53	74	44	53

Source: Donald G. Hay and Robert A. Polson, *Rural Organization in Oneida County, New York* (Cornell: Agricultural Experiment Station, Bulletin 871, 1951), p. 31.

the farmers' cooperatives were originally small and organized on a family basis. As their memberships increased, their enterprise became characterized by a drive for aggrandizement. These cooperatives have been caught up in the spirit and character of urbanized social organization. Participation in them has become intensely formal rather than informal.

General farm organizations include the Farm Bureau, the Farmers'

TABLE VI. PERCENTAGE DISTRIBUTION OF HEADS OF SAMPLE OPEN-COUNTRY HOUSEHOLDS* AS TO MEMBERSHIP† IN SELECTED TYPES OF ORGANIZATIONS: 1946

Household Characteristics	Number of Households	Church	Farmers' Economic Organization‡	Farmers' General Organization§	Civic Patriotic Organization	Fraternal Organization	Adult Extension Service Organization
All households	405	66.2	54.3	13.8	13.8	13.8	49.6
Occupational status							
Full-time farmers	279	66.7	63.4	33.6	16.8	14.7	57.7
Part-time farmers	42	59.5	45.2	27.3	7.1	14.3	54.8
Nominal farmers	41	58.5	29.3	26.6	2.4	9.8	17.1
Hired laborers	4	#	#	#	#	#	#
Rural residents	39	76.9	30.8	17.9	10.2	12.8	25.6

Source: Donald G. Hay and Robert A. Polson, *Rural Organizations in Oneida County, New York* (Cornell: Agricultural Experiment Station Bulletin 871, 1951), p. 33.

* Data for 405 open-country households in Boonville, Camden, Hollard Patent-Barneveld, and Vernon communities.
† Membership of male and/or female head. If both heads belonged to the same organization, the household was credited with only one membership in the organization.
‡ Farmers' cooperative organizations for milk marketing, purchasing, and other goals.
§ Grange, "Cornell" club, Farmers' Union.
|| Farm bureau and home bureau.
Number of instances too few to figure percentages.

Union, and the Grange. From some points of view they are political pressure groups, and from other points of view they are economic organizations. Consequently, in this context they can be designated as general organizations, even though they have multiple programs any one of which is highly specific. Indeed, these organizations did develop specific membership programs for men, women, boys and girls.

Civic patriotic organizations in rural America include volunteer firemen's associations, commercial clubs, service clubs, women's clubs, historical societies, and many others. In Oneida County, New York, it was reported that 14 per cent of the farm household heads and 21 per cent of the village household heads participated in civic patriotic organizations (see Table VI).

Fraternal and social organizations found more members among small-town and urban people than among rural people. Nevertheless, participation on the part of rural people was significant and ever increasing. In Oneida County, 14 per cent of the heads of farm households and 37 per cent of the heads of village households were members of fraternal lodges. Lodge and social club memberships were held in approximately equal proportion by full-time and part-time farmers and rural residents. Large-scale farm operators tended to be more frequent participants in organizations of this type. Most lodges were located in towns rather than open-country areas. Consequently, membership in lodges on the part of farm people was, in most cases, a significant index of social participation between rural and urban people. Indeed, it was often an index of the deterioration of boundary maintenance between rural and urban areas.

Recreational organizations and associations were widespread among open-country, small-town, and urban people. These included such organizations as rod-and-gun clubs, riding organizations, wild game conservation clubs, bowling leagues, winter sports groups, and fishing clubs. Many of the riding clubs and winter sports organizations represented the invasion of city people into open-country areas. In most cases they were actively supported and joined by more urban than rural people. On the other hand, there was some evidence that farm people found it profitable to promote such recreational organizations. They rented land for recreational purposes, provided guides, operated outfitting services, and owned lodging facilities.

SUMMARY

Farm people have long been the American prototype, but by the second half of the twentieth century they constituted one of America's newest numerical minorities. The decline of numerical importance of the nation's farmers is part of the society's food and fiber success story. It is also an index of the continuing urbanization of the entire nation.

The farm population has traditionally sent people, as well as food and fiber, from the farms to the cities. Only in the depression years of the 1930's and briefly in the post-World War II period did farms receive more persons than left them.

Definitions of farms and farm people have changed over the years. Consequently, some of the recent decline in the farm population is primarily a function of changed definitions. The recent definition, more sociologically and economically rigorous, has had the effect of eliminating many "hobby" farmers from the farming category.

Demographic characteristics of the farm population reveal that it is becoming more urbanized. However, the sex ratio remains higher in rural than urban areas, and farm areas continue to have a disproportionate number of people under age twenty. It was recorded in the 1960 Census that farm people were still less well educated than urban people, and that farm men were less well educated than farm women. The occupational experience of farm people has come to be strikingly similar to that of other segments of the population. More employed rural people were in blue collar occupations than engaged in farming. Geographically, the greatest number of farm people were concentrated in the South. The North-Central region had the second-largest number of farm people and still held claim to being the bread basket of the nation. It had proportionately more of the large commercial farms than did the South. Hired farm workers continued to play an important role in food and fiber production. Their future is precarious, however, due to gradual displacement by mechanization and vertical integration efficiencies.

The historical, family-centered, social participation of farm people has diminished in importance as a distinguishing characteristic of rural life. Farm people have been found to engage regularly and widely in formal social participation, in addition to traditional family-centered interaction.

In sum, the profile of the farm population shows some distinguishing characteristics including age, sex, and education, but as a whole it is blending into the national urbanized profile.

NOTES

1. Donald J. Bogue, *The Population of the United States* (Glencoe: Free Press, 1959).

2. Agricultural Marketing Service, *Farm Population Migration to and from Farms 1920–1953* (Washington: U.S. Department of Agriculture AMS-10, 1954); *Farm Population Estimates for 1955* (Washington: U.S.D.A., AMS-80, 1955); *Farm Population Estimates for 1956* (Washington: U.S.D.A., AMS-80, 1956); and *Farm Population Estimates for 1957* (Washington: U.S.D.A., AMS-80, 1958).

3. "Revised Estimates of the Farm Population of the United States, 1910–1950," *Farm Population* (Series Census BAE, Number 16, March 9, 1953).

4. Calvin L. Beale and Gladys K. Bowles, *The 1960 Definition of Farm Residence and Its Marked Effects on Farm Population Data* (Washington: U.S.D.A., Agricultural Marketing Service, 1961); "Effect of Definition Changes on Size Composition of the Rural-Farm Popuplation: April, 1960 and 1959," *Farm Population* (Washington: Series Census-AMS, No. 28, 1961), p. 27.

5. *Farm Population,* Series Census-AMS, No. 28, p. 1; Charles H. Elliot, Jr., and Glenn H. Beyer, *The Changing Farm Housing Inventory* (New York Agricultural Experiment Station Bulletin 930, 1958).

6. Beale and Bowles, *op. cit.,* pp. 3 ff.

7. Louis J. Ducoff, "Changing Occupations and Level of Living of Rural People." Talk presented at the 40th Annual Agricultural Outlook Conference, Washington, 1962.

8. Beale and Bowles, *op. cit.,* p. 10.

9. U.S. Bureau of the Census, *U.S. Census of Agriculture: 1959.* Vol. II, General Report Statistics by Subjects, Chapter 11 (Washington: U.S. Government Printing Office, 1962).

10. *The Hired Farm Working Force of 1960* (Washington: U.S.D.A., Economic Research Service, Agricultural Information Bulletin 266, 1960).

11. W. A. Anderson, *Some Factors Associated with Family Informal Participation* (Cornell Agricultural Experiment Station, Department of Rural Sociology, Mimeographed Bulletin 36, 1953). See also: W. A. Anderson and Harold E. Smith, *Formal and Informal Participation in a New York Village* (Cornell Agricultural Experiment Station, Department of Rural Sociology, Mimeographed Bulletin 28, 1952).

12. Anderson, *op. cit.,* p. 18.

13. Donald G. Hay and Robert A. Polson, *Rural Organizations in Oneida County, New York* (Cornell Agricultural Experiment Station Bulletin 871, 1951).

14. *Ibid.,* p. 31.

SELECTED READINGS

Phelps, Harold A. and David Henderson. *Population in its Human Aspects.* New York: Appleton-Century-Crofts, 1958.

See especially Chapter 4, "Rural People," a capable summary of the vital processes, compositional factors, and social correlates of the rural population.

Price, Paul H. "The Rural Population," in Alvin L. Bertrand (ed.), *Rural Sociology.* New York: McGraw-Hill Book Co., 1958.

This chapter is a compact treatment of the number, distribution, composition, migration, and vital process characteristics of rural people.

Smith, T. Lynn. *Fundamentals of Population Study.* New York: J. B. Lippincott, 1960.

See especially Chapter 4, "Rural or Urban Residence," a summary of rural and urban population trends in the United States with international comparisons.

Taylor, Carl C., *et al. Rural Life in the United States.* New York: Alfred A. Knopf, 1955.

See especially Part III, "Rural People," a provocative and informative treatment of such subjects as "Occupational Patterns of Rural Population," "Farm Laborers," "Landowners and Tenants," "Rural Population Characteristics," and "Dynamics of Rural Population."

5 RURAL NONFARM AND SUBURBAN RESIDENTS

By 1960, most rural residents in the United States were not engaged in farming. The typical country people in America were rural nonfarm, fringe, or suburban residents. The complete study of rural populations must, therefore, include a detailed consideration of rural nonfarm and suburban people in addition to farm people. Most human relations in rural America concern nonfarm activity. In farm areas human relations have come to be dominated by science, mechanization, and agribusiness. In short, most human relations in rural America have been widely influenced by urbanized social organization. This chapter presents a description and analysis of the largest categories of rural people, namely, nonfarm and suburban people.

URBAN INFLUENCES ON RURAL PEOPLE

A persuasive body of evidence has been assembled which indicates that rural people differ in their behavioral characteristics depending on whether they are close to or remote from major urban centers and metropolitan contacts.[1] One of the comprehensive studies of the dominance of urban life over rural areas is Bogue's analysis of the impact of hinterland cities on rural counties.[2] Based upon a study of 1950 Census data, Bogue's conclusion was that most central cities were located in counties which also had some rural nonfarm and rural farm population. Only 37 of more than 3,000 counties were completely urban; even 61 of the

93

counties which were the seats of central cities had some rural population. The remaining majority of American counties contained no major cities. Bogue's findings were:

Both the rural-nonfarm and the rural-farm populations occupy more intensively those counties which contain a large hinterland city than they occupy in counties which contain a small city. With each increase in size of the largest city contained, the average level of land occupancy tends to rise. In spite of these marked and uniform differences, which are attributed only to the influence of the local hinterland cities, the elements of the metropolitan pattern remain in each of the distributions. It is concluded that, to the extent that population distribution is related to population organization, the rural-nonfarm and the rural-farm populations are organized with respect both to the metropolis and to the hinterland.[3]

Bogue classified all counties as either metropolitan or nonmetropolitan, and hypothesized that the greatest urban influence would be experienced by the rural populations in metropolitan counties with urban centers of 250,000 or more. It was found that the nonmetropolitan counties with cities under 250,000 contained about four-fifths of the rural farm population. In contrast, only three-fifths of the rural nonfarm people lived in the nonmetropolitan counties. At the other end of the continuum, one-sixth of the rural nonfarm population was located in the metropolitan counties with urban centers of 250,000 or more. Urban counties had only one-twentieth of the rural farm population but they had a disproportionate share of the rural nonfarm population.

RURAL NONFARM PEOPLE

Since 1920, the census has identified rural nonfarm residents. This category has included individuals whose place of residence was outside the corporate limits of cities of 2,500 or more, and who did not live on or operate farms. The delineation of the rural nonfarm population has involved complexities in several specific instances, but essentially it has meant including those persons in the country who were not operating farms.

Age, sex, and education. In 1950, Duncan and Reiss [4] constructed population pyramids for the rural nonfarm and rural farm populations by type of county (see Fig. 6). These age-sex pyramids indicated that proximity to large urban areas influenced both the rural nonfarm and the rural farm

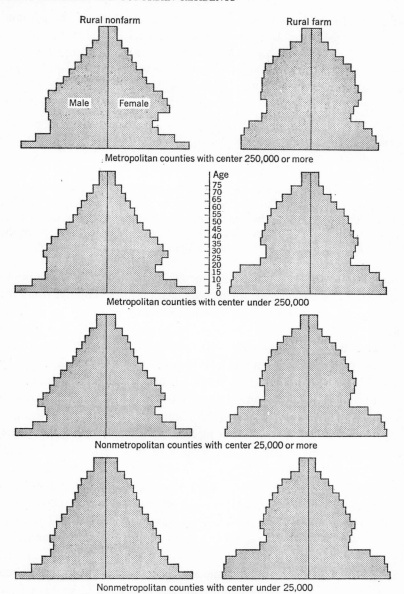

FIGURE 6. POPULATION PYRAMIDS FOR THE RURAL–NONFARM AND RURAL–FARM POPULATION BY TYPE OF COUNTY: 1950

Source: Otis D. Duncan and Albert J. Reiss, Jr. *Social Characteristics of Urban and Rural Communities, 1950* (New York: John Wiley and Sons, 1956), p. 156.

populations. In the least metropolitan counties, the base of the pyramid rose precipitously, indicating a disproportionately greater number of young children in those populations which were most remote from the major urban areas. The categories of rural people in the counties with population centers of 250,000 or more had a proportionately smaller number of young children. Duncan and Reiss's analysis also revealed that, for the United States as a whole, the median age of the farm populations by county declined as one moved away from those with major metropolitan centers to those with centers of under 25,000.

Thus, in metropolitan counties, the rural-farm median age exceeds that of the rural-nonfarm population—by nearly three years in the case of metropolitan counties with large centers. In nonmetropolitan counties the reverse is true, particularly in those counties whose largest center is under 25,000, where the rural-nonfarm median is two years greater than the rural farm median.[5]

In short, these findings revealed that median age of the rural farm population clearly reflected the degree of urbanization in the county, while the median age of the rural nonfarm population was relatively more independent.

The Duncan and Reiss analysis reported insignificant differences between the rural nonfarm and rural farm sex ratios when classified by county. There was a downward progression of sex ratios from the metropolitan to the nonmetropolitan counties. This trend was observed for both nonfarm and farm populations, but the differences were not significant.

Educational attainment, like the median age of the rural populations, tended to reflect the extent of urbanization of the county. For the rural nonfarm population the median number of school years ranged from a high of 10.0 in the metropolitan counties to a low of 8.7 in the nonmetropolitan counties. For the rural farm population the range of school years completed was not so great, but the drop was similar—from 8.8 years in the metropolitan counties to 8.3 years in the nonmetropolitan counties.

Labor force. More rural nonfarm males were in high prestige occupations when they came from metropolitan counties with large cities than from nonmetropolitan counties with small cities (see Table VII). The occupational distribution for the rural nonfarm population varied most widely in the farm and farm labor categories. In those metropolitan counties with the largest urban centers, only 1.4 per cent of the male labor force was engaged in farming; in counties with the smallest urban areas, nearly 4

TABLE VII. PERCENTAGE DISTRIBUTION OF THE RURAL NONFARM-EMPLOYED MALE
LABOR FORCE BY MAJOR OCCUPATION GROUP, BY TYPE OF COUNTY: 1950

Major Occupation Group	All Counties	Metropolitan by Size of Largest Place in Standard Metropolitan Area		Nonmetropolitan by Size of Largest Place in County	
		250,000 or More	Under 250,000	250,000 or More	Under 250,000
Professional, technical, and kindred workers	6.1	8.1	5.9	6.0	5.5
Managers, officials, and proprietors, except farm	10.7	10.9	9.7	10.1	10.9
Clerical and kindred workers	4.3	5.7	4.9	4.4	3.8
Sales workers	5.1	5.7	5.3	5.2	4.9
Craftsmen, foremen, and kindred workers	21.6	26.1	24.3	23.0	19.6
Operatives and kindred workers	25.0	23.6	27.3	25.4	24.9
Private household workers	0.2	0.3	0.2	0.2	0.2
Service workers, except private household	4.3	4.6	4.1	4.8	4.2
Laborers, except farm and mine	11.8	9.4	10.3	11.1	12.9
Farmers and farm managers	3.0	1.4	1.8	2.3	1.9
Farm laborers, unpaid family workers	0.5	0.1	0.2	0.3	0.6
Farm laborers, except unpaid and farm foreman	6.0	3.0	4.8	5.9	7.1
Occupation not reported	1.4	1.1	1.2	1.3	1.5
Total	100.0	100.0	100.0	100.0	100.0

Source: *1950 Census of Population,* Vol. II, Characteristics of the Population, Parts
2 to 50, Table 48.

per cent of the labor force worked in agriculture. Similarly, the proportion of farm laborers in the nonmetropolitan counties was more than
double that in the metropolitan counties, 7.1 per cent and 3.0 per cent,
respectively.

RURAL-URBAN FRINGE

The growth and expansion of rural-urban fringe areas—buffer zones, as
it were, between farms and cities—has constituted one of the most sig-

nificant effects of urbanization on rural life. The term *rural-urban fringe* applies to the developing set of human relations between farm and city.[6] The rural-urban fringe development was prompted largely by increased mobility due to the automobile and other means of rapid transportation, and by advanced communication techniques. The people who formed this fringe moved there from two directions—namely, from farms and cities.[7]

The development of the rural-urban fringe was still a comparatively new phenomenon in the 1960's. Much conjecture of its scope was offered by the literature. But, while the concept itself was embryonic, certain of its components were clear. For example, the study of the rural-urban fringe specifically involved the description and analysis of community life on the periphery of cities and of farms. Human relations in the fringe had a spatial location but lacked a clear relationship with older established lines of governmental jurisdiction. The fringe social organization was not political; indeed, one of the key characteristics of the fringe was the absence of political organization. If cities had been able to keep abreast of the developments in the dynamic urbanized social organization, many of the areas regarded as rural-urban fringes might well have become integral parts of the cities. In most cases, however, the political boundaries of cities have not expanded to incorporate them.

The fringe area has been visualized as a belt of land extending all the way around cities. Its population is typically heterogeneous. It is a concentration of nonvillage, rural nonfarm people adjacent to larger urban areas, a place where urban and rural activities are interwoven.[8]

In addition to an identification of the land and an interpretation of land use within the fringe, an assessment must be made of the adjustment of people in this area, their living conditions, awareness of community life, conditions of social participation—in short, their various types of social interaction. Two early studies of the fringe described and analyzed the social interaction there to some extent.

In 1941, Andrews [9] made an extensive study of the fringe around Janesville, Wisconsin. Some individuals had migrated to the fringe because of job layoffs in the city, desire for lower rents, and desire to be near family and friends. Others migrated in search of a new environment. These people were antiurban; they believed the fringe was superior to the city for child rearing, sought gardening as a hobby, looked upon the fringe as a more healthy place to live or went there for retirement. A set of so-called "fringe problems" developed, including: high transportation cost, deficient utilities, inadequate government, and continued fringe expansion which, in turn, resulted in the loss of characteristics that had served to make the fringe area so attractive for its earlier residents. Human relations in the fringe were complex and subject to extensive changes.

In a study of a rural-urban fringe area in Williamsport, Pennsylvania, Blizzard and Anderson delineated the typical characteristics of the fringe:

The fringe is an area of land use contrast. Rural and urban, agricultural, commercial and residential land uses are intermixed. In any of these mixtures the uses may be of high intensity and are often found adjoining or in close proximity.

One may see contrasts in economic enterprises and in levels of living in the fringe, again, in many cases, adjoining or in close proximity. Family-built houses and modern, urban-type dwellings; jerry-built houses, trailers, squatters, and country estates; junk-yards and clean, modern farms—all these may be found in the urban oriented area around central cities. . . .

The rural-urban fringe has been found to contain many unfinished structures, some occupied, some unoccupied. Occupied roofed-over cellars may be found. Several cellar houses and two cellar churches, all occupied, were found in the Williamsport fringe. . . .

Of high incidences in the fringe are houses with paper or other temporary siding. There are houses that indicate that the owners have hired professional labor to do the major portion of the work, but left details for themselves to finish at their convenience. . . .

Undeveloped plotted land is a dominant fringe phenomenon. Real estate speculators often guess wrong and leave land marked off but unoccupied. Often the mistakes are costly when streets, sidewalks, and sometimes even utility installations are abandoned because of the building boom which has collapsed.[10]

Duncan and Reiss made an extensive case study of the Chicago fringe using 1950 Census data. They designated

the urban component of the fringe to include that portion of the urbanized area within the metropolitan district, but outside of incorporated places of 2,500 or more. Thus defined, Chicago's urban fringe includes some 46,000 residents of incorporated places under 2,500 and about 77,000 inhabitants of incorporated urban territory. The rural component of the fringe includes all persons residing in the metropolitan district outside of urban territory. It contains nearly 92,000 rural-nonfarm and about 11,000 rural farm fringe population. The separation of rural-urban fringe into urban, rural-urban, and rural farm components was made possible by the fact that the Bureau of the Census prepared a separate summary card for each of these parts of each census tract in the metropolitan districts.[11]

In the area of Chicago, and in the case of many other fringe areas, the rural fringe extends greater distances from the central city than do suburbs or the urban fringe. Most of the city of Chicago was located within a ten-mile radius. Much of the fringe population, on the other hand, occupied a belt area between 10 and 25 miles distant from the central city. Satellite cities were more remote, occupying a space between 25 and 50 miles from the central area.

Age-sex characteristics. Differential age-sex characteristics between the central city and the fringe were quite precise. The highest median age (33.6) was recorded in the central city. The median age was 27.4 in the urban fringe, 27.9 in the rural nonfarm fringe, and 31.9 in the rural farm fringe. The sex ratio was lower in the central city and higher in the fringe areas.

Educational attainment. The lowest median educational attainment was recorded for the rural fringe area, and the highest median educational attainment was reported for the suburbs. In the Chicago area the median number of school years completed for people in the rural farm fringe was 8.6, the rural nonfarm fringe 9.8, and the urban fringe 10.0. In contrast, the suburbs with populations between 2,500 and 50,000 had inhabitants reporting a median educational attainment of approximately 11.9 years. The suburbs significantly surpassed the central city, where the recorded median educational attainment was 9.5 years.

Labor force and the fringe. One of the most striking trends in the organization of labor within the fringe as compared with that in the central city was the declining proportion of working women as one moved from the central city to the fringe. Another distinguishing characteristic was the number of white collar workers, which was highest in the suburbs, second-greatest in the central city, and lowest in the urban and rural nonfarm fringes.

In concluding their study of the Chicago rural-urban fringe, Duncan and Reiss stated that the traditional rural-urban continuum represents an oversimplification of human behavior. The rural population was a mixture. It had a high sex ratio, similar to the farm areas, but a low fertility ratio, similar to the cities. Rural fringe people like farm people, had low educational attainment. On the other hand, white collar work experience was more common to them than to farm people. Even more important was the close similarity between the urban and the rural nonfarm fringe. The rural nonfarm population in proximity to large cities was primarily an urban-oriented body of residents, while the more remote rural nonfarm populations were relatively more rural in their orientation.

A case study of a rural-urban fringe in Baton Rouge, Louisiana, corroborated the findings of the Chicago case study.[12] The authors of the Louisiana study reported a merging of the rural-urban populations. They found that farmers did not ascribe to values significantly different from those of urban people. In the Louisiana fringe, differential occupational behavior as well as differential family size were observed. The merging was far from complete, but the trend toward it was clear.

Human organization in the rural-urban fringe provides another striking example of the expansion of urbanized social organization throughout the nation. The dominant cultural universals are clear; they originate in the cities and expand outward. They are modified in their expansion so that they become a combination of cultural traits which are both urban and rural. There is an interplay and reciprocity between the polar types of social organization, even though the abiding character remains city-generated.

SUBURBS AND SUBURBANIZATION

American suburbs first came into existence in the late nineteenth century. Their accompanying way of life, namely suburbanization, came into existence in the first quarter of the twentieth century. Neither of the concepts, *suburbs* or *suburbanization,* has yet become precisely articulated in the research literature. Suburbanization was established as a subject of study in the late 1930's, with the Connecticut, Rhode Island, and New York studies.[13]

The primary difference between the conceptualization of suburbs and fringe areas is that the former usually constitute a specific political area outside a major metropolitan area but within its zone of dominance. The fringe, by contrast, may or may not be under the direct dominance of a metropolitan area, but in either event it is typically not an incorporated area.[14]

Duncan and Reiss analyzed the suburban areas around American cities, using data from the 1950 Census. They suggested that the most appropriate definition of suburb would be "all places of 2,500 inhabitants or more, within urbanized areas but outside central cities." The 1950 Census provided for the delineation of a category called the *urban fringe,* which included all populations in the urbanized area but outside the central cities. Due to the method by which the statistics were reported, the authors necessarily *treated as suburbs the population included in the urban fringe.* They estimated that at least seven-tenths of the urban fringe population lived in suburbs, using the more restricted definition to include places of 2,500 or more. Sixty-nine million people were reported as residents of all urbanized areas in 1950. Seventy per cent of these people were residents of the central cities, 21 per cent of the suburbs, and 9 per cent of the urban fringe.

Age, sex, and education. The sex ratio of all the nation's urbanized areas was low—94 men per 100 women. Cities also had proportionately more females than did the suburbs. Their sex ratios were 93.5 and 95.1, respectively. The suburban population was typically younger than the urban population. The median age for the central city's population was recorded at 33 years, compared to 31 years for the suburbs. Higher fertility ratios were recorded for suburbs than for central cities. The 1950 Census reported some 452 children under five years of age for 1,000 women of child-bearing age in the central cities, compared to 534 children for 1,000 women of child-bearing age in the suburbs.

Educational attainment was typically higher for the suburban population than for the central city population. The 1950 Census reported the median number of school years completed by persons 25 years of age and over as 9.9 in the central cities, compared with 11.1 in the suburbs. Differential educational attainment was even greater between the largest central cities and the suburbs than between the smaller central cities and suburbs.

Labor force and occupations. Labor force participation was high both in the central cities and in the suburbs. Fifty-seven per cent of the people in the central cities were in the labor force, compared to 54 per cent of the suburbs' population. Analysis of the major occupation of employed persons in the suburbs revealed the number of individuals in the upper socioeconomic work statuses to be higher than in the cities. In contrast, greater proportions of the central city population were employed in clerical and service types of work. Approximately equal proportions of the central city and suburban labor forces were employed in sales work, operative work, and laboring work.[15]

Suburbanization long has been associated with general affluence. Occupational analysis reveals that many suburbanites are in the professional and managerial categories. On the other hand, an increasing number of suburban residents are in blue collar work positions. Some entire suburbs have become characterized as blue collar areas.[16]

In the urbanized social organization of the United States, suburbs, rural-urban fringe areas, and small hamlets indirectly and sometimes directly stand as indexes of the bucolic values which never have been obliterated by the urbanization process. Land use outside the central cities is perhaps the most economically inefficient that man can imagine. But the meaning of land in America is a matter of more than efficiency. It originally entailed a love for nature, later a symbol of political right and economic well-being, and more recently the combination of all of these in the urbanized society's prestige and status system. Expensive suburban and fringe area homes with extensive park-like yard areas are marks of prestige, costly, and symbols of conspicuous consumption. Studies of human behavior and value orientations of individuals in the suburbs and fringe areas reveal the intricate relationship of rural and urban values contained within them.

SOCIAL PARTICIPATION

A detailed study was made of social participation of rural nonfarm adults in four New York localities.[17] The inhabitants of these rural nonfarm areas were typically in the middle years of life—between 25 and 54; both males and females had slightly more formal education than farmers; the household size of three or four persons was slightly smaller than that of their neighboring farmers; finally, the rural nonfarm people had lived for a shorter period of time in their localities than had the farm families. The average number of organizations to which the rural nonfarm residents belonged was 2.6 for the males and 2.4 for females. Rural nonfarm residents whose occupational positions were professional or proprietory had more memberships, 4.3 for the men and 3.2 for the women. Skilled workers and retired couples had fewer organization memberships than the average in the rural nonfarm area.

When comparisons were made between the number of organization memberships of rural nonfarm people and farm people, it was discovered that farmers reported memberships in three organizations, or slightly more than the number reported by the rural nonfarm males. Rural farm wives reported an average of 2.2 organization memberships, or slightly less than the number reported by the rural nonfarm wives. In both cases the differences were not significant. As urbanized social organization comes to dominate the nation, increased organization memberships are bound to characterize rural as well as urban America.

Rural nonfarm people belonged to slightly more than two organizations on the average, but they regularly attended meetings of only one organization. When this pattern of attendance for rural nonfarm people was compared to that of farmers in the area, no significant difference was found. The most significant difference in attendance was found between members of various occupations. Those at the upper end of the occupational ladder attended organization meetings with significantly higher frequency than those at the lower end.

Analysis of the financial contributions to organizations revealed no significant difference between the pattern of making donations or the number of organizations supported by rural nonfarm and rural farm people. As in the case of attendance, significant differences in support were greater among the occupational than among the residential categories. Again, the white collar, and particularly the professional workers, tended to support more organizations than did those in the non-white-collar occupations. Anderson summarized his findings as follows:

Adults in the professional-proprietorial-managerial occupations take part in these activities to a greater extent and in larger numbers than adults in any other occupational classes. Clerical and kindred workers are next in the extent of their activities, farmers third, skilled-semiskilled and unskilled persons fourth, and retired and unemployed persons fifth.[18]

A study of suburbanization in Michigan revealed that its impact on social participation took the form of community problems.[19] Moore and Barlowe studied two suburban areas near the city of Lansing. They interviewed 224 individuals, 58 per cent of whom were not farmers. Most of the residents of this suburban fringe had moved into the area because of its lower housing costs, health and retirement conditions, and their desire to raise children in an open area, as well as the family's general desire for more freedom than was available in either the city or the open country. Social interaction between the indigenous farm residents and the new in-migrants was not always amiable. The in-migrants had brought to the suburb the desire for open space, but also the generally contradictory desire for urban conveniences. The authors reported the ensuing social interaction patterns as follows:

Most part-time farmers felt that suburbanization had very little impact upon community life. Some full-time farmers, however, argued that the new residents were urban-oriented and that their influx into the community had disrupted the neighborly spirit that had formerly prevailed. Suburbanization was credited with part of the rise of properly values . . . also, there was a general feeling that suburbanization was partly responsible for the upward trend in property taxes.[20]

Demands on the part of the new residents for improved roads, city bus service, more adequate schools, extension of natural gas facilities, and other conveniences all contributed to social distance between the new and the indigenous residents. The social interaction pattern did not reach the level of conflict intensity, but relations were often strained.

A study of the suburban fringe development around the city of Milwaukee led to a description of social interaction patterns as temporary and provisional.[21] Dewey discovered that membership in formal organizations was often provisional and that informal interaction in friendship groups was often temporary. People in the fringe areas were seldom anchored; indeed, they were often marked by rapid mobility. Characteristically, they held salaried positions or did work that involved transfer to other locations. Home ownership was typified by possession of mortgages and repeated sale and resale of property. The families were younger than average and child-centered.

In a study of the fringe area development around Columbia, Missouri, it was discovered that the so-called "decentralized" in-migrants to the fringe most often continued their participation in city organizations and, in addition to this activity, participated in a selected number of fringe and open-country organizations.[22]

Questions have been raised concerning the failure of fringe in-migrants to assume their proper share of leadership responsibilities in the new environment. A study in New York reported no failure of in-migrants to participate in leadership.[23] In the particular area studied in New York, it was reported that approximately an equal number, namely one-third, of farm families and of nonfarm families typically participated in local community leadership activities. Moreover, it was reported in the same study that an approximately equal number of farm and nonfarm families participated in local fraternal organizational work. Both farm and nonfarm families were found to be interested in recreational activities. The new rural residents were more active leaders in their new communities than in the communities of the larger central cities from which they had migrated.[24]

The social relationships between the farm and nonfarm people in the fringe area were often potential conflict situations. Overt conflict, however, seldom occurred. Some research has suggested that conditions of tension between these two groups were often tempered by the fact that many of the in-migrants were born on farms, and socialized in the open-country environment for a period of years before they migrated to the central cities and eventually back to the fringe. In short, it was observed that many of the in-migrants were far from newcomers, as it were, to the open country. Many in fact were returning to native grounds.[25]

SUMMARY

By the middle of the twentieth century it has become clear that most nonurban people live not on farms but in a diffuse fringe zone outside the corporate limits of major metropolitan areas. Social organization and land use between farms and cities have been variously designated as urban fringe, rural fringe, suburban, and rural nonfarm. These concepts are not yet adequately formulated or widely accepted. Indeed, the absence of a clear conceptualization of human relations between the city and the farm complicates research in these areas. The thesis expounded in this book, however, is that the boundary between rural and urban is diffuse and unclear. The conceptual difficulties which complicate research lend support, by default, to this thesis.

In this chapter, emphasis is placed on patterns of interaction that are widely observed outside of metropolitan areas but not on farms. Most, if not all, of these relationships can only be adequately understood in the light of two factors, that is, rural location and the value orientation of the bucolic way of life. Social relations in rural America clearly include those involved in the operation of farms and those of the ever increasing number of rural nonfarm inhabitants.

The behavior of both farm and rural nonfarm people pointedly illustrates the advanced condition of urbanized social organization in the United States. These social relations are the product of the reciprocal interaction of people and ideas from remote rural areas and metropolitan centers, and the various degrees of population density between these two extremes. The fringe developments above all else serve as strong evidence of urbanized social organization. The condition of life in the fringe cannot be subsumed under either the urban or the rural category. Yet there is no adequate evidence that life in the fringe constitutes a third behavioral type, and that instead of the historic dichotomy between rural and urban life there is now a trichotomy of city life, fringe life, and farm life. There has been some suggestion of such a trichotomy, and research has been conducted for the purpose of ascertaining its usefulness. Evidence of a confirming nature, however, remains far from convincing.

When demographic characteristics of people in the rural-urban fringe and in the suburban areas are reviewed, some important differences are observed. High fertility rates, high mobility, high educational attainment, and often high status or white collar occupations characterize the fringe areas. But even these characteristics are not clear and precise. Other researchers have produced evidence of the extreme heterogeneity of life in the fringe. Aristocratic suburbs and working class suburbs have been delineated. Affluent estates have been found adjacent to tar-paper shacks. Country clubs may be seen in close proximity to garbage dumps. In the absence of systematic zoning, suburban tracts and farm enterprises are often juxtaposed. In short, the fringe is a complex labyrinth of human relations, ideologies, and patterns of land use.

Studies of social participation in the fringe provide further evidence of the dynamic social structures evolving in these areas. The norms of social participation in the fringe areas are still fluid, still developmental. The patterns that are observed are more embryonic than mature. The boundary maintenance that once obtained between country and city no longer exists. The power struggle in the norms of social interaction is centered upon the degree and character of urbanized social organization rather than upon isolationism. The dynamics of social behavior in the rural-urban fringe no longer characteristically involve the separation of farm and city, but, juxtaposing them, involve experimental attempts at working out the mechanisms of compatible social interaction.

NOTES

1. Edmund deS. Brunner and J. H. Kolb, "Rural and Urban Relationships," in *Rural Social Trends* (New York: McGraw-Hill, 1933); E. T. Hiller, "Extension of Urban Characteristics into Rural Areas," *Rural Sociology*, 6 (Sept., 1941), 242–57; Roland S. Thompson and Nelle G. Jackson, "Fertility in Rural Areas in Relation to Their Distance from Cities, 1930," *Rural Sociology*, 5 (June, 1940), 143–62.

2. Don J. Bogue, *The Structure of the Metropolitan Community: A Study in Dominance and Subdominance* (Ann Arbor: University of Michigan Press, 1949), pp. 115–29.

3. *Ibid.,* p. 129.

4. Otis Dudley Duncan and Albert J. Reiss, Jr., *Social Characteristics of Urban and Rural Communities, 1950* (New York: John Wiley and Sons, 1956), pp. 151–69.

5. *Ibid.,* p. 157.

6. T. Lynn Smith, *The Population of Louisiana: Its Composition and Changes* (Louisiana Agricultural Experiment Station Bulletin 293, 1937); Samuel W. Blizzard and William F. Anderson, *Problems in Rural-Urban Fringe Research: Conceptualization and Delineation* (Pennsylvania Agricultural Experiment Station Progress Report 89, 1952); and Charles E. Lively *et al.,* "The Sociological Significance of the Rural-Urban Fringe," *Rural Sociology,* 18 (June, 1953), 101–20.

7. Myles W. Rodehaver, "Fringe Settlement as a Two Directional Movement," *Rural Sociology,* 12 (March, 1947), 49–57; see also J. M. Gillette, "Some Population Shifts in the United States, 1930–1940," *American Sociological Review,* 6 (Oct., 1941), 619–28; and Vincent H. Whitney, "Rural-Urban People," *American Journal of Sociology,* 54 (July, 1948), 48–54.

8. John D. Black, "The Soul and the Sidewalk," *American Planning and Civic Annual, 1939* (Washington: American Planning and Civic Association, 1939).

9. Richard B. Andrews, "Urban Fringe Studies of Two Wisconsin Cities: A Summary," *Journal of Land and Public Utility Economics,* 21 (Nov., 1945), 375–82.

10. Blizzard and Anderson, *op. cit.,* pp. 23–4; and William F. Anderson, *A Method for Delineating the Rural-Urban Fringe Surrounding Small Cities* (Unpublished Master's Thesis, Pennsylvania State College, 1941).

11. Duncan and Reiss, *op. cit.,* pp. 136–50.

12. Paul H. Price and George A. Hillery, Jr., *The Rural-Urban Fringe and Louisiana's Agriculture: A Case Study of the Baton Rouge Area* (Louisiana Agricultural Experiment Station Bulletin 526, 1959).

13. N. L. Whetten and E. C. Devereux, Jr., *Studies of Suburbanization in Connecticut, One: Windsor: A Highly Developed Agricultural Area* (Connecticut Agricultural Experiment Station Bulletin 212, 1936); N. L. Whetten and R. F. Field, *Studies of Suburbanization in Connecticut, Two: Norwich: An Industrial Part-Time Farming Area* (Connecticut Agricultural Experiment Station Bulletin 226, 1938); N. L. Whetten, *Studies of Suburbanization in Connecticut, Three: Wilton: A Rural Town in Metropolitan New York* (Connecticut Agricultural Experiment Station Bulletin 230, 1939); W. R. Gordon, *Satellite Acres* (Rhode Island Agricultural Experiment Station Bulletin 282, 1942); W. R. Gordon and Gilbert S. Meldrum, *Land, People, and Farming in a Rurban Zone* (Rhode Island Agricultural Experiment Station Bulletin 285, 1942); Earl L. Koos and E. deS. Brunner, *Suburbanization in Webster* (Rochester: University of Rochester Studies of Metropolitan Rochester, No. 1, 1945).

14. Duncan and Reiss, *op. cit.,* p. 117. See also Chauncy D. Harris, "Suburbs," *American Journal of Sociology,* 49 (July, 1943), 1–13.

15. *Ibid.,* pp. 128–9.

16. Bennett M. Berger, *Working Class Suburb: A Study of Auto Workers in Suburbia* (Berkeley: University of California Press, 1960).

17. Walfred A. Anderson, *Social Participation of Rural-Nonfarm Adults* (Cornell Agricultural Experiment Station Bulletin 928, 1958).

18. Anderson, *op. cit.*, p. 24. See also Walfred A. Anderson and N. Sibley, *The Social Participation of Fringe Families: A Second Study* (Cornell Agricultural Experiment Station, Rural Sociology Publication No. 50, 1957).

19. E. Howard Moore and Raleigh Barlowe, *Effects of Suburbanization upon Rural Land Use* (Michigan Agricultural Experiment Station Technical Bulletin 253, 1955).

20. *Ibid.*, p. 4.

21. Richard Dewey, "Peripheral Expansion in Milwaukee County," *American Journal of Sociology*, 4 (Sept., 1948), 118–25.

22. Noel P. Gist, "Ecological Decentralization and Rural-Urban Relationships," *Rural Sociology*, 17 (Dec., 1952), 328–35.

23. C. E. Ramsey, "Flight to the Fringe Affects Social Participation and Leadership," *Farm Research*, 23 (July, 1957), New York Agricultural Experiment Station.

24. Compare also W. A. Anderson, "Flight to the Fringe—Effects on Rural New York," *Farm Research*, 22 (July, 1956), New York Agricultural Experiment Station.

25. See especially Charles H. Elliott, Jr., *The Changing Farm Housing Inventory* (Cornell Agricultural Experiment Station Bulletin 930, 1958).

SELECTED READINGS

Anderson, Walfred A. *Social Participation of Rural-Nonfarm Adults.* Cornell Agricultural Experiment Station Bulletin 928, 1958.

An analysis of the extent and intensity of participation in organizations by nonfarm families in New York rural areas.

Blizzard, Samuel W., and William F. Anderson. *Problems in Rural-Urban Fringe Research: Conceptualization and Delineation.* Pennsylvania Agricultural Experiment Station, Progress Report 89, 1952.

The authors deal with recent attempts to conceptualize the contemporary phenomenon of rural-urban fringe development and with various methods for delineating the fringe areas for research purposes.

Duncan, Otis Dudley, and Albert J. Reiss, Jr. *Social Characteristics of Urban and Rural Communities in 1950.* New York: John Wiley and Sons, 1956.

An important comparative demographic analysis of communities of different sizes, types, and locations in American society, using concepts and hypotheses from human ecology.

Gist, Noel P. "Ecological Decentralization and Rural-Urban Relationships," *Rural Sociology*, 17 (Dec., 1952), pp. 328–35.

The author discusses the social implications of urban decentralization, the relocation of urban families in the open country surrounding the urban center, and the social interaction of decentralized families with urban people.

Gordon, W. R. *Satellite Acres*. Rhode Island Agricultural Experiment Station Bulletin 282, 1942.

A study of rural Rhode Island households which combine agricultural with non-agricultural employment.

Koos, Earl L., and E. deS. Brunner. *Suburbanization in Webster*. Rochester: University of Rochester Studies of Metropolitan Rochester, No. 1, 1945.

The problems of suburbanization in a metropolitan area, adjustment of immigrants in surrounding fringe towns, the cause of emigration from metropolitan areas, and implications for community organization planning are discussed by the authors.

Moore, E. Howard, and Raleigh Barlowe. *Effects of Suburbanization upon Rural Land Use*. Michigan Agricultural Experiment Station, Technical Bulletin, 235, 1955.

This study shows the impact of the suburbanization movement upon the use of farm land in a sample area in Michigan, and indicates the effects suburbanization has had on property values, taxes, and the attitudes of residents.

Whetten, N. L. *Studies of Suburbanization in Connecticut, Three: Wilton: A Rural Town in Metropolitan New York*. Connecticut Agricultural Experiment Station Bulletin 230, 1939.

———, and E. C. Devereux, Jr. *Studies of Suburbanization in Connecticut, One: Windsor: A Highly Developed Agriculture Area*. Connecticut Agricultural Experiment Station Bulletin 212, 1936.

———, and R. F. Field. *Studies of Suburbanization in Connecticut, Two: Norwich: An Industrial Part-Time Farming Area*. Connecticut Agricultural Experiment Station Bulletin 226, 1938.

These are significant pioneering studies of suburbanization in American Society. They deal with the problems and conflicts of suburban movements when population groups of wide socioeconomic diversity come together in residential areas.

6 DECENTRALIZED INDUSTRY AND RURAL NONFARM EMPLOYMENT

Throughout modern history, industrial development and urban growth have been closely associated. Yet, from the Industrial Revolution to the present, agriculture has not always been viewed in relation to industrial development. Industry has been and continues to be, ecologically as well as in terms of human relations, closely affiliated with rural and urban areas and people. Indeed, in the urbanized social organization of the United States, there is a tendency for industry to locate in rural areas and for these industries to utilize rural people in their labor force. The purpose of this chapter is to call special attention to the industrially employed population in rural areas.

HISTORY AND IDEOLOGY

Agriculture and industry were still interrelated at the beginning of the eighteenth century in England. The division of labor between farming and manufacturing was simple and scarcely suggested the complexity by which it would be characterized more than a century later. Rural-urban differences were minimal compared to what they were to become in the nineteenth century. Industry was rural and decentralized. Of the early 1700's in England, Arnold Toynbee wrote:

When we turn to investigate the industrial organization of the time, we find that the class of capitalist employees was as yet in its infancy. A large part of our goods were still produced on the domestic system. Manufactures were

111

little concentrated in towns, and only partially separated from agriculture. The "manufacturer" was, literally, the man who worked with his own hands in his own cottage. Nearly the whole cloth trade of the West Riding, for instance, was organized on this system at the beginning of the century.[1]

Production during this period was accomplished by small master manufacturers who combined the resources of capital and land. These operators had small enclosures, usually less than ten acres, with a house on the land.[2] Manufacturing activities were located in the house. A horse was kept on the land and used to transport the product to market. A cow and some poultry were also maintained on the land for the manufacturer's family.

By the middle of the eighteenth century, master manufacturers were enlarging and centralizing their operations. The "putting-out" system was developed, and, in turn, was soon replaced by a more authentic urban industry. Thus, local and regional markets declined in the face of ascending national markets and advancing technology.[3] In the United States the centralization of markets easily changed into urbanized social organization.

After approximately a century of experience with city centralization of industrial manufacturing, a new integration of field, factory, and intellect was called for. Kropotkin wrote:

The importance of such a combination . . . was eagerly discussed some fifty years ago under the names of "harmonized labor," "integral education," and so on. It was pointed out at that time that the greatest sum total of well-being can be obtained when a variety of agricultural, industrial, and intellectual pursuits are combined in each community; and that man shows his best when he is in a position to apply his usually-varied capacities to several pursuits in the farm, the workshop, the factory, the study or the studio, instead of being riveted for life to one of these pursuits only.[4]

Kropotkin believed that fields and gardens should be located at the gates of factories and workshops, and that the same labor force should be employed in both. Much of the effort to move factories into low-income rural areas in the United States in the past twenty years has implemented this notion, even though unintentionally. The great majority of America's part-time farmers combine work in factories and in fields. In the United States, however, this has been less directed toward providing adequate food than it has been toward providing a gratifying living experience. Some part-time farmers have achieved a unique adjustment to urbanized social organization through this combination of work experiences.

A recent study of the depopulation of rural England revealed major difficulties in the provision of services to sparsely settled areas.[5] The position was taken by some that rural communities were not to be preserved but to be developed:

While it may be agreed that there are some villages, and some rural areas, which ought to be kept "unspoilt" for the sake of amenity, it would indeed be unfortunate if we were to accept as inevitable a general cleavage of interest between town and country. . . . Much of the isolation of rural communities has, of course, been broken down by the development of motor transport, wireless, and the telephone; and it would be difficult to deny that a great deal of the change has been for the better. In any case, "for better or worse," it will continue, and I see no reason why the benefits of economic progress should not be further extended to the countryside. Indeed it is by the introduction of some industrial development that there is most hope of the improvement of the social and economic conditions in the countryside, in the future as in the past. . . .

These various grounds constitute a strong case against any view that the introduction of new industries or other construction into villages or the countryside should be restricted as a general principle; our duty is to foster the "well-being" of rural communities, and not to "preserve" them. Indeed, the most difficult cases in any scheme of planning will not be those rural areas where new development is likely to occur, but those where employment and economic activity remain comparatively static.[6]

There was also a strong preservationist view in England. Spokesmen for this view rejected the scheme to bring industry into rural England.

The history of the integration of agriculture and industry is longer than that of their separate developments. Arguments for and against integration or separation of agriculture and industry have long been expounded. The contemporary trend in plant location indicates the existence of a tendency for integration of industry with rural life, but with little conscious ideological guidance.

PLANT LOCATION

The systematic planning of plant location is advanced in an urbanized society. Manufacturing has become a systematizing and rationalizing force in human endeavor, predicated on the collection and analysis of facts. Consequently, the earliest plants were located close to markets, raw materials, transportation, and a labor force. As the complexities of contemporary societies increase, the factors which enter into the determination of plant location also increase. Ten factors are listed in a recent issue of

Plant Location as guides for site appraisals. These are: labor and manufacturing, raw materials, power and fuel, transportation, taxes and labor
laws, finance, climate, industrial development, and general factors.[7] Under
these major categories, such diverse items are included as population,
housing, school facilities, family income, labor turnover, labor history,
strikes, work stoppages, unions, recreational facilities, cultural facilities,
hospitals, churches, newspapers, police and fire service, zoning, political
awareness of citizens, solicitations for donations, and living conditions.

Problems of industrial location have become so complex that both
government and private agencies assist in site selection. In the Industrial
Location Division of the Office of Area Development in the U.S. Department of Commerce, a clearinghouse service has been provided for technical advice on problems of plant location. The government's Industrial
Location Division has maintained a complete inventory of planned industrial park locations. The Division has published a monograph entitled
Organized Industrial Districts: A Tool for Community Development. In
addition to the federal government's service various states have appointed
industrial development directors. The American Industrial Development
Council (1925) was organized to provide services similar to those of the
government. The Council now has more than 700 members located in
every state as well as Canada and Puerto Rico. The Society of Industrial
Realtors has offered similar services. Multitudinous small communities
now have developed industrial corporations or other programs to encourage and nurture industry in their areas.

RECENT TRENDS IN INDUSTRIAL LOCATION

In the second half of the twentieth century the most urgent reasons for
determining plant location have undergone significant modifications. With
rapid transportation and rapid communication, high mobility of the population, widespread threats of military conflict, and with mass markets, the
problem of plant location becomes uniquely different from that in earlier
periods of history. The net impact of these changes in social organization
was that an estimated 30 per cent of all industrial plants established in the
1950's were located in small towns or in the open country near small
towns of less than 10,000 inhabitants.[8]

Many of the plants located in small communities were related to the
farming enterprise or were an integral part of agribusiness. Other plants
have little or no direct relationship to agribusiness. Robock [9] reported that

rural industries constitute an important source of employment for farm people. His study also presented evidence that rural industrial employment alone would not be sufficient to provide enough jobs for all rural youth. Between 1939 and 1947, rural industrial jobs increased at a slower rate than all manufacturing jobs. During this eight-year period, only 360,000 new jobs were created in rural industries, compared to more than 2,500,000 workers who were underemployed.

In seven Southeast states the need for off-farm employment was even more critical than in other areas of the nation. Those states annually added approximately 70,000 new entrants to the labor force over and above those needed on farms. Rural industries in the Southeast annually provided only about 11,000 new jobs. Many of the nonfarm jobs were in forestry, but advances in technology were reducing the size of the needed labor force in that industry.

In general, rural industries provide only a few jobs per plant. The plants are usually small, and their wage rates are lower than those of larger city plants. The decline in the number of "agricultural rural industries" has been more alarming (see Table VIII). "Forestry rural industries" and "rural market industries" have increased; but they employ proportionately fewer people.

IMPACT OF INDUSTRIALIZATION ON RURAL LIFE

Modern industrialization has invaded the rural areas through an urban-oriented pattern of life. Ironically, however, most research findings have revealed that rural residents are generally favorable to this pattern. For the rural people it has meant increased income, suitable part-time or even full-time employment, and employment for farm youth who would otherwise have to leave home to seek work in the large cities. The impact of industry in rural areas also furthered the expansion of secondary or contractual human relations in an environment where the people have historically prided themselves on warm, personal relationships. In short, industries brought with them ethics of competition and urbanized social organization. The human relations involved, however, were reciprocal. Rural workers brought a traditionalist ethic to their work in plants. Moreover, there is some evidence that plant management found the rural environment a more desirable location because of the competence and other craft-oriented values allegedly associated with the work ethic of rural people. Thus, decentralization of industry is another social factor

TABLE VIII. RURAL INDUSTRIES IN THE UNITED STATES AND SEVEN SOUTHEASTERN STATES[a]

Industry Groups	Number of Establishments				Number of Production Workers			
	Number 1947		Change in Number 1939-47		Change, 1939-47 (In Thousands)		Per Cent Change, 1939-47	
	United States	Southeast	United States	Southeast	United States	Southeast	United States	Southeast
All manufacturing industries	240,881	24,627	67,079	8,898	4,108.0	411.9	53	45
All rural industries	38,214	10,631	11,560[bc]	5,134[cd]	357.8[bc]	90.2[cd]	41[bc]	48[cd]
Agricultural rural industries	13,783	1,421	-1,601[b]	-126[d]	153.2[b]	10.5[d]	40[b]	12[d]
Meat packing wholesale	2,153	224	761	94	52.0	4.2	45	68
Canning and preserving (excl. fish)	2,265	218	366	40	28.3	1.6	30	32
Flour and meal	1,243	372	-900	-214	6.0	0.1	24	4
Cigarettes	28	14	-7	-5	-1.9	-2.0	-7	-8
Tobacco stemming and redrying	163	128	n.a.	n.a.	n.a.	n.a.	n.a.	n.a.
Poultry dressing wholesale	557	46	-195	26	5.2	1.8	37	519
Pickles and sauces	743	44	232	12	6.1	0.5	49	41
Frozen foods	291	39	230	32	12.4	1.3	373	404
Creamery butter	2,157	36	-1,349[g]	-70[g]	7.2[g]	0.05[g]	40	7
Concentrated milk	562	28	—[g]	-3[g]	9.9[g]	0.5[g]	102	60
Cottonseed oil mills	315	122	-132	-50	-3.1	-1.8	-20	-26
Beet sugar	74	—	-11	—	1.2	—	12	—
Natural cheese	1,811	48	-871[g]	-12[g]	7.7[g]	0.5[g]	153	193
Corn products	55	1	20	—	3.4	n.a.	50	n.a.
Chewing and smoking tobacco	73	23	-59	-8	0.5	1.7	6	40
Liquid, frozen and dried eggs	154	5	113	4	7.3	0.1	527	404
Wines and brandy	418	13	70	6	3.5	0.1	149	386
Soybean oil mills	133	15	86	10	3.6	0.4	242	171
Vegetable oil mills, N.E.C.	84	32	46	17	3.4	1.2	399	351
Raw cane sugar	82	—	4	—	-0.2	—	-5	—
Dehydrated fruits and vegetables	146	4	n.a.	1	n.a.	0.3	n.a.	1,322
Rice cleaning and polishing	88	1	16	—	0.9	n.a.	39	n.a.
Malt	53	—	1	—	0.6	—	42	—

Linseed oil mills	17	—	—8	—	—0.8	—	—36	—
Vinegar and cider	118	8	—14	—6	—0.2	—0.06	—22	—33c
Forestry rural industries	21,038	8,699	11,764c	5,157c	172.0c	73.7c	39c	75c
Sawmills and planing mills, gen.	19,039	8,298	11,719	5,180	115.4	57.6	46	81
Paper and board mills	665	44	15	9	13.5	4.1	12	46
Pulp mills	226	34	32	8	18.5	5.4	69	101
Plywood mills	162	46	64	11	11.3	2.2h	86	87
Paper coating and glazing	182	6	42	3	7.7	0.3	104	438
Cooperage stock mills	250	122	—70	—52	3.3	2.4	39	66
Veneer mills	156	75	17	10	1.9	0.5	25	14
Softwood distillation	32	13	7	—2	1.7	1.0	73	68
Shingle mills	184	—	—42	—	—1.3	—	—35	—
Hardwood distillation	27	2	—16	—1	—0.2	—0.1	—9	—25
Natural tanning and dyeing	28	10	—7	—5	—0.09	0.2h	—7	36
Excelsior mills	56	25	3	—4	0.2	—0.02	17	—6
Gum naval stores (steam distilled)	31	24	n.a.	n.a.	n.a.	n.a.	n.a.	n.a.
Rural market industries	3,393	511	1,397	103	32.6	6.0	95	60
Prepared animal feeds	2,689	249	1,306	155	24.9	4.4	161	285
Fertilizers	187	88	16	10	6.3	2.0	58	44
Fertilizers (mixing only)	517	174	75	—62	1.4	—0.3	18	—8

Source: Stefan H. Robock, "Rural Industries and Agricultural Development," *Journal of Farm Economics*, 34 (Aug. 1952), 348–50.

a Alabama, Georgia, Kentucky, Mississippi, North Carolina, Tennessee, and Virginia.

b Does not include "dehydrated fruits and vegetables," and "tobacco stemming and redrying" industries because of changes in census coverage.

c Does not include change in "gum naval stores (steam distilled)" industry because of changes in census coverage.

d This figure does not include "tobacco stemming and redrying," which was not considered a manufacturing industry in 1939.

e Does not include wages in "dehydrated fruits and vegetables," "rice cleaning and polishing," and "corn products" industries because of disclosure regulations of the census.

f Does not include wages in "paper coating and glazing," "hardwood distillation," and "gum naval stores" because of disclosure regulations of the census.

g Figures for 1939 include dairy plants distributing fluid milk. Such combination plants are not covered in the 1947 Census.

h Estimate based on size of firm data. Actual employment not reported due to disclosure regulations of the census.

n.a. Not available because of disclosure regulations or changes in coverage of census.

which has furthered the integration of the previously dichotomized rural and urban way of life into new commonplace cultural universals.

Provision for nonfarm employment has been a major advantage of the industrialization of rural areas. In some cases, industry has deliberately been located in the country to utilize the already existing labor force. In other instances, local community leaders have worked systematically to promote the establishment of plants in their area in order to increase the level of living of the local people. Plants in rural areas have sometimes utilized large numbers of relatively unskilled and semiskilled workers. The indigenous labor forces found in most rural communities have historically been characterized by a minimum of technical training. In some cases the establishment of industry in local communities made for an acceleration of vocational training programs to increase the level of skill of the labor force to the point demanded by industrial occupations.

Industrialization and family life. The process of industrialization in rural areas has affected all members of the local community. Both those who have worked in rurally located plants and those who have served them have been directly influenced by the industrialization process, and most of the other people in the community have been indirectly influenced by it. The industrial payroll is one of the most tangible influences upon the lives of the people.

Specific inquiry has been made to delineate the differential characteristics of plant-employed families and nonplant-employed families in rural communities. These studies report differences in level of living, family incomes, community participation, and attitude toward fringe benefits between plant employees and nonemployees.[10] A majority of these studies conclude that plant workers are younger than other residents in the community; a greater proportion of the plant than the nonplant workers were under age thirty. This age-specific pattern of employment had serious implications for many rural communities. High birth rates in rural areas generally result in an excess number of people in the young age categories. Historically, most of the young people migrated to cities for employment after they completed their educational experience. Now, the presence of industries in their local environment enables many of these youths to remain in their homes.

Many smaller rural nonfarm areas, on the other hand, are characterized by a large proportion of older people whose presence often complicates the structure of the labor force. Elderly people are usually not prepared to compete in the labor marketplace. In most cases they are inadequately trained and can serve only as unskilled workers. Due to age, their physical and intellectual endurance is also limited. The presence of industry in rural areas which employs a disproportionately large number of young people leaves such communities to face the challenge of an increasing number of aging persons with few employment opportunities.

Women have been employed regularly in industries located in rural areas. The proportion of women employed is determined primarily by the type of industry, the employment policies, or their availability for work. The willingness of women to work in rural areas is an established fact. But, since many of the employees of rural plants are young, many of the wives are still in the child-bearing age. Consequently, their availability for work is more often limited by pregnancy and child care than by other factors.[11]

The need for more educational and vocational training on the part of rural plant employees has been underscored by research findings indicating that the educational attainment of employees in almost all cases was below the average attainment for persons age twenty-five and over in the U.S. When the national average of educational attainment was eleven years, it was found in several case studies that plant employees had a median educational attainment of seven years in Louisiana, ten years in Iowa, ten years in Mississippi, and twelve in Utah. In some areas it was discovered that more than two-thirds of the plant employees had received no vocational training to prepare them for nonfarm jobs. Moreover, those few who had received vocational nonfarm training obtained it while in the military service and not as a regular part of their education in their local communities. On-the-job vocational training was consequently of great importance to the plant employees.

Plant employees in rural areas typically are commuters. With modern all-weather roads and a great number of private automobiles, employees have little difficulty in commuting from surrounding farm and rural nonfarm areas. Greater residential mobility is found among plant employees than farm operators. Many plant employees leave farms for rural nonfarm residence. This was observed particularly in studies of the Middle Atlantic States where, as farms became larger, the farmsteads were renovated and used as places of residence for rural nonfarm families.

Social participation patterns in rural areas have historically included few formal organizational memberships. By contrast, participation in formal organizations was reported to be greater in cities. Accordingly, it was suspected that, as plant employment was extended into the rural areas, social participation patterns might undergo significant changes. Some differential participation was observed between the plant and non-plant employees, but in most cases the differences were not great. It was generally concluded that the establishment of plants in local areas had not been accompanied by major social changes in organizational membership. Participation in religious organizations was most frequent for both plant and nonplant employees, but few respondents were found to participate in secular organizations only. In many cases the differential participation that was observed could be more accurately explained in terms of age and occupational differences than employment differences.

Level of living. Many plants are located in low-income rural areas. In such localities there is much subsistence farming, with few opportunities for nonfarm employment prior to plant development. Consequently, one of the most tangible effects of plants in rural areas is a material increase in family incomes and a substantial increase in consumer spending. Even the smallest of plants contributes to larger payrolls. Research findings revealed that, commensurate with increased payrolls, there was an accelerated purchasing of household equipment, automobiles, and other commodities associated with higher levels of living.

The level of living for plant workers increased more rapidly than for other residents in the area involved. Acquisition of more material goods had a cumulative affect. As plant employees obtained more material goods they more accurately perceived the goals and values of American society than others in their area. They were opportunity- and success-oriented, and, therefore, most willing to accept plant employment to continue achieving the goals acceptable in the national society.

Mobility. Plant employees were found to be more mobile than nonemployees. But the concept of mobility used in much of this research did not always differentiate between geographical and occupational mobility. Therefore, in the remarks which follow, unless otherwise specified, mobility will include both the geographical and occupational connotations.

Ability to obtain a working force for the new plants may be taken as evidence of the greater mobility of plant as opposed to nonplant employees. Those who initially accepted employment from the local area were willing to change jobs. In many cases, plant employees continued to be part-time farmers and thereby only partially altered their work situation. Most of the indigenous population was reported to have remained in their place of residence for ten or more years. A larger proportion of the plant workers were found to have changed their place of residence within a ten-year period. Farm residents in the area were found to be least mobile; rural nonfarm second-least mobile; and plant employees most mobile. In sum, it was found that local employees had moved 2.8 times in ten years compared to about 4.4 moves for in-migrant employees.[12] The greater residential and occupational mobility of plant as contrasted to nonplant employees is illustrated in Figs. 7 and 8.

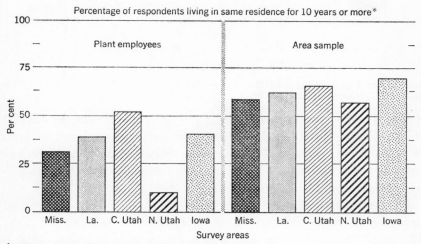

FIGURE 7.   RESIDENTIAL MOBILITY

Source: *Rural Industrialization.* (Washington, D.C.: U.S.D.A., Agriculture Information Bulletin 252, November, 1961), p. 21.

Part of the high mobility among plant workers was explained by the general findings that unskilled and semiskilled workers are more mobile than highly skilled and professional workers. Most of the employees in the rurally located plants were of the unskilled and semiskilled type. Part of the differential mobility was also explained by the fact that the resident area employees are typically older than the plant employees, and higher social mobility is associated with younger ages.

Work situation conceptions. Attitudes toward work and knowledge of the occupational market place in rural areas have been the subjects of detailed

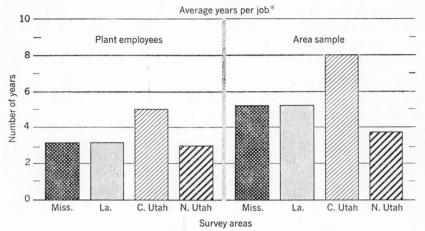

FIGURE 8.   OCCUPATIONAL MOBILITY

Source: *Rural Industrialization.* (Washington, D.C.: U.S.D.A., Agriculture Information Bulletin 252, November, 1961), p. 22.

studies. In some rural areas the local people do not accept the cultural universal norms governing the occupational market place. In other cases, local people do perceive the advantages and disadvantages of various types of jobs and seek the appropriate occupational training which will prepare them for the positions they desire.

Plant workers indicated that, in the work situation, job security and steadiness of employment were the single factors most important to them. The next-highest value was placed on adequate monetary remuneration and on good working hours.[13] The high value placed upon satisfactory working hours is a reflection of the dislike for night-shift work. In the case of many part-time farmers, shift work often complicated the operation of the farming enterprise.

Respondents were asked what they would do if they were laid off from their factory employment. In most cases they indicated that they would seek other plant employment rather than return to full-time agricultural enterprises. Many of the workers were keenly aware of the difficulty in securing additional plant employment in their local areas.

INDUSTRIALIZATION AND FARM ORGANIZATION

Approximately one-third of the nation's farm operators, as listed in the 1959 Census of Agriculture, worked away from their farms 100 days or more per year. This amount of off-farm work, by definition, resulted in the fact that they were listed as part-time farmers. More than one-third of these farmers indicated that their families had more income from nonfarm than from farm sources. Industrialization in their communities afforded an opportunity to enter into the nonfarm labor market. Some have viewed this combination of part-time farming with part-time industrial work as a mechanism for facilitating the shift from agrarian to urban occupations.

The type of farming enterprise people engaged in was found to be related to their availability for industrial work. Farm operators with smaller capital investments and less farming skill more frequently gave up their farming enterprises for industrial work. Many of these lowest-income farmers, however, were also in the poorest position to make a shift from farming to nonfarming employment.

Cash renters were found to be freer to obtain off-farm work than were share croppers. Farm ownership was more prevalent among the factory workers than among the full-time farm operators. It has become a typical pattern for full-time farm operators to be part-owners. This enables them to expand their operations and to have greater investment flexibility. The earlier values placed upon full ownership become conservative and traditionalist in the urbanized social organization.

Part-time farmers working in local industries operated smaller farms than did farmers not involved in industrial employment. Moreover, most of the part-time farmers who worked in industry engaged in farming enterprises which required a minimum of labor. Specific adjustments were observed in the farming operations of those individuals who worked part-time in industries. They used more family labor or hired labor. They also reduced the amount of the acreage tilled and substituted crop for livestock operations. Reduced labor input on the part of the farmer is widely associated with employment in local industry, particularly when the industrial work involves forty hours or more per week.

Whether or not the part-time farmers who worked in industry desired to continue in both occupations indefinitely seemed to be a matter of conjecture. Some of the respondents indicated that part-time farming is an ephemeral enterprise. As they became firmly established in industrial employment, they desired to move out of farming completely. Others indicated that their part-time farming enterprise would be continued indefinitely. Some indicated that the continuation of part-time farming was an assurance of security in the face of limited industrial occupational opportunities.

INDUSTRIALIZATION AND COMMUNITY DEVELOPMENT

Resistance to the development of industries in local communities has not been widespread. Nearly 95 per cent of the plant workers in four communities indicated that industrialization was an asset in their area. Residents in the communities who were not employed in industry also indicated their approval, although the proportion favoring industrialization was smaller than in the case of those who worked in the factories (see Table IX). Farmers were the least decisive in their judgments concerning the assets or liabilities of industrialization. Generally they believed that the impact of industrialization in the local community improved the condition of the schools and contributed to the improvement of the condition of churches. Most respondents believed that industrialization made little impact on neighborliness.

The study of industrialization in rural areas is incomplete unless some indication is made of its impact on those who continue their farming operations. One of the most immediate consequences is a greater amount of sophistication in social relationships, indicated by changes in the manner of dress and the social significance of clothing.[14] In urbanized society, type of dress becomes a status symbol, thus the concepts of white collar and blue collar work. Farm operators fare badly in this development of status symbolism. Because their work is often out-of-doors and involves exposure to the elements, white collar dress is most inappropriate. In small and relatively isolated rural communities, with an absence of specialists and of industrial workers, the range of styles of dress is limited, and more rural than urban. With industrialization, managers and technical experts introduce a new style of dress, and the workers themselves dress in a manner that is recognizably different from that of the farmer. Finally, farmers tend to change their manner of dress from a rural to an urban type as they go into town.

As industries locate in the larger rural communities, the various trades and services there become more complete than in the nonindustrial communities. Farmers accordingly tend to patronize the larger rural communities for both technical services and social activities. As farm operations become more mechanized, the services for maintaining them are located in the larger rural communities. Industrialization of rural communities and mechanization of farms constitutes an aspect of the condition of urbanized social organization in rural areas.

TABLE IX. PERCENTAGE DISTRIBUTION OF RESPONDENTS BY OPINIONS ON THE EFFECT OF THE FACTORY ON THE COMMUNITY AND ON CHANGES IN SELECTED ASPECTS OF COMMUNITY LIFE IN RECENT YEARS, FIVE-AREA STUDY

	Area					
	Mississippi		Louisiana		Central Utah	
	Plant Employees	Area Sample	Plant Employees	Area Sample	Plant Employees	Area Sample
	(per cent)	(per cent)	(per cent)	(per cent)	(per cent)	(per cent)
Effect of factory on community:						
Total	100	100	100	100	100	100
Helpful	97	71	96	61	96	65
Not helpful	1	4	1	11	2	21
No opinion	2	25	3	28	2	14
Opinion on changes in community:						
Schools had improved	54	49	65	70	51	44
Churches had improved	59	41	50	49	65	55
Neighborliness						
Was about the same	67	62	60	57	62	73
Had improved	17	16	20	20	13	14
Was worse	10	17	20	20	24	15
Community pride had improved	37	31	40	44	66	58

	Area					
	Northern Utah				Iowa	
	Plant Employees*	Area Sample			Plant Employees	Area Sample
		Total	Nonfarm	Farm		
	(per cent)	(per cent)	(per cent)	(per cent)	(per cent)	(per cent)
Effect of factory on community:						
Total	100	100	100	100	100	100
Helpful	83	72	79	55	94	80
Not helpful	—	—	—	—	5	17
No opinion	17	28	21	45	1	3
Opinion on changes in community:						
Schools had improved	68	60	†	†	40	50
Churches had improved	46	54	†	†	†	†
Neighborliness						
Was about the same	84	78	†	†	75	59
Had improved	13	12	†	†	8	10
Was worse	2	10	†	†	17	22
Community pride had improved	47	40	†	†	†	†

Source: *Rural Industrialization* (Washington: U.S.D.A., Agriculture Information Bulletin No. 252, 1961), p. 29.

* Applies only to local respondents.

† Not available.

SUMMARY

The location of processing plants and industries in small rural communities and the open countryside was accelerated in the United States in the post-World War II years. Many considerations enter into the final decision about plant location; the more important ones are the location of markets, labor force, raw materials, and transportation. With the mass urbanized society now a virtual *fait accompli,* the advantages of plant location in smaller communities are often substantial. There is a large indigenous labor force in many rural areas. With ever more school consolidation and expansion of curriculums, plus adult extension education, the rural labor force is continually better trained and more valuable to nonfarm enterprises. Transportation and communication have become so advanced technologically that even the smaller rural communities now can attract industry to their areas.

Research has indicated that industrialization in low-income rural areas is generally beneficial to the local population Resistance to such industrialization is little, and sometimes nonexistent. Patterns of local life are not usually disrupted by plant location. Some of the plant employees wish to continue some part-time farming as a matter of security. In many rural areas there is only one plant, or one type of plant, or a limited number of plants; hence the opportunity for continued employment is not great if a worker loses his job. The community's problem of dependence upon a single type of industry is still great in many of the rural areas where plants are located.

In most rural communities the need continues for more adequate vocational training, if the workers are to take full advantage of industrial opportunities. In many cases this includes not only the original training of workers, which may often be given through regular secondary school courses, but also the retraining of adults in special vocational courses.

The role of industrialization in rural areas is largely to transfer the labor force from farm to nonfarm employment, while at the same time retraining most workers. In the absence of industrialization in the community, the migration of the labor force to other places of employment is a frequent pattern.

NOTES

1. Arnold Toynbee, *The Industrial Revolution* (Boston: Beacon Press, 1957), p. 25.

2. Daniel Defoe, *A Tour Through the Whole Island of Great Britain,* Vol. III. (7th ed., London: J. and F. Rivington, 1769), pp. 144–6.

3. John Saville, *Rural Depopulation in England and Wales, 1851–1951* (London: Routledge and Kegan Paul, Ltd., 1957), p. 30.

4. P. Kropotkin, *Fields, Factories and Workshops: Industry Combined with Agriculture and Brain Work with Manual Work* (rev. ed., New York: G. P. Putnam's Sons, 1913), p. x.

5. Saville, *op. cit.*

6. *Ibid.,* p. 162.

7. *1959 Plant Location* (Chicago: Simmons-Boardman Publishing Corporation, 1959), pp. 17–30.

8. "Ruralized Industry," *Rural Electrification News,* 16 (June–July, 1951), 12–13.

9. Stefan H. Robock, "Rural Industries and Agricultural Development," *Journal of Farm Economics,* 34 (Aug., 1952), 346–60.

10. Wade H. Andrews *et al., Benchmarks for Rural Industrialization: A Study of Rural Development in Monroe County, Ohio* (Ohio Agricultural Experiment Station Research Bulletin 870, 1960); J. M. Stepp and J. S. Blaxico, *The Labor Supply of a Rural Industry: A Case Study of the McCormic Spinning Mill* (South Carolina Agricultural Experiment Station Bulletin 376, 1948); Ward Bauder, *Effects of Industrial Development on the Agricultural and Urban Sectors of an Iowa Community* (in press); Alvin L. Bertrand and Harold W. Osborne, *Rural Industrialization in a Louisiana Community* (Louisiana Agricultural Experiment Station Bulletin 524, 1959); Therel R. Black *et al., Rocket Age Industrialization of Box Elder County* (Utah Agricultural Experiment Station Bulletin 420, 1960); John R. Christiansen *et al., Industrialization and Rural Life in Two Central Utah Counties* (Utah Agricultural Experiment Station Bulletin 416, 1959); Sheridan T. Maitland and George L. Wilbur, *Industrialization in Chickasaw County, Mississippi: A Study of Plant Workers* (Mississippi Agricultural Experiment Station Bulletin 565, 1958). The last five of these studies are summarized in *Rural Industrialization* (Washington: U.S.D.A., Agricultural Information Bulletin 252, 1961). This section of the chapter draws heavily from the summary bulletin.

11. George Bauder, "Effect of Nonfarm Employment of Farm Wives on Farm Family Living" (Paper presented before the Rural Sociological Society, State College, Pa., 1960).

12. *Rural Industrialization,* p. 21.

13. *Ibid.,* p. 23.

14. W. H. Form and G. P. Stone, *Social Significance of Clothing in Occupational Life* (Michigan Agricultural Experiment Station Technical Bulletin 247, 1955).

SELECTED READINGS

Andrews, Wade H. *et al., Benchmarks for Rural Industrialization.* Ohio Agricultural Experiment Station Bulletin 870, 1960.

Report of a study of the impact of industrialization on a low-income rural community. The purpose of the research was to describe the rural social organization at the beginning of the industrialization and afterward.

Bertrand, Alvin L. and Harold W. Osborne, *Rural Industrialization in a Louisiana Community.* Louisiana Agricultural Experiment Station Bulletin 524, 1959.

This study reports the impact a small box factory made on a small rural Louisiana community.

Black, Therel R. *et al., Rocket Age Industrialization of Box Elder County.* Utah Agricultural Experiment Station Bulletin 420, 1960.

Reports the impact made by a chemical company on a local rural community.

Christiansen, John R. *et al. Industrialization and Rural Life in Two Central Utah Counties.* Utah Agricultural Experiment Station Bulletin 416, 1959.

Reports the impact of a rubber plant on workers and nonworkers in rural communities.

Kropotkin, P. *Fields, Factories and Workshops.* New York: G. P. Putnam's Sons, 1913.

In this monograph the author calls for a reunification of work in fields and factories, of manual and mental labor.

Robock, Stefan. "Rural Industries and Agricultural Development," *Journal of Farm Economics,* 34 (Aug., 1952), 346–60.

A systematic statistical analysis of industrial development and labor force utilization in seven Southeastern states.

7 VACATIONING ITINERANTS IN RURAL AREAS

Vacationers have come to constitute a new population in rural areas. They are an itinerant population moving into the open country in mass for holidays and vacations. Never before have so many people taken their recreation outdoors into the countryside. Annually the vacationing itinerants outnumber both farm and rural nonfarm families. In 1960, the number of visits to the national forests alone totaled 92,500,000.

New patterns of social interaction are becoming widespread in rural America as a result of this itinerant population. There is social interaction among the vacationers and between them and the resident rural people. There is economic interaction as the indigenous rural people establish services to fill the needs of the vacationers.[1] There are changes in church organization to provide for religious worship in the open country, small towns, and national parks.[2] There are changes in political organization which provide for zoning for recreation and wilderness areas.[3] Human relations in contemporary, urbanized, rural America include the experiences of this new and expanding itinerant population.

Historically, the major demand for rural land use has been for the production of food and fiber. Now recreation has become a major consideration in land use planning for both urban and rural parts of the nation. Leisure and recreation are becoming more structured; indeed, they are taking on the form of social institutions. The organization of recreation in urbanized society is more specialized than that in ruralized society. This

129

chapter is devoted to an analysis of the human relations of recreation in rural areas.

HISTORY AND MEANING OF RECREATION

Recreation and leisure are integral parts of the total social organization of a society. Their definitions and roles are relative to the cultural configuration of societies, and their contraction or expansion is related to the level of development of societies. In all societies, man has had some form of recreation or leisure, but during most of the long course of human history the distinction between labor and leisure has not been sharply drawn. Many societies have existed and remain at the subsistence level, which gave little opportunity for recreation specialization. In fact, at this level, recreation and leisure are scarcely separated from work.

As ancient societies reached high points of civilization, recreation became more specialized and differentiated from other activities. Greek and Roman societies specified the nature of recreational activities, the types of people who engaged in them, the types who were spectators, and the types who were neither.[4]

The teachings of Christianity glorified work and presented it as a way of piety. The mundane activities of spinning, weaving, hoeing and carpentry were idealized by St. Jerome, St. Basil, and St. Benedict. The idea of leisure time was rejected; such use of time contaminated godliness. Athletic sports and athletic events were frowned upon. Music, drama, dancing, and dicing were considered avenues to the devil. St. Jerome admonished young ladies against singing the songs of the day, sporting in the dance, and learning to play the lyre, harp or flute.[5]

An austere depiction of the Christian Middle Ages is more or less "official," but it is not definitive. Social histories suggest that men, then as now, worked for daily bread, worshiped, and relaxed in song, drink, and merriment. There was joyful singing by workers in the fields and at other daily duties. Church holidays as well as the Sabbath were times of both worship and leisure. But the pleasure of dancing, wrestling, and cock shooting were considered to be particularly sinful on church holidays.[6] The complaint was often made that those who danced on religious holidays committed a mortal sin, yet many who should have been at vespers were often found dancing.[7]

By the thirteenth century humanists began a long campaign to restore recreation to respectability. By the seventeenth century in England and

Colonial America there had developed a conflict between the ascetics and the pleasure-lovers. This conflict reached a point of bitterness between the Puritans and King James I. The Puritans opposed sporting on the Sabbath while the king upheld the right of lawful recreation after divine service. In 1618, King James issued a proclamation, now known as the Book of Sports, asserting the right of the people to participate in dancing, archery, leaping, vaulting, and other harmless recreations on the Sabbath after worship.[8]

In New England a strong ascetic influence emanated from Puritans, Quakers, and German pietistic sects. By contrast, cavalier Virginians knew how to dance, hunt, and play music without a twinge of conscience. There were also those in New England who did not uphold pietistic ideals. Their festive activities, including a Maypole, wine, and songs, are revealed in the following verse:

> Drinke and be merry, merry, merry boyes,
> Let all your delight be in the Hymens joyes,
> Joy to Hymen now the day is come,
> About the merry Maypole take a Romme.
> Make greene garlons, bring bottles out
> And fill sweet Nectar freely about.
> Uncover thy head and fear no harme,
> For hers good liquor to keepe it warme.[9]

Puritanism eventually did succeed in inhibiting the colonists' urges for play. Early Northern colonists were audience to a thundering from pulpits against dancing, sports, and merrymaking of all kinds. These admonitions were in several respects similar to those uttered in the Middle Ages.

With the coming of the eighteenth century, American colonists had achieved some measure of economic security so that more time was free for the pursuit of leisure. Their outlook on life was broadening, and the colonists took up once more the sports and games beloved by their English countrymen.[10] There was an uneven development of recreation in the colonies; where Puritanism, Calvinism, and Quakerism were weak, recreation flourished, and where these religions prevailed, it was minimal. Hunting and fishing were enjoyed as sports by townsmen and farmers from Carolina to New England. Squirrel and raccoon hunts were popular in Massachusetts and Connecticut. In Virginia, hunting for opossum and wild horses was frequent. In Maryland even servants were provided with guns and powder and allowed the sport of hunting on holidays.[11] In addition to hunting and fishing, there were husking bees, sewing bees, and barn raisings, the latter combining both gainful work and recreation.

Between 1800 and the Civil War, industrialization was accelerated, and with it came the concentration of greater numbers of people in central cities. Among the many changes brought about by the growth of industry and the shift in population were demands for more recreation. Before the Civil War such demands were forcefully discouraged by moral condemnation. The church rejected the theater and commercial amusement. Evangelism on the part of the nineteenth-century Presbyterians, Baptists, and Methodists generally revived the earlier Puritan repression of gambling, card playing, and dancing. In spite of moral opposition, however, the theater was established by the middle of the nineteenth century. Spectator sports were also developed, with horse racing, boat racing, and foot racing being particularly popular forms of recreation.

Throughout times of ruralized social organization and, for all practical purposes, up to the twentieth century, recreation was limited. At times, recreation was dominated by the religious institutions of the society. In the urbanized social organization of the twentieth-century, forms of play, like those of other human experiences, became specialized and tended to reach an institutional level of development.

OUTDOOR RECREATIONING IN URBANIZED SOCIETY

Recreation activities range from the passive spectator to the active participator type. The former type of recreation is illustrated by attendance at athletic events, reading, music, art, dance, and movies. It requires a minimum of physical space. By contrast, many active participator forms of recreation, exemplified by boating, fishing, hunting, canoeing, and camping, require large amounts of land space. In contemporary social organization, most participator recreationing takes place in open-country rural areas.

Emergence of specific recreational customs or norms has been gradual. In the 1880's the *New York Tribune* devoted hundreds of columns to sports. It also published a *Book of Open-Air Sports*. In 1896 Hearst's *New York Journal* inaugurated a special page for amateur sportsmen.[13] The idea of the sports page was adopted rapidly. It became a normative pattern in the social structure of recreation. Newspaper space given to recreation was paralleled by periodicals devoted entirely to sports, from the *American Canoeist* to the *Bicycling World,* from the *Ball Players' Chronicle* to *Archery* and *Tennis News.*[14]

Outdoor recreation gained increasing popularity. Hiking, mountain climbing, fishing, and camping all became fads. Canoeing held a special place, and railroad trips into country water areas were arranged with specially equipped freight cars which hauled canoes and other outing materials.[15] The summer resort came into vogue. This was the beginning of outdoor recreation in rural America. Participants were typically non-farm people making a tour into the open country. By the middle of the twentieth century, outdoor recreation was a firmly established pattern in which the masses of the population participated.

Social structure and outdoor vacationing. Several elements of social structure have contributed to the growth and expansion of outdoor vacationing. They influenced the amount, place, and type of outdoor recreation and vacationing chosen by an individual or group.[16]

Changes in the nation's population constituted the first major structural element which made an impact on recreational organization. The population grew from just under 4,000,000 in 1790 to over 179,000,000 in 1960. The number of people per square mile increased from fewer than five in 1790 to more than fifty in 1960.[17] The population was still growing at a rapid rate. The people of the nation were not dispersed uniformly over the land. In 1960, about half of the nation's population was located in New England, the Middle Atlantic, and the East-North-Central areas. Taken together, these Eastern areas constituted less than 14 per cent of the nation's territory. At the other extreme, the Mountain states had 28 per cent of the land and less than 4 per cent of the people. Densities of population ranged from nearly 750 people per square mile in Rhode Island to fewer than two people per square mile in Nevada.

Population pressure in the United States is increasing as the number of people multiply and as they demand to use the land for gainful employment and for recreational leisure. The pressure of overpopulation is increased by the concentration of people in the Eastern and major urban areas. Megapolis areas are most often not located in proximity to the major outdoor recreation areas. The result is overcrowding of the recreational land in and near the major population centers. Some of the park areas are becoming so congested by masses of people that they take on slum characteristics. The nation has a considerable amount of land area in the Southwest, the Mountain States, the Great Lakes Cutover area, and the Southeastern mountain areas that is potentially valuable for outdoor recreation. It is not yet possible to move great masses of the population for short-term periods from the major urban centers to remote outdoor recreation areas. Consequently, there is considerable planning to make available greater land acreages near urban centers for full-time recreation use.[18]

Changes in the age structure of the population constitute a second major factor which contributed to the growth of recreational institutions. Increased longevity in and of itself meant a potentially greater number of years during which individuals could participate in leisure experiences. The type of recreation needs varies with the three major sociobiological age periods, the preproductive years (under age 20), the productive years (ages 20 to 65), and the postproductive years (after age 65). Expansive areas for outdoor recreation are generally required for people in productive and preproductive years. Less expansive land areas are required for those in postproductive years.

Higher living standards provide a third incentive for the growth of leisure and recreation. The reduction of hours in the average work week and the increase in disposable income combined to produce a situation amenable to a rapid increase in recreational opportunities. The standard work week was seventy hours in 1870 and fewer than forty hours in 1960.[19] The average annual per capita disposable income has increased from $1,025 in 1930 to $1,450 in 1950. This income is expected to increase to more than $1,700 by 1975.[20] The work routine in mass society typically requires little creativity and is characterized by maximum rigidity. The greatly specialized division of labor in the assembly line operation has been both maligned and extolled. But regardless of what else might be said of it, such a work experience provided an opportunity for the worker to plan leisure activities. Many of the nation's employers have come to appreciate the value of recreation. They have provided recreation facilities in their companies and encouraged participation.[21]

Improved travel facilities constitute a fourth factor in increasing outdoor recreation. By the end of the nineteenth and the first part of the twentieth centuries, trains brought people to out-of-doors recreation areas. But the advent of the automobile provided the major breakthrough in transportation. The increase in automobile ownership started during the second decade of the twentieth century and continues to the present. Privately owned automobiles increased from 8,000 in 1900 to nearly 50,000,000 in 1954.[22] The automobile has greatly increased Americans' range of travel. It also has increased the number of visits to parks and forests in the more remote locations. All-weather highway construction was a concomitant part of the impact which the automobile had on recreation. In recent years both commercial and private planes have contributed to recreation, particularly in the utilization of remote areas.

In short, more people, longer life, longer retirement, longer paid vacations increased mobility, more freedom from household duties, and changes in values have all contributed to the development and specialization of recreation as a social institution.

RECREATION LAND AREAS AND THE VACATIONERS

Data on recreation land areas and the number and characteristics of persons using them have not been accumulated systematically for many years. What data are available frequently come from reports of those agencies which administer recreational areas. The types of reports vary, and they often do not contain all the information that is important from a human relations point of view.[23] Nevertheless, the best available data do present an important and reasonably valid picture of human relations in this new form of rural experience.

Recreation land areas. About 10 per cent of the nation's land area is utilized for nonagricultural purposes.[24] Nonagricultural land uses include residential, commercial, industrial, transportation, recreational, and military areas. Among these various nonagricultural land uses, 32,000,000 acres are set aside primarily for recreation. This is exceeded only by the 33,000,000 acres used for transportation (see Table X). Increased demands for outdoor recreation and other nonagricultural land uses are expected to continue. Projections for these increases by population size are reported in Table X. Much of the increased pressure for recreational land will be in or near urban areas. Accordingly, the National Recreation Association has recommended that ten acres of land be provided for leisure purposes for every 1,000 residents in cities of 10,000 or more, and one acre for every forty residents in smaller cities. The National Recreation Association further advised that an additional ten acres per 1,000 persons should be provided around larger cities for county and metropolitan parks and that still more facilities should be provided within a distance of two hours' drive from the major cities.[25]

Greater amounts of recreational land would have only a minor effect upon the over-all physical land use situation of the nation during the next forty years. In the area of human relations, however, the effect of more

TABLE X. LAND USE AND ANTICIPATED LAND USE FOR A POPULATION OF 300 MILLION PEOPLE

Types of Land Use	Millions of Acres Used in 1954	Millions of Acres Needed for a National Population of	
		225 million	300 million
Residential lands	18.6	26.2	33.8
Commercial and industrial	3.0	4.5	6.0
Transportation areas	33.0	40.4	47.4
Recreational lands	32.0	35.3	39.8
Military and defense	21.5	21.5	21.5
Service areas and other	20.0	22.5	25.0
Areas in nonagricultural uses	128.1	150.4	173.5
Wasteland areas not included in farms	55.5	54.5	53.0
Total nonagricultural land	183.6	204.9	226.5

Source: *Land: The Yearbook of Agriculture, 1958* (Washington: U.S. Government Printing Office, 1958), p. 478.

recreational land will be greater. Much additional land for recreation will come from areas currently used for farming, grazing, or forestry. Conflicts are anticipated in the shift of land use from farm to nonfarm activities.

There are various types of land available for recreational use (see Table XI). All of the land in the national forests is potentially available for recreation activity, but Clawson estimates that only 14,000,000 of

TABLE XI. TYPES AND UTILIZATION OF RECREATIONAL LAND

Recreation Areas	Available for Recreation	Primarily for Recreation
	(Million acres, incl. Alaska)	
National forests	188.1	14.0
National park system	24.4	24.4
National wildlife refuges	17.2	?
TVA reservoirs	0.98	0.2
Corps of Engineers reservoirs	4.7	3.3
Bureau of Reclamation reservoirs*	0.4	?
State parks	5.1	5.1
Municipal and county parks	0.7	0.7

Source: Marion Clawson, *Statistics on Outdoor Recreation* (Washington: Resources for the Future, Inc., 1958), p. 3.

* Excluding areas under administration of agencies reported here.

the 188,000,000 acres are used primarily for recreation. Much of the national forest land is too remote or unattractive, or unused for some other reason. Only a small proportion of the national forest areas have facilities developed specifically for recreation. Most of the area used for recreation is of the wilderness variety. Land utilization in national parks is similar to that in the national forests. All land in the national parks is intended mainly for recreation; however, most of it is very little used in the sense of people actually walking on the land. Wildlife areas, TVA reservoirs, and Corps of Engineers reservoirs are not primarily designed for recreation purposes, yet recreation is allowed in practically all of them. In terms of number of visits, there is more frequent utilization of municipal and county parks than all other areas combined.

The various recreational land areas are not distributed equally over the nation. Areas administered by the federal government are located more extensively in the Rocky Mountain states. State parks are more commonly found in the Eastern part of the nation. Municipal recreational land area is more related to size of city than to region.

Overnight facilities serve as the most commonly used index for reporting the degree of development or improvement in recreation areas (see Table XII). The types of overnight accommodations vary from luxury resort hotels to relatively unimproved campgrounds. The best estimate of the number of people using the nation's park and recreation system is made by checking on the number of visits or visitor days spent at these areas during any given time. Such statistics, however, may be misleading. For example, if the same person makes several visits to a park during the

TABLE XII. OVERNIGHT FACILITIES IN RECREATIONAL AREAS

Recreation Areas	Overnight Capacity (1,000 persons)
National park system	77
National forests	400
National wildlife refuges	?
TVA reservoirs	12
Corps of Engineers reservoirs	36
Bureau of Reclamation reservoirs	?
State parks	195
Municipal and county parks	?

Source: Marion Clawson, *Statistics on Outdoor Recreation* (Washington: Resources for the Future, Inc., 1958), p. 5.

TABLE XIII. NUMBER OF VISITS AND PER CENT INCREASE OF VISITS

Recreation Areas	Million Visits (or Visitor Days) 1955–1956	Average Annual Per Cent Increase Since World War II
National park system	55	8
National forest	53	10
National wildlife refuges	8*	12
TVA reservoirs	40*	15
Corps of Engineers reservoirs	71	28
Bureau of Reclamation reservoirs	4†	—
State parks	201	10
Municipal and country parks	1,000 or more	4

Source: Marion Clawson, *Statistics on Outdoor Recreation* (Washington: Resources for the Future, Inc., 1958), p. 7.
  * Million visitor days.
  † Estimated visits recorded in the area.

year, the record of his visits will appear more than once in the statistics. Table XIII reports the number of visits and the per cent increase of visits to the various recreation areas.

National park organization. The establishment of national parks has developed gradually over the years since 1872 when Yellowstone was founded. The number of parks has increased to 29 with a combined land area of some 13,500,000 acres. The National Park Service was established as a bureau in the U.S. Department of Interior in 1916. It provides the central administration for more than 175 areas totaling 23,000,000 acres. In addition to the national parks, the system includes historical parks, monuments, military parks, memorial parks, battlefield parks, battlefield sites, historic sites, memorials, cemeteries, seashore recreational areas, parkways, and national capital parks.[26]

Operating the National Park Service involves complexities of an order which parallel those of the U.S. Department of Agriculture. The National Park Service headquarters' offices are located in Washington, D.C. In addition to five regional offices, there are two branch offices of the Division of Design and Construction. Personnel are stationed at each of the national parks, monuments, and other sites.[27] The director of the National Park Service, its highest ranking administrative officer, is responsible to the Secretary of the Department of Interior. Under him there are regional directors and superintendents of each of the local units. There are associate and assistant directors and technical administrative personnel. Specialists are employed in the areas of finance, personnel, property and records management, safety, engineering, landscape, and architecture.

National forest organization. There are 149 national forests, located in 44 states, which total more than 180,000,000 acres. The primary purpose of the national forests is timber production. However, their importance as recreational areas has increased both in popularity and in the services which they render to the vacationing itinerants. In 1957 it was reported that some 150,000,000 visits to the national forests were made by casual motorists driving through, and an additional 60,000,000 visits were made to the forest areas for periods of longer duration.[28] Between 1950 and 1957 the Forest Service reported a 92 per cent increase in recreational utilization. As a result of inadequate funds and lesser use during the war years, recreational facilities in the national forests area have generally deteriorated; they were grossly inadequate for the recent upsurge of visitors. To meet the developing need, the U.S. Forest Service inaugurated a program called Operation Outdoors. This was a five-year development and rehabilitation program to be completed in 1962 at a cost of $85,000,000. It was followed by a related program, Operation Multiple Use.[29]

The legal status of the national forests is based upon an 1891 act which authorized the President to reserve by proclamation specific lands from the public domain to be known as forest reserves. The U.S. Forest Service was organized as a bureau in the Department of Agriculture, with headquarters in Washington, D.C. Its top administrative officer, the Chief Forester, has a staff of specialists concerned with specific aspects of the administration of the national forests. Among them is a recreation specialist. The U.S. Forest Service is divided into ten regions with a forester in charge of each. Each forest in the region, in turn, has a forest supervisor.

National forests were differentiated from national parks primarily on the basis of the fundamentally utilitarian nature of the former and the fundamentally recreational nature of the latter. Moreover, they were under different administrative units, the national forests under the direction of the U.S. Department of Agriculture, and the national parks under the U.S. Department of Interior. In spite of these original differences in purpose and administrative alignment, the U.S. Forest Service has an extensive recreational policy.[30] Its recreational objectives state:

1. The recreational resources of the forest areas will be managed in conjunction with other recreation areas to avoid duplication of services and facilities.
2. Every effort will be made to preserve the rugged natural environment of the forest as a distinctive characteristic.
3. The Forest Service will discourage the development of such facilities as would bring about urbanization in the forest areas.
4. The Forest Service will permit a minimum of artificial installations in the woods areas.
5. It is intended that the recreation appropriate for forest areas will involve participation rather than spectator enjoyment.
6. Expansion of facilities will be aimed at providing for large numbers of people rather than small groups.
7. Specific charges will be made for such services as charcoal, electricity, checking clothes, renting swim suits and towels, renting boats, use of skis and ski tows and similar services.
8. Special attention will be given to the development of facilities for low-cost recreationing. Other facilities are for organized camp site areas, winter sports, scenic areas, and summer home sites.

National wildlife refuge organization. National wildlife refuges have been established to provide suitable habitats for various species of wildlife. They are a twentieth-century development, the first dating back to 1903. Three major types of wildlife sites include refuges primarily for water fowl (199), colonial refuges (41—many of these are small islands), and refuges primarily for big game (18). Nearly two-thirds of the wildlife refuges are under the administration of the Bureau of Sport Fisheries and Wildlife of the U.S. Department of Interior. The others are divided administratively under a variety of governmental agencies.

Wildlife refuges are distributed more equally over the nation than either national parks or national forests. Like the national forests, the wildlife refuges have experienced a heavier recreational use (51 per cent increase) since the midpoint of the century.[31] The greatest impact has been felt in the Great Lakes and Corn Belt states. By recreational use the areas are classified as hunting, 6 per cent; fishing, 37 per cent; other uses, 57 per cent. The latter include picnicking, swimming, and wildlife observation.

TVA organization. The Tennessee Valley Authority system of dams, reservoirs, and other installations was primarily intended for purposes of flood control and electric energy production. TVA's services did not provide specific recreational facilities. Nevertheless, in 1956 some

40,000,000 visitors * were reported around the TVA's land and water areas for recreation. Many recreation facilities are located on this site under arrangements whereby land rights are transferred to federal, state, and local government agencies for operating public recreational facilities. Land sites are also sold to clubs and summer residents at public auction. The system of human organization of recreational facilities within and around the TVA areas is strikingly less centralized than that in other major outdoor recreation areas.

Corps of Engineers reservoirs organization. Many of the nation's rivers and other waterway systems are under the jurisdiction of the Corps of Engineers. Their main functions are navigation control, flood control, and often the production of hydroelectric power. Like so many other government organizations that administer land areas, the Corps of Engineers has been recently faced with servicing recreation demands as an important function. Visits to the reservoirs have increased from 26,000,000 in 1952 to 70,000,000 in 1956.[32] The Corps of Engineers' recreational policy has been aimed at maintaining scenic value of and public access to reservoirs and other locations when this is not in contradiction with its original programs. Like many other agencies that are not primarily in the recreation business, the Corps of Engineers organizes its areas for recreational use in cooperation with many other units of local government. For example, the Dennison Reservoir (Lake Texoma) between Oklahoma and Texas was organized into a wildlife refuge, two state parks, and several city and county parks, all of which are located on the Corps of Engineers' project lands.

Bureau of Reclamation. The Bureau of Reclamation under the U.S. Department of Interior is charged primarily with the development of water irrigation and hydroelectric power production. Tangential to these major purposes is the development of large dams and reservoir areas. These bodies of water are heavily used for purposes of recreation, but the administering of such recreation services is under the jurisdiction of the National Park Service, the Forest Service, or other agencies in the area.[33]

State park organization. Visits to the state parks far exceed those to the national parks and national forests. In turn, visits to municipal and county

* Since return visits were not held constant, the same visitor may have been counted more than once.

parks exceed those to state parks, visits to which increased from 92,500,000 in 1946 to more than 200,000,000 in 1957.[34] Extensive use of the state park system is largely due to the fact that such systems are most developed in states having large populations. Compared with the national parks and the national forests, the state parks are in closer proximity to large populations. Geographic availability is thus an important factor in choosing sites for state parks; because of this, they become keystones in the outdoor recreation system.

Types of recreational utilization of state parks are reported in Table XIV. In order of frequency they were day visitors, overnight visitors,

TABLE XIV. STATE PARK RECREATION UTILIZATION: 1952–1960

Type of Use	1952	1960
Day visitors	139,577,727	238,431,744
Overnight visitors	7,812,163	20,569,257
Campers	4,618,194	16,216,670
Organized campers	1,683,872	2,235,496
Cabin and hotel users	1,507,347	1,696,591
Total	149,255,417	259,001,001

Sources: *State Park Statistics, 1952* (Washington: U.S. Department of Interior, National Park Service, 1953); and *State Park Statistics, 1960* (Washington: U.S. Department of Interior, National Park Service, 1961), p. 18.

campers, organized campers, and cabin and hotel users. State parks are primarily utilization areas with services developed for swimming, boating, picnicking, camping, and winter sports. They are not characteristically locations of historic, geographic, or archaeological interest. Administration of the parks varies considerably from state to state. In some cases these parks have their own autonomous departments, and in other cases they are administered as part of parks, forests, and game departments. Their organization is complicated by the states' general lack of public domain land and by insufficient sources of revenue for acquiring land and supporting its operation. State parks have typically found it difficult to obtain and keep adequate personnel. The number of state park employees continues to be grossly inadequate for the amount of service desired.

TABLE XV. NUMBER OF VISITS TO NATIONAL FORESTS BY PRIMARY
RECREATIONAL PURPOSE: 1956

Recreational Purpose	Number of Visits (in thousands)	Per Cent
General enjoyment	14,190	27
Picnicking	12,822	24
Fishing	9,499	18
Hunting	4,436	8
Camping	3,516	7
Winter sports	2,673	5
Swimming	1,609	3
Hiking and riding	1,353	3
Other	2,458	5
Total	52,556	100

Source: Marion Clawson, *Statistics on Outdoor Recreation* (Washington: Resources for the future, 1958), pp. 42–3.

TYPES OF RECREATION

In post-World War II years the outdoor recreation boom has brought millions of people into rural America to seek a variety of experiences. In order to provide more appropriately for the interests and demands of national forest users, the U.S. Forest Service surveyed the major uses of its recreation areas in 1956 (see Table XV). This survey revealed that the most popular open-country recreation usages involved general enjoyment and picnicking rather than the more specific activities of fishing, hunting, camping, canoeing, and the pursuit of scientific hobbies. This type of participation pattern resulted in part from the historic social structure which produced negative judgments of recreation and leisure. To be a systematic participant in hunting, camping, canoeing, and similar types of activities involves a greater commitment and positive value orientation to things recreational. General outings and picnicking require a minimum of cost in recreating, a minimum of specialized equipment, and less emotional commitment to recreation as a significant form of human behavior.

Another element of social organization which contributes to the pattern of general rather than specific outdoor recreation participation is the predominantly city life experience of great masses of the population. Their socialization provides them with only a minimum knowledge of wilderness travel, canoeing, systematic hunting trips, and other types of outdoor recreation quite removed from life in the metropolis. Consequently, daily living in a remote, undeveloped wilderness area may precipitate more danger and frustration than gratification and enjoyment for the itinerant metropolitan individual. As the total society continues to become more urbanized, the socialization structure is broadened. It now provides for the training of the younger generation in the various forms of camping and outing trips. Youth of the future will have sufficient knowledge of wilderness areas to enjoy greater participation in outdoor recreation.

Camping. Camping has been an experience of humankind through the ages. Organized camping, on the other hand, has grown by gigantic proportions since the midpoint of the twentieth century. In 1951 there were some 12,600 camps, both day and resident, serving over 4,000,000 campers.[35] Organized camping was developed in the United States. Frederick William Gunn, headmaster of a Connecticut boys school, has been credited with being the originator of organized camping in the 1860's. In the 1880's, church camps were established, and from these early origins camping continued to develop after the turn of the century. The Boy Scouts and Girl Scouts have contributed to the rapid growth of camping. Associations of camp directors were organized, and in 1935 the American Camping Association was established to promote the programs of camping. Organized camping is participated in mostly by children between the ages of nine and fourteen. Much of the program is described as an outstanding educational experience. The American Camping Asociation's purposes include: one, the development of a feeling for the natural world; two, development of capabilities in out-of-door living; three, education for healthful living; four, training in constructive use of leisure; five, personality, character, and spiritual development. The objectives of a camping program are a logical product of a social structure in which leisure has become acceptable. Constructive recreation, rather than random recreation, appeals to the pragmatic American.[36]

Hunting and fishing. Hunting and fishing, as forms of recreation, have been a part of American life since pioneer times. In 1955 a survey was made of hunting and fishing practices in the United States.[37] Slightly more than 20 per cent of the population over twelve years of age had participated in hunting or fishing during that year. Both of these sports were male dominated. The following data indicate the proportion of participators.

	Per Cent Who Fished	Per Cent Who Hunted
Men	26	19
Women	9	1
Both	18	10

Both sports tended to be somewhat more popular in rural than urban areas.

	Per Cent Who Fished	Per Cent Who Hunted
From big cities	10	2
From small cities	16	6
From towns	21	12
From rural areas	21	16

There were regional variations in participation in these activities. Individuals living in the Mountain and West-North-Central states participated more frequently than those living in the Middle Atlantic and New England states. Both hunting and fishing were typically participated in by younger age persons. Fishing was most popular from the teen-ages through the young adult years. Hunting continued to be popular from the teens to the middle ages, but declined sharply after age 45. Some two-thirds of the hunters went after small game, the next most popular hunting was for large game; the least frequent hunting was for water fowl. Interest in hunting and fishing has generally expanded in post-World War II years for both city and rural people, males and females, and persons in all age categories.

Boating. Recreational boating has been characterized as the nation's family sport.[38] In 1957, some 30,000,000 Americans spent part of their recreational time boating. Americans operated 6,500,000 pleasure craft in their luxury armada. The cost of these craft and their upkeep reached the staggering total of $1,500,000,000 by the late 1950's. Though boating was once the sport of the rugged individualistic *nouveau riche* of the 1880's and 1890's, it is now popular among the middle classes. The pleasure craft industry was just getting under way at the turn of the century. Fifty years later it constituted one of the nation's principal recreation businesses. Among the middle classes the most popular boat is the outboard run-about, ranging in size from ten to twenty feet. It lacks sleeping, cooking, and toilet facilities, but it provides the average man with an opportunity for low-cost boating.

Recreational travel. Americans have come to be among the most avid travelers found in any society.[39] Travel has become a national pattern, pursued for both business and pleasure purposes. To come and go at one's desire has been facilitated by freedom to cross state boundaries, as well as by expanded automobile, rail, and air facilities. Social structures like high incomes and short work weeks further contributed to the popularity of travel. Americans have spent in the magnitude of $18,000,000,000 for domestic travel and $2,000,000,000 for foreign travel per annum in recent years. More than 60,000,000 Americans have annual paid vacations of one week or more. Typically they are joined in vacation travel by members of their family. National holidays extend the ordinary weekend periods and further contribute to extensive travel.

Many other forms of outdoor recreation experiences are known to exist. Unfortunately there is a minimum of systematic information about the social norms associated with such activities. Regardless of how it is viewed, however, out-of-door recreation is widespread in America. It is highly organized in terms of government management of much of the land area utilized. Industrial and economic markets were developed to produce recreation equipment. Recreation organizations were established to socialize people for recreationing experiences. Increased demands for outdoor recreational facilities and services, and increased participation on the part of the masses of the population have led to the proliferation of regional surveys of outdoor recreation.

REGIONAL STUDIES OF OUTDOOR RECREATIONING

Studies of vacationing itinerants in specific geographical areas varied considerably in scope and purpose. Studies in the New England-Middle Atlantic region, the Pacific Coast area, the South, and the Great Lakes area revealed many folkways and normative patterns of vacationers.

New England-Middle Atlantic studies. A study of summer home residents in rural New Hampshire revealed social interaction among the indigenous and the itinerant residents which ranged from extreme social distance to accommodation and, finally, to integration.[40] As early as 1939, the recreation industry in New England was recognized as second only to manufacturing. Half a billion dollars resulted from recreationing in pre-World War II years. That was more than twice the income from all agricultural production. Summer and winter recreation both were increasing in New

Hampshire. Summer home purchases constituted one of the major aspects of the recreation industry. Growth in this form of recreation was expanded greatly as middle-income groups tended to become owners of leisure property. Real estate agents introduced urban itinerants to remote areas of the state and thereby contributed to the development of summer vacation colonies. Waterfront sites became particularly popular. Abandoned rural homes were purchased by vacationing itinerants and renovated to provide adequate summer cottages. Demand for recreational cottages in an area where agriculture was declining contributed to the stability of local property values and generally bolstered the local community's economy.

Summer home residents were important contributors to the local public revenue and minimum users of the public services. The new itinerant residents disturbed old residents' visiting patterns and brought about modifications in local community organization. New accommodation and integration patterns were gradually established. The local community people discovered that the new residents provided a market for their produce and services.

Pacific Coast studies. On the Pacific Coast, the California Public Outdoor Recreation Plan (1960) represents an important example of the normative growth of recreation.[41] The purposes of the plan were to provide a system for protection and preservation of the natural resources and wildlife of the state; to provide people with recreational space along the state's coastal waters; to facilitate the acquiring of land and the development of parks, beaches, and campgrounds; to propagate game, and to improve wildlife habitation for the recreation of hunters and fishermen. Need for the plan grew out of the state's explosive increase in population. Outdoor recreationers showed very little regard for local political boundaries; hence, planning for out-of-door recreation required administrative direction from a central government agency.

The California survey was designed to investigate: pleasure travel, sightseeing and study, picnicking, camping, riding and hiking, swimming, boating, fishing, hunting, and winter sports. In spite of the emphasis placed on this kind of casual recreation, needs for wayside travelers were hardly considered. Outdoor recreation, aside from travel, was water-centered. No lake, stream, or waterway was considered too remote to be used by the state's population for pleasure purposes. One of the pressing demands in supplying recreational facilities in this regard was the provision for greater public access to the waterways. In sum, the findings revealed that the 1960 demand for outdoor recreational areas was 30 per cent greater than the supply.

California's inventory of recreational land resources finds an ample supply of open-country area for recreationists. However, like many other states it is faced with an uneven distribution of population and recreation resource areas. Over half of its population is concentrated in the southern part of the state and the area of greatest recreational potential is located in the northern part of the state.

Camping in the state of Washington was reported to have increased by skyrocket proportions since 1950.[42] The total number of visitors to the state's parks was 1,640,000 in 1950, and 5,790,000 in 1956. Persons using overnight facilities increased from 138,000 in 1950 to 510,000 in 1956. The 1956 survey of overnight campers revealed a number of folk-ways. Most of the campers were in family groups of four. Ninety per cent of the campers used tents, and 10 per cent had trailers. Over 60 per cent were residents of Washington. Most of the campers spent their vacation in Washington's parks. The length of their stay was typically a week, and their average expenditure was $150 per party. In most cases the income of the campers ranged between $5,000 and $6,000. Campers were particularly pleased with the parks' clean camping sites and wilderness atmosphere. Their complaints centered around overcrowding of camp areas and a desire for more facilities such as hot showers and related sanitary services.

The Washington survey revealed economic and social interaction between vacationing itinerants and the resident open-country and small-town people. Many of the vacationers utilized the services of motels and restaurants. Their gas purchases contributed significantly to the economic prosperity of local businessmen.

Another study in Washington revealed social interaction between hunters and farmers through arrangements which allowed the multiple use of land for recreation and systematic agriculture.[43] Farmers had some knowledge of the type of habitat required for game birds. Their primary interest, however, was in systematic farming. Provisions for birds and hunting were secondary in their value system. Many farmers had already removed cover area used by birds, and they planned to continue removal of cover areas in the interests of systematic agriculture. According to the game biologists' knowledge of bird habitat practices, conflict prevailed between the practices of systematic farming and the utilization of land for recreational hunting. Farmer-hunter relationships were more affable.

Farmers generally expressed a favorable attitude to hunters. A majority of the farmers allowed hunting on their land. Some had experienced property damage, but the general feeling of farmers was respect for the sportsmanlike conduct of the hunters.

Lake states studies. Numerous surveys have been made of the impact of outdoor itinerants on the Great Lakes area.[44] These studies report a general wilderness, an undeveloped character of the area. Surveys of the persons who vacation there showed their desire to preserve the wilderness lands; however, the vacationers also criticized such management practices as placing bans on private air flights, providing for only minimum roads, placing restrictions on logging and commercial developments —all of which are aimed at wilderness preservation. The idea was frequently expressed that the area might be more fully developed, and suggestions were made that wells for drinking water should be provided, sanitation facilities and parking facilities at camp grounds should be improved, camp sites and space for individual campers should be expanded, and more adequate firewood sources should be provided.

Most of the vacationers in this area come from the Midwest, in particular the metropolitan areas in the northern Midwest, such as Detroit, Chicago, and the Twin Cities. In the Quetico-Superior area a survey indicated that vacationers are largely from the upper middle class in that they tended to have higher educational attainment, higher occupational attainment, and higher levels of income than the national average.[45]

Canoers in this area were predominantly in the late teens to the late middle ages. Most canoe parties were made up of men. Most campers were in family groups, a fact which has led to some inaccurate judgments concerning the value of camping for increased family togetherness. Another penetrating research finding concerning families from an urbanized society undertaking the outdoor camping experience was its disruptiveness of family unity.

SUMMARY

Outdoor types of recreationing are among the age-old experiences of mankind. But throughout most of human history, men have lived so near the subsistence level that they have not developed specific recreational norms. In the ruralized social organization of the Middle Ages, patterns of outdoor recreation were scarcely differentiated from patterns of work.

In the urbanized social organization of contemporary America, recreation has come to have specific norms which distinguish it from other forms of social life. Having grown out of a society which placed negative value on recreation and leisure, normative patterns are now being established to make vacationing acceptable. Such a shift in the social structure has been one response to the minimum human energy put into economic production. It is also a result of extended longevity, which results in an increase of time spent performing some activity other than gainful employment. Recreation, as a rapidly developing social institution, is providing for the meaningful use of otherwise unused time.

Outdoor vacationing is one of the major forms of the developing social institution of leisure. It is a phenomenon of rural areas and is participated in by nearly half of the nation's people. The newest and most expansive forms of human behavior in rural America are associated with vacationing, rather than food and fiber production. Vacationing itinerants far outnumber rural populations. The structure of outdoor vacationing is becoming highly organized in the form of forest development and national, state, and county parks.

Surveys of vacationers in various regions reveal the proliferation of normative patterns of recreation. Most outings are for picnicking, travel, or sightseeing. Campers are usually composed of family groups. Canoeing and hunting parties are predominantly young male adults from the higher socioeconomic classes. Boating, like camping, is mainly a family experience.

NOTES

1. John C. Blum, *Land Utilization in New Hampshire* (New Hampshire Agricultural Experiment Station, Bulletin 344, 1942); Robert F. Lazillotti, *The Washington Tourist Survey, 1951* (State College of Washington, Bureau of Economic and Business Research, Bulletin 20, 1952); I. V. Fine and E. E. Werner, "Private Cottages in Wisconsin," *Wisconsin Vacation-Recreation Papers* (April, 1960); "Economic Significance of Hunters in Wisconsin," *Wisconsin Vacation-Recreation Papers* (July, 1960); and "The Economic Significance of Skiing in Wisconsin," *Wisconsin Vacation-Recreation Papers* (Aug., 1960).

2. Lauris B. Whitman and William G. Mather, *The Rural Churches of Four Pennsylvania Counties* (Pennsylvania Agricultural Experiment Station, Progress Report No. 76, 1952); Gibson Winter, "The Church in Suburban Captivity," *The Christian Century* (Sept. 28, 1955), 1112–14; *A Christian Ministry in the National Parks: Opportunities Unlimited* (New York: National Council of Churches, n. d.); "Worship in America's Wonderlands," *Presbyterian Life* (May 1, 1959), 20–22.

3. Erling D. Solberg, *The Why and How of Rural Zoning* (Washington: U.S.D.A., Agriculture Information Bulletin, No. 196, 1958); Louis A. Wolfanger, *Rural Zoning in a Nutshell* (Michigan Cooperative Extension Service, Extension Folder F-272, 1958).

4. Thomas Woody, "Leisure in the Light of History," *The Annals of the American Academy of Political and Social Science*, 313 (Sept., 1957), 4–10.

5. "Letter CVII," 4, 8, *Selected Letters of St. Jerome*, Translated by F. A. Wright (London: William Heinemann, 1928).

6. G. Coulton, *The Medieval Village* (Cambridge: Cambridge University Press, 1931), p. 255; see also Woody, *op. cit.*, p. 6.

7. G. R. Owst, *Literature and Pulpit in Medieval England* (Cambridge: Cambridge University Press, 1933), p. 395.

8. Foster Rhea Dulles, *America Learns to Play: A History of Popular Recreation, 1607–1940* (New York: D. Appleton-Century Co., 1940), pp. 8–13.

9. Thomas Morton, *The New English Canaan* (London: 1637; Reprints Society Publications, XIV, Boston, 1883), p. 279.

10. Dulles, *op. cit.*, p. 22.

11. Mary N. Stannard, *Colonial Virginia* (Philadelphia: 1917), p. 259; John Bernard, *Retrospections of America, 1797–1811* (New York: 1877), p. 206; George Alsop, *A Character of the Province of Maryland* (London: 1666, reprinted by N. D. Mereness, ed., Cleveland, 1902), p. 58.

12. Thorstein Veblen, *Theory of the Leisure Class* (New York: Mentor Books, 1953).

13. William H. Nugent, "The Sports Section," *American Mercury*, 16 (1929), 329–38.

14. Dulles, *op. cit.*, p. 201.

15. *Ibid.*, p. 202.

16. C. Frank Brockman, *Recreational Use of Wild Lands* (New York: McGraw-Hill Book Co., 1959), pp. 12 ff.

17. U.S. Bureau of the Census, *U.S. Census of Populations: 1960, Number of Inhabitants, U.S. Summary*. Final Report PC (1) 1A (Washington: U.S. Government Printing Office, 1961), p. xiii.

18. Edward L. Ullman, "Amenities as a Factor in Regional Growth," *The Geographical Review*, 44 (1954), 119–32.

19. *Annals*, p. 17.

20. Brockman, *op. cit.*, p. 17.

21. *Ibid.*, pp. 368–9; and Don L. Neer, "Industry," *Annals*, pp. 79–82.

22. *Ibid.*, p. 20.

23. Marion Clawson, *Statistics on Outdoor Recreation* (Washington: Resources for the Future, Inc., 1948), pp. 1–8.

24. Raleigh Barlowe, "Our Future Needs for Nonfarm Lands," in *Land* (Washington: Yearbook of Agriculture, 1958), pp. 474–9.

25. *Ibid.*, p. 477.

26. *Areas Administered by the National Park Service* (Washington: U.S. National Park Service, 1958).

27. Brockman, *op. cit.*, p. 126.

28. *Ibid.*, p. 147.

29. *Operation Outdoors: Part I, National Forest Recreation* (Washington: U.S. Department of Agriculture, Forest Service, 1957); and *Report of the Chief of the Forest Service* (U.S.D.A., 1960).

30. "National Forest Protection and Management, Recreation," Vol. III of *Forest Service Manual* (Washington: U.S. Department of Agriculture, Forest Service, n.d.).

31. Clawson, *op. cit.*, pp. 46–9.

32. *Ibid.*, pp. 55–7.

33. *Ibid.*, p. 58.

34. Brockman, *op. cit.*, pp. 84–109; and Clawson, *op. cit.*, pp. 62–75.

35. Reynold E. Carlson, "Organized Camping," *Annals*, pp. 83–6.

36. C. Wright Mills, *White Collar* (New York: Oxford University Press, 1956), pp. 235–8.

37. *National Survey of Fishing and Hunting, 1955* (Washington: Fish and Wildlife Service, U.S. Department of Interior, Circular 44, 1956).

38. Joseph E. Choate, "Recreational Boating: The Nation's Family Sport," *Annals*, pp. 109–12.

39. James L. Bossmeyer, "Travel: American Mobility," *Annals*, pp. 113–6.

40. John C. Blum, *op. cit.*, Part II.

41. *California Public Outdoor Recreation Plan* (Sacramento: State of California, Document Section, Printing Division, Parts I and II, 1960).

42. *We Came to Camp in Washington State Parks: Overnight Camping Survey, 1956* (Olympia: Washington State Parks, Recreation Commission, 1957).

43. Walter L. Slocum and LaMar T. Empy, *The Role of the Farmer in Upland Game Production and Hunting in Whitman County* (Washington Agriculture Experiment Station Bulletin 552, July, 1954).

44. Gordon Bultena *et al.*, in "Recreation in the Upper Great Lakes Areas: A Summary of Social Research," *Outdoor Recreation in the Upper Great Lakes Area* (Minnesota Lake States Forest Experiment Station Paper 89, 1961).

45. Marvin Taves, William Hathaway, and Gordon Bultena, *Canoe Country Vacationers* (Minnesota Agricultural Experiment Station Miscellaneous Report 39, June, 1960).

SELECTED READINGS

Blum, John C. *Land Utilization in New Hampshire.* New Hampshire Agricultural Experiment Station Bulletin 344, 1942.

One of the early descriptive studies of urban residents purchasing rural vacation property. It reports the patterns of social interaction between vacationers and indigenous residents.

Barlowe, Raleigh. "Our Future Needs for Nonfarm Lands," in *Land.* Washington: Yearbook of Agriculture, 1958.

A critical analysis of the need for nonagricultural land utilization in the United States.

Brockman, C. Frank. *Recreational Use of Wild Lands.* New York: McGraw-Hill Book Co., 1959.

Recreational programs in various types of open-country areas are described in some detail.

Clawson, Marion. *Statistics on Outdoor Recreation.* Washington: Resources for the Future, Inc., 1948.

One of the most comprehensive accumulations of statistics concerning outdoor recreation in the United States. Individual chapters are devoted to national parks, national forests, national wildlife refuges.

Dulles, Foster Rhea. *America Learns To Play.* New York: D. Appleton-Century Co., 1940.

A study of the growth of popular recreation in the United States. Emphasizes changes in recreation as the society shifted from agriculture to industry.

The Annals of the American Academy of Political and Social Science, 313. Sept., 1957.

This issue of *The Annals* is devoted to the subject of recreation. Of special interest for this chapter are the essays: "Organized Camping," "Recreational Boating," and "Travel: American Mobility."

III SOCIAL STRUCTURES OF FOOD AND FIBER PRODUCTION

8 SOCIAL SIGNIFICANCE
OF SETTLEMENT PATTERNS

The meaning of land and its resources varies from one society to another and from time to time in history. This diversity of meanings derives from the fact that land is directly or indirectly necessary for human survival. For nomadic and seminomadic tribes who do not systematically cultivate land, infringement upon their rights to its use is considered to be justification for retaliation and protection of their right to survive. For sedentary man, however, community or private ownership, or other legal or customary rights to land are essential to the livelihood of the group.

In American society both nomadic and sedentary types of land use have prevailed. Nomadic and seminomadic Indian tribes once battled for their right to move over the land in order to secure food, shelter, and clothing. Early farmers had to defend their rights to a homestead on which they raised grain or grazed livestock. Early ranchers, in contradistinction to both of the above, at first were concerned with unrestricted and open ranges on which to graze their cattle, and only secondarily and later were they concerned with the fencing in of their claims to range land.

In contemporary America there are several specific dimensions to the social meaning of land. One important meaning is the prestige element which accrues to those with propeprty. Status and social rank differentiation are associated with the possession or lack of land. The norms of this dimension involve not only ownership rights but also certain responsibilities of the landowner to his land. In the Western World, and growing out of the era of ruralized social organization, land became a symbol of power, nobility, and wealth. The absence of control over land reduced one to the low social ranks. In the early history of the United States, and on to the contemporary period of urbanized social organization, land ownership and property possession were and are measures of prestige and often wealth.[1]

An analysis of land utilization requires some systematic judgments concerning the productivity and resource potential of various areas of the earth. Utilization practices reflect the value judgments of the inhabitants of an area, the productive potential of the area and, in certain instances, the national welfare. As an increasing number of natural resources have been discovered, new notions of land utilization have become more specific. Certain normative patterns now characterize the use of land for industry, agriculture, cities, residences, recreation, transportation, and defense.[2] The utilization of land is increasingly influenced by demands for recreation, particularly out-of-door recreation. An increasing amount of land is being set aside for the construction of transportation arteries. Values of suburban living, reflected in suburban architecture, community shopping centers, industrial parks, country clubs, and playgrounds, have modified land utilization practices in contemporary America. The importance of land clearly reflects the condition of a developing society.

Ideas of multiple types of land utilization are found to be most extensive among people of the urbanized societies. Yet even among the urbanized societies, the unequal distribution of people over the land (see Table XVI) limits some of its multiple uses. Currently about 1.2 acres of crop land are needed to support each individual.[3] While approximately that amount of land is available, it is not equally available, due to the uneven

TABLE XVI. ACRES PER HEAD OF POPULATION

Area	Acres
World	12.6
Canada	140.0
Brazil	34.0
United States	10.6 (12.7)*
Great Britain	1.1
England and Wales	0.8
Japan	1.1

Source: L. Dudley Stamp, "Planning the Use of Land," *The New Scientist,* 8 (Aug. 25, 1960), p. 514.

  * Including Alaska.

distribution of the world population. In many areas of the world there is insufficient land for food and certainly insufficient land for alternative multiple uses. In contemporary American society, land utilization and settlement patterns have undergone considerable change, and their social significance is discussed in this chapter.

THE AMERICAN DOMAIN

Between 1781 and 1867, the young nation acquired an extensive domain of 1,807,681,920 acres which now include the continental United States and Alaska.[4] The land of the original thirteen colonies officially became that of the new nation by the Treaty of 1783 with Great Britain. State land continued to be ceded to the United States from 1781 through 1802. The original area was supplemented by the Louisiana Purchase from France in 1803; the North Red River Basin, including primarily parts of Minnesota and North Dakota, in 1818; the cession of Florida and part of Louisiana by Spain in 1819; the Oregon Compromise with Great Britain in 1846, including essentially the states of Washington, Oregon, Idaho; the Southwest cession by Mexico in 1848, including California, Nevada, Utah, most of Arizona, and parts of Wyoming, Colorado, and New Mexico; and the Gadsden Purchase from Mexico in 1853 of the southern parts of Arizona and New Mexico.[5]

Rapid removal of land from the public domain to private ownership has long been a normative pattern in American society. Disposal has been implemented by land grants, cash sales, military bounties, veterans' privileges, pre-emption, and homesteading. Less than 25 per cent of the national domain remains under federal ownership, and this only because of the small demand for low-grade land as well as the national interest in retaining some land in the public ownership. Federal ownership of land is greatest in the Mountain and Pacific States—50 per cent and 45 per cent, respectively.[6] Most of the public land in the Western States is of the rough, mountainous, arid, and semiarid type. All other regions have less than 10 per cent of their land in public ownership. There are some federal landholdings in all states of the nation, varying from 85 per cent in Nevada to 3 per cent in Iowa.

Ninety per cent of the public domain has been continuously in federal ownership. The other 10 per cent of public land has been reacquired by the nation, after having once been in private ownership. Most of the acquired lands have been brought back into public ownership by the Department of Agriculture for national forests, by the Department of Defense for military purposes, and by other agencies for flood control, national parks, wildlife refuges, reclamation areas, and related federal uses. Nearly half of the public domain in the continental United States was disposed of through homestead policies, direct sales, and grants to private individuals (see Table XVII). About 15 per cent of the public domain was given to educational institutions, and an additional 6 per cent was granted for the development of railroads. Nearly 12 per cent of

TABLE XVII. FEDERAL DISPOSALS OF PUBLIC DOMAIN IN CONTINENTAL UNITED STATES TO 1956

	Millions of Acres	Percentages
Disposals:		
Homesteads, sales, and grants chiefly to private individuals	715.8	49.6
Granted to railroads to aid construction of railways	91.3	6.3
Granted to states for education and public improvements	223.8	15.5
Total disposals	1,030.9	71.4
Indian tribal and trust lands	52.8	3.7
Reserved for public purposes: national forests, parks, wildlife refuges, reclamation, power and national-defense areas	187.8	13.0
Unreserved and unappropriated public domain:		
Within grazing districts	142.6	9.9
Outside grazing districts	28.1	2.0
Total	170.7	11.9
Total federal	358.5	24.9
Grand total, original public domain *	1,442.2	100.0

Source: U.S. Department of the Interior, *Report of the Director of the Bureau of Land Management,* Statistical Appendix, June 30, 1956; U.S. Senate, Doc. 25, 85th Cong., 1st sess., *Inventory Report on Real Property Owned by the United States,* as of June 30, 1956; and U.S. Senate Doc. 100, 84th Cong., 2nd sess., *Inventory Report on Federal Real Property in the United States,* as of June 30, 1955, prepared by General Services Administration.

* The total area of the original public domain is given as computed in 1912 by a committee representing the General Land Office, the Geological Survey, and the Bureau of the Census (see U.S. Department of the Interior, Office of the Secretary, *Areas of Acquisitions to the Territory of the United States*). The total has not been adjusted for recomputation of the area of the United States which was done for the 1950 Decennial Census.

the public domain remains available for disposal to private individuals.

The largest acreage of federal land (178.6 million acres) is reserved for grazing districts and unappropriated use. Over 167,000,000 acres of public land are included in the national forests and related areas. Nearly 22,000,000 acres of the government land is utilized for national defense; 16,000,000 acres for reclamation, flood control, and power areas; 15,000,000 acres for national parks and historical sites; and nearly 10,000,000 acres for wildlife refuges and institutional uses.[7]

Total land utilization in the United States since the turn of the century has tended to become stabilized. There have been some shifts in utilization patterns and more are expected in the future, but, according to Clawson, land utilization dynamics are decreasing.[8] Acreages of land utilization by type of use for 1910, 1950, and 2000 are reported in Table XVIII. The greatest land acreages were utilized for grazing; forestry acreages were the second-largest land utilization areas and agriculture the third largest. Between 1950 and 2000, it is anticipated that all three of these major land utilization areas will decline. By contrast, increases are expected for urban uses (up 140 per cent), public recreation purposes (up 107 per cent), reservoirs and water management (up 100 per cent), wildlife (up 43 per cent), and transportation (up 20 per cent). [9]

SYSTEMS OF LAND SETTLEMENT

Colonial settlement patterns. Land settlement in America was designed for speculative and exploitive purposes of the kings of Spain, France, England, and Holland.[10] The first British colonial charters were granted in 1606 to the Plymouth Company and the Virginia Company. These were joint stock companies composed of knights, gentlemen, merchants, and others. They were also trading corporations, by provision of their charters, given considerable measures of self-government. The original charters made no mention of Indian rights to the land and established no particular procedure for distributing the land to subsequent owners.[11]

During the early period of colonial establishment, both in Plymouth and Virginia, there was a village-oriented system of land utilization. As the colonists increased in number, and as the danger of Indian attacks decreased, the settlers dispersed over the land. From that time, patterns of "land grabbing" became part of the social organization. Settlements of Pilgrims in early New England were characterized by close communal living due to their religious belief, their experience as a minority people

TABLE XVIII. USE OF LAND IN THE UNITED STATES (NOT INCLUDING ALASKA AND HAWAII), SELECTED YEARS, 1900–1950, AND PROJECTIONS FOR 1980 AND 2000 IN MILLIONS OF ACRES [a]

Use of Land	1900	1910	1920	1930	1940	1950	1980	2000
Cities of 2,500 or more population [b]	6	7	10	12	13	17	30	41
Public recreation areas [c]	5	9	12	15	41	46	72	95
Agriculture: crops [d]	319	347	402	413	399	409	389	389
pasture [e]	77	84	78	73	68	69	69	69
other [f]	53	57	58	45	44	45	45	45
Commercial forestry:								
continuous management [g]	0	30	60	200	300	359	385	405
little or no management	525	482	440	295	188	125	90	50
Grazing [h]	808	775	730	735	740	700	700	680
Transportation	17	19	23	24	24	25	28	30
Reservoirs and water management [i]	*	1	2	3	7	10	15	20
Primarily for wildlife	*	*	1	1	12	14	18	20
Mineral production								
Deserts, swamps, mountain tops, some noncommercial forest, etc.	94	93	88	88	68	85	63	60
Miscellaneous and unaccounted for								
Total	1,904	1,904	1,904	1,904	1,904	1,904	1,904	1,904

Source: Marion Clawson, "Land Use and the Demand for Land in the United States," in *Modern Land Policy* (Urbana: University of Illinois Press, 1960).

ᵃ The data in this table are necessarily estimates in several instances, sometimes on a relatively scanty basis of fact. This table emphasizes land use, as separate from land ownership or control or from vegetative cover.

ᵇ Includes municipal parks.

ᶜ Excludes municipal parks. Includes national park system, areas within national forests reserved for recreation, state parks and acreages around TVA and Corps reservoirs reserved for recreation. Excludes all areas used primarily for other purposes even though they provide much recreation. Excludes actual water area of reservoirs, which is shown later under its own heading. Excludes also wildlife areas, which are shown below. We have assumed that only part of the increased potential demand will be met.

ᵈ Cropland harvested, crop failure, cultivated summerfallow, and cropland idle or in cover crops. See Tables 11 and 12, Agriculture Information Bulletin No. 168, U.S. Department of Agriculture (1957).

ᵉ Only pasture on land which is considered cropland is included. This corresponds to the 1949 and 1954 Census of Agriculture definition. The 1900 figure is an estimate. The acreages for 1910 through 1940 are the difference between crops, as shown above, and estimates of cropland potential which included cropland pastured, given in Table 1 of Agriculture Information Bulletin 140 (1955).

ᶠ Farmsteads, farm roads, and other land not in crops, pasture, or woods. See Tables 11 and 12. Agriculture Information Bulletin 168 (1957).

ᵍ This is a roughly estimated figure. For 1950, it excludes commercial forest land that is poorly stocked, or has no fire protection, as shown in *Timber Resources for America's Future* (Washington: Forest Service, U.S.D.A., Forest Resource Report No. 14, 1958). For earlier years, it is our estimate of comparable definition area.

ʰ Includes some noncommercial forest land used primarily for grazing.

ⁱ Excluding land around reservoirs and conservation pools of reservoirs, which are included in recreation areas.

* Less than 500,000 acres.

in Holland, and the need for protection against the Indians whose land they had appropriated. As their numbers increased, the Pilgrims spread out on the land but continued to follow the system of "town settlements." The New England town approximated the English village; both existed in the fading shadow of the feudal system. Under that system, land was allotted in individual strips to be cultivated by individual families, but in the colonies land was held by free ownership rather than through the tenant system.

Dutch settlers established themselves in the area of New York (New Amsterdam) under the auspices of a charter similar to that of the British companies. The Dutch were oriented to trading, but they also provided for colonization of large landholdings under feudal or manorial conditions. The lords of this feudal system, known as patroons, had absolute right over the land; settlers on it existed in something of a serfdom, holding their rights to the land under the quit-rent system.[12]

Early land settlement patterns in the colonies were a mixture of the traditional settlement characteristics of the Old World countries with new ones resulting from the abundance of land and Indians. Systems of feudalism, tenancy, and quit-rents were all modified and generally unsuccessful in the New World.[13]

In the second half of the eighteenth century the colonies had grown both in population and land area, so that there was continual pressure to cross the Allegheny Mountains and settle the Western areas. After the French and Indian War, the English Crown sought to overcome corrupt land grabbing. A royal order was issued in 1763, which prohibited governors from granting land patents west of the headwaters of rivers emptying into the Atlantic. This constituted a major grievance among the land-hungry colonists. Indeed, it was never fully accepted, and ultimately became one of the injustices mentioned in the Declaration of Independence.[14] The system of village settlement and irregular dispersal throughout the land, following rivers and other natural geographic boundaries, prevailed until the time of the Revolution.

LAND SETTLEMENT IN THE NEW NATION

Colonial experience provided precedents for the traditional village pattern of land settlement, and for the more unusual dispersed pattern. This dispersed form of settlement became commonplace in contemporary America, to the virtual exclusion of the village system.

Opposition to the norms of feudalism and the manorial system were widespread in colonial America. The Revolution abolished these norms in almost all cases. The norm of primogeniture which prevailed in New York and several of the Southern States (and in modified form in New Jersey, Pennsylvania, Delaware, and several New England States) allowed the eldest son a double share of the inheritance. Between 1784 and 1796 the practice of primogeniture was generally abolished.[15] Other developments that grew out of the Continental Congress and the forming of the new nation were the limiting of entails and the abolition of land ownership as a qualification for voting.

Types of land settlement. The two major patterns of agricultural land settlement used throughout the world are the nucleated and the dispersed pattern. The nucleated or village pattern is the most universal. The dispersed settlement, with residence on the farm land, is found most often in the United States. There are several variations of each of these forms of settlement. In the village agricultural systems, buildings which house cattle and equipment may be on the land or in the village. In the dispersed settlement pattern the individual houses or farmsteads may be randomly located on the land, or they may be settled in specific patterns to provide some clustering for purposes of achieving sociability and services. The two major types of land settlement have been subdivided into these four complex patterns: one, individual locations or scattered settlement; two, crossroad settlement; three, line settlement; four, village settlement. In each of the first three cases, the farmstead is placed at some location within the boundaries of the farmland itself. In the fourth case, the farmsteads are nucleated on plots of land separated from the farm areas.

Scattered settlement has been most widespread in the United States. It has been used most frequently in the major land developments since 1800. This settlement type was popular because of its occupational advantages, since it placed the farm operator in the greatest possible proximity to his area of work. The scattered pattern of settlement was further supported by the quadrangle survey method and the early Homestead Acts. As the population flow moved westward into Kentucky, across the Ohio River, across the Mississippi River, through the Plains States, and on to the Pacific Coast, the size and shape of farms came to follow survey lines.

The Ordinance of 1785 provided for the surveying of the West into townships. Each township was six square miles and contained 36 sections to the square mile. This system of land survey led to the fixing of boundaries at right angles, and the development of straight roads and fences. It is the so-called *checkerboard system*.[16]

As this settlement pattern first developed, there was a tendency to locate the farmstead approximately in the center of the land, allowing easy access to all of the fields and pastures. Some consideration was given also to the strategic location of the farmstead for natural drainage, scenic views, and availability of water supply. In areas where a road system was established, the farmstead was usually located in proximity to it. Various considerations entered into locating the farmstead, but in practically no case did they include nearness to one's neighbors.[17] With the continual development and improvement of roads, accessibility to highways has been a factor in the relocation of farmsteads; however, such relocation has been slow, and generally does not alter the dominant pattern of scattered farmsteads.

Scattered settlement is essentially indigenous to America, although some of the early Dutch settlers in New York were dispersed on the land in a pattern similar to it. In the early days of the nineteenth century, the scattered pattern of settlement separated farm families by an average of a half-mile in all directions from the nearest neighbor. When the Homestead Acts provided larger acreages, the dispersion and separation of farm families were increased proportionately. (Fig. 9 illustrates the scattered settlement pattern.)

Crossroad settlement, or partial nucleation (see Fig. 10), has not been a typical aspect of the rural landscape in the United States, although it does appear occasionally. The location of three or four farmsteads at a crossroads, when it does occur, has been designed most often so that its residents might take advantage of some trading or transportation facility.

Other variations on the crossroad or partially nucleated settlement cluster have been suggested (see Figs. 11 and 12). In the first case, a triangular or hexagonal land survey was projected so that farmsteads could be located at the center or most acute section of the angles. William Penn advocated such a land settlement pattern, and in the 1890's surveys were initiated in Nebraska. In both of these cases, this pattern of settlement was never realized.[18] The second semiclustered pattern, the so-called "F" settlement, brought eight farmsteads together. It was a further modification of the crossroads and the hexagonal settlement plans. Both of these variations of the crossroad settlement were particularly unacceptable

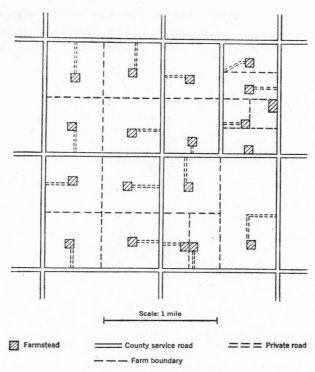

Scale: 1 mile

▨ Farmstead   ══════ County service road   ═ ═ ═ Private road
                   ─ ─ ─ ─ Farm boundary

FIGURE 9.   SCATTERED SETTLEMENT PATTERN

Source: Carl C. Taylor, *et al., Columbia Basin: Pattern of Rural Settlement, Problem 10* (Washington, D.C.: U.S. Department of Interior, Bureau of Reclamation, 1947), p. 8.

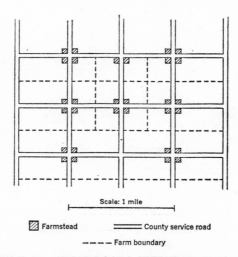

Scale: 1 mile

▨ Farmstead   ══════ County service road
                   ─ ─ ─ Farm boundary

FIGURE 10.   CROSS–ROADS SETTLEMENT PATTERN

Source: *Ibid.,* p. 9.

167

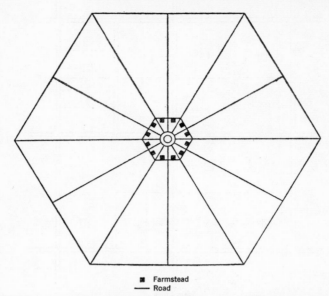

■ Farmstead
— Road

FIGURE 11.   A TYPE OF COMMUNITY AND FARM LAYOUT WHICH IS
PERFECT GEOMETRICALLY BUT QUITE UNACCEPTABLE FROM THE
STANDPOINT OF FARM MANAGEMENT AND OPERATION

Source: *Ibid.*, p. 10.

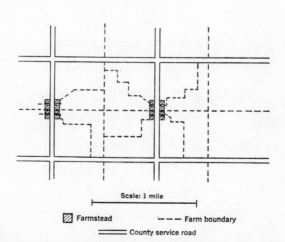

Scale: 1 mile

▨ Farmstead   – – – Farm boundary
═══ County service road

FIGURE 12.   CROSS–ROADS SETTLEMENT: "F" PATTERN

Source: *Ibid.*, p. 11.

to farmers. Their objection was that such fields involved turning too many sharp angles in the process of planting and cultivating.[19]

Line settlement patterns are sometimes called "string towns." These are a variation of the dispersed and of the village settlement patterns. In line settlement areas, square farm plots give way to the long, narrow, rectilinear type of holding. One end of the narrow plot of land is located on a major transportation artery—a stream, highway, river, or bayou. Widespread use of the line village is made in the areas of southern Louisiana settled by the French. A second use of the line village is in the Connecticut Valley.[20] In the line settlement, houses are systematically nucleated or settled randomly, but in either case they are close to neighboring farmsteads (see Fig. 13).

The village settlement pattern was widespread in early colonial America, particularly in New England and the Dutch areas along the Hudson River.[21] Later experiences with village settlement include those of the Mormon communities, Utopian communities, Amana communities in Iowa, and Amish communities, particularly in Pennsylvania.[22]

Farm villages are established by removing the farmsteads from the agricultural land to a common cluster area near the farms (see Fig. 14). Numerous advantages accrue to the village settlements when settlers place value on social organization and the amenities of material conveniences. However, these are sharply offset when the system of social organization is viewed from the perspective of efficient operation of farmland for economic and production records. The advantages often include the provision of more complex educational and religious systems at a lower cost for the individuals involved. Social gatherings and community activities of practically all types are facilitated and promoted by the village residential plan which brings people into more frequent and intense social interaction. A second advantage of the village plan is the reduced cost of providing the tangible, material benefits of high levels of living to large numbers of people. For example, the provision of electricity, telephones, water, sewage, roads, fire protection, health facilities, and a variety of other services all become more feasible and economical when major lines for transmitting such services can be focused in a central community rather than spread over great distances. A third advantage of the village type of organization is the flexibility it allows in determining the size, shape, and organization of farms.

Disadvantages of the village system include the necessity for regular travel between the place of residence and the fields. This is costly in terms

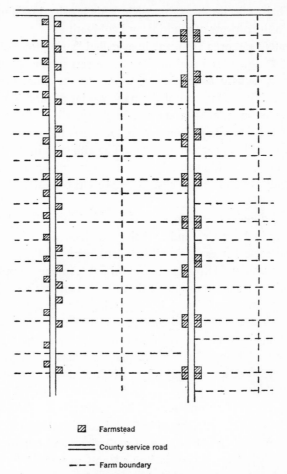

Farmstead

County service road

— — — Farm boundary

FIGURE 13. LINE SETTLEMENT PATTERN: FREE AND CLUSTERED

Source: *Ibid.*, p. 15.

of both time and equipment necessary to move operators, animals, and machinery. Further, this system reduces the amount of supervision possible in the land and livestock areas.

The importance of settlement patterns is clearly apparent in the case of the land pattern of Canyon County, Idaho. There the historic pattern of scattered settlement was used extensively and little attention was given to topographic features or to road-mileage minimization.[23] Canyon County had 74 farms with 70 houses located on them in a six-section area. Several of the farms followed the traditional square shape, but 36 farms

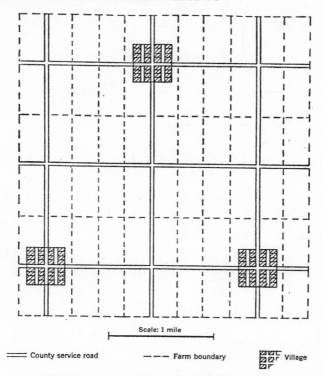

Scale: 1 mile

═══ County service road   — — — Farm boundary   Village

FIGURE 14.   VILLAGE PATTERN SETTLEMENT

Source: *Ibid.*, p. 13.

were at least twice as long as they were wide; in addition, there were a
few irregular shapes. The irregularities of the land shapes were due
essentially to adjustments between occupants of the land. To serve these
scattered farmsteads, a total of seventeen miles of road was required (a
peripheral roadway counted as half its length because it served houses
on both sides). Figure 15 illustrates this layout of the land. Systematic
planning, involving a minimum of changes, could have reduced to less
than ten miles the amount of road required to serve this same number of
farmsteads (see Fig. 16). The plan would have involved splitting many
of the eighty-acre tracts into long forties; that is, making them rectilinear
rather than square. The ultimate plan would approximate that of the line
arrangement. To take advantage of this savings in road mileage would
have required boundary changes for 24 farm units and different locations
for fourteen houses. These minor changes would not only have reduced
the road mileage by nearly half but, in addition, would have reduced the

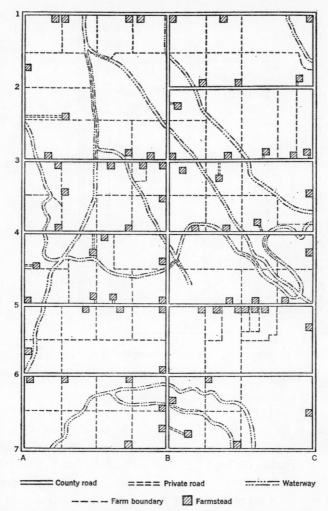

FIGURE 15. SETTLEMENT PATTERN: PART OF CANYON COUNTY,
IDAHO, SAMPLE

Source: *Ibid.*, p. 31.

cost of travel for farm operators and the cost of bringing services for
house-to-house delivery. This plan would have involved arranging farmsteads along service roads located a mile apart and along crossroads that
are from two to three miles apart.

Another system of planning land settlement is based upon consideration of the natural topography of the land. This is in contrast to an arbi-

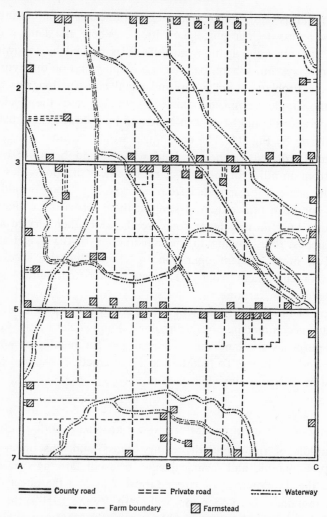

FIGURE 16. DEMONSTRATION OF ECONOMIES WHICH MIGHT HAVE
BEEN EFFECTED: CANYON COUNTY, IDAHO, SAMPLE

Source: *Ibid.* p. 32.

trary checkerboard survey system. In this system, planned land settlement
could be at maximum efficiency by developing farm areas in accordance
with the type of farming anticipated—for example, irrigated or dry
farming. Illustrations are provided by a study of four sections of land in
Owyhee Project Area of Malheur County, Oregon.[24] There the traditional
system of establishing farm boundaries was the checkerboard pattern.

Most of the farms had regular square or rectilinear shapes, cutting indiscriminately across topographical conditions. Where the land was level and at all suitable for irrigation, no difficulties ensued by following this regular survey system. Where the land was sloping and on different levels, however, the problem of irrigation and canal construction was complicated by the simple rectilinear boundaries. In this case, the efficiency of farming operations could have been increased by following natural boundaries, as shown by Fig. 17. The advantages would include: one, elimination of small isolated patches of land which could be more naturally irrigated from an adjacent farm; two, arrangement of boundaries so that land in one slope to be irrigated from a single high point would be included in one farm rather than in several; three, provision of more land for irrigation by removing fence rows, roads, and other service areas to the high slopes; four, savings in the construction of the irrigation canal system; five, more efficient operation by eliminating the necessity for movement of equipment from one isolated patch to another, and six, adoption of contour farming.

The type of farm land settlement which is most desirable in urbanized society must accommodate both technological and social needs. For technological purposes the land must be arranged for maximum utilization of science and machines. To facilitate social interaction, the land arrangement must be such as to obviate isolation.

CONTEMPORARY LAND SETTLEMENT AND URBANIZED SOCIAL LIFE

By the middle of the twentieth century, most land was under private ownership. Economic and technical efficiencies in farming continued to encourage the development of larger farms. This had the effect of separating the remaining farm operators still more. By the 1950's, the average distance from the farmstead to the nearest trading center was six miles, and nearly 80 per cent of the nation's farms were within ten miles of such a center.[25] Road conditions have been continually improved for service distribution efficiency and family touring. As a result, two-thirds of the nation's farm homes are located within two-tenths of a mile of all-weather roads. The combination of good roads and automobiles placed practically all of the nation's farmers within twenty minutes' reach of a trade center. Time and difficulties involved in travel are being reduced, but accessibility of service and social isolation are still serious problems. School bus rides often involve trips of nearly an hour to and from consolidated schools.

Selected area of four sections, Owyhee project
Malheur County, Oregon

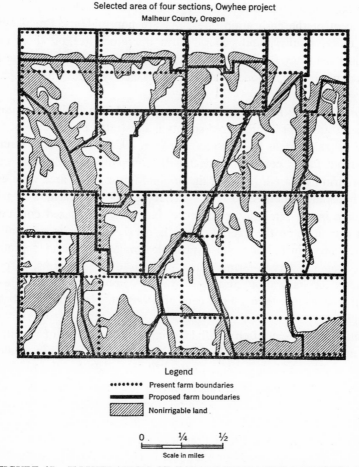

Legend

••••••• Present farm boundaries

▬▬▬▬ Proposed farm boundaries

//////// Nonirrigable land

0   ¼   ½

Scale in miles

FIGURE 17.   ILLUSTRATION OF FARM BOUNDARIES MODIFIED TO
FIT NATURAL FEATURES

Source: Carl P. Heisig and Marion Clawson, *Migration and Settlement on the Pacific
Coast: New Farms on New Land* (Washington, D.C.: U.S. Department of Agriculture,
Bureau of Agricultural Economics, Oregon Agricultural Experiment Station and Farm
Security Administration, Report No. 4, 1941), pp. 86–88.

Excessive and costly mileage is accumulated in the great number of trips
that are made by open-country families to central meeting places for social
gatherings.

Less than 5 per cent of the nation's farmers are nonresident; their
homes are often located in a nearby village or town. Most of the nonresident farmers are engaged in some type of plant production rather than
in animal production. For example, nearly 15 per cent of the fruit and nut

farm operators, 12 per cent of the vegetable farm operators, and just over 10 per cent of the cash grain operators are nonresidents. Practically all of the dairy, poultry, and general farm operators live on their farms. There is a tendency for more large than small farm operators to be non-residents, but on the national scale farming is clearly a resident occupation.

Off-farm residence in Montana: A case study.[26] The high social cost of dispersed settlement in urbanized society is illustrated by the case of farm-ing and ranching areas in Montana. Between 1920 and 1950, the number of Montana farms continually declined. Concomitantly, the size of the average farm increased. Many of the original farms in the area were estab-lished by homesteading 320-acre sites. Even this size farm was grossly inadequate in the semiarid area; hence, farm sizes increased continually. At the present time the average farm is nearly double its original size. Improved mechanization made it possible for a single farm operator to manage a much larger farm. These patterns of large farms, dispersed settlement, mechanization, and social values combined to develop a situ-ation in which more than 10 per cent of Montana's farmers have become nonresidents.

Montana farms can often be divided into the categories of wheat, live-stock, and general farming. Nonresident farm operators were studied in all three types of farming areas. In the districts studied, over 14 per cent of the wheat operators, over 7 per cent of the general farmers, and 6.5 per cent of the stock ranchers were all nonresidents. In those operations in which care for cattle is not a factor, off-farm residence is feasible. Nevertheless, considerable variation was found in off-farm residence in the various wheat districts. For example, in eight of the 33 wheat districts studied, there were no off-farm residents; at the other extreme, in one of the wheat districts, 77 per cent of the operators lived in town rather than on their land.

Nonresident farming in Montana is different from much of the world's historic village agriculture in that places of residence are maintained both on the farms and in the towns. In Montana over half (58 per cent) of the nonresident farmers lived on their farms part of the year. In most cases, farmers and their families lived on the land during the summer months, and in situations where they were sufficiently close to the town to transport their children to school, they continued to live on the land during part of the fall and part of the spring.

The most important factor motivating farmers to move families off the land was their desire to provide better school facilities for their children. Two-thirds of the nonresident farm operators moved to towns primarily because of educational advantages. Nearly 11 per cent moved because of health, and others moved to escape poor weather and inadequate roads, or to have town conveniences available. Most of the nonresident farm operators migrated at a young age; this corresponds to their desire for better schools for their children.

The advantages of moving off the farm included better school facilities for children, modern conveniences of electricity, running water, indoor bath facilities, and other related items which are valued in the urbanized society. Also, more social life, greater participation in organizations (among the adults and particularly among the children), and more extensive medical facilities were available in towns. The primary disadvantages of living away from the farm included an increased cost of living, inability to keep livestock, complications in doing farm work and maintaining equipment, and less time for family life.

Off-farm residence was highly correlated with acceptance of the dominant values of the urbanized society in both social life and economic efficiency of the farm operation. The typical off-farm resident operated a larger and more efficient farm, and accomplished this at an earlier date than other Montana farmers. The off-farm residents had more highly mechanized farms than resident operators.

Attitudes toward the farm operator as a town resident were generally favorable in the judgment of businessmen and government leaders. Often, town leaders and businessmen have opposed the retirement of farm families in the towns because the retired have traditionally been hostile to programs designed for progress. The farm operator, by contrast, was an active and interested citizen, and a strong supporter of good schools and modern public facilities—even when these involved increases in taxation. Often the farm operators built modern homes in the towns and took pride in the attractiveness of their residences. Many of the off-farm resident operators already had become members of town organizations prior to moving off their farms. Their participation was great but not strikingly changed as a result of their relocation.

New nonfarm residents. A high density of population per square mile is a major social cost in providing many of the institutional organizations of urbanized society, such as consolidated schools, large churches, recreational facilities, and club meeting facilities. These institutional organizations by nature require large numbers of people to live close together. The trend toward larger farms and a smaller number of farm operators intensifies this problem. A countertrend—the movement of exurbanites into open-country areas—sometimes compensates for the out-migration of farm people. When nonfarm people become integrated into a community of farm people, many urbanized social patterns of behavior are introduced into its social organization.

Sprawling cities are encroaching upon rural areas at an ever accelerated rate.[27] While urban expansion into the open country does not present a critical problem in terms of the amount of land used, problems do arise concerning the use of land in a specific way. There appears to be adequate land in the United States for both urban expansion and food and fiber production, in the foreseeable future. Nevertheless, the movement of city people into rural-urban fringe areas has often involved the division of farms into small units, especially when adequate zoning was not provided. Consequently, farm and nonfarm residents often became incompatible neighbors. The social cost of land utilization in the fringe areas necessitates perceptive planning to integrate the residents in such a way as to support the urbanized social institutions without interfering with the agricultural enterprise. In New York, parts of New England, and other areas, nonfarm residents have made effective use of farmsteads vacated by farm families.

SUMMARY

The meaning and utilization of land are related to the type of social organization prevailing in a given society at a certain time. Land may have a general or a collective use for subsistence purposes, or it may be intensely meaningful as private property. This latter use identifies political rights and social status. Land may have intrinsic value for the poet, the nature lover, and the humanist. Also, it can be viewed as something to be manipulated, exploited, or conserved for the systematic accomplishment of man's economic goals.

Since the period of ruralized social organization in Medieval Europe, land has been utilized for food and fiber production, political rights, and social status. Where urbanized social organization predominates, man has adopted these meanings of land. Concurrent with the development of urbanized social organization are specific patterns of land use including recreational, transportational, residential, military, and industrial purposes.

Land settlement from colonial America to the present has been oriented toward sustaining multiple uses. Nevertheless, land settlement patterns in the United States have been modified over a period of time. The scattered farm settlement, which grew largely out of the survey system adopted by the Continental Congress in the 1780's, became inefficient for the provision of many social institutions such as education, religion, recreation, health, and economics. Much of contemporary rural America has been characterized by school and church consolidation and programs for construction of all-weather roads, as well as the provision of electricity and telephones to remote rural areas. Where these programs are not accomplished with sufficient haste, some farm operators are moving off their land and relocating in towns and cities. A compensatory current to the shifts in traditional rural areas is the flow of exurbanites into fringe areas, as they take up residence in older farmsteads and in suburban developments.

The meaning of land settlement is no longer determined only by efficiency in food and fiber production. It has now become influenced greatly by conditions of social organization. Governmental programs which have contributed so much to record-breaking production of food and fiber are now being challenged by a modification in the meaning of land. As land has become less necessary for food and fiber production, it has become more important for urbanized living.

NOTES

1. Aaron M. Sakolski, *Land Tenure and Land Taxation in America* (New York: Robert Schalkenbach Foundation, 1957) and *The Great American Land Bubble: The Amazing Story of Land-Grabbing, Speculations and Booms from Colonial Days to the Present Time* (New York: Harper and Brothers, Publishers, 1932).

2. L. Dudley Stamp, "Planning the Use of Land," *The New Scientist,* 8 (Aug. 25, 1960), 514–16; Marion Clawson, "Land Use and Demand for Land in the United States," in *Modern Land Policy: Papers of the Land Economics Institute* (Urbana: University of Illinois Press, 1960), pp. 3–16.

3. Stamp, *op. cit.,* p. 514.

4. Marion Clawson, *The Public Domain in 1953* (Washington: U.S. Department of the Interior, Bureau of Land Management, 1953).

5. *Ibid.,* p. 3.

6. John B. Bennett *et al.,* "The Heritage of Our Public Lands," in *Land: The Yearbook of Agriculture, 1958* (Washington: U.S. Department of Agriculture, 1958), p. 44.

7. Bennett, *op. cit.*, p. 48.

8. Clawson, "Land Use and Demand," p. 4.

9. *Ibid.*, p. 13.

10. Sakolski, *The Great American Land Bubble,* p. 1.

11. Sakolski, *Land Tenure,* p. 21.

12. *Ibid.*, pp. 30 and 31, sections 30 and 32.

13. Beverley W. Bond, Jr., *The Quit-Rent System in the American Colonies* (New Haven: Yale University Press, 1919); C. N. Andrews, *The Colonial Period of American History,* Vol. I (New Haven: Yale University Press, 1934).

14. *Ibid.*, p. 51.

15. John Fiske, *The Critical Period of American History* (New York: Houghton Mifflin and Co., 1882); Amelia C. Ford, *Colonial Precedents of Our National Land System as It Existed in 1800* (Madison: University of Wisconsin Press, 1910); Marshall Harris, *Origin of the Land Tenure System in the United States* (Ames: Iowa State College Press, 1954); Beverley W. Bond, Jr., *op. cit.*

16. Wayne D. Rasmussen, ed., *Readings in the History of American Agriculture* (Urbana: University of Illinois Press, 1960), p. 35.

17. Carl C. Taylor *et al., Columbia Basin: Pattern of Rural Settlement,* Problem 10 (Washington: U.S. Department of the Interior, Bureau of Reclamation, 1947), p. 7.

18. T. Adams, *Rural Planning and Development* (Ottawa: Canada Commission of Conservation, 1917), pp. 62 ff.

19. Taylor, *op. cit.*, pp. 8–11.

20. T. Lynn Smith, "An Analysis of Rural Social Organization Among the French Speaking People of Southern Louisiana," *Journal of Farm Economics,* 16 (Oct., 1934), 680–88; Horace Miner, *St. Denis, A French-Canadian Parish* (Chicago: University of Chicago Press, 1939), Chapter 3; Edna Scofield, "The Origin of Settlement Patterns in Rural New England," *Geographical Review,* 28 (Oct., 1938), 652–63; Martha Krug Genthe, "Valley Towns in Connecticut," *Bulletin of the American Geographical Society* (New York: 1907), Chapter 39.

21. H. B. Adams, *Village Communities of Cape Ann and Salem* (Baltimore: Johns Hopkins University Studies in Historical and Political Science, Series 1, Nos. 9 and 10, 1883); Irving Elting, *Dutch Village Communities on the Hudson* (Baltimore: Johns Hopkins University Studies in Historical and Political Science, Series 4, No. 1, 1886); F. W. Blockmar, *Spanish Institutions of the Southwest* (Baltimore: Johns Hopkins University Press, 1891).

22. Lowry Nelson, *The Mormon Village: A Study in Social Origin* (Provo: Brigham Young University, Study No. 3, 1930); Bertha M. H. Shambaugh, *Amana: The Community of True Inspiration* (Des Moines: Iowa State Historical Society, 1908); Walter M. Kollmorgen, *Culture of a Contemporary Rural Community: The Old Order Amish of Lancaster County, Pennsylvania* (Washington: U.S. Department of Agriculture, Bureau of Agricultural Economics, Rural Life Study 4, 1942); L. E. Deets, "Data on Utopia," *Sociology* (New York: Hunter College, Dec., 1940), Vol. III; L. E. Deets, *The Hutterites: A Study in Social Cohesion* (New York: Hunter

College, 1939); and E. F. Row, *Communist and Cooperative Colonies* (New York: T. Y. Crowell Co., 1930).

23. Taylor, *op. cit.,* p. 30 ff.

24. Carl P. Heisig and Marion Clawson, *Migration and Settlement on the Pacific Coast: New Farms on New Land* (Washington: U.S. Department of Agriculture, Bureau of Agricultural Economics, Oregon Agricultural Experiment Station and Farm Security Administration, Report No. 4, 1941), pp. 86–8.

25. Ronald L. Mighell, *American Agriculture: Its Structure and Place in the Economy* (New York: John Wiley and Sons, Inc., 1955), p. 149.

26. E. A. Wilson, *Off-Farm Residence of Families of Farm and Ranch Operators* (Montana Agricultural Experiment Station Bulletin 530, 1957).

27. Jerome D. Fellman, "Some Agricultural Consequences of the New Urban Explosion," *Modern Land Policy, op. cit.,* pp. 157–62; Erling D. Solberg, "Zoning to Protect Agriculture," *Soil Conservation,* 26 (Nov., 1960), 76–8.

SELECTED READINGS

Bertrand, Alvin L., and Floyd L. Corty (eds.). *Rural Land Tenure in the United States.* Baton Rouge: Louisiana State University Press, 1962.
   In this study of land tenure the perspectives of sociology and economics are integrated. Part 4 which deals with the impact of change on tenure is of particular interest.

Harris, Marshall. *Origin of the Land Tenure System in the United States.* Ames: Iowa State College Press, 1953.
   Detailed attention is focused on the land tenure system prior to the establishment of the national government.

Heisig, Carl P., and Marion Clawson. *Migration and Settlement on the Pacific Coast: New Farms on New Land.* Washington: U.S. Department of Agriculture, Bureau of Agricultural Economics, Oregon Agricultural Experiment Station and Farm Security Administration, Report No. 4, 1941.
   A report of settlement on a new irrigation land development.

Sakolski, Aaron M. *Land Tenure and Land Taxation in America.* New York: Robert Schalkenbach Foundation, 1957.
   This monograph provides a comprehensive treatment of land ownership from its European background through land reform in the United States.

Taylor, Carl C., *et al. Columbia Basin: Patterns of Rural Settlement,* Problem 10. Washington: U.S. Department of Interior, Bureau of Reclamation, 1947.
   The main purpose of this study was to determine the social and economic advantages and disadvantages in farm layout and farm work resulting from the concentration of residents in small communities.

Wilson E. A. *Off-Farm Residence of Families of Farm and Ranch Operators.* Montana Agricultural Experiment Station Bulletin 530, 1957.
   The report of an empirical study designed to determine the extent of migration of farm families from farm to town residence while they continued to operate farms, and also to discover the major reasons for this migration.

9 GOVERNMENT AGRICULTURAL PROGRAMS: A NATIONAL SUCCESS STORY

Government's roles in agriculture have had a substantial impact upon food and fiber production in the United States. Farm production usually has been a matter of government concern, policies, and programs. As early as 1796, George Washington suggested that a national agricultural agency be established. John Quincy Adams gave governmental support to agriculture when he directed overseas naval officers to send seeds and improved breeds of animals to the United States. In 1836, Patent Commissioner Ellsworth used his own initiative and his office facilities to distribute seeds obtained from abroad. Three years later, Congress made its first appropriation for agriculture, giving a total of $1,000 to the Patent Office for collecting agricultural statistics, conducting agricultural investigations, and distributing seeds. All three of these programs were soon advanced, and by 1854 a chemist, botanist, and entomologist were employed.[1] Two years later a small plot of ground was obtained and used for experimental purposes.

Yet, like most situations involving benevolent aid, the government's programs and its financial assistance to agriculture brought with them alliance and interaction. This prevented the establishment of a boundary maintenance system for agriculture. Governmental concern and intervention at an early date had pervaded agricultural organization to the extent that agriculture was denied the character of an independent organization. Boundary maintenance for agriculture, as for other elements in society, is never complete. In order to contribute to an ongoing society, agriculture

182

cannot exist in a vacuum. The food and fiber needs of the country prevent agriculture from becoming a separate and independent segment of society.

There have been many arguments and counterarguments concerning governmental support of agriculture. Some persons have opposed any government assistance, while others have maintained that agriculture should be represented by a special bureau. The United States Agricultural Society (nongovernmental) assumed leadership in calling for a U.S. Department of Agriculture ten years prior to its establishment. The reasons given for the proposed department, though lacking vision in terms of the ultimate course of agriculture, were quite practical for the short-run development of food and fiber production. The eventual result proved to be record quantity and quality of food and fiber production. Government's substantial contribution to overabundance in food and fiber production is also a national success story.

U.S.D.A.: GOVERNMENT'S FORMAL DEBUT INTO AGRICULTURE

The work of the United States Agricultural Society and the pledges of the Republican Party for agrarian reform in 1860 set the stage for the establishment of the new department. In 1862, Lincoln signed a bill creating the U.S. Department of Agriculture. From 1862 to 1889 it was headed by commissioners responsible to the President. In 1889, the U.S. Department of Agriculture was promoted to cabinet status, and its chief administrator since has been given the title Secretary of Agriculture.

The 1862 law provided the basic authority for the department. Its scope was broad and allowed for the acquisition and dissemination of information concerning all aspects of agriculture. The U.S.D.A. was charged with responsibility for procuring, propagating, and distributing new and valuable seeds and plants. It was to preserve all information concerning agriculture contained in publications and reports of all practical scientific experiments. It was also to accumulate statistics concerning food and fiber production and make them available to general use.

The initial work of organizing the U.S. Department of Agriculture was the responsibility of Commissioner Isaac Newton. Newton was chief of the Section of Agriculture in the Patent Office when the U.S. Department of Agriculture was established. He was appointed the first Commissioner of Agriculture and given control of the new department's property in the Patent Office.

Organization proceeded slowly in the beginning, but in time the department's various properties were brought under its own control. Under the new commissioner, a departmental chemist was appointed, as was a superintendent to direct the activities of an experimental garden. In 1863 further expansion brought the appointment of a statistician and an entomologist. Crop conditions were reported in a newly founded monthly publication, and the study of climate and weather conditions was advanced.[2]

Newton's organization of the department was neither farsighted nor dynamic. The demands made on it were more political than in the farmers' interests. Gentleman farmers, who had been instrumental in promoting the department's establishment, were more concerned with specialized scientific developments than with practical programs for agriculture.[3] In spite of its precarious beginnings, however, the U.S. Department of Agriculture became an important scientific research agency.

The department has grown by vast proportions. In 1937, peak employment was attained, with over 100,000 workers. By 1961 the U.S.D.A. employed over 80,000 workers. Nearly 12,000 of the department's employees worked in Washington, D.C., while the others were located in every state and territory of the nation as well as in many foreign cities.

Contemporary organization of the U.S.D.A. From the point of view of its social organization, the functions of the U.S.D.A. may be summarized under the headings of research, education, and regulation, although in the course of its operations a great number of more specific purposes become evident. Nevertheless, changes are the quintessence of its goals, which are generated by its many specific subdivisions.

The organization of the U.S. Department of Agriculture is presented in Fig. 18. The Secretary is the chief administrator. Legal advice and assistance in the enforcement programs are provided by the Office of the General Counsel. Administrative offices organize and implement the department's records, paper work, and other administrative duties. The Agricultural Research Service coordinates the research activities, conducts research concerning production and utilization, and administers grants of federal funds for research in the state experiment stations. The principal educational unit is the Federal Extension Service, which coordinates the educational activities of the department. It also works in cooperation with state extension services, county agents, home demonstration agents, 4-H Club agents, and others. The Office of Information is an educational and communication service providing reports through the

FIGURE 18. HOW U.S.D.A. IS ORGANIZED

Secretary

Under Secretary

Staff Assistants

Office of the General Counsel

Departmental Administration
  Administrative Assistant Secretary
    Administrative Management, Office of
    Budget and Finance, Office of
    Hearing Examiners, Office of
    Information, Office of
    Library
    Personnel, Office of
    Plant and Operations, Office of

Federal-States Relations
  Assistant Secretary
    Agricultural Research Service
    Cooperative State Experiment Station Service
    Farmer Cooperative Service
    Federal Extension Service
    Forest Service
    Soil Conservation Service

Marketing and Foreign Agriculture
  Assistant Secretary
    Agricultural Marketing Service
    Commodity Exchange Authority
    Foreign Agricultural Service

Agricultural Stabilization
  Assistant Secretary
    Agricultural Stabilization and Conservation Service
    Commodity Credit Corporation
    Federal Crop Insurance Corporation

Agricultural Economics
  Director
    Economic Research Service
    Statistical Reporting Service

Agricultural Credit Services
  Director
    Farmers Home Administration
    Office of Rural Areas Development
    Rural Electrification Administration

press, radio, and television. It is concerned with the printing and distribution of the departmental publications, the provision of motion picture services, and the arrangement of exhibitions. The U.S.D.A. Library is an important adjunct to the educational enterprise of the department. It collects and organizes the literature of agriculture and related sciences from the world over. It disseminates information through department publications, for example through bibliographies and indexes, reference service, loans of publications, and microfilms, and often engages in exchange programs with foreign countries.

The major policy making agencies of the department are found in the Agricultural Conservation Program Service, Forest Service, and Soil Conservation Service. Regulatory programs are primarily prepared by the Commodity Stabilization Service, which has directed acreage allotments, marketing quotas, soil bank programs, and price support systems. The Agricultural Research Service directs the meat inspection control program. More specific types of control are directly related to other divisions.

TYPES OF AGENCIES

Government agencies may be classified into three types, namely, grant-in-aid, line action, and loan. Grant-in-aid agencies have gained general public approval. In this type of organization the federal government makes a grant of money to state or local units of government. Frequently, it is the practice for the federal funds to be supplemented or matched by funds appropriated at the state or local level. Federal funds are typically granted with specifications indicating the way the money should be spent, and the government sends employees to inspect the operations for which this money is utilized. Beyond the point of the original specifications and the periodic inspections, the federal government generally exercises no direct control over local authorities in the expenditure of such monies.

The Agriculture Extension Service is a grant-in-aid type of organization. In this case the federal government makes annual appropriations to the local state extension services. Local governments, often both state and county, contribute matching funds. This means that the salaries of persons employed in the county agent's office are supported by federal, state, and local money. In such an organization, county agents must satisfy multiple bosses, the local people, and the director of the state extension service. Neither the county agent nor the state director are directly accountable to the federal government.

Agricultural experiment stations provide another example of grant-in-aid organization. Annual appropriations are distributed through the Office of Experiment Stations, which is part of the U.S. Department of Agriculture's Research Service. Additional funds are appropriated for state experiment stations by local government, and in some cases from nongovernmental agencies and private parties. Aside from the federal funds, the experiment stations are administratively state agencies. State directors are their top administrators.

Many U.S. Department of Agriculture agencies are of the line action type. Authority extends from the federal government, with the U.S.D.A. as its agent, in cooperation with state and county officials, to the individual farmer. Local representatives of such agencies are federal employees. Funds for their salaries and expenses are appropriated by the federal government. The Soil Conservation Service, Forest Service, Agricultural Stabilization and Conservation Service, and Farmers Home Administration are examples of line action organizations.

In line action agencies, for example the Soil Conservation Service, the chief administrator works under the Secretary of Agriculture. There are state organizations which are headed by state soil conservationists. These individuals are responsible to the federal office in the U.S. Department of Agriculture. Typically, the work of the state office is divided into a series of areas, each of which is subordinate to a county soil conservationist. State and county conservationists direct conservation planning of farmers. Authority is communicated from Washington down to the local county offices. In the case of the Soil Conservation Service, a local three-man board of trustees presides. These are farmers who usually meet each month with local officials, and together constitute a local policy-making body. From the point of view of social organization, this so-called local policy-making group functions as a buffer, interpreting policies to the local community and supervising their implementation on behalf of the local people.

Line organization is exemplified by the Farm Credit Administration and the Rural Electrification Administration. This type of federal organization makes loans at relatively low interest rates to state and local organizations. Loans are to farm cooperatives, or, in the case of rural electrification, to local community cooperatives or small businesses which provide or agree to provide electric and telephone services.

PUBLIC ATTITUDE TOWARD AGRICULTURAL AGENCIES

In spite of the information released by agricultural news services, the public remains relatively uninformed concerning government programs for agriculture. In urbanized society, technology has made possible vast communication accomplishments. Mail service, radio, telephone, television, and the press bring the news to the people throughout the land. But the people do not, in return, respond to all the mass media. Among the restrictive aspects of the development of urbanized social organization is man's limited capacity to assimilate a complex amount of culture. Success has been attained in presenting the masses of the population with diverse cultural stimuli—from headlines reporting catastrophes, war, peaceful use of atomic energy, and exploration of outer space to the scientific study of fish diets for mink. Despite the great amount of news which is disseminated daily, it has been found that farmers and others throughout the society often do not absorb enough information to develop informed opinions.[4] Frequent exposure to new information is required before it is used in the formation of opinions and actions based upon them. In a New York study it was found that only half of 1,500 farmers knew about the Farmers Home Administration. Four out of ten farm operators in counties without soil conservation believed they had con- servation districts. Many farmers in counties with soil conservation dis- tricts had no knowledge of them. Similarly, in Ohio it was found that only a third of a sample of farmers knew there was no direct connection between the Farm Bureau and the Extension Service. Only 68 per cent of the Ohio farmers in the sample understood the direct connection be- tween the 4-H Clubs and the Extension Service.[5]

Evidence exists which suggests that farmers' attitudes are becoming more favorable toward government agencies in agriculture. The rate of acceptance of new ideas which lead to increased production and efficiency has been accelerated.[6] Soil conservation programs and the Agricultural Extension Service programs are both coming to be more readily accepted by farmers.[7]

LAND-GRANT COLLEGES *

Throughout the first half of the nineteenth century, social forces were emerging which supported a new type of free school education. During the second quarter of the nineteenth century, the American lyceum movement gained rapid acceptance. Along with the lectures and interest in popular subjects there was a growing demand for more rigorous teach- ing of science. The older colleges were accused of being oriented more to curriculums of earlier centuries than to contemporary subjects. In 1824, Steven Van Rensselaer founded an institute in Troy, New York, which was dedicated to articulating science in terms of the common pur- poses of life. The institute also provided the sons and daughters of farmers and mechanics with instruction in chemistry, philosophy, agriculture, do-

---

* See Chapter 19 for the influence of land-grand colleges upon rural life.

mestic economy, and manufacturing.[8] In 1859 the Sheffield Institute was established at Yale. The movement to science education was under way. Agriculture science was a systematic part of this new educational trend.

The Gardiner Lyceum was the first school primarily devoted to agriculture. It was establshed in 1823 and lasted barely a decade. In 1837 the University of Michigan was established for the purpose of teaching practical farming and agriculture. The decade 1840 to 1850 was characterized by a general proliferation of schools oriented toward agriculture. In spite of this development of schools, popular support from rank and file farmers was conspicuously absent. When they did acknowledge the development, it was more with antagonism than praise. Such passivity or antagonistic interest on the part of farmers was typical of their attitude toward the new developments which have come strategically to influence the course of the food and fiber system in the nation.

Schools, like other developments in agriculture, were little deterred by lack of interest among farmers and were espoused by articulate citizens of the time. The ultimate drive for the establishment of the land-grant colleges was beset with difficulties. There was resentment, trial and error, and failure up to 1862 when Lincoln signed the Morrill Act establishing the land-grant colleges. Even passage of the act was not heralded as of extraordinary importance. The significance of the uniquely American land-grant colleges and universities, however, is not to be overlooked. These schools are an integral part of the government's agricultural program designed to teach agriculture. Yet, from their very inception they were not exclusively agricultural schools. They were charged with the responsibility of teaching general science, classical studies, and military tactics, as well as agriculture and the mechanical arts.[9] Their contribution to the American story of abundant agricultural production constitutes a chapter in itself.

AGRICULTURAL RESEARCH SERVICE

The Research Service of the U.S. Department of Agriculture is the principal agency providing basic practical research at the national and regional level in agriculture. Complementary research is also carried out by the Farm Cooperative Service, Forest Service, Agricultural Marketing Service, and Foreign Agricultural Service. Historically, the Agriculture Research Service has been oriented toward technical work in the area of food and fiber growth and production. In more recent years, the programs of research have been greatly expanded into the areas of agricultural economics and marketing. Most of the private and industrially supported research in agribusiness has been largely oriented to farm suppliers, manufacturers of machinery and other consumption commodities, and to farm product processors and distributors.

The department's major areas of research are: agricultural organization, land utilization, home economics, farm product marketing, and forestry. The first three of these research programs have been under the administrative jurisdiction of the Agricultural Research Service. There are deputy administrators for farm and utilization research and a director for home economics research. The Agricultural Marketing Service designs and supervises most of the projects related to marketing. The Farmer Cooperative Service also engages in marketing research in those specialized areas that involve co-ops. Research concerning foreign markets is conducted by the Foreign Agricultural Service. All phases of research concerning forestry production, protection, utilization, and marketing are administered by the Forest Service.

The department's research, regardless of the area where it is ultimately conducted, is coordinated through the Agricultural Research Service. Coordination involves examination of all ongoing research activities, review of all proposed projects, approval of new projects, and assistance in planning projects. Research development is supported by the Agricultural Research Policy Committee, Commodity Committees, Agricultural Research Council, and other special bodies which provide systematic review and suggest areas where research is needed.

The Agricultural Research Policy Committee has functioned since 1946. Its members guide the department's research efforts into the areas of most immediate value. Decisions made by the committee are often based on shifts in the social structure. For example, changes in public consumption practices alter market demands for products from some of the older so-called staples to an increased consumption of fruits, vegetables, meats, and milk. Accordingly, new research is demanded concerning these products, their transportation, handling, processing, and distribution. The Agricultural Research Policy Committee has met regularly to discuss shifts in the structure of food and fiber production and consumption, and to make recommendations for new research directions on the basis of their findings.

In recent years the policy committee has called for more emphasis on both basic and applied research. Areas of emphasis have included: one, new industrial uses for agricultural products; two, more efficient marketing techniques; three, expansion of both foreign and domestic markets; four, systematic measures of product quality and the improvement of maintenance of high quality; five, more systematic use of food to contribute to better health; six, mechanisms for achieving equilibrium in production and in markets; and seven, the acquisition of more primary information to be utilized in the development of agricultural policies.[10] Several of these new research directions could lead to the expansion of the department's research program to include farm supplying and farm product processing, the other major components of agribusiness. Aims two, four, six, and seven suggest new research horizons bordering on the area of agribusiness.

Commodity and functional advisory committees. The 25 commodity and functional advisory committees are composed of representatives selected from groups that utilize the findings of the department's research. These individuals are knowledgeable in specific problem areas and use their intensive experience to evaluate ongoing research programs, suggest areas where new research would be profitable, recommend priorities of research projects, and acquaint themselves with the total research operations of the department in order to develop better public understanding of it. Their special committees function in the areas of citrus and subtropical plants, cotton, dairy, deciduous fruits and tree nuts, economics, farm equipment and structures, feed and forage, food distribution, food and nutrition, forest, grain, home economics, livestock, oilseeds and peanuts, potatoes, poultry, refrigerated and frozen products, rice, seeds, sheep and wool, soil, water and fertilizers, tobacco, transportation, and vegetables.[11] Their policy planning is supported by departmental members who are specialists in those areas. The departmental personnel assist in preparations for advisory committee meetings and help to carry out recommendations made there.

Finally, the Agricultural Research Council is concerned with those policies that affect all areas of the department's research. It is composed of department personnel who are directly responsible for the experiment stations, the farm research program, utilization research, home economics, forestry, and other areas.

The project system. Federally supported agricultural research, as well as state experiment station research, has been organized into projects. This system provides for uniformity in the outline of research proposals, the approval of research design, and the organization of progress reports. It eliminates duplication of research effort, and allows for maximum effectiveness in the review of research progress and the report of findings. Project statements are utilized by departments doing related types of work, in order to facilitate consolidated efforts. They are also used by subject matter specialists in the state experiment station divisions, and they are reviewed by the secretaries of the research advisory committees.

The department tries to attract the most capable scientists for research work, to provide them considerable freedom and facilities for their work, and at the same time to coordinate their activities both in terms of teamwork and the department's total research program.

Research facilities in the form of laboratories, equipment, and physical housing are centralized or decentralized in terms of requirements related to climate, soil, plants, animals, and other considerations. A major agricultural research center at Beltsville, Maryland, is primarily designed for basic research and research involving interdisciplinary programs. Nearly 700 of the department's research scientists are located at the Beltsville Center, over 600 others in Washington offices. More than 3,000 of the department's research scientists are located at some 300 research centers in all the states across the nation (see Fig. 19).[12]

Demand for research information is great and continues to increase. The department's dissemination of findings is closely associated with the adult education and extension program and with college and high school agricultural training programs. The research findings are published in technical and popular bulletins, in leaflets and circulars, in farm and daily papers, and reported by radio and television.

AGRICULTURAL EXPERIMENT STATIONS

In 1887, 25 years after the U.S. Department of Agriculture was established, the Hatch Act was passed. This legislation established the basis for federal and state cooperation in support of agricultural research at the state experiment stations.

State experimental farms prior to federal support. Requests for experimental farms in several states were repeatedly made from the 1840's until the passage of the Hatch Act. This was part of the general movement which led to the U.S. Department of Agriculture and the land-grant colleges. State geological and agricultural surveys were progressing, and

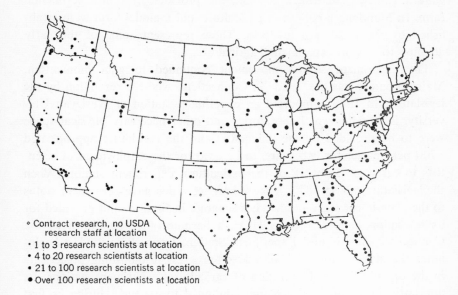

Contract research, no USDA research staff at location
· 1 to 3 research scientists at location
· 4 to 20 research scientists at location
· 21 to 100 research scientists at location
● Over 100 research scientists at location

FIGURE 19. LOCATIONS OF U.S. DEPARTMENT OF AGRICULTURE
RESEARCH, 1958

Source: *The Research Program of the U.S.D.A.* (Washington, D.C.: U.S.D.A, Agricultural Research Service, Miscellaneous Publication 779, 1958), pp. 44–45.

their success led the allies of agriculture to request farms and laboratories in order to carry out systematic research. Requests were fostered by publications in which the application of science to agriculture was suggested.

European research attracted the attention of American students and agriculturists, and encouraged them in their drive to establish similar investigations in this country.[13] Outstanding early work in Europe includes Liebig's *Chemistry and Its Applications to Agriculture and Physiology* (1840) and Boussingault's *Économie rurale* (1844). In Moeckern, Saxony, an experimental farm was established in 1851.

Agitation for systematic agricultural investigation was strong in New York. The New York State Agricultural Society encouraged the establishment of agricultural colleges. By 1841 the society was receiving state appropriations for some of its own work, including the distribution of premium money to county agricultural societies and the publication of its transactions as documents of the New York Legislature.

The California Constitution of 1849 provided support for agriculture. By 1854 the California State Agricultural Society was incorporated and authorized to establish a model experimental farm. The Michigan Agricultural College, established in 1855, was provided with an experimental farm. In Maryland a college of agriculture and a model farm were established by the legislature in 1856. These represent some of the early attempts to support experimental agriculture.

The experiment station movement continued to gain momentum. Major progress was next made in Connecticut, where a resolution by the legislature, in 1875, supported an experiment station at Wesleyan University, in Middletown. Laboratories and other necessary physical space were to be provided by the university, and the legislature appropriated $700 per quarter for two years, to be used for the employment of scientists to carry on the work of the agricultural experiment station. When the legislature met in 1877, it passed an act which gave permanent status to the experiment station, made it a separate institution, and provided for its relocation to New Haven. There it became officially known as the Connecticut Agricultural Experiment Station. From these modest beginnings the station enjoyed a decade of progress, establishing precedents in the organization and operation of agricultural experiment stations. Its appropriations, staff, and research continued to expand. During its first ten years, the station issued 93 bulletins, which were widely noted and acclaimed by the agricultural press.

Prior to federal assistance, agricultural experiment stations were supported by state money in California, North Carolina, New York, New Jersey, Ohio, Tennessee, Alabama, Wisconsin, Maine, Louisiana, Kentucky, and Vermont. Agricultural experiments were also carried out in other states which did not yet have experiment stations as such.

Active agitation for federally supported agricultural experiment stations continued to grow with the establishment of state stations. In 1871, a convention of friends of agricultural education was held in Chicago. This meeting was dominated by professors from land-grant colleges, who called attention to the much needed support for agricultural experiment stations. There was continued promotion of this proposal, bolstered by reports of the advances of the European experiment stations. In 1882, the Commissioner of Agriculture called a convention of agriculturists in Washington, D.C. One of the results of this convention was the drafting of a bill by Seman A. Knapp to establish national experiment stations in connection with the agricultural colleges. The bill was introduced into the House of Representatives in the same year. In 1883 it was formulated as the Holmes Bill, but it was not supported by the land-grant colleges since it appeared to put the experiment stations under the control of the

Commissioner of Agriculture. For several years Congress was presented with petitions for federal support of agricultural experiment stations. The National Grange joined in support for the experiment stations in 1885.[14]

In 1887, William H. Hatch, chairman of the House Committee on Agriculture, introduced a bill which provided federal aid for state agricultural experiment stations. Its passage marked an end to several years of heated discussion concerning the primary authority and the place of first responsibility of institutions receiving continual federal aid. The Hatch Act established a new normative pattern whereby federal monies were granted to institutions whose first responsibility was distinctly to the state and not to the federal government. This was of particular importance to social development, since it contributed further to the trend of fragmentation of the agricultural system into state and territorial units. The implementation of the federal government's subsidy to the state agricultural experiment stations was organized through the Office of Experiment Stations established in the U.S. Department of Agriculture.

Three-quarters of a century after the provision of federal support to the state agricultural experiment stations, approximately three-fifths of all public supported agricultural research was conducted by these stations. Over the years their funds have been supplied by both federal and private sources. By the 1960's the state agricultural experiment stations had annual appropriations in excess of $35,000,000. Approximately one-fourth of this amount was appropriated by federal grants.[15]

The magnitude of this program is illustrated by the more than 12,000 federally and state supported annual projects which are reviewed and recorded in the office of the State Experiment Station Division. In addition to state and federal research projects, a program of regional research has been established. Over 12 per cent of the funds available for research are devoted annually to about 200 regional projects. Such projects are cooperatively planned by representatives of the states in the region and by representatives of the U.S. Department of Agriculture.[16]

VOCATIONAL AGRICULTURE AND HOME ECONOMICS

By the end of the nineteenth century the demand for practical training in farming and homemaking included secondary education. Between 1890 and 1917 the focus of attention in the socialization of people for the pursuit of agriculture had shifted from land-grant colleges and agricultural experiment stations to what practical training was being offered in the secondary schools. In 1909, at a meeting of the Land-Grant Colleges Association, a paper was presented which reviewed the conditions of agricultural education in the secondary schools. The general conclusions were: one, agriculture, horticulture, and forestry should be a regular part of the secondary education; two, the basic educational curriculum should be continued and expanded to include the practical subjects needed by the people; three, the agricultural courses should be organized to conform to general state programs; four, the agriculture curriculum should not be exclusively vocational, but sufficiently expansive to prepare pupils for a progressive, broad-minded, intelligent life as farmers and homemakers.[17]

In 1917, federal support for vocational agriculture and home economics was provided by the Smith-Hughes Act. This involved a grant-in-aid program administered by the U.S. Office of Education in the U.S. Department of Health, Education, and Welfare. These vocational teachers are not directly related to the U.S. Department of Agriculture. Like other of their colleagues in the teaching profession, they are allowed a high degree of autonomy, regardless of federal support of their duties. They are, of course, given some directives by the supervisors of the Vocational Education Program.

Over 10,000 high schools across the country offer courses in vocational agriculture and home economics. The instruction is practical and involves supplementing classroom work with home projects. The Future Farmers of America and the Future Homemakers of America are student organizations associated with this curriculum. The abiding purpose of the vocational agriculture program has been to train high school boys to enter farming. The realization of this purpose has been greatly impeded by the limited and rapidly declining opportunities to enter profitable farming operations. In some cases the vocational agriculture programs are being shifted to prepare students for careers in agribusiness. Such shifts in purpose and orientation, however, have had only limited success.

AGRICULTURAL DEVELOPMENT AND STABILIZATION AGENCIES

Major development programs have covered a wide range of areas. They have included such agencies as the Federal Extension Service, Commodity Exchange Authority and the Foreign Agriculture Service, Federal Crop Insurance Programs, and Farm Home Administration. Indirectly, of course, one can view all of the government's agricultural programs in terms of their contributions to the development of the food and fiber system. These particular programs, however, are most specifically responsible for some aspect of food and fiber development and only peripherally for research activities.

Federal Extension Service. The national extension program has been an integral segment of the U.S. Department of Agriculture since 1914, the date of its establishment by the Smith-Lever Act. The Federal Extension Service has been charged with responsibility for leadership in all of the department's education programs. This service is often referred to as the cooperative extension work because of its interactional alignment with the department, the land-grant colleges, and the county governments. National, state and county governments all share the financing of this program. Extension agents often work directly with local people in all aspects of their daily living from 4-H Clubs to marketing. Practically all of the nation's counties have extension personnel located in their area. The program of extension work has been broadened in recent years to include rural nonfarm people, and to some extent urban people, in its scope of services. In addition to serving the nation's citizens, the Agricultural Extension Service, in cooperation with the Foreign Agricultural Services, provides training programs for agricultural visitors from other nations.[18]

Commodity Exchange Authority. The Commodity Exchange Authority has existed since 1936. Unlike the cooperative extension program which serves a great mass of people, the commodity exchange program is highly specific. Its primary purpose is developmental: to maintain fair and competitive pricing. It also functions to prevent the spreading of false market and crop information, to protect market users, to provide market privileges to cooperative associations, and to provide information to the public concerning trade on the contract markets. The Authority supervises trading on sixteen commodity exchange contract markets.[19] It is highly directive and regulatory, and provides a formal structure for the marketing of a large number of products.

Foreign Agricultural Service. The U.S. Department of Agriculture's continued interest in market operations and development has been expressed by the more recent establishment (1954) of the Foreign Agricultural Service. Among the major functions of this service is the development of foreign markets for American food and fiber products. The foreign market is advanced by continually appraising foreign agricultural marketing opportunities and through the improvement of international trade conditions. In addition to its marketing interests, the Foreign Agricultural Service is concerned with the compilation of statistics and other information needed by American farmers, business, government, and other interested parties. The Service also assists in programs for the dissemination of technical assistance and the training of foreign visitors who come to the United States.[20]

Federal Crop Insurance Corporation. Crop insurance is among the most revealing programs of urbanized social organization in agriculture. In addition to manipulating the production of plants and animals, the conditions of marketing, and the development of technology, the crop insurance program provides still another type of structure which greatly removes food and fiber production from a subsistence to a highly rational level. The concept of insurance, if broadly conceived, dates from the guild system of the late Middle Ages and possibly had strong precedents from still earlier eras. However, the application of such systems of social organization to food and fiber production, which historically has been viewed as closely related to things biological and physical, provides a valid index of the development of ideology which leads man to manipulate not only his own social relationships but his ecological relationships as well.

In 1938 the Federal Crop Insurance Act was passed. The purpose of the program was to provide financial strength and security for the farmers' expenditure of money in the production of crops against losses still beyond their control, namely, weather, insects, and disease. As currently organized, this program does not insure profit or cover losses due to neglect. It has set maximum limits of coverage at the level of cost of the particular crop production in a given area.

Since 1949, the number of counties covered by all-risk crop investment insurance has increased to about one-third of all agricultural counties. The corporation insures wheat, cotton, tobacco, corn, flax, dry eatable beans, soy beans, barley, grain sorghums, oats, rye, rice, citrus fruit, and peaches, and offers a combined crop protection plan. The insurance is organized so that premiums paid by farmers will cover the losses of those who suffer crop failure. The program is thus designed to operate on a sound actuarial basis. Administrative costs of the program have been covered by annual governmental appropriations, but in 1956 it was provided that some of the payment for adjusters and some other administrative costs should come from premium income. The rates of premium vary from county to county, depending on local conditions. Policy holders who have experienced no loss over a consecutive three-year period receive insurance discounts.[21]

Farmers Home Administration. In 1946 the Farmers Home Administration Act added another dimension to governmental programs in agriculture. The purpose of the program is to provide credit for some types of farmers unable to procure financing through other agencies at reasonable rates. Loans are made through local Farmers Home Administration offices, which are generally located in county seats. A local committee composed of two farmers and one other local citizen typically determines the applicant's eligibility. After a loan is made, the committee reviews the borrower's progress. This type of loan includes money for the purchase of livestock, equipment, feed, seed, and fertilizer. Another type of loan is designed to facilitate entering farming or expanding farm operations. These loans are intended for the purchase or expansion of family type farms and cannot be granted for the acquisition of farms that have a value greater than the average economically efficient farm in the county. The loan program is designed so that the money can be repaid in forty years.

This loan program offers a highly structured norm supporting family farms or small entrepreneurial units. Throughout other areas of the government's agricultural programs, efforts have been made to promote agriculture in ways which supersede the family farm type of operation. It is a curious ambiguity, at least from one perspective, to have government programs support contradictory ends.

Other phases of the work of the Farmers Home Administration are to provide loans to assist farmers in improving soil conservation, water development, and other land use programs. The program is also extended to provide financing for the construction and repair of farm residences and other primary farm buildings. Specific uses of this phase of the program include the provision of bathrooms, utility rooms, modernization of kitchens, and other forms of material development.[22]

Agricultural stabilization programs. Two principal stabilization and regulatory programs are the Commodity Credit Corporation, established in 1933, and the Commodity Stabilization Service, established in 1953. The Commodity Credit Corporation was brought under the jurisdiction of the U.S. Department of Agriculture in 1939. It is managed by a board of directors with the approval of the Secretary of Agriculture. Price support programs for certain products come under its jurisdiction.

Food and fiber items acquired through the program are utilized in the domestic and export sales market, transferred to other government agencies, and specific donations are made to welfare use. This program purchases and maintains granaries for the storage of products, makes loans for the construction or expansion of farm storage units, and in other specific ways serves the price support programs.

The Commodity Stabilization Service is responsible for acreage allotments and marketing quotas; a soil bank; price supports; disposal through domestic and foreign sales; barter, transfer, and donation of government-owned surplus farm products; the International Wheat Agreement Act; storage, shipping, and related service activities; administration of the Shipper Act; and assigned mobilization planning.[23] The same personnel and facilities are utilized by both the Commodity Stabilization Service and the Commodity Credit Corporation.

LAND AGENCIES

The principal rural land agencies are the Forest Service, established in 1905, and the Soil Conservation Service, established in 1935. The Forest Service administers over 150 national forests and some related areas which collectively account for nearly one-third of the nation's land area. The program has a dual purpose of conservation and production. It is concerned with the growing and harvesting of timber. The scientific regulation of cattle grazing is provided on the forest service lands, and watersheds are managed to control stream flow and reduce soil erosion. Research and recreational aspects of the Forest Service are discussed in Chapter 7.

The Soil Conservation Service is responsible for permanent national soil and water conservation programs. Much of the program is carried out in the form of specific assistance to farmers and ranchers through local soil conservation districts. Technicians and specialists are employed to assist local landowners in making acre-by-acre soil surveys. After the survey, the specialist and the landowner design a conservation plan. The soil conservationist continues to use necessary technical guidance in making the plan operative; finally, he continues to consult with the farm owner to keep the plan in operation and to modify it as changes become necessary.

SUMMARY

The success of the government's agricultural programs is demonstrated by the abundance of food and clothing for the population. This accomplishment is notable, notwithstanding the existence of slums and the hunger that still prevails in certain areas.[24] Record outputs in food and fiber production continually headline the nation's agricultural story.

Some overtures for government participation in agriculture have been made ever since the founding of the nation, but the government's major movement into agricultural organization took place during the Civil War years. Both the U.S. Department of Agriculture and the land-grant colleges, established in 1862, have grown by gigantic proportions since that time. The U.S. Department of Agriculture's major contribution to this success has been in the area of research. Findings have been disseminated through its adult education program, land-grant colleges, and vocational agriculture programs. A new dimension was added to the federal programs in the 1930's by the organization of regulatory agencies for development and stabilization of agricultural production.

The success of the government's agricultural programs has been great. It rests on two major developments: first, the supply of food and fiber which now reaches levels of overproduction; second, the government's big business in agriculture, which has only lately been recognized. This second aspect certainly was not overtly part of the government's original planning in agriculture. Much of the original planning and several aspects of the current program are oriented to small independent farm units. But the development of government programs has inadvertently been an integral part of urbanized social organization. Though not recognized in the latter half of the nineteenth century, centralized research and the government's regulatory support of agriculture have been instrumental in breaking down the boundaries around the social organization of agriculture. The federal program has continued to be a social force for integration of all phases of agriculture. More recently, it has been faced with the problem of coordinating farm supply with product processing and distribution. The combination of these with farming is now viewed as agribusiness. Its notorious success in providing adequate food and fiber is a dubious victory for the American family farm. The very system of benevolent systematic planning supported by the government has overwhelmed the farming enterprise and, in the social milieu of urbanized society, brought it close to a point of dissolution. The boundaries between the farm supplier, the farm grower-producer, and the farm product processor and distributor are vanishing. The system of abundant food and fiber production in mass ubanized society has led to big organization and agribusiness.

NOTES

1. Wayne D. Rasmussen, *Reading in the History of American Agriculture* (Urbana: University of Illinois Press, 1960), p. 105.

2. Charles H. Greathouse, *Historical Sketch of the U.S. Department of Agriculture: Its Objectives and Present Organization* (Washington: U.S. Department of Agriculture, 1907), pp. 9 ff; Alfred Charles True, *The History of Agricultural Experimentation and Research in the United States, 1607 to 1925* (Washington: U.S. Department of Agriculture, Miscellaneous Publication 251, 1937), pp. 41 ff.

3. T. Swann Harding, *Two Blades of Grass: A History of Scientific Development in the U.S. Department of Agriculture* (Norman: University of Oklahoma Press, 1947), pp. 23–4.

4. Edward O. Moe, *New York Farmers' Opinions on Agricultural Programs* (Cornell Agricultural Extension Bulletin 864, 1952); *Power To Produce: 1960 Yearbook of Agriculture* (Washington: U.S. Department of Agriculture, 1960), pp. 89–100.

5. Everett M. Rogers and Harold H. Capener, *The County Extension Agent and His Constituents* (Ohio Agricultural Experiment Station, Research Bulletin 858, 1960).

6. Moe, *op. cit.;* Horace Miner, *Culture and Agriculture: An Anthropological Study of a Corn Belt Community* (Ann Arbor: University of Michigan Press, 1949), p. 87.

7. Julian Prundeanu and Paul J. Zwerman, "An Evaluation of Some Economic Factors and Farmers' Attitudes That May Influence Acceptance of Soil Conservation Practices," *Journal of Farm Economics,* 40 (1958), 903–14; Everett M. Rogers and George M. Beal, *Reference Group Influences in the Adoption of Agricultural Technology* (Iowa Agricultural Experiment Station Mimeographed Bulletin, 1958).

8. Edward D. Eddy, Jr., *Colleges for Our Land and Time: The Land-Grant Idea in American Education* (New York: Harper and Brothers, 1957), p. 10.

9. Eddy, *op. cit.,* pp. 33–5.

10. *The Research Program of the USDA* (Washington: U.S.D.A. Miscellaneous Publication 779, 1958) p. 8.

11. *Ibid.,* p. 9.

12. *Ibid.,* p. 12.

13. True, *op. cit.,* p. 67.

14. *Ibid.,* pp. 120–23.

15. *The Budget of the United States Government for the Fiscal Year Ending June 30, 1963.* Appendix (Washington: U.S. Government Printing Office, 1962), p. 86.

16. *Ibid.*, pp. 3–4.

17. Rufus W. Stimson and Frank W. Lathrop, *History of Agricultural Education of Less Than College Grade in the United States* (Washington: U.S. Department of Health, Education and Welfare, Vocational Division Bulletin 217, Agricultural Series 55, 1954), pp. 5–7.

18. *United States Government Organization Manual for 1960 to 1961* (Washington: Office of the Federal Registrar, National Archives and Records Service, General Services Administration, June, 1960), p. 265.

19. *Ibid.*, p. 272.

20. *Loc. cit.*

21. *Ibid.*, p. 276.

22. *Ibid.*, p. 277.

23 *Ibid.*, p. 274.

24. Josué de Castro, *Geography of Hunger* (London: Victor Gollancz, Ltd., 1952).

SELECTED READINGS

Eddy, Edward D., Jr. *Colleges for Our Land and Time.* New York: Harper and Brothers, 1957.
   This comprehensive volume deals exclusively with one government-related program, namely, the land-grant colleges.

Harding, T. Swann. *Two Blades of Grass: A History of Scientific Development in the U.S. Department of Agriculture.* Norman: University of Oklahoma Press, 1947.
   A semipopular treatment of the history of scientific research in agriculture.

Moe, Edward O. *New York Farmer's Opinions on Agricultural Programs.* Cornell Agricultural Extension Bulletin 864, 1952.
   This study of 1,500 New York farmers indicated generally favorable opinions toward government agricultural agencies.

True, Alfred C. *The History of Agricultural Experimentation and Research in the United States, 1607 to 1925.* Washington: U.S. Department of Agriculture, Miscellaneous Publication 251, 1937.
   This history deals specifically with the U.S.D.A., state movements to establish agricultural research facilities, the Hatch Experiment Station Act, and increased federal aid to agricultural research.

10 AGRIBUSINESS

American food and fiber production has undergone a metamorphosis from agricultural self-sufficiency to agribusiness. This dramatic change represents the American response to the challenge of feeding its people.

Every society is faced with the problem of providing and distributing food to its members. Much of the history of mankind is an account of this struggle. American society, along with very few other societies, has achieved overproduction in food and fiber. This achievement is remarkable but beset with difficulties. Small farms, low-income farms, price supports, and controversial policy programs all stand between the success of food production and the final victory of integrating the food and fiber system into the total urbanized society.

Ideology, land settlement patterns, and government programs stand out as particularly important among the many factors behind American food and fiber accomplishments. From colonial times to the present, Americans have adhered implicitly, and most often explicitly, to the ideology that nature is something to be studied systematically. Ideas of science have been widely accepted and implemented in the utilization of land for farming. From the late colonial period, and throughout virtually all of the national period, settlement on the land has been dispersed rather than nuclear. This is the most efficient system possible from the point of view of producing plants and animals. It places the farmer in immediate proximity to his work. Unlike the agricultural villages of most other parts of the world, dispersed settlement frees the farmer from the necessity of moving animals and equipment from his village residence to the fields and back again. During the colonial and early national period, the notion of efficiency was more often expressed in the form of competition with one's neighbors than an image of collective or societal accomplishment. The normative patterns which motivated early Americans to work for gold and silver plaques awarded by the Philadelphia Society for the Advancement of Science, and those normative patterns which motivate men in contemporary society to work for higher corn and wheat production per acre are basically the same. Only the elements of the situation have been changed; its competitive nature remains.

In recent years the dispersed form of land settlement has attracted study of both its social and economic characteristics. From the point of view of providing schools, churches, and social gathering places for the people of the agricultural community, the dispersed form of settlement is grossly inefficient. From an economic point of view, large-scale mechanization (begun a century ago) requires larger acreages if its utilization and efficiency are to be profitable. As agricultural mechanization moved forward, the small farm, unable to keep pace with new production rates and marketing needs, came increasingly to be considered a problematic aspect of the national economy. One of the primary reasons for the establishment of the U.S. Department of Agriculture was to provide assistance to small farmers in dealing with problems of production and marketing. Its major functions today have shifted to the conducting of scientific research and the dissemination of the findings.

The key development in farming which led to abundance of production has been the growth of organizations involving complex interrelationships with off-farm businesses. Food and fiber production has become more than a matter of farming. It has become agribusiness.

ORIGIN OF AGRIBUSINESS

Subsistence farming. From the founding of Jamestown throughout most of the eighteenth century, food and fiber production in the North American colonies was at a subsistence level. As late as 1790, less than 5 per cent of the new nation's population resided in towns and cities. Family farms dominated the way of life. Market production was an exception rather than the rule. The subsistence farmer produced goods for himself and his family with the assistance of the family members. His farm constituted a virtually closed economic and social unit.

Subsistence farming in Plymouth Colony in the 1620's involved the division of land into tillable portions of about twenty acres per family; additional land was to be used as a refuge or commons.[1] Animals were distributed so that there was one cow, two goats, and a larger number of swine for each group of six families. Hand cultivation of maize prevailed. The system was essentially the same as that used by the Indians except that the colonists used better hoes and replaced the labor of women with that of men. An area of ground was loosened by the hoe and several kernels were planted. Following the Indian pattern, a fish or two were deposited in the soil near the seed. Corn was planted four to six feet apart, and the intervening area was hoed to control the weeds. At a later date, when plows and animal power were introduced, corn was planted in rows and the area between them was cultivated to control weeds. Wheat was grown in New England, but mildew damaged the crop so severely that it was of little value. Rye was more durable and more widely used as a bread grain in the New England area throughout the colonial period. Fish and pork constituted the major portion of the meat diet. Sheep were kept but were constantly threatened by predatory animals.

Home industries provided the meager needs of furniture and clothing used by the colonists. Furniture was crudely fashioned from the abundance of available wood. Clothing was provided from homegrown wool and flax. Many agricultural tools—particularly the wooden parts of plows, harrows, hand tools, carts, and yokes—were made by the farm family during the winter months. There was need of some cash to procure items like salt, sugar, tea, coffee, iron, tin, and leather goods which were not available locally. In addition, there were some annual sums due the church and the commonwealth. Farmers made a few items for sale, such as shakes, barrel staves, hoops, treenails, wagon wheel spokes, bowls, and other wood articles. In some cases they were able to sell salt pork, smoked ham, and other meat, and occasionally apples, cider, and vinegar. When sleds were used on winter snows, the New England colonists often managed to trip to Boston, New Haven, or New York to sell any surpluses of the season.

The condition of subsistence farming varied somewhat in the South and in frontier areas. But wherever it was found it was characterized more as a way of existence than as a method of systematic farming. The primary goal among subsistence families was to provide those items necessary for their own living. Only secondarily, if at all, were they concerned with providing surpluses for market sales.

Agriculture. The shift from subsistence farming to systematic agriculture was gradual. The turning point was reached during the first part of the nineteenth century with the development of agricultural technology. The cast iron plow and the cotton gin both made their appearance before the end of the eighteenth century. During the nineteenth century, as agriculture moved westward, new developments in farm machinery were frequent. By the midpoint of the nineteenth century, the variety of farm implements included plows, harrows, planters, disks, stalk cutters, baling presses, feed grinders, cultivators, mowers, reapers, and threshers. Their use yielded quantities of food and fiber that far exceeded the farm family's requirements. Markets for agricultural products were growing, but they generally lagged behind production records. This created widespread unrest in farming. The Civil War was partly an outgrowth of the tumultuous shift from subsistence farming to systematic agriculture. The war itself was a factor which created a major market for farm products.

The concept of farming as a commercial enterprise was developing but on an uneven front. Some subsistence operations continued to exist. Nevertheless, those farmers who used the new machinery and who considered it advantageous were systematically developing the idea that food and fiber production is a basic function in the total society. Yet, as in the development of other occupational images, farmers could not by themselves promulgate the concept of agriculture as an occupation. Technological innovations in the processing and marketing of food and fiber products contributed to this new notion of the social role of farming. By the end of the eighteenth century and the early part of the nineteenth, the basic processes of mechanical production of textiles were established. These developments had the effect of further decentralizing the family subsistence farm. Weaving was removed from the home to factories. With the expansion of the textile market, manufactured cloth became available at lower prices for both city and farm consumption.

The mass processing and distribution of foods developed at a slower rate than those of the textile industry. The systematic development of agriculture was necessarily concomitant with the development of processing and distribution centers away from farms. Another major stimulus to these developments was the demand of an enlarging urban population which worked in occupations other than farming. A significant proportion of the increase in the urban population was due to the continual migration of rural people to towns and cities. The rural labor force which met the food demands of the urban population continued to diminish in size. In

1790 it is estimated that some 80 per cent of the labor force was required in farming; in 1820, 72 per cent; in 1860, 59 per cent, and in 1960, 6 per cent.

The concept of agriculture as a way of life and as a commercial enterprise has prevailed in most of American rural life for the past century and a half. The way of life aspect of agriculture, generally embodied in the notion of the family farm, has been at the same time the greatness and the major weakness of American farming. The commercial spirit of agriculture was never able to sever the umbilical cord, as it were, from the family experience of early subsistence days. The idealization of the family farm has held several million small rural land units to the place of diminishing returns in the twentieth century. In urbanized society no other major occupation or economic enterprise is similarly segmented into millions of units. This segmentation has come to be agriculture's undoing. Even with mass communication of science, technology, and marketing news, the ability of several million independent entrepreneurs to evaluate the condition of their market has yet to be demonstrated. Decision making in urbanized society is achieved through the combined reports of specialists or experts rather than by generalists. The man engaged in agriculture on a small entrepreneurial unit is a generalist.* The staff in the U.S. Department of Agriculture and its related state branches has been developed to provide him with at least part of the specialized information which he must have at his disposal.

Major industries produce the supplies and equipment needed for the operation of the contemporary farm. Other related industries process and distribute the food and fiber produced on the land. These organizational units (the U.S.D.A., the farm suppliers, and the processors-distributors) are organized more centrally than agriculture itself and are, consequently, better equipped to utilize the services and information of specialists. The great number of generalist farmers are ill-prepared to plan their operations as a major industry or occupation in such a way as to bargain successfully with the organized segments of society which are related to their enterprise. In fact, large numbers of decentralized and generalist farmers often have been used as a shock absorbing mechanism during major shifts in

---

* The farmer is a generalist even when 50 per cent or more of his sales are reported in a single commodity, which thereby causes his operation to be reported in the specialized categories. In management terms he is a generalist in that he still must plan his operation, review market conditions, be his own cost accountant, and perform other tasks for which industry would have individually trained personnel.

the socioeconomic organization of the society. Specifically, this is reflected in the low income of many farmers. Big businesses organized by specialists are often able to take advantage of the small, dispersed generalist farmers.

Agribusiness. Agriculture as a whole has failed to develop as a centralized or horizontally integrated economic unit. Yet many of its supplier and processor-distributor enterprises have been integrated horizontally and vertically. They are now prepared to take the last step in order to integrate the farm grower-producer aspect of food and fiber into their structure. This brings the food and fiber aspect of the society to a stage of development called agribusiness.[2]

The concept of agribusiness includes, by definition, the total food and fiber operation. There are three specific aspects of agribusiness: one, the manufacture of farm equipment and other agricultural supplies; two, farm grower-producer operations, and, three, storage, processing, and distribution of these commodities.

The word *agribusiness* was coined by John H. Davis and first presented in a public lecture in 1955. It grew out of a research program in agriculture and business that was planned initially at Harvard University in 1944. The original program faced a number of difficulties before it was finally launched in a modified form in 1952. It was intended that studies be conducted of the relationships between agriculture and industry with particular emphasis on the processes of decision making. Systematic thinkers who viewed urbanized society with a broad perspective had been aware of the interdependence between farming and manufacturing.[3] Yet the impact of management decisions on farm operations had never before been studied. The first major undertaking of the Harvard program was a description of the extent of the interrelationship between farming and manufacturing. The findings were summarized in terms of the concept agribusiness.

The roots of agribusiness have been developing for a century or more. They are part of the very concept of urbanized social organization. Viewed in this way, the total food and fiber operation constitutes but one part of the nation's greater economic institution. There is little or no social space in urbanized social organization for agriculture to continue its existence as a free-standing unit. The family farm is only a manifestation of the transition from ruralized to urbanized social organization.

The shift of agriculture to agribusiness has involved the development of whole new industries which relate to farm production. These include farm implement companies, meat processors, food canneries and freezers, and a variety of others. In some other cases, existing industries have been modified to provide specific commodities for farmers. This has been the case in rubber manufacturing, chemical and pharmaceutical production. Aspects of manufacturing and processing in farming have been extracted from the local independent farming units and centralized as major industries.

Even agribusiness is not destined to become a free-standing social institution. It has no centralized control, no president, and no board of directors. Its three major types of enterprises—supplying, growing, and processing—are each integral components of the nation's economy. Each of the components of agribusiness has experienced centralization into fewer and larger businesses. The food industry has experienced many mergers in recent years.[4] By mid-twentieth century many food and fiber companies were reported among the nation's 500 largest corporations.[5] Four meat packing firms controlled over 40 per cent of the nation's meat slaughtering, and eight flour milling businesses accounted for 40 per cent of the industry's operation.[6] Four per cent of the nation's food retailing stores controlled nearly half of the business.[7] Thirteen farm supplying enterprises were listed among the nation's 500 largest corporations.[8] It is reported in the Census of Manufacturers that over a quarter of all prepared animal feeds came from eight large companies, and that eight farm machinery producers controlled approximately 70 per cent of the dollar value of that industry.[9] In farming the large operations are growing rapidly. In this phase of agribusiness some 102,000 operators of large farms, out of a total of more than two million commercial farmers, accounted for more than 30 per cent of the farm products sold. Compared to big business in farm supplying and farm food processing, the big grower-producer operations are relatively small. Nevertheless, the trend toward bigness remains, and agribusiness constitutes a new social force leading toward an integration of the food and fiber operation into the national economy.

NATURE OF AGRIBUSINESS

Agribusiness is one of the major aspects of the national economy, both in terms of its volume of business and its essential contribution to food and clothing. It is complex and, in several respects, decentralized. Unfortunately, few data concerning agribusiness exist, and those which are available have been obtained with much difficulty. Such data are generally inadequate in the analysis of the great magnitude of agribusiness. Accordingly, most considerations of manufacturing and farming are still based on the spurious notion of a dichotomy between farming and business. This dichotomy is reflected in the distinct cabinet offices, Secretary of Commerce and Secretary of Agriculture, as well as in the separate legislative committees concerning these aspects of the economy. The secondary educational system continues to develop separate programs for vocational agriculture and vocational business training. Colleges separate business schools and institutes of agriculture. Trade and labor organizations also generally reflect this historical separation of farming and business.

Basic dimensions. In 1954, farmers purchased over $16,000,000,000 worth of manufactured supplies to operate their businesses. These supplies included the staple items of manufactured feeds, seeds, farm machinery and equipment, fertilizer, transportation, power, and a variety of lesser items. By 1960, purchases of the American farm plant had increased to approximately $17,000,000,000 annually.[10] Sale of farm products reached a magnitude of nearly $30,000,000,000 in 1954 and about $34,000,000,000 by 1960. Processor-distributors sold food and fiber products for nearly $70,000,000,000 in 1954 and nearly $80,000,000,000 in 1960. The difference between this sales volume and the consumer cost of some $93,000,000,000 in 1954 was attributed to wholesale and retail price margins and to such items as fish, synthetic fiber and imported foods, none of which come directly from American farm units.

The massive nature of agribusiness in the total national economy is illustrated by these consumer expenditures which constituted 40 per cent of the $236.5 billion total consumer expenditures in 1954. Food and fiber expenditures occupy a place only half as large in the national economy today as 150 years ago. Nevertheless, their share of the national economy continues to be of vast significance.

Agribusiness labor force. Agribusiness workers constitute a major proportion of the total United States Labor force. They were estimated at over 30 per cent of the total labor force in 1954. The number of agribusiness workers remained at about 24,000,000 people between 1947 and 1954, but the national labor force increased from about 60,000,000 people in 1947 to 64,000,000 in 1954. This resulted in a relative decrease

TABLE XIX. AGRIBUSINESS LABOR FORCE: 1947 AND 1954

	1947	1954	Per Cent Change
Farm suppliers	5,000,000	6,000,000	+20.0
Farm workers	10,000,000	8,000,000	−20.0
Processor-distributors	9,500,000	10,000,000	+5.3
Agribusiness labor force	24,500,000	24,000,000	−2.0

Source: John H. Davis and Ray A. Goldberg, *A Concept of Agribusiness* (Boston: Harvard Business School, Division of Research, 1957), p. 14.

in the proportion of agribusiness workers (see Table XIX). Farm supply workers increased from 5,000,000 to 6,000,000 between 1947 and 1954, or a 20 per cent rise. Farmers decreased in number from 10,000,000 to 8,000,000, a 20 per cent drop during the same period. Processor-distributors increased in number from 9,500,000 to 10,000,000, or a 5 per cent gain during the seven-year period. Within the agribusiness triaggregate, farm suppliers were 20 per cent of the total in 1947 and 25 per cent in 1954. Farm producer-growers constituted nearly 41 per cent of the total in 1947, or the largest single category in the triaggregate. In 1954 they had declined to 33 per cent, placing them in an intermediate position between farm suppliers and processor-distributors. In 1947 the processor-distributors constituted approximately 39 per cent of all agribusiness workers, and by 1954 they constituted nearly 42 per cent, or the largest single category of agribusiness workers. By 1954 this meant that two-thirds of the agribusiness workers were employed off the farm and only one-third were involved with classic farming operations.

Capital structure. A most important development has been the growth of the farm plant as a major market for manufactured and processed goods. In their historic subsistence operations the farm families produced practically all of their own fuel, power, and fertilizer. By the 1960's, farmers annually used 6,500,000 tons of finished steel, an amount greater than that used in a year's production of passenger cars. With increased understanding of scientific agriculture, farmers used 45,000,000 tons of chemicals in 1960, or about five times the amount used in the mid-1930's. Widespread use of tractors was accompanied by the use of 18,000,000 gallons of crude petroleum. No other single industry uses petroleum in such a large quantity. Rubber utilization has increased rapidly to

285,000,000 pounds. This was equal to the amount needed for the manufacture of 6,000,000 automobile tires. Electricity was utilized on more than 95 per cent of the nation's farms. The total consumption was 22,000,000 kilowatt hours, or enough to serve the cities of Chicago, Detroit, Baltimore, and Houston for a year.[11]

Organizational structure. It must be emphasized that agribusiness is decentralized into three component parts. There is no formal organizational structure which gives one part jurisdiction over the others, or which specifies the authority of the parts. Their interrelationships grow out of a free enterprise system rather than one of centralized governmental authority. By the late 1950's the farming aggregate had some 4,000,000 units. Approximately 60 per cent of these farms were extremely small and often ineffectual in their operations. They generally contributed less than 10 per cent of the nation's total marketed food and fiber products. At the other extreme there were nearly 150,000 large farms which produced well over one-fourth of the nation's marketed food and fiber. Many of the large farms were horizontally integrated and some of them vertically integrated. Yet, regardless of their specific type of organization, most of the large farms were still relatively small businesses in comparison to the nation's other corporate enterprises. It is estimated that about 20 per cent of farm commodities and farm supplies are handled through cooperatives at one stage or another in the production cycle. When one takes into consideration the aspects of processing and distributing, it is probable that less than 5 per cent of the agribusiness enterprise is vertically integrated into the nation's economic social institution.

In sharp contrast to farmer grower-producers, the farm supplier and processor-distributor aggregates are extensively integrated both horizontally and vertically. The major corporations engaged in manufacturing farm supplies and equipment, as well as those engaged in processing and distributing farm food and fiber, are well represented in that small category of the nation's 500 largest corporations. Extensive centralization and integration of the supplier and the processor-distributor aggregates is continuing. Expansion of factory preparation of foods reduces the work of women in the home and frees them for other roles in the labor force.

One of the important aspects of agribusiness organization is the shift in manpower from farm to off-farm jobs. These jobs are a direct outgrowth of research advances and technological development. Paralleling these developments has been the increased productivity of workers on the farm and the accompanying requirement for additional workers in the supplier and processor-distributor aggregates. A higher level of living for both farm and nonfarm people has been one of the major rewards of this specialization in agribusiness. Food commodities have been expanded in number so that the public can select from greater varieties. The quality of preserved food items has been improved greatly. Preservation of food has been extended. Marketing and distributing of food items has become national in scope. People are no longer dependent upon their local food suppliers for subsistence. Thus, the threat of famine has virtually been eliminated.

Food and fiber production has been increased, and technology has contributed to the improved quality of the products. Both natural and synthetic fibers have contributed to lowering the price of ready-made garments as well as to extending available varieties. Level of living increases have accrued for both farm and nonfarm people as a result of this specialized production, processing, and distribution.

On the liability side of the organizational structure of agribusiness are the imbalances and maladjustments resulting from uneven progress in the development from agriculture to agribusiness. These imbalances in the system are exemplified by glutted markets, unstable prices, uneconomic farm units, poor managerial training, and the lack of any broadly conceived agribusiness policy.[12] From time to time these imbalances have reverberated throughout all three aggregates of agribusines, but most often they have converged on the farm production aggregate. A concrete example of accumulating inequities of this type is seen in the Census of Agriculture reports which distinguish between commercial and noncommercial farming enterprises. Such a differentiation in the census is, in effect, an official concession of the point that a great number of farmers face problems of serious maladjustment to major shifts in the agribusiness organization. The inability of many farmers to adjust to the organization of agribusiness is much more serious than that suggested by the distinction of commercial and noncommercial farms in the census reports. Moreover, from a purely economic point of view, many of the commercial farms in the smaller classes could be more appropriately placed in the noncommercial category.

In the case of the commercial farm the current complex of problems centers around the cost-price squeeze. Several dimensions of this problem influence the income of farm families, the rate of capital formation, and hence the degree of progress of the farming aggregates. In the main, this problem is a result of the farmer's inadequate management ability to relate output and capital accumulation to market demand. This is largely due to his occupational role which casts him as a generalist rather than as a specialist. It is also a product of the total social milieu of farming, which brings into focus the need for central planning. There is a failure to achieve this planning even among the 2,000,000 major economic farm producers.

Due to the organization of agribusiness into multiple aggregates, and particularly due to the large number of entrepreneurs in the farming aggregate, it is most difficult for management accurately to relate output to market demand at a price which is comparable to national economic levels. Other industries, in addition to agribusiness, are subject to abrupt shifts in the economy which bring about overproduction. In the case of most other industries where there are a smaller number of major producers, it is possible for management to arrange output cuts until the balance of supply and demand is again achieved. However, the diversified management of agribusiness is unable to balance production and consumption in a relatively short period of time.

Part of the difficulty in the case of food and fiber production is due to its biophysical nature. Farm production is still very much related to weather conditions and to the life cycle of animals. Science and technology have helped to decrease, but not remove, the dependence of food and fiber production on the elements of weather and biology. The farm investment which motivates farmers to produce as long as they can pay for the short-range operations and their living expenses is relatively fixed. This fact further complicates relating production to consumption. Research and agriculture extension programs tend to stimulate greater efficiency and greater production, often irrespective of market conditions. The fact that the three major sections of agribusiness are separate frequently results in the isolation of management decisions within the respective aggregates. For example, in the short run, even in the face of declining markets, farm suppliers may continue to make efforts to step up their sales of machinery and other supplies. In the long run, the continued limbo of farm production operations will ultimately mean that farm suppliers will be caught in the economic imbalance to which they have contributed. Often decisions to continue sales promotion are internal. They are made within the given aggregate of agribusiness and not in light of the total agribusiness operation or the total national economy.

Farm cooperatives are prone to behave in a similar short-range manner. A cooperative may endeavor to contribute to the farmer's efficiency in some particular type of production operation without being sufficiently cognizant of the state of expansion or contraction of the market for a more efficiently produced commodity. Similarly, the processor-distributor or marketing aspect of agribusiness is concerned primarily with the sale of food and fiber products. Management of this aggregate, like that of the others, is prone to make decisions which are based more on internal organization of its operations than on the total agribusiness operation and the total economy.

Agribusiness is still in the process of formation. The concept is based on an interdependence of the various parts of food and fiber production. It still awaits the systematic development of social norms and structures through which the interrelatedness of the triaggregate can be regulated and by which food and fiber production can become acutely sensitive to the shifts and changes in the nation's economic institution. The costs of food and fiber production have become firmer as the result of increased dependence on advanced forms of machinery and the expanded use of artificial fertilizers and other chemicals. Basic production levels have reached such a high point for so many years that consumer patterns have become highly stable in amount but more discriminating and variable in terms of quality and exotic taste. The variability of plant and animal production has also become more exact as a result of scientific breeding, fertilization, cultivation, and the use of insecticides. To a great extent, harvest returns can now be predicted when certain acreages are planted in specific crops. In like manner, the number of animals needed to provide for a given consumption can be predicted. The development of agribusiness is consequently concerned with bringing together these three major aggregates and programing for them simultaneously.

The situation of the low-income farmers is continually being studied for the possibility of developing more systematic structures for moving them into other areas of agribusiness or other areas of the national economy.[13] Some of them will be able to move into systematic and economically profitable farming operations, but the great majority will be faced with increasing their earnings by part-time or full-time productive work in off-farm enterprises.

From the viewpoint of agribusiness, the extensive participation of government assistance in agriculture is considered to be the result of conspicuous absence of systematic planning between the various units in the total food and fiber production system. Throughout the era of agriculture, and more recently with the development of agribusiness, food and fiber interests have been well represented in government from the point of view of political action. There was the Grange movement of the 1870's, the Populist movement of the 1890's, the Agricultural Marketing Act of 1929, the Agricultural Adjustment Acts of 1933 and 1938, and a more recent continual unfurling of agriculture price support programs, and acreage programs. These various movements and programs have been typically oriented to a specific inequity. When some amelioration was provided for the particular problem at hand, the movements went out of existence or came to be of secondary importance. At no time have they sought to promulgate an image of the integration of farming and business and to plan an agribusiness program accordingly.

Systematic research in food and fiber has continued to reach new heights, and until recently most of it has been focused on production rather than marketing. In terms of total dollar sales, research in the non-farm aggregates of agribusiness is relatively less than that in the nonagribusiness industries. Even the large governmental expenditures for farm production research lag behind the amount of money spent on research in the nation's total economy. In 1956, industry spent an average of two dollars for research for every $100 of sales. Agriculture spent only fifty cents for research for every $100 of sales.[14]

AGRIBUSINESS AND OTHER ELEMENTS OF THE SOCIAL STRUCTURE

For over half a century, nonagricultural business enterprises have been oriented in the direction of national markets and toward making decisions based on the industry's total operation within the national economic structure. The growing pains have been many, marked by labor-management conflicts, ideas of scientific management, the development of trusts and interlocking directorates. The national approach in agribusiness has been hesitantly accepted. The development of an adequate agribusiness policy necessarily awaits a widespread emergence of this national role.

Agribusiness policy. Systematic dissemination of the concept agribusiness has moved ahead quietly but rapidly since 1955. In 1960, the *Yearbook of Agriculture* contained a section entitled "Agribusiness in the Machine Age," [15] and a Federal Extension publication in 1960 explained the manpower distribution in agribusiness.[16] In 1959, the North Carolina Agricultural Extension Service published a folder entitled *Agriculture:*

Industry's Growing Business Partner, in which there was a discussion of agribusiness as big business in North Carolina. The Texas Agricultural Experiment Station has published a bulletin explaining the significance of agribusiness to Dallas in 1959. In 1963 a Louisiana Agricultural Experiment Station bulletin was published concerning agribusiness and the labor force.[17] Articles concerning agribusiness abound in the trade magazines, the popular farm magazines, and farm papers. Also, the subject of agribusiness has been considered at symposiums and other meetings. This suggests that the communication mechanisms which concern food and fiber organization are reporting the concept agribusiness and soliciting discussions concerning its advantages and disadvantages.

Davis and Goldberg report that the role of government in agribusiness policy may be developed in one of three ways: first, by continuing the excessive reliance on the governmental superstructure as a mechanism for achieving balance in the otherwise loosely organized enterprise; second, by integrating the sectors of agribusiness so that they can provide their own superstructure and achieve their own economic balance or, finally, by following a middle ground combining elements of the first two.[18] But in any event and whatever the outcome, due to the recent conceptualization of agribusiness and the infancy of its development, it is probable that the role of government in agribusiness policy will be of major significance for some time to come.

Agribusiness policy can be applied to the broad national scene or, on a more limited scale, to specific regions or to specific commodities. In an ongoing dynamic society and out of a social milieu which provides for a great multiplicity of entrepreneurs, it is probable that the first agribusiness policies will be promulgated on regional and commodity bases. At a later stage of development they may be elevated to a national level and integrated into the urbanized social economic institution.

Research and agribusiness. Only a preliminary profile of the agribusiness structure may be obtained from the facts that are currently accumulated. Research, surveys, and statistical compendiums have generally not been assembled to examine the agribusiness structure. Historically, research in agriculture has been oriented toward the extermination of plant and animal diseases, improved breeding practices, development of hybridization, socioeconomic organization, processing, and marketing. Such research has served a real purpose and provided answers to basic questions appropriate to the area of agriculture. As the various elements of agribusiness became conceptually and structurally integrated, new kinds of research questions are necessarily raised. New research directions will involve team work and interdisciplinary research between institutes of agriculture and schools of business administration, between the U.S. Department of Agriculture and the U.S. Department of Commerce, between farm organizations and organizations of American manufacturers. Agribusiness considerations will have to be added to the programs of the Agricultural Extension Service, vocational agriculture, and other organizations which seek to make an impact on the food and fiber production of the land.

Agribusiness research does not by design suggest the curtailment of existing technical research programs. Instead and simultaneously, agribusiness research will seek to provide information for integrated decision making.

Antitrust legislation and agribusiness development. Agribusiness planners anticipate questions from, if not conflict with, antitrust regulation in the growing integration of the food and fiber system. Systematic planning by farm and nonfarm businessmen of the course of food and fiber development may be subject to question in terms of the intent of antitrust legislation. It may be that regulative social structure can be shifted from government to the economic institutions within the framework of agribusiness. But agribusiness has arrived so recently on the human landscape that its validity in planning and control remains to be determined.

Agribusiness and vertical integration. Agribusiness brings a broad integration of the parts of the food and fiber system into a single organization. Vertical integration and, similarly, horizontal integration are specific mechanisms for combining various production stages of a commodity or for making one stage into a mass operation. Such mechanisms are not intended to bring all the basic elements of the food and fiber operation into a common system of social organization. Theoretically, agribusiness, when fully developed, would generate an organized segment of the national economy which would maintain a distinct identity. For example, it would be separate from the organization of forms of transportation, the organization of recreation, and the organization of defense. These and other segments of the national, urbanized economy are interrelated in terms of division of labor specialization, and of supply and demand. Yet, such respective segments of the economy can maintain clearly articulated and more systematic structures within their own system of operations than between their system and that of some other segment of the economy. However, forms of vertical integration, if completely developed, would break down the boundary maintenance around otherwise integrated special segments of the economy. The character of the national economic institution would be that of a broad superstructure composed of a gross number of vertically integrated steps in the production and distribution of various basic items, rather than the collective organization of primary areas of economic production and distribution.

Another possible effect of vertical integration on agribusiness is the interrelation of specific stages of the food and fiber system within agribusiness rather than between agribusiness and some other segment of the economy. In short, vertical integration may constitute a major structural development in the economic institution. It may become a specific mechanism for combining parts of the agribusiness operation with parts of the transportation system, the recreation system, the military defense system, or other basic segments of the economy.

Examples of vertical integration are found both within the agribusiness organization and between agribusiness and other segments of the economy. Vertical integration between segments of the economy is found in some parts of the sugar and vegetable industries. The processors provide their own production, processing, and marketing. By contrast, most of the vertically integrated seed production is well within the agribusiness system itself. High-quality seed is often specifically contracted for by farmers and used by farmers. This involves a minimum of contact with the nonagribusiness elements of the economic institution. Wage structure and labor organization relate this form of vertical integration to nonagribusiness segments of the economic institution, but these aspects of the operation are secondary to the primary purpose of seed production.

SUMMARY

The history of American agriculture reports continual change. There was a brief era of heavily ruralized social organization in the early colonial period when subsistence farming prevailed. This form of food and fiber production was a transitory stage from its inception. Ruralized social organization already had declined in Europe, and the founders of the new nation were cognizant of more systematic forms of food and fiber production. Subsistence farms were developed for a short period of time in the colonies wherever the rugged wilderness could be brought under control. The conceptualization of agriculture as a business enterprise and, later, as a systematic occupation developed during the nineteenth century. By the middle of the century, and with the Civil War, agriculture was dealt a devastating blow. It became clear that the American society would be characterized by urbanized social organization. Agriculture was to constitute a basic segment of the society but as a supporting rather than a dominating influence. During the latter part of the nineteenth century and the first half of the twentieth, social forces were pressing the leaders of agriculture to integrate food and fiber production completely into the national economy. This would obliterate small farm identity and subsume it under other economic structures. One of the alternatives was the development of a new image of the food and fiber system which was consistent with the broad nature of urbanized social organization. The most vigorous statement of such a new image is agribusiness. Shifts in the economic organization of farming and business have developed over the past twenty years in such a way as to make such a new integrative organization between farming and business clearly possible.

A careful statement of agribusiness was formally promulgated in 1955, and since that time it has been quietly and systematically permeating the food and fiber production system. Further refinement of the concept agribusiness remains a task for the future. The folkways and mores of the agribusiness structure are far from precise; indeed, many have not yet been generated. But in any event, it appears that in contemporary, urbanized social organization there exists social space for such an image of food and fiber production as agribusiness, and that its more complete development will come in the future.

NOTES

1. William Bradford, *History of Plymouth Plantation* (New York: C. Scribner's Sons, 1903); Joseph Schafer, *Social History of American Agriculture* (New York: Macmillan, 1936), pp. 44–69.

2. John H. Davis and Ray A. Goldberg, *A Concept of Agribusiness* (Boston: Harvard Business School, Division of Research, 1957); John H. Davis and Kenneth Hinshaw, *Farmer in a Business Suit* (New York: Simon and Schuster, 1957).

3. Address by T. V. Houser, Chairman of the Board, Sears, Roebuck and Co., at the National Institute of Animal Agriculture Conference, Apr. 15, 1955.

4. *Business Conditions* (Chicago: Federal Reserve Bank, July, 1955).

5. *Fortune,* 54 (July, 1956, supplement).

6. Davis and Goldberg, *op. cit.*, p. 19.

7. "Facts in Grocery Distribution," *Progressive Grocer,* 35 (1956), 12.

8. *Fortune.*

9. Davis and Goldberg, *op. cit.*, p. 19.

10. Earl L. Butz, "Agribusiness in the Machine Age," in *Power To Produce: Yearbook of Agriculture, 1960* (Washington: U.S. Department of Agriculture, 1960), pp. 380–84.

11. *Ibid.,* p. 381.

12. Davis and Goldberg, *op. cit.,* pp. 20 ff.

13. William A. Wayt and Thomas J. Dix, *Adjusting the Commercial Family to Part-Time Operation in Southeastern Ohio* (Ohio Agricultural Experiment Station, Research Circular 97, 1961).

14. Davis and Goldberg, *op. cit.*, p. 23.

15. Butz, *op. cit.*

16. Richard G. Ford, *Manpower in the 1960's: Number Needed and Training Required* (Washington: U.S. Department of Agriculture, Federal Extension Service, 1960).

17. Lee Taylor and Arthur R. Jones, Jr., *Louisiana's Human Resources, Part II, Agribusiness and the Labor Force* (Louisiana Agricultural Experiment Station Bulletin 562, 1963).

18. Davis and Goldberg, *op. cit.*, p. 75.

SELECTED READINGS

Butz, Earl L. "Agribusiness in the Machine Age," in *Power To Produce: Yearbook of Agriculture, 1960.* Washington: U.S. Department of Agriculture, 1960.

This brief article summarizes the major statistics concerning agribusiness and puts its contribution into a meaningful perspective.

Davis, John H., and Ray A. Goldberg. *A Concept of Agribusiness.* Boston: Harvard Business School, Division of Research, 1957.

The first major effort at conceptualizing agribusiness in its economic aspects.

Davis, John H., and Kenneth Hinshaw. *Farmer in a Business Suit.* New York: Simon and Schuster, 1957.

A popular treatment of the historical shift from subsistence farming to agriculture, and to agribusiness.

Schafer, Joseph. *Social History of American Agriculture.* New York: Macmillan, 1936.

The chapters entitled "Primitive Subsistence Farming," "Big Business Farming," and "Professional Farming" are particularly relevant to the subject of agribusiness.

Taylor, Lee, and Arthur R. Jones, Jr. *Louisiana's Human Resources, Part II, Agribusiness and the Labor Force.* Louisiana Agricultural Experiment Station Bulletin 562, 1963.

Develops a sociological concept of agribusiness and specifically contrasts it with the economic concept.

11 SCIENCE AND AGRIBUSINESS

The history of American agriculture is a remarkable account of scientific development. The ideas and patterns of cognition of farmers are those of a sensate society. Agricultural accomplishments are many, supported by the concept of progress as well as by the work of the U.S. Department of Agriculture, agricultural experiment stations, and farm organizations. Literature on this subject is replete with the statements of acceptors and rejectors, of rationalistic and traditionalistic farmers. But overshadowing all of this is an enthusiasm for agricultural progress. The goals, motives, and drives of agricultural societies' founders, agricultural journalists, agricultural inventors, agricultural experiment station directors, and agricultural fair supporters are those of men who have bypassed notions of ruralized social organization. There are those who wax sentimental about country life, all the while supporting the very activities which are reducing dissimilarities between rural and urban patterns of life.

HISTORICAL LEGACY

The first application of science to agriculture could be variously dated, depending on one's definitions of science and of agriculture, and one's perception of the given social milieu. An exact dating is, however, not necessary and would be of doubtful value from the point of view of human relations. With the advent of the Industrial Revolution, inhabitants of the growing towns created a new and extended demand for meat.[1] This demand led to large-scale systematic breeding of cattle and, in quick succession, to greater production of higher-quality milk. The rigorousness of the scientific design of the early experiments might be questioned, but out of that social milieu grew the unquestionable application of science to agriculture. This social situation, which involved the movement of people out of rural areas into towns and cities as a part of the early Industrial Revolution, brought a requirement for more food. A systematic and scientific examination of the nature of food and fiber production was the response to this situation. It was a rationalistic and consumption-oriented pattern of cognition which ultimately led agriculture to become a specialty area within a larger society.

The great breeding experiments in England were begun in the latter half of the eighteenth century. Robert Bakewell (1725–95) is lauded by many as the founder of the art of animal breeding. There are differences of opinion on the significance of Bakewell's work; but, in preparing for the time when sheep and cattle were to be more important for wool and food than for power as draft animals, Bakewell was one of the first systematic students of animal breeding.[2] His principle was essentially that of inbreeding rather than crossbreeding. He collected animals for some particular characteristic, often taking them from the same family. Bakewell was particularly interested in breeding animals that would have small bones in proportion to a large amount of meat. The details of his breeding experiments were kept secret, but his general practice of selective breeding of domestic animals is still used. In the course of the eighteenth century, both cattle and sheep breeds were significantly improved. They were bred for earlier maturity, greater weight in proportion to smallness of bones, and greater yields of milk in proportion to the time that the cow was producing milk.[3]

From the point of view of ideological history, it must be noted that the Bakewell experiments were precisely oriented toward the consumer and to the market which was developing in the eighteenth century. As an interactional pattern, this was based on the notion of farming for production rather than as a way of life.

In colonial America a related concern with systematic agriculture was also operating. George Washington was one of the systematic farmers of early America. At one time he controlled some 70,000 acres of land and in the immediate estate of Mount Vernon some five farms totaling approximately 8,000 acres. Washington was not only concerned with the management of his immediate farms but with the promotion and improvement of agriculture. He began fertilizer research in 1760, and he intensified his scientific efforts in the growing of grain in 1763. He developed methods of grafting trees in 1765, and in 1770 he restricted growing of tobacco because of his observation that it was depleting the soil. Between 1768 and 1774, his interests were focused on diversified farming and crop rotation. The last of his major accomplishments, in 1786, was to invent a combined plow and drill seeder.[4]

Dies reports that Washington was a painstaking experimenter:

He experimented endlessly with fertilizer available on the plantation. He mixed with minute care the excrements from various animals, marl from the gullies, and the black mold from the creek sides, with soil from his numerous fields. In detail he entered various concoctions in his diary, related how each of ten mixtures was placed in a separate compartment, and then added: 'In each of these divisions were planted three grains of wheat, three of oats, and as many of barley—all at equal distances in rows, and of equal depth (done by a machine made for the purpose).' [5]

This illustrates the nature and detail of the activities of one of the first scientific farmers in the new nation. In addition to Washington's own experiments, it was reported that he carried on a lengthy correspondence with Arthur Young of London, who at that time was the editor of the *Annals of Agriculture.*

Another of the systematic early American farmers was Thomas Jefferson. He called agriculture a science of the first order: "It counts among its handmaidens . . . chemistry, natural philosophy, mechanics, mathematics, natural history and botany." [6] Jefferson was a tireless experimenter in the breeding and raising of livestock. His goal was to develop better breeds of sheep and to improve his specially imported Calcutta hogs. Like Washington, Jefferson was concerned with systems of crop rotation and, accordingly, on his four farms he divided the fields into seven distinct areas, marking the boundaries between them with peach trees. Crops were then rotated in the various areas. Notable in his system of crop rotation was that he did not leave any soil unplanted because he believed it would cause deterioration of the land.[7] Jefferson was also distressed by the inadequate type of agricultural equipment available. Accordingly, one of his most notable accomplishments was the invention of a new type of plow.

Soil chemistry was among the early scientific practices in the United States. The title, Father of Soil Chemistry, is given to Edmund Ruffin, who began his soil experiments in 1813.[8] He was a gentleman farmer from Virginia who carried on extensive experiments. He published the *Farmer's Register* and other materials which promoted the ideas of soil science and soil chemistry. The *Farmer's Register,* a monthly magazine regularly published between 1833 and 1844, was a potent force in rebuilding agriculture, particularly in the South. About half of this magazine was regularly writen by Ruffin. Its importance is not to be underrated, and experts today still rank its editorial quality as among the best ever in agricultural journalism.[9]

Another pioneer leader in the application of chemical science to soil was Samuel W. Johnson. He conducted chemical experiments on his farm in the late 1840's, did graduate work in chemistry at Yale in the early 1850's, studied chemistry in Germany in the middle 1850's, and taught at Yale from 1855 to 1896.[10] In the 1870's Johnson was instrumental in getting the Connecticut Legislature to enact a law establishing the Connecticut Agricultural Experiment Station, the purpose of which was to promote the scientific study of agriculture. Johnson became its director in 1877 and published its first bulletin. For several years the experiment station was located at Yale's Sheffield School. In 1882 the experiment station was provided with its own building, and it continued to progress under Johnson's direction.

Scientific agriculture was advanced still further by Johnson's student, Wilbur Olin Atwater. Atwater took his Ph.D. at Yale's Sheffield School under the direction of Johnson. His thesis on the chemical composition of sweet corn represented the first attempt to apply modern chemical methods to American food products.[11] Like Johnson, Atwater studied in Germany after going to Yale. Between 1875 and 1877, he served as director of America's first agricultural experiment station, at Wesleyan College. Under his guidance the Connecticut Agricultural Experiment Station grew to become an agricultural college. Atwater's major contributions in the area of nutrition led to definitive studies of human diets which were undertaken in Indiana, Missouri, Tennessee, and Illinois at schools and other public institutions, in hotels and private homes, and among rich and poor.[12] In 1894 he published his findings and thereby popularized the word *calorie*. This type of scientific endeavor was particularly important not only for its technical contribution but also because it illustrated the type of problem which researchers sought to define in the late nineteenth century. Such systematic and penetrating concern with problems of diet illustrated the specialization and division of labor which were to become so characteristic of urbanized social organization.

In addition to Atwater's technical achievements were his devoted administrative accomplishments. He was an ardent advocate of the Hatch Act of 1887 which provided federal financing of experiment stations. He was appointed the first Chief of the Office of Experiment Stations when the bill became law.[13] The establishment of agricultural experiment stations, identified with Johnson as well as Atwater, ushered in a new dimension to the social organization of urbanized society. Structurally, the agricultural experiment stations brought more public support, both federal and state, to scientific research in agribusiness. The role of public research in agriculture at this early time not only contributed material advancement but, sociologically speaking, also helped define the role of agriculture as a specialty area within a larger society. In an era of ruralized social organization there was yet no need for a social structure such as public support for scientific research. It has already been pointed out that the Homestead Act (1862), the Land Grant College Act (1862), and the U.S. Department of Agriculture (1862) all contributed to the broad definition of the function of agriculture within a larger society. By the 1870's, with the establishment of agriculture experiment stations, a further refinement and specification of this role took place.

Science, as a new structural element in agriculture, brought the historical legacy to an end. Scientific development was accelerated by two major changes or shifts in the social structure: one, the need for more food for nonagricultural people resulting from the early developments of the Industrial Revolution in Europe, and two, an ultimate answer to this new market need which defined the role of agriculture in terms of public support.

AGRICULTURAL SOCIETIES FOR IMPROVING FARMING

Developments in European agriculture, few as they might have been, were known in the colonies. Continuous streams of information connected Europe to the new nation. The agricultural societies were among the specific social mechanisms for disseminating agricultural information from Europe to the new country. For example, the American Philosophical Society, founded in 1743, and the American Academy of Arts and Sciences, founded in 1780, both encouraged and promoted investigation of European ideas and experimentation in agriculture.[14] Other societies devoted entirely to agriculture were soon organized. The first agricultural society was founded in New Jersey in 1781. Better known was the

Philadelphia Society for Promoting Agriculture, which was organized in 1785 and which published the results of its work. In the same year the South Carolina Society for Promoting and Improving Agriculture was founded. This was followed by the Society of Maryland (1786), established for the improvement of agriculture. Many more societies were founded thereafter.[15]

Membership in the societies was composed of men from all occupations who were sufficiently affluent to give time to experimentation. They were men interested in seeking knowledge of agricultural experiments in Europe and in applying the new accomplishments to the American situation. Among the 23 charter members of the Philadelphia Society for Promoting Agriculture, none were completely dependent upon the production of their farms for a living. Several were signers of the Declaration of Independence, others served as officers in the Revolutionary War, some served in the Continental Congress, a few were physicians, and one was a professor at the University of Pennsylvania.[16]

It was the practice of various societies, particularly the Philadelphia Society, to award premiums to individuals who made notable accomplishments in the development of agriculture. Some premiums awarded by the Philadelphia Society were:

1. For the best experiment made of a course of crops, either large or small, or not less than four acres, agreeable to the principles of the English mode of farming, mentioned in the aforegoing address—a piece of plate of the value of $200 inscribed with the name and the occasion: and, for the experiment made of a course of crops next in merit,—a piece of plate, inscribed on the value of $100. Certificates to be produced by the 20th of December, 1790.

2. The importance of complete or fold-yards, for sheltering and folding cattle,—and a preferable method of conducting the same for producing great quantities of compost or mixed dung and manure within the husbandman's own farm, induces the Society to give for the best design of such a yard and method of conducting it suitable to this climate and circumstances of common farmers—a gold medal:—and for the second best, a silver medal. The design to be presented to the Society by the 20th of December next.

3. For the best method of counteracting the injurious effects of frost in heaving or spewing up ground and exposing roots of wheat to the drying winds of the spring,—founded in experience, a gold medal: and, for the second best a silver medal. The account to be presented to the Society by the 20th of December next.

4. The best method of raising hogs, from the pig in pens or sties, from ex-

perience, their sometimes running in a lot or field not totally excluded if preferred,—a gold medal: and, for the second best a silver medal to be produced by the 20th of December next.

5. The best method of recovering worn-out fields to more hearty state, within the power of common farmers, without dear or far-fetched manures; but by judicious culture the application of materials common to the generality of farmers; founded in experience;—a gold medal and, for the second best a silver medal. To be produced by the 20th of December, 1786. . . .[17]

The major concern of these agricultural societies until approximately 1860 was with the scientific and technical problems of food and fiber production.[18] Many of the members of the earliest agricultural societies were primarily not farm leaders; some were not farmers at all. Often as not they were urban dwellers and national leaders interested in agriculture because it was one of the nation's basic enterprises. The directional force and the role of these agricultural societies was implicitly aimed at developing cultural universals which were to integrate farming into a larger national economy. There were, however, other social goals implicit in improving the welfare of the farm population. Notions of progress were central in the American ideology of success. High standards of living and the accomplishment of high levels of living were intended for all the people, not only city people.

The earliest agricultural societies faced numerous problems and often experienced failure in endeavoring to arouse interest in their programs. Bidwell argued that they were largely unable to interest common farmers in their efforts at scientific improvement, because the farmers were unable to perceive any market for the surpluses they might thereby be able to achieve.[19] Farmers ridiculed some of the early societies for their efforts at scientific advancement in the years that were coterminous with such conflicts as Shays' Rebellion. Rebellions such as Shays' reflected the immediate interests of many farmers; [20] the interests of science were broader, and thus more remote.

These contrasts revealed two aspects of the structure of the society. First, the farmers were apparently not antagonistic to the notions of science. In American fashioned pragmatism they wanted first to have markets identified, with which the scientific effort would be rewarded. Second, a power structure dominated by nationally oriented political leaders was developing. These men were visionaries who saw the total society in broad perspective. This type of perspective was inconsistent with what one might have found in the earlier medieval societies with their localisms. The situation of early national America was complex, and the formal governments of the nation and the states had been organized to provide a maximum of local control. Less conspicuous, however, was the informal organization which, if not admittedly oriented toward strong central government, was from the point of view of social structure oriented toward broad cultural universals that would guide and direct the behavior of all members of the society. Building an early scientific agriculture was appropriate to those ends.

Scientifically oriented societies attracted the attention of the federal government by means of the first President. As a part of Washington's last annual message to Congress, he cited the existence of such societies in other nations.[21] Washington's suggestion for an official government agricultural organization was taken up in the House of Representatives, and a committee recommended the establishment of a national society to promote agriculture. It was to be called the American Society of Agriculture and its membership would have included no less than the members of Congress, the Supreme Court Justices, the Secretaries of State, Treasury, and War, and the Attorney General, plus others who might be appointed. Such a national society was to hold annual meetings, elect officers, and have a governing board, which would have been known as the Board of Agriculture, along with a secretary who would carry on the details of the society's work.[22] Action was never taken on this committee report because Congress's attention was absorbed with matters of taxation. Local societies continued to proliferate; by 1852 they numbered approximately 300 and by 1860, almost 1,000. In 1852 the (nongovernmental) United States Agricultural Society was established in Washington, D.C. This society carried on a program of scientific work for ten years, until the U.S. Department of Agriculture was established.[23]

JOURNALISM AND THE PRESS CONTRIBUTE TO SCIENTIFIC AGRICULTURE

Scientific interest and the progress orientation in agriculture were substantially encouraged by journals and scientific publications from the first decade of the nineteenth century to the present.[24] Many of the journals served as official publications for the agricultural societies. They published dates and places of fairs, reported scientific research findings, and generally spearheaded interest in agricultural progress. The *Agricultural Museum* was the first journal devoted exclusively to the subject of agriculture. This publication was issued at Georgetown, D.C., starting in July of 1810. David Wiley, a Presbyterian minister, principal of the Columbian Academy of Georgetown, postmaster, mayor of Georgetown, and secretary of the Columbian Agricultural Society, was its editor and publisher. This journal lasted for nearly two years, appearing on a monthly and bimonthly basis. It published the proceedings of the Columbian Agricultural Society and, in some cases, of other societies. The focus of the *Agricultural Museum* was directed toward the raising of sheep, but all agricultural subjects were given some space.

John Stuart Skinner is often considered the founder of agricultural journalism in the United States. In 1819 Skinner published the *American Farmer* in Baltimore. His publication was the first farm periodical in the United States to achieve a real measure of permanence. Also published in 1819 was the *Plough Boy,* in Albany, New York. From these modest beginnings, agricultural journalism was launched.[25] It was the intention of the editor of the *Agricultural Museum* to have the magazine become an important means of communication for both farmers and manufacturers, a channel for the free exchange of their ideas and sentiments.[26] Such a conviction by an early editor suggests interest not only in systematic agriculture but also in the interrelationship between agriculture and manufacturing as two specific elements of an ongoing society. Such expressions were not illustrations of agrarianism or ruralized social organization; rather, they were statements which implicitly recognized the early development of urbanized social organization.

From the early journals the agricultural press has grown in many directions. Agricultural journalists now publish their communications in daily newspapers, weekly papers, popular periodicals, technical journals, agriculture experiment station bulletins, and extension publications. The broad impact of this agricultural press is largely responsible for the metamorphic change of agriculture from a horse-and-hand-labor occupation to a dynamic mechanized and scientific business.[27] The press reaches rural and urban people alike in communities, large and small, across the nation from Springdale to Wasco, to Plainville, U.S.A. America publishes more newspapers and periodicals than any other nation of the world. The aggregate circulation reaches some 57,000,000 people. Ten thousand weekly papers with a circulation of several million are aimed at a local level. Over 400 publications are devoted primarily to agriculture. They have a circulation of more than 30,000,000, a number greater by far than the total farm population. Eighty per cent of the nation's farm families subscribe to a daily or weekly newspaper, and 70 per cent take at least one magazine. Moreover, it is reported that farm people read an average of thirty to sixty minutes daily.[28]

The American press is one of the vital mechanisms which serves to bring about rapid and widespread dissemination of information. In the case of agriculture, it advances scientific farming and homemaking practices. Magazines with titles such as *Successful Farming* illustrate the universality of the ideology of material achievement. The notion of success used in this way is not urban or rural, but American. In the U.S. Department of Agriculture there is an Office of Information. The purpose of this office is to disseminate as rapidly and as expediently as possible agricultural news and reports of scientific research to the daily, weekly, and periodical press. Through this mechanism farm news reaches more than 3,000,000 people weekly.[29] Similar provisions are made for news releases concerning research programs at the various agricultural colleges and experiment stations. Childers writes that American farmers are interested in new ideas, that science is news, and that farming is a science. One function of the complex of agribusiness is dissemination of the news from laboratories and research stations, as well as about the development of new products and marketing procedures.

The dissemination process often involves reading a technical paper at a professional meeting of scientists, publication of the paper in one of the scientific learned journals, and interpretations of this publication to non-scientific readers in the form of condensed articles in daily newspapers and magazines and on radio and television programs. Finally, precise information in how-to-do-it publications and leaflets is issued directly to the people through county agent offices.

The important role of the agricultural press was revealed in a study conducted at North Carolina State College, in which it was found that nine exposures to new information were necessary before a new idea was put into practice.[30] Accompanying this expanded use of the agricultural press was an increase in the prestige of the science writer and the farm editor.

Publications have been continuously a basic part of the U.S. Department of Agriculture program. In 1889 Secretary of Agriculture Rusk advised that a comprehensive system of publication be established to bring the results of research as quickly as possible to the people. By the late 1950's, millions of copies of publications were issued by federal and state agricultural agencies. Agricultural experiment stations published 8,500 titles, the U.S. Department of Agriculture published 725 titles, and private industry published at least 1,000. More than 30,000,000 copies of these various publications were distributed by over 11,000 extension agents. College research scientists wrote 5,500 technical articles and published 1,150 journal articles in 1958–9.[31]

Apart from reports of scientific research in agriculture, scientific investigation is also being conducted in the area of journalism itself as a mechanism of communication. The Department of Agricultural Journalism at the University of Wisconsin has conducted studies which reveal the extent to which farmers understand the various terms and concepts used in agricultural publications. One study reported that, for some 25 words which scientists asserted were necessary in their writing about dairying, misunderstandings occurred on the part of 30 per cent or more of the farmers.[32]

AGRICULTURAL FAIRS ADVANCE FARM AND HOME

The agricultural fair was another early development which contributed to the advancement of scientific agriculture. It came into its own in the first decade of the nineteenth century, or at approximately the same time as the advent of agricultural journalism. Its predecessors can be traced back to the Middle Ages and ruralized social organization.[33] The agriculture fair was an established part of medieval rural society where it served the purpose of providing a seasonal market place. In colonial America there were a number of cattle fairs and, in Berkeley County, South Carolina, a Strawberry Fair. The nation's capital had an agricultural exhibition in 1804. This was followed in Arlington, across the Potomac River from Washington, with public sheep shearings from 1810 on.

The real impetus for the modern county fair came from Elkanah Watson, a man of considerable energy, imagination, and wealth. After traveling in Europe and becoming acquainted with the advances being made in agriculture there, he returned with his head and notebook crammed with ideas for the advancement of agriculture and spent considerable time in conversation with George Washington about the matter.[34] It was his belief that American farmers were not tilling the soil but mining it. He went on to Albany, New York, where he became a prominent and successful businessman. He amassed a sufficiently large fortune from his banking enterprise to retire at 49. He moved to Pittsfield, Massachusetts, where he acquired a large farm. There Watson devoted his energy and resources to agricultural education. He imported a pair of Merino sheep from France in 1807 and exhibited them in the town square. There was great interest in these fine sheep, and he inculcated the viewers with an appreciation of America's need to develop its own sheep raising and wool industry. To implement his grandiose plans, Watson, along with his farm neighbors, organized the Berkshire Agricultural Society in 1811. The major purpose of this society was to sponsor an annual cattle show or fair. The early fairs were organized around the principle of competition. Farmers came to the fair, entered their animals, and enthusiastically competed for the highly coveted awards for outstanding livestock and grains and other products from the fields or orchards.

The idea of the cattle show and fair spread rapidly through New England, and by 1820 agricultural societies sponsoring fairs were organized in practically all of the New England counties. In the early 1820's the various states made grants to the societies to help support the fairs. Such grants were used to pay for the various products that were exhibited. The purpose of the awards was to emphasize the growing of larger and better crops and fatter animals.[35] Agricultural fairs have had their periods of prosperity and their lean years, but the movement has continued to grow. By the middle of the twentieth century it was estimated that more than 60,000,000 people attended some 2,000 agricultural fairs annually.[36] The emphasis of the fair has expanded into all areas of homemaking, demonstrations of new machines, and entertainment and recreation.

AGRIBUSINESS RESEARCH IN URBANIZED SOCIETY

Scientific research is the Rosetta Stone by which the rapid, at times almost breathtaking, advances of American agriculture have earned it a place among the most successful producing businesses in the United States. The discovery of this explanation of the social organization of agriculture had been slowly understood, often painful to some and still resisted by a few. The family farm ideology caught the imagination of the American people in the early days of the country, and they have upheld it with nearly as much tenacity as they uphold the ideal of democracy. The individual family owning its own land and operating it in the yeoman sense, often barely subsisting, was really an abstract sentiment to which only nominal allegiance was given. Indeed, there have been some people, most often those in the nation's cultural islands, who have been overcome with the notion of the family farm and who actually tried to live the simple, bucolic, and romantic life it suggests. Such people are few. Now as always, the masses of the nation's farmers, in conjunction with the nonagricultural population, support the family farm ideology glibly. Yet, in action, they have participated in the various mechanisms for promoting systematic agriculture, in many cases to the extent of engaging in serious scientific agricultural research.

In urbanized societies it appears acceptable to adjust and readjust one's behavior, following the trends, if not the bandwagon, of social configurations. Consequently, it is not surprising now to discover a "modern" definition of the family farm concept. It is now a commercial enterprise, sometimes, although not often, incorporated; it is a mechanized operation involving a large capital investment and a minimum human energy input. Typically, one family still owns the farm, makes the managerial decisions, and provides most of the labor. These are the rationalistic operations in which business entrepreneurs are market-oriented, success-oriented, and participants in the mainstream of middle- or upper-class American society. Such farm operators and their families would disdain the thought of a subsistence operation. The Industrial Revolution and the mass population have justified, if not demanded, science in agriculture; and the scientific developments, in conjunction with other shifts in the social structure, are the key to understanding food and fiber production today.

Numerous attempts have been made to establish some measure of the productivity or value of the various forms of agricultural research. The task is a gigantic one, and most often unrewarding because of the changing criteria throughout the long course of history. Nevertheless, the best judgments which can be made concerning the value of such productivity are: in 1787, when the Constitution of the United States was being framed, nineteen farmers were required to produce food for themselves and one additional city person; between 1930 and 1940, the output increased so that nineteen farm people could produce enough food for 56 nonfarm people plus ten people living abroad.[37] According to Mighell, farm output rose about 75 per cent between 1910 and 1950. A more penetrating observation of the increased production is that, while it was continuous between 1910 and 1930, the proportions were relatively modest. Between 1930 and 1940, due to drought and other disadvantageous conditions, there were at times some recessions in the production rate. With the crisis of World War II in the 1940's, expansion of agricultural production came in gigantic proportions. Science and improvements in technology in one form or another rank among the primary reasons for this acceleration in farm output from 1920 to the current dates.[38] Between 1918 and 1953 the substitution of tractor power for horse power released to human food production approximately 70,000,000 acres of land which had previously been used in the production of food for animal energy.

Farm production can also be analyzed by using sales as an index. In the 1840's, farmers probably sold less than one-fourth of their food and fiber. A century later, they sold seven-eighths of all farm products.[39] Such a record clearly indicates farms came to be operated for business rather than subsistence purposes.

The question can still be raised how much of this impressive farm output should be attributed to better techniques and scientific developments and how much to additional inputs of land and other resources. Schultz provides carefully derived estimates on this subject, indicating that between one-half and three-fourths of the increased agricultural output is appropriately attributed to technology alone. The range which Schultz reports is explained on the basis of the definitions and indexes used.[40] Questions are also raised concerning the cost to the public for agricultural science research. Schultz estimates that the value of inputs saved in one year as the result of scientific research is greater than the total amount expended for farm research and extension work by the federal and all state governments since 1910.

Agricultural research is a cost to the general taxpayer, and in some cases it appears to be a burden. From the point of view of social organization and the reward of a well-fed and well-clothed population, the price paid to operate the U.S. Department of Agriculture and its research and extension programs has indeed been minimal. In spite of the fact that the agricultural budget of the nation has for several years been one of the large items in the federal government's operation, few other societies have experienced the general overproduction of food and the freedom from malnutrition which are the materialistic advantages of this urbanized society.

Investments in food and fiber research and the programs for disseminating this information involve one of the biggest success stories of the nation. The explanation for extensive government support of agricultural research, furthermore, provides one of the most dramatic examples of the power of a social structure available to the student of contemporary society. In a nation where an ideology supporting small agricultural units, namely, the family farm, prevails, there is a need for large-scale agriculture to produce mass quantities of food and fiber items in a standardized way to meet the marketing demands of large wholesale and retail firms. The small-farm ideology conflicts with mass market consumption. Some reconciliation was required by compromise or by a power struggle through which one would come to dominate the other. In the ongoing organization of American society, the pendulum of the power struggle has swung in the direction of the mass consumption market. However, there has also been some compromise. As long as the society was sufficiently affluent to afford the luxury of small-scale agriculture which is markedly inefficient in producing for mass markets, the ideology of the family farm could be supported while, at the same time, the needs of the mass urbanized society could be met. This has been accomplished in the United States through the government which fulfills the research role for agriculture. The nation's farmers, many of whom are sizable operators, are nonetheless typically much too small in resources and land units to carry on the research programs that are needed to enable agriculture to fill the mass markets. But, rather than bringing about a consolidation of farms by political action, the American prefers to enlist government support in providing research and thus permitting the farmers to remain, at least ideologically, free entrepreneurs. This situation is in marked contrast to that of the large manufacturing businesses, where it is continually reported in recent years that about 500 of the largest corporations dominate the manufacturing sphere of the nation. Paralleling these large operations is the ability of private industry to provide a major part of its own research needs.

In the study of social organization in American society, two developments now become clear. First, science in its complex ramifications is one of the largest single factors contributing to advances of agriculture. Second, the formal organization of science itself is developed within identifiable and precise elements of the social structure, involving an interplay between the family farm ideology and the mass market as aspects of urbanized social organization. There are multiple ways of accomplishing social goals. Given urbanized mass society as an accepted value, large-scale organization is required for the production of goods. In industry, big corporate enterprise is the mechanism used. It is large enough to provide much of its own research. Government's role is essentially limited to regulatory functions. The masses are potentially stockholders, but they have very little management power. In agriculture the family farm, in conjunction with government supported research, has been the mechanism.[41] In this case the owner-operator has maximum managerial control. There is a minimum of incorporation and stockholding in farming. Both of these types of business organization, the corporate industry and the owner-operator farm, have worked. But the norm of bigness is powerful in American society, and it appears that vertical integration may become more widespread in agriculture and thereby become a mechanism for bigness in agribusiness.

Examination of some of the specific areas of scientific research in agriculture and the rationale for their existence further reveals the nature of agriculture's role as it expands to become, more accurately, agribusiness. Scientific research in agriculture affects the lives of all the people, not only those engaged in farming. There is not a separate field of agricultural sciences. Research in the agricultural laboratories is carried on using the same principles that are basic to science wherever it is practiced. The term *agriculture science* is useful only if it is understood in a shorthand manner as referring to basic science applied to matters of food and fiber production.[42] This research is illustrated in the several examples which follow.

Animal research. Research advances in thyroprotein for cows [43] have been important from a technical point of view, and they are also important for illustrating the type of development which takes place in an urbanized social milieu. Technically, the matter of the thyroid gland affects milk production. Researchers learned some years ago that the removal of this gland from a cow would decrease milk production approximately 75 per cent. When such a gland was replaced in the cow in the form of dried thyroid tissue or synthetic hormone thyroxine, the milk yields returned to normal. Among the difficulties in this situation for increasing milk production were the high cost of dried thyroid tissue and the inadequacy of the supply. The problem was clearly the need for a cheaper substitute, and German scientists in 1938 discovered that the addition of iodine to proteins under specified chemical conditions would provide a material which, in terms of milk production in the cow, would function like thyroid tissue. In the United States, at the University of Missouri, scientists in the dairy department discovered that they could produce a similar result by adding iodine to skimmed milk. This new material has several names but most often is referred to as thyroprotein. Until recently thyroprotein was used essentially by experiment stations for further research in the increase of milk production.

Milk is often called one of nature's most valuable foods. Consequently, the concern for greater and higher-quality production is believed to be justifiable. This research illustrates man's attempts to improve on nature. It also points out the widespread, in this case even international, concern in agricultural science matters.

Artificial breeding is another area where scientific advances have been great. It is reported that, under natural conditions, a bull can service some thirty to fifty cows per year. With each of these natural fertilizations millions of sperm are expended for the fertilization of a single egg. Artificial insemination is a process whereby semen is taken from the male animal, diluted, and finally injected by manual process into the uterus of the female. By this process of semen collection and artificial insemination scientists are able to have 500 to 1,000 cows impregnated a year from one bull. The great advantage of this practice is that it extends the usefulness of good male animals and, at the same time, curtails the spreading of disease.

Artificial insemination has been a twentieth century experience in the United States, but the practice itself has been known for a far greater period of time. In 1780 the Italian scientist Lazaro Spallanzani artifically inseminated a bitch to prove that semen by itself was sufficient for pregnancy.[44]

Dairy cattle breeders' associations have been using artificial insemination since 1939. At that time they had over 600 members, with 33 bulls and over 7,500 cows. By 1946 the associations had proliferated to some 336, with a membership of well over 73,000. The members owned nearly 600,000 cows and were using approximately 900 bulls.[45]

Research is continually being conducted on the processes of artificial insemination, the shipment of semen, and its preservation. The advantages that accrue to an urbanized society from this type of scientific endeavor are many. There is a reduction in the number of bulls necessary to farms and a corresponding increase in cows. Improvements in feeding and management practices are precipitated, systematic keeping of records is promoted, and contacts with technicians and other farmers are increased. Health and fertility of animals are improved. Eventually, eugenics comes to be the accepted practice.

Progress in hog production [46] has taken many directions. One of the most interesting, from the point of view of society, is the attention given to the market and to the consumer of pork. Swine breeders some years ago realized that if pork was to remain profitable it would be necessary to develop leaner meat. Research findings from the 1930's indicated that an intermediate type of animal best suited the needs of the American producer and consumer. This meant that the hogs which are most marketable are those between 200 and 240 pounds rather than those of 300 pounds or more. This size animal provided for wider ranges of practice in the production aspects and offered the consumer a greater amount of lean meat. In 1934 the Iowa Agricultural Experiment Station imported several head of Landrace hogs from Denmark. For years this breed had been raised under testing methods in Denmark and had produced a bacon that was favored on the London markets. Progress in market-oriented hog production is continuing at a rapid pace.

The poultry industry is another that has experienced a similar metamorphosis. A few generations ago the average hen laid 86 eggs a year; today the average is over 118 and in some cases twice that amount.[47] Improved management, systematic trap-nesting, and scientific breeding are among the important explanations for this improved egg production. The business of farming is calculated in these terms; when egg production increases, income increases more rapidly than food costs for the birds, and higher production means lower cost per dozen of eggs to the consumer. Related types of research have been conducted in egg production to eliminate blood spots and to provide more durable shells.

The approach to the production of chickens for meat is strikingly different from that for eggs. Poultrymen who raise broilers select their birds for fast feathering, rapid growth, and superior conformation. The reasons for this selection are market-oriented. Fast feathering is associated with a reduction in the number of pin feathers in the marketed birds. Rapid growth, of course, is simple economics; it means getting them to market at an earlier date. Superior conformation concerns the amount of meat that will be avalable to the consumer; often as not this means larger breasts. Science has discovered that crossbreeds produce more meat than do pure breeds and, therefore, crossbreeding is widespread in the broiler industry.

Turkey research is also market-oriented. Much attention is devoted to the development of a small bird with good conformation, that will be more suitable for small family consumption. If comparative historical data were available, it might be found that profits have increased in the turkey industry in recent years as a result of the increased size of families since the 1930's.

The poultry industry is one of the most keenly market-oriented in terms of scientific research. In terms of management, it is one of the most vertically integrated agricultural businesses.

Another norm is lucidly illustrated by the research that is still being conducted concerning horses and mules. Science, like other forms of human behavior, is not immune to resistance to change. By 1947 Americans owned less than 8,000,000 horses, the lowest number reported during the last 75 years. "Nevertheless," one researcher writes, "those of us who believe there will always be a place for horses in the rural scene have gone ahead with tests and experiments to breed better horses and to learn more about them." [48] Research concerning the horse is systematic, even though the horse has been replaced by the tractor. This represents one of the many changes that have come about in the agricultural landscape in recent years. Science is most often at the vanguard precipitating the changes. In this case it reveals itself as a very human enterprise, defending the traditional rather than spearheading the innovative.

Plant research. The application of scientific investigation to plant production is enormous. Again, the extreme sensitivity of agricultural scientific research to the shifts and directions of the mass market is apparent. Among the best illustrations is the specialization taking place in the growing of tomatoes. The tomato is an indigenous American plant, but for many years it was hardly considered a proper food. All of this has changed in recent times. Now the tomato is prized so greatly that specialization in the industry has grown to the extent that tomatoes are produced in the winter under greenhouse conditions. The use of the greenhouse involves many problems, most of which have been met and overcome through scientific research. Without the winds of nature the plants are, nevertheless, fertilized. Pollenization is provided in such a way as to allow for or eliminate seeds in the tomatoes. Market research has been performed to determine the size of tomato most desired by the housewife, and tomatoes are produced to these dimensions. All of this is to say, in these modern times you can have your tomatoes when and where you like them.[49]

Flowers in an urbanized society are not allowed to grow in their natural manner. They are not even allowed to have simple aesthetic value.

Flowers are caught up in the status symbol race. The raising of flowers and the scientific research related to this process illustrates the cultural norm of bigness. The American gardener, hobbyist or professional, boasts at length about his giant pansies, his enormous petunias, or his gladiolus spikes six feet tall with flowers six inches across.[50] In a similar way, vegetable gardeners manifest the norm of bigness as they strive to have more corn, giant radishes, four-pound onions, turnips as big as pumpkins, and pumpkins as "big as a house." Large size is prized even though big vegetables are often inferior.[51] Through the advances of science the size of flowers and vegetables is something over which their producer can have a great amount of control. At this point it becomes unquestionable that the cultural norms guiding agriculture are those universally accepted throughout the society.

The hybrid onion illustrates the accomplishments of science in accordance with the norm of size and bigness. The process of the hybridization of the onion was systematically undertaken as early as 1925. At the University of California's agriculture campus at Davis, researchers brought together the Italian Red and the Lord Howe Island onions to produce what is now known as the California Hybrid Red Number 1.[52]

The quality of cotton means many different things to different people.

To the farmer it means a high yield and ease in picking; to the cotton broker quality means above-average classer's grade and staple length; the technologist may define it as a strong, reasonably long, and fine cotton; the spinner's definition may include a smooth running, uniform cotton that produces a nap-free, strong yarn; the finisher looks for something that will bleach and dye uniformly; and the consumer wants a product that will survive repeated washings and ironings.[53]

In spite of this range of criteria for good cotton, science has been able to develop types of cotton which embody these great diversities.

Other subjects in the area of plant research include: hydroponics, new types of blueberries, new varieties of sugar cane, new kinds of tobacco, improved clover, better alfalfa breeding, improved timber crops, and hybrid forest trees. The range of human inquiry into the production of plants reflects the full scope of the imagination.

Soil research. Differential fertility of soils has long captivated the curiosity of the scientist. Ideas of crop rotation have existed through the ages. Systematic attempts in the application of fertilizers date from antiquity. More systematic application of science to the understanding of soil is a relatively recent development. Just a little more than a century ago, Sir John Lawes of England produced the first soluble phosphate fertilizers. A quarter of a century later, the process was attempted in the United States, and over the years it has become increasingly successful. Now over 4,000,000 tons of phosphate rock are mined annually in the United States for the production of superphosphate fertilizers or for direct application to the soil.[54]

The problem of phosphate fertilization is not simply one of adding to soils an amount of phosphorus equal to that removed by crops or lost by erosion. Soils differ greatly in the kinds of phosphorus compounds they contain and in their ability to pass along to the plant the phosphate added in fertilizers. Moreover, crops vary in their ability to use the phosphorous compounds of the soil and in their response to phosphate fertilizers. The kinds of phosphate fertilizers used and the way in which they are applied are other factors that affect the returns that are obtained.[55]

Because of the great complexities of soil, it can be said that some of the most scientific research on phosphate fertilizers has been concerned with determining the amounts required by the various soil types.

Nitrogen fertilizers are coming to be widely used in the United States. During the World War II years, American farmers used more nitrogen than ever before in their history. The desire for continued use has increased in more recent years. Nitrogen is used in differential amounts in the various regions of the nation. Some of the factors involved in the use of nitrogen include its original content in the soil, rainfall, cropping or system of farming, and the value of the crop per acre. Nitrogen is used extensively in the Southeast because of high rainfalls and high temperatures. It is used less in the area west of Minnesota, Iowa, and Missouri, where rainfall is low. In those areas where livestock farming is involved, the amount of legumes grown and the farm manure return much of the nitrogen to the soil. By contrast, the removal of cash crops from the land depletes the nitrogen content of the soil. All of these factors influence the amount of nitrogen fertilizers used.[56]

Other systematic research concerning land utilization which has achieved spectacular results includes irrigation. Irrigated farming is one of the oldest practices known to mankind and dates from the earliest civilizations. Yet it has been systematically improved in the urbanized society. The modern farmer using irrigation needs to know at the beginning of a season about how much water will be available to him so that he can plan accordingly. In the Western States snow is measured, and a system of forecasting stream flow is widely used. Systematic studies have been made to reveal the amount of water flow and water loss due to various types of irrigation ditches. In order to get the maximum amount of efficiency from irrigation, the water must be evenly spread over the soil at a uniform rate. For maximum results, the farmer must know the water-holding capacity of the land and the area of the plant root zone, measure the water applied, and limit it to the amount that can be profitably used according to these indicators.[57]

Science leads to new products. In 1938, the Congress of the United States formally authorized agricultural research specifically designed to promote new uses for farm commodities.[58] The results of this research are widespread and make a great impact on individual lives across the length and breadth of the nation. Just a few of the accomplishments include the production of penicillin, methods of making sweetening materials from wheat flour, and sweet potato starch.

The federal government's support for new products research is organized in such a way that it reveals much about urbanized social organization. Four regional laboratories were established at Peoria, Illinois; Wyndmoor, Pennsylvania; New Orleans, Louisiana; and Albany, California. Different tasks were assigned the various laboratories. In Peoria, research was directed toward new uses for corn, wheat and other cereal crops, soybeans and other oil seed crops of the area. Research in the Southern region dealt primarily with cotton. This was due largely to the competition cotton faced from the synthetic fibers. The Eastern laboratories focused on milk, tobacco, animal fats and oils, vegetables, apples, hides, leather, and tanning materials. In the West, attention was directed toward fruit, vegetables, alfalfa, poultry, and wheat. Not only, therefore, is the organization of agriculture coming to be centralized within the social structure, but scientific research, which is at the vanguard of urbanized agriculture, is most systematically and centrally planned.

Food research. Advances in home economics research are almost without number. They include proper methods of canning and preserving food, the uses of dried food, developments in freezing of foods, and the preparation of fabrics for protection against mildew and insects. Experimentation in the cooking of poultry has been a subject of research at the University of Missouri.[59] Rapid acceptance of precooked frozen and canned foods creates the need for new information concerning methods for final preparation of the food. The purpose of this particular research was to ascertain cooking losses, degrees of tenderness with and without salts, and other factors.

The details of these types of research are many, but the subjects mentioned illustrate the integration of their findings into an urbanized social organization.

New research horizons. One of the most interesting and promising new types of scientific research concerns the role of ionizing radiation in the preservation of foods. It is still in the research stage, and the preservation of food by radiation remains a task for the future. Bruce H. Morgan writes:

Now let's jump on cloud 39 and project ourselves to October 4, 1978 and take a glimpse at a shopping list of a woman on her way to the store and pick out the products that have been treated by radiation: 1. TV-type dinner for four foods in a ready to serve dish. Package is dated and should be used within three months at room temperature. Heat the package in oven just before serving. 2. Pre-cooked canned lamb chops that need warming just before serving. Keep can no more than a year at room temperature. 3. Dates that would last twice as long at room temperature without fermenting. 4. Onions that could be held three months at home without sprouting and resistant to bacterial rot. 5. Peaches shipped across country and free of brown rot and black mold. 6. Cold slaw that can keep crisp for two weeks or more in the refrigerator.[60]

It is Morgan's belief that the housewife of 1978 will find irradiated foods in the supermarkets. One must also note that a guiding principle to which Morgan subscribes is Emerson's motto, "The future belongs to those who prepare for it." Such an ideology reveals the type of cognition and the role perception of researchers in urbanized societies.

Atomic energy in agriculture is an inevitable development, according to Willard F. Libby.[61] The application of atomic energy, of radioactive isotopes, to agriculture is new. But conferences are already being held at the state colleges and experiment stations concerning this very matter. The ultimate possibilities are myriad; some have already been visualized and others are yet unknown. Libby does not recommend that at this time every farmer should carry a Geiger counter, but it is his admonition that every farmer should know that some of the results of applying Geiger counters are being oriented to his food and fiber production. There is no question that direct application of isotopes or radiation to everyday farming and food handling is within the foreseeable future. The food irradiation business is one of the most likely prospects. In addition, some of the mutations produced by radiation will gradually become important for food production.

ROLES OF PRIVATELY AND PUBLICLY SUPPORTED RESEARCH IN AGRIBUSINESS

Public support of agricultural research has value not only for farmers but for the total population. Writing shortly after the time when hybrid corn was developed, Blaisdell cited this accomplishment as one of the outstanding returns on research investment. The new hybrid corn was producing about 20 per cent more per acre than regular varieties. As a penetrating observer of human society, Blaisdell could not help but be mindful of the fact that this increased corn production came at a time when the government was endeavoring to get farmers to reduce their acreage in corn. The two government programs, namely, scientific production of hybrid corn and acreage controls, appeared in the short run to be working at cross purposes.[62] This is one example of many situations that could be cited where the manifest and latent functions of the government programs in agriculture tend to be contradictory. Yet in light of the long-range accomplishments and the contribution of agriculture to the affluence of the society, these contradictions appear to have a minimum measure of inefficiency. It does not appear likely that a scientific holiday or moratorium will be called in order that research contributions to increased production can be brought into line with acreage control policies. Lauren K. Soth has suggested,

. . . that United States agriculture could "spare" a third or more of its overhead production-improvement organization—namely the United States Department of Agriculture technical research and educational services, combined with the state land grant college experiment stations and extension services—without strain.[63]

Byron T. Shaw, as a research administrator in the U.S. Department of Agriculture, explained the system as one of our great national resources.[64] It was Shaw's contention that the advancement of farming efficiency through scientific research has contributed not only to progress in food and fiber production, but, in a no less important way, has made possible the release of farm workers to other industries. In short, the advancement of farming is a contribution to the development of an industrial nation.

Research in agribusiness contributes to the advancement and prosperity

of farming. This is certainly one of its goals and one of its accomplishments. But a second goal and accomplishment is probably of even greater
magnitude. This is the benefit of agribusiness research to the entire population. Shaw asserts that the nation is greatly indebted to the planners of
the national system of agricultural research. Such a program was designed to accelerate efficient food and fiber production for a growing
industrial nation.[65]

Government's research authority. The federal government first supported
agricultural research activities in 1839. At that time it appropriated $1,000
to the Patent Office to enable it to gather statistics, to collect and distribute
seeds, and to conduct agricultural investigations. From this initial authori-
zation, chemical and entomological research received their first support.
The next major occasion for government to participate in agricultural
research followed the establishment of the U.S. Department of Agriculture
in 1862. As a consequence, the already developed chemical and entomological research increased in proportion to productivity. Shortly after the
turn of the twentieth century, in 1902, the Division of Chemistry became
a Bureau. The Division of Entomology continued to grow, and it became
a Bureau with the passage of the Plant Quarantine Act in 1912. The
1884 research work in animal pathology was specifically authorized when
the Bureau of Animal Industry was established. In 1885, appropriations
were made available to establish a section of mycology, and in 1888 funds
were provided for research in the larger field of plant diseases. The Department continued to make advancements through the end of the nineteenth century. The first 20 years of the twentieth century, however, were
relatively limited in terms of expansion.

Some important peripheral contributing programs to governmental
research in agriculture include the Hatch Act in 1887 which authorized
the experiment stations, the Adams Act in 1906 which provided additional government support for research, the Purnell Act in 1925 which
provided research in the human sciences, and the Bankhead-Jones Act
in 1935 which further extended research support at the federal, state,
and territorial levels.

SUMMARY

The history of social relations in American agriculture offers an impressive
account of scientific development. The advance of scientific agriculture

has not been smooth; there have continually been many persons who rejected new ideas. But change has prevailed, as agents and mechanisms in the society supported and promoted it.

Among the great historical stimuli for science in agriculture was the Industrial Revolution in England, which precipitated a movement of people out of agriculture into the shops. The new industrial workers needed to be supplied with food and thereby provided the demand for market-oriented agriculture. In the eighteenth century the first animal breeding experiments were performed in England.

European advances in agriculture were taking place at the time the American colonies became a nation. Among the Founding Fathers of the new nation, men like George Washington and Thomas Jefferson were systematic, scientifically oriented farmers. They carried out experiments on their own farms, and they were in correspondence with those conversant with advances in European agriculture. Soil chemistry originated early in the nineteenth century in America. By mid-century it was incorporated into the study and research program at Yale. American scholars of that time studied soil chemistry in Germany as well as America.

Agricultural societies from the earliest times supported change and scientific approaches to farming. In 1743 the American Philosophical Society encouraged systematic farming, and other organizations, some exclusively devoted to agriculture, followed in quick succession.

Agricultural journalism dates from the first quarter of the nineteenth century. Its growth has been continuous, and its contribution almost without measure in the support and communication of scientific ideas. Since the establishment of the U.S. Department of Agriculture, journalism has been systematically supported by the government. The findings of scientific investigations are quickly communicated to food and fiber producers.

Agricultural fairs are another means for bringing the latest scientific and other information to the attention of farmers and homemakers. Like agricultural journalism and soil research, such fairs originated in the first decade of the nineteenth century.

Most scientific agricultural research is supported by government. Since the 1830's the federal government has provided financial support, first informally and then formally with the founding of the U.S. Department of Agriculture. The U.S.D.A., the land-grant colleges, the state departments of agriculture—all individually and cooperatively support scientific research in agribusiness. In recent years private industry has increased its support of agricultural research.

The range of research problems is all-inclusive. Animal, plant, and soil research have long histories. Food, clothing and new product research are more recent. Investigations into economic and social organization, along with marketing research, are primarily twentieth century developments. All agribusiness, including food and fiber production, processing, distribution and consumption, is directly and significantly influenced by scientific research.

NOTES

1. L. Dudley Stamp, *Man and the Land* (London: Collins, 1955), p. 124.

2. *Ibid.,* p. 128.

3. *Ibid.,* p. 129.

4. Edward J. Dies, *Titans of the Soil: Great Builders of Agriculture* (Chapel Hill: University of North Carolina Press, 1949), p. 15.

5. *Loc. cit.*

6. *Ibid.,* p. 25.

7. *Loc. cit.*

8. *Ibid.,* p. 56.

9. *Ibid.,* p. 61.

10. *Ibid.,* p. 96.

11. *Ibid.,* p. 108.

12. *Ibid.,* p. 111.

13. *Ibid.,* pp. 109–10.

14. Wayne D. Rasmussen (ed.), *Readings in the History of American Agriculture* (Urbana: University of Illinois Press, 1960), p. 41.

15. *Loc. cit.*

16. *Ibid.,* pp. 41–2.

17. *Ibid.,* pp. 44–5.

18. Carl C. Taylor, *The Farmer's Movement, 1620–1920* (New York: American Book Co., 1953), p. 71.

19. Percy W. Bidwell, "The Agricultural Revolution in New England," *American Historical Review,* 26 (July, 1921), 686.

20. Taylor, *op. cit.*, p. 72.

21. James D. Richardson (ed.), *A Compilation of the Messages and Papers of the Presidents,* Vol. I, "Eighth Annual Address, George Washington, December 7, 1796," p. 199 (New York: Bureau of National Literature, 1912), cited in Taylor, *op. cit.*

22. Taylor, *op. cit.*, pp. 75-6.

23. *Ibid.*, p. 77.

24. Rasmussen, *op. cit.*, p. 51.

25. *Ibid.*, p. 52.

26. *Ibid.*, p. 53.

27. L. E. Childers, "The Role of a Free Press," in *Power To Produce: Yearbook of Agriculture, 1960* (Washington: U.S. Government Printing Office, 1960), p. 95.

28. *Ibid.*, p. 95.

29. *Ibid.*, p. 96.

30. *Ibid.*, p. 97.

31. Lyman J. Nordhoff, "The Place of Publications," in *Power To Produce,* p. 98.

32. *Ibid.*, p. 99.

33. Paul H. Johnstone, "Old Ideals Versus New Ideas in Farm Life," in *Farmers in a Changing World: Yearbook of Agriculture, 1940.* (Washington: U.S. Government Printing Office, 1940), p. 114.

34. Dies, *op. cit.*, p. 36.

35. Rasmussen, *op. cit.*, p. 55.

36. Dies, *op. cit.*, p. 34.

37. Donald C. Blaisdell, *Government and Agriculture: The Growth of Federal Farm Aid* (New York: Farrar and Rinehart, Inc., 1940), p. 132.

38. Ronald L. Mighell, *American Agriculture: Its Structure and Place in the Economy* (New York: John Wiley and Sons, Inc., 1955), p. 6.

39. Blaisdell, *op. cit.*, p. 137.

40. Theodore W. Schultz, *The Economic Organization of Agriculture* (New York: McGraw-Hill Book Co., 1953), pp. 109-20.

41. C. Wright Mills, *White Collar* (New York: Oxford University Press, 1956), pp. 40-44 ff.

42. Charles E. Kellogg, "What is Farm Research?" in *Science in Farming: Yearbook of Agriculture, 1943-1947* (Washington: U.S. Government Printing Office, 1947), p. 18.

43. L. A. Moore and J. F. Sykes, "Thyroprotein for Cows," in *Science in Farming,* p. 107.

44. Ralph W. Phillips, "Artificial Breeding," in *Science in Farming,* p. 113.

45. *Ibid.,* p. 114.

46. John H. Zeller, "Progress in Hog Production," in *Science in Farming,* p. 201.

47. Theodore C. Byerly, "Breeding Better Poultry," in *Science in Farming,* p. 225.

48. William Jackson, "Horses and Mules," in *Science in Farming,* p. 239.

49. John W. Mitchell, "Plant Growth Regulations," in *Science in Farming,* p. 259; also see Marshall R. Godwin and William T. Manley, *Preference for Sizes of Florida Tomatoes* (Florida Agricultural Experiment Station, Agricultural Economics Report 58–5, 1957).

50. S. L. Emsweller, "Flowers as You Like Them," in *Science in Farming,* pp. 284 ff.

51. *Loc. cit.*

52. H. A. Jones and A. E. Clarke, "The Story of Hybrid Onions," in *Science in Farming,* pp. 320–23.

53. E. E. Berkley and H. D. Barker, "What Makes Good Cotton?", in *Science in Farming,* p. 369.

54. W. H. Pierre, "Phosphate Fertilizers," in *Science in Farming,* p. 554.

55. *Ibid.,* pp. 554–5.

56. F. W. Parker, "Uses of Nitrogen Fertilizers," in *Science in Farming,* pp. 561–3.

57. George D. Clyde, "Irrigation in the West," in *Science in Farming,* p. 603.

58. H. T. Herrick, "New Uses for Farm Crops," in *Science in Farming,* p. 689.

59. O. J. Kahlenberg and E. M. Funk, *Experiments in Cooking Poultry for Pre-Cooked Poultry Products* (Missouri Agriculture Experiment Station Research Bulletin 748, 1960).

60. Bruce H. Morgan, "The Role of Ionizing Radiations in the Future Preservation of Foods," *Symposium Papers on the Role of Agriculture in Future Society, 1957* (Geneva, N.Y.: Agricultural Experiment Station, 1957), p. 24.

61. Willard F. Libby, "Atomic Energy in Agriculture," *Symposium Papers,* pp. 41–8.

62. Blaisdell, *op. cit.,* p. 124.

63. Lauren K. Soth, "Farm Policy, Foreign Policy, and Farm Opinion," *The Annals of the American Academy of Political and Social Science,* 331 (Sept., 1960), 105; see also F. F. Hill, "Scientific Manpower for the Less-Developed Countries," and Mervin G. Smith and Joseph Ackerman, "Contributions of Colleges of Agriculture in Making Human Capital Available in Foreign Economic Development," both in *Annals.*

64. Byron T. Shaw, "The Role of Publicly Supported Agricultural Research in Future Society," *Symposium Papers,* p. 64.

65. *Ibid.,* p. 63.

SELECTED READINGS

Childers, L. E. "The Role of a Free Press," in *Power To Produce: Yearbook of Agriculture, 1960*. Washington: U.S. Government Printing Office, 1960, pp. 95–97.
A concise article which traces the impact of journalism on agriculture.

Dies, Edward J. *Titans of the Soil: Great Builders of Agriculture*. Chapel Hill: University of North Carolina Press, 1949.
A classic study of the scientific imagination of the early leaders in American agriculture.

Eddy, Edward D., Jr. *Colleges for Land and Time*. New York: Harper and Brothers, 1956.
A history of land-grant colleges, including an account of scientific research programs by the colleges and their affiliated experiment stations.

Farmers in a Changing World: Yearbook of Agriculture, 1940. Washington: U.S. Government Printing Office, 1940.
The impact of science on farming is clearly illustrated. Part V is entitled, "What Some Scientists Have To Say."

Rasmussen, Wayne D. (ed.). *Readings in the History of American Agriculture*. Urbana: University of Illinois Press, 1960.
Several of the readings in this book are of early agricultural scientists.

Science in Farming: Yearbook of Agriculture, 1943–1947. Washington: U.S. Government Printing Office, 1947.
This entire yearbook is devoted to a review of the many scientific research programs in food and fiber production.

Symposium Papers on the Role of Agriculture in Future Society, 1957. Geneva, N.Y.: New York Agricultural Experiment Station, Dec., 1957.
This symposium reports some specific features of the scientific research horizons in agriculture.

12 TECHNOLOGY, MECHANIZATION, AND AGRIBUSINESS

Technology has been a historic part of agricultural development in the West generally and in the United States particularly. From the earliest times in this nation, specific mechanical advances have been made to facilitate farming and to make its operation more efficient.[1] These developments have become so advanced in the second half of the twentieth century that they are integrating farming in the form of agribusiness into the total national economic system.

TECHNOLOGY AND SOCIAL CHANGE

The rate at which agricultural technology can proceed is well illustrated by the introduction of the tractor. Tractors were first counted in 1910, when only 1,000 were reported. In the same year 24,000,000 work stock were reported. By 1959 the Census of Agriculture reported more than 4,000,000 tractors (on 3,700,000 farms) and less than 4,000,000 work stock animals. Some of the small farmers still had no tractors, while many of the large commercial farmers had several, thus accounting for the fact that there were more tractors than farms by 1959. The nature of this technological advance has had a major impact on the social organization of farming. Less animal energy and less human energy are required in food and fiber production. Accordingly, the agricultural labor force has been greatly reduced, and in come cases even displaced, by the shift to technological energy.

253

Some indexes of change in human relations. Technological advances have contributed to the increased size of farms throughout the nation.[2] Concomitant with the increased size of farms is the mass migration of rural young people away from the country into cities. Thus the city has exerted a "pull" influence; but the "push" of technology which displaces human labor in farming has contributed even more to this migration pattern. While the size of farms has increased, their number has declined precipitously. One farm operator with an understanding of technology, utilizing machines, can now operate hundreds of acres of land, where multiple operators and many farms laborers were required for the same task in past decades.

Part ownership of farms has increased with technological advances. In past generations, full rather than part ownership was most desired and afforded most prestige. By the second half of the twentieth century, full ownership in many cases was an index of a traditionalistic rather than a scientific orientation. Large-scale operators often have found that they can expand their operations and have more financial flexibility by investing in multiple land and machine units with borrowed money while remaining part owners.

Technological advances also have helped to solidify stratification systems. Now it has become commonplace to distinguish between those who accept and those who reject new technological developments. Operators in the former category most often have large holdings, a scientific orientation, high education, and an urbanized ideology. Those of the latter type typically have small holdings and traditionalistic orientations which do not predispose them to accept innovations in agricultural technology.

Informal mutual aid practices, widely reported among farm families in the past, are abandoned as technological developments are incorporated into the production of food and fiber. Technological operations are, by definition, formal and rationalistic rather than informal and traditionalistic. Formal organization of technology is based upon a contractual urbanized ideology rather than a ruralized social organization.[3] Increased use of technology also results in liberal attitudes as well as in a reduction of ritualism and fatalism.[4]

Advances in technology have shifted agricultural enterprises in the direction of commercialization. Systematic farm management becomes part of the operation. Farmers shift their business transactions from rural villages to cities. Farm equipment and other supply businesses related to the new mechanization are more readily available in urban centers.

Marketing and the utilization of services in the larger population centers precipitates changes in the mode of dress. More sophisticated wearing apparel replaces the traditional rural overalls, as farmers and their families interact in the larger communities. Similarly, the range and types of foods are increased as the technological developments engender social interaction on the larger urban scale.

The acceptance of technology engenders changes throughout major social institutions. For example, in order to prepare individuals to understand the meaning of technological changes, the structure of educational institutions must necessarily be modified. Acceptance of technology has been accompanied by school consolidation, expansion of technical curriculums, and broadened educational experiences. Family life becomes more rationalistic, and those who accept technological advances have smaller families similar to those of the urban middle classes. Governmental institutions are modified, and new organizations are developed to supplant old ones. For example, electricity districts, irrigation districts, telephone districts, and a host of other special districts are all part of the social configuration in the areas of advanced technology.

Farm people who accept new technology are also more frequently participants in a host of associations. They are the most active participants in school and adult educational activities. They carry a larger burden of work in civic and recreational programs. Further, they are active in special interest groups, and, on the whole, often shift their participation from the level of the local neighborhood to the larger community,

These are but a few of the indexes of social change associated with developments in technology. Other secondary and tertiary changes are also attributable to technological advance.

Technology and capital investment. Advances in technology have been made at a high economic price. The total capital investment per farm in the United States increased more than 60 per cent between 1940 and 1958, in terms of 1940 dollars. Between 1940 and 1958, investments in machinery and equipment increased more than 200 per cent.[5]

Capital investment in new technology was first made in wheat farming. By 1940, mechanization of the nation's wheat farms was extensive. The size of wheat farms was increased to facilitate more effective use of new equipment. Between 1940 and 1958, the size of wheat-fallow farms increased 35 per cent, in contrast to an increase from 12 to 24 per cent for other types of farms during the same period. Various types of farming enterprises have rapidly followed the pattern established for wheat farming.

One of the major ramifications of the advancing technology is the increasing dependency of farmers on purchased input materials. Traditionally, subsistence family-farm operators produced virtually all of their own supplies and materials. Modern scientific farm operators, almost by definition, purchase their supplies and materials. Purchasing of supplies contributes to the integration of agriculture into the national economic system. In addition, it also creates an interdependence between the farmer and the national economic system. The price of purchased implements has been less flexible than that of implements produced by farmers. Therefore, as more input items are purchased, farmers become more dependent upon the rigid national economic system.

ENGINEERING, MACHINES, AND FARMSTEAD AUTOMATION

Twentieth century engineering advances are refashioning agriculture. Management practices, layout and arrangement of facilities, and types of equipment—all influence agricultural work routines and potential profits.[6] Agricultural engineers have made many trips to farms to study work operations in order to design equipment that will be immediately serviceable. In the first decade of the twentieth century, experiment stations began to construct research designs for farmstead buildings. During the 1920's the U.S. Department of Agriculture implemented similar research. During the depression years of the 1930's this type of research was continued on several fronts. By the 1940's, laboratory studies were being made to explain the physiological responses of cattle, hogs, and poultry to their environment. Marketing research initiated in 1946 extended these inquiries to include the preparation and storage of agricultural products. The net result of this research was an industrially organized farm from production to processing. Buildings were designed as productive tools. Animals were grouped together to provide increased efficiency in machine servicing of their feeding and cleaning.

Agricultural engineers have studied the layout of farmsteads. The purpose of these studies is to promote the smooth flow of materials and animals in an orderly and efficient performance of detailed tasks. The operation involves handling and storage of feed, movement and cleaning of animals, removal of waste, and handling of the final product. Electronically operated feeding equipment has been developed on the basis of such research findings, as have feed grinders, conveyers, milking machines, and machines for the removal of animal wastes.

Farm engineering has been a byproduct of urbanization. This is illustrated in the case of dry-lot dairy operations. Electrical energy and machines replace human energy and hand labor. Animals are confined in specifically shaped enclosures. Food is purchased commercially, delivered according to time schedules, and mixed on the premises according to the farmer's specifications. Drinking water for the animals is piped to the appropriate place. Power scrapers and water are used to remove manure.[7]

The milking machine was introduced early in the twentieth century. By the middle of the twentieth century, approximately 90 per cent of all dairy operators utilized milking machines. Heavy milk pails have been eliminated, and milk is generally carried by pipelines to bulk tank storage.

Advances have been made in the engineering of the milking parlor, which further eliminates hand operations and improves sanitary conditions. Pie-shaped or wagonwheel-shaped corrals have been designed to replace the older rectilinear ones. These new designs reduce the required travel by about one-third. The milking facility is at the center of the hub, and feeding is provided on the perimeter of the corral where fence-line bunkers are filled from self-unloading wagons.[8]

Poultry operations have been engineered to provide for extreme mechanization and a high level of market-oriented efficiency. Birds are most often raised in multilevel apartmentlike buildings where they may never touch the ground.

Mechanization had lagged in the fruit and specialty crop industries. Accordingly, in post-World War II years, increased attention was given to experimental research in these areas. The immediate goals were increased efficiency and reduced labor costs. During these years, labor costs in the harvesting and handling of such crops as berries and tart cherries reached more than 50 per cent of the total production cost. The need for mechanization in these areas was clearly apparent. In the 1950's, cooperative research was initiated at Michigan State University, the University of California, and Washington State University to invent labor-saving devices for this type of harvest. Handling and harvesting were not separable processes in this industry; hence, complete systems were developed whereby great proportions of diverse types of fruit crops could be harvested by machine. The equipment typically consisted of tree shakers and collecting frames. The mechanical tree shakers removed the fruit which was then caught in frames sealed around the tree trunks. The fruit was removed from the frames by conveyors and placed in bulk boxes or tanks. Three-men crews were reported to harvest 60 trees an hour, and labor costs were reduced from twelve to two dollars per ton.[9]

Scientific and engineering research in soil tillage is one of the most advanced of the agricultural research areas. In 1935, the U.S. Department of Agriculture built the National Tillage Machinery Laboratory at Auburn, Alabama. This laboratory included nine soil bins, each 20 feet wide and 250 feet long. Engineers and soil scientists combined their efforts to design equipment, measure the force that tillage tools apply to the soil, and analyze the way that they break the earth. Advances in tillage which control a maximum number of variables have been achieved through this type of research.

Work simplification. The goals of engineering experimentation and mechanization in agriculture include work simplification for farmers and laborers, greater efficiency in production, and higher quality of goods. Such goals are well-known in other operations. In the late nineteenth century, Frederick Taylor expanded and implemented these goals in the pig iron industry of Philadelphia. Vertical integration in the steel industry during the same period was a further manifestation of the ideal of efficiency.

Following the precedent set by Taylor for time and motion studies, Carter published a bulletin [10] in 1943, reporting the first such study in agriculture. Carter's study focused on the systematic milking of dairy cows before the time of the modern milking parlors. His research demonstrated how daily chores could be reduced from five hours and 44 minutes to three hours and 39 minutes, thus saving two hours and five minutes a day. Following his plan, walking could be reduced from 3.25 miles to 1.25 miles, or a savings of two miles daily. This was a total of 720 man-hours and 730 miles of walking saved per year, through a cash investment of fifty dollars or less.

The importance of time and motion studies and work simplification procedures has been widely recognized. In 1943 a national work simplification project which focused on agriculture was established, and many similar studies have followed. Buildings have been rearranged, remodeled, and relocated after a study of work routines, in an effort to abbreviate the number of steps taken and to relieve the burden of various types of workloads. Handwork or piecework is being eliminated wherever possible. Although much research remains to be done to reduce the workload further at the farmstead, the advances already made have been substantial.

Research conducted at Purdue University has demonstrated that energy requirements for the average farm worker are moderate. Peak stress periods, however, remain a problem. The workload in such instances is still sufficiently great to cause trouble for cardiac patients.[11]

It is believed by agriculture research specialists that much of the major physical work which continues to be associated with farming can be reduced, and some of it completely eliminated. Heavy expenditure of physical energy has been reduced to a minimum in the two-level cow milking parlors. Some strenuous activity is still directly associated with work that involves the use of tractors. Efforts are being made to equip tractors with power steering as well as with more comfortable seats. Before horse power was replaced with tractors, regular rest periods were required for the animal. Thus a rest period for the farmer was also provided. The tractor's operation can, for all practical purposes, continue for long hours; in this way, the need for rest periods is eliminated. In the short run, some mechanization has contributed to heavier workloads and greater fatigue. Research is now being conducted to find methods of reducing these fatigue situations. Automation appears to be the ultimate result of research findings.

Technology and machines in the homes. Household equipment has been modified at an unprecedented rate. Major household developments are brought about through home economics research divisions of federal and state governments. Although research centers are located in the agriculture agencies, there is little basis for arguing that the development of technology in the area of household equipment is different from rural and urban areas. With electric service now available to virtually all of the nation's homes, such items as electric sewing machines, clothes washers, hand irons, vacuum cleaners, cooking utilities, water heaters, air conditioners, and refrigerators are more or less universal in mid-century America.

Multiple types of services have been invented for many of the domestic machines. The latter are now often automatic or semiautomatic, operating with electric timers and thermostats. Time and motion studies and simplification of work details have been no less aggressive when employed in experimental kitchens by home economists than throughout the various other technological laboratories for farming. Arrangement of facilities for space-saving kitchens has been widely adopted. Mechanical advances which lead to central home organization tend to contradict the adage that a woman's work is never done. As agricultural laborers are largely displaced by mechanization, the domestic household servant is also largely displaced by mechanization in the efficient organization of small homes. In the second half of the twentieth century the domestic servant, when utilized at all, is more a status symbol than a person of functional necessity to home management.

Automation and systems farming. Knowledge of engineering and acceptance of the machine are now combined so as to leave automation as a next horizon for farming. *Systems engineering* and *linear programming* are not yet household words, but the frequency of their use is increasing. They imply, in effect, a degree of automation, a type of vertical integration, and a particular system of agribusiness.

Notions of systems are not new. The sciences of astronomy, physics, and biology, led researchers to the study of so-called natural systems and to the discovery of natural laws. Researchers were concerned primarily with explaining the relationships between interacting but distinct parts. The application of science and technology to agriculture also involves systems building. New assemblages are created, new correlations are observed, and new systems members are constructed. The ultimate result may be the creation of completely new methods for producing and processing materials.[12] Systems organization is not as rigid in agriculture as in some other industries. For example, there are time lapses between some of the various stages, such as that between the planting of a crop, and its harvest. Such time lapses allow for, or create, some flexibility in the systems.

Systems are still segmental and do not typically involve comprehensive planning. The argument in favor of systems engineering, however, is the recurrent one that many advances can be made even though certain information or variables remain unknown. The progress may be partial, but it is preferable to an absence of any systems planning. The variables for systems engineering in agriculture are particularly complex. They include not only the usual mechanization and electronic processes but, in addition, and peculiar to plant and animal growth and development, chemical utilization, bacterial development, and many other processes that are a known part of scientific agriculture. The systems engineering of agriculture is primarily concerned with materials, machines, labor, and energy—all of which are combined to modify the natural processes of the environment in the production of food and fiber.

In agriculture many single units of operation constitute small systems within themselves. The tractor is viewed by some as a system involving the complex unification of liquid fuels for mechanical power and the integration of a variety of tillage tools and other equipment. Farm supply services now constitute additional systems in many cases. They include delivery of bulk feed, custom service in the application of fertilizers and insecticides, and the sale and distribution of farm products.

Systems analysis in agriculture begins with the selection of goals and a criterion for judging their attainment processes, commonly used in systems analysis in other industries. In the case of the farming enterprise, a systems analysis might be aimed at minimizing soil loss, maximizing output, minimizing the costs of given outputs, or maximizing the profit for a particular farm. A systems analysis may include one or all of these goals. Specific examples of systems research were reported by the California and Oregon Agricultural Experiment Stations in 1958 for the plant assembly of lima beans and peas for freezing.

A further and perhaps final development in systems programming would be the integration of comprehensive systems to solve production and marketing problems. As agribusiness expands, these operations necessarily become integrated into single, inseparable units. Systems agriculture represents one way of directly implementing this process.

"Push-button" agriculture, or mechanization in the form of automation, is another step in efficient production. It is said that push-button agriculture is not a dream but a reality. It is already in the experimental stage, but widespread implementation has not yet been achieved. There are many variables, not the least of which is the need for more training on the part of farmers and others involved in automation.

The concept of automation was first applied to industry in the early 1950's and appeared in agricultural publications in the middle 1950's. Automation is already characteristic of the nation's nonagricultural industries, and it is now used experimentally in agribusiness as well. In the post-World War II years, labor costs for farming have increased, as they have for other industries. Much of the merit of automation consists of the potential reduction of labor costs through the elimination of laborers in some cases and less extensive utilization of labor in others.

Farming specialization and mechanization have developed in a parallel fashion. There is a continual combining of operations to bring production nearer to automated control.

Automation will develop—tractors, self-propelled units, and implements that operate according to preset directions and adjust themselves for variations in soils and crops. Sensing devices will be developed to determine depth of top soil, moisture content, soil cover, crop growth, height of crop, and height of heads of crops. Feelers for sensing the locations of plants—sugar beets, corn, cotton—will be used for cultivation and harvest.[13]

Automation already has become a reality in the complete operation of small feed mills. The dairying industry approximates a point of complete automation. Some of its individual component parts are automated. Automation from field to storage for various crops has not been achieved yet, but experimental advances are being made in that direction.

AGRIBUSINESS AND TECHNOLOGY

The systematic farming ideas that have been advanced reflect the incorporation of agriculture into an industrial society. Technology and mechanization on farms have led to the integration of food and fiber production into the total national economic system. As urbanized social organization has come to characterize the society, these developments and their ramifications in agriculture can be seen as a phase in the process of social change. The impact of agribusiness and technology upon marketing and the farm labor force remain to be considered.

Marketing as an ultimate goal of mechanized agribusiness. Marketing processes are influenced by the number of persons whom the product reaches and by the number involved in the processing and distribution of the product. Human relations in marketing are therefore twofold, that is, those that involve the consumer and those that involve sales. Both aspects have been intensively studied. In the case of sales, it has been observed that one of the high costs of marketing is labor. Technological innovations are, therefore, concentrated in the area of labor-saving devices. They are oriented to minimizing the number of times that individuals must pick up and put down items as they are moved from the farm through the processing plants to the consumer. Although most of this handling of products is still manual, machines are now being designed to eliminate the handwork. In addition, power lifts, loaders, conveyors, and related equipment all are contributing to reduced handwork.[14]

Large-scale mass markets continue to require more standardized products from large-scale mechanized farming enterprises. Farmers' markets are expanded greatly, and distribution of products is no longer limited to the local communities. The inauguration of the supermarket depended upon a complex of human relations, and an extensive technology which combined the results of large-scale, standardized agricultural production, large-scale processing, and large-scale distribution. None of these stages of development has yet reached a point of maturity. Many farmers are aware of the fact that they are only in the introductory stage of a techno-logical revolution. The final integration of producing systems, processing systems, and distributing systems, all in an automated series of relation-ships, is a foreseeable consequence of the processes already in motion. Supermarket retailers welcome specialized production of uniform com-modities. Similarly, the producers can welcome the mass market as an assured market for their processed product.

Harbingers of things to come are cow pools, in which groups of farm owners turn over their cows to pool operators for feeding and milking at central points, and in pig hatcheries and pig put-out systems that are used to assure a steady flow of pigs to market outlets. Beef cattle feeding operations are also conducted on a contract or custom basis for market agents, such as packer or chain stores, who want an assured supply of beef of a particular quality for their customers.[15]

Labor efficiency resulting from mechanization. During the fifty years between 1910 and 1960, farm output per man-hour rose an average of nearly 3 per cent per year. During the period between World Wars I and

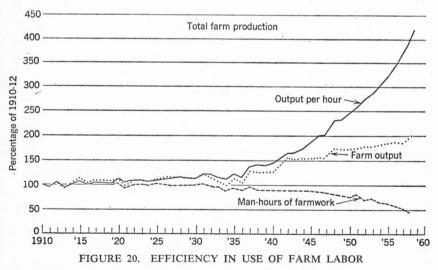

FIGURE 20. EFFICIENCY IN USE OF FARM LABOR

Source: *Power to Produce: Yearbook of Agriculture, 1960* (Washington, D.C.: U.S. Gov-ernment Printing Office, 1960), p. 318.

II, there was a consistent trend toward smaller numbers of farm workers. World War II brought about an acceleration in agricultural production of a magnitude unprecedented in previous national history. Farm output rose approximately 3.3 per cent annually, and production per man-hour also rose to record levels. The efficient use of farm labor between 1910 and 1960 is illustrated by Fig. 20. In recent years increased efficiency in labor has resulted from modern mechanized equipment, increased farm acreages, and specialization. Indexes of farming efficiency in terms of labor utilization also have been supported by advancing scientific experiments in fertilization and in crop and animal production.

SUMMARY

Ideas for technological advances in agriculture have been germane to American society through the long course of history. The majority of the population has been receptive to new ideas and to the concept of change itself. Consequently, indexes of technology suggest high levels of living, dominant social orientations, and systematic rationalistic operations. Technological advances require large-scale capital investments and systematic planning.

The experts for many technological advances in farming are typically agricultural engineers. They have held key positions in the development of both manually and automotively operated agricultural machines. Their research has been conducted in the spirit of the national culture—to reduce the energy input of individuals and to increase the quality of products produced. Automation in agribusiness is already in a developing stage. It should result in further labor reductions and higher production for the individuals remaining in the industry.

NOTES

1. *Science in Farming: The Yearbook of Agriculture, 1943–1947* (Washington: U.S. Department of Agriculture, 1947).

2. Otis D. Duncan, "Economic Changes in American Rural Life," in *1955 Yearbook of Rural Education* (Washington: Department of Rural Education, N.E.A., 1955), pp. 316–25; Alvin L. Bertrand *et al.*, *Factors Associated with Agriculture Mechanization in the Southwest Region* (Arkansas Agricultural Experiment Station Bulletin 567 and Southwestern Regional Bulletin 6, 1956); Alvin L. Bertrand, *Agricultural Mechanization and Social Change in Rural Louisiana* (Louisiana Agricultural Experiment Station Bulletin 458, 1951).

3. Walter Goldschmidt, *As You Sow* (New York: Harcourt, Brace and Co., 1947).

4. Alvin L. Bertrand (ed.), *Rural Sociology* (New York: McGraw-Hill, 1958), pp. 408–9; Bertrand *et al., Factors Associated with Agricultural Mechanization in the Southwest Region.*

5. Wylie D. Goodsell, "Technology and Capital," in *Power To Produce: 1960 Yearbook of Agriculture* (Washington: U.S. Government Printing Office, 1960), pp. 370–75.

6. John W. Rockey *et al.,* "Progress at the Farmstead," in *After a Hundred Years: 1962 Yearbook of Agriculture* (Washington: U.S. Government Printing Office, 1962), p. 411.

7. *Ibid.,* p. 414.

8. *Ibid.,* p. 415.

9. *Ibid.,* p. 420.

10. R. M. Carter, *Labor Saving Through Farm Job Analysis* (Vermont Agricultural Experiment Station Bulletin 503, 1943).

11. *Power To Produce,* p. 402.

12. L. L. Sammet, "Systems Engineering in Agriculture," *ibid.,* p. 428.

13. *Ibid.,* p. 418.

14. Harry C. Trelogan, "Marketing in the Future," *ibid.,* p. 447.

15. *Ibid.,* p. 449.

SELECTED READINGS

Bertrand, Alvin L., *et al., Factors Associated with Agricultural Mechanization in the Southwest Region.* Arkansas Agricultural Experiment Station Bulletin 567 and Southwestern Regional Bulletin 6, 1956.

    This bulletin illustrates the type of empirical research which is being carried out to study, report, and accelerate mechanization of farms.

Goldschmidt, Walter. *As You Sow.* New York: Harcourt, Brace and Co., 1947.

    A classic study of an industrial farming community in Southern California. The essence of the monograph is poignantly suggested in the author's phrase, "From industrialized sowing of the soil is reaped an urbanized rural society."

After a Hundred Years: 1962 Yearbook of Agriculture. Washington: U.S. Government Printing Office, 1962.

    An entire section is devoted to the subject of "technologies."

Power To Produce: 1960 Yearbook of Agriculture. Washington: U.S. Government Printing Office, 1960.

    A succinct review of recent research developments which further industrialize and urbanize agriculture. The particularly illustrative chapters are: "Engineering the Farmstead," "Agribusiness in the Machine Age," "Mechanization and Automation," and "Machines for New Crops."

Science in Farming: The Yearbook of Agriculture, 1943–1947. Washington: U.S. Government Printing Office, 1947.

A nontechnical report which briefly treats the history of agricultural research and, in more detail, recent research developments regarding animals, plants, trees, soils, insects, food and clothing, and new products.

13 PROFESSIONALS AND SPECIALISTS IN AGRIBUSINESS

A new and unobtrusive core of workers is primarily responsible for changing agriculture to agribusiness. These workers are professionals and specialists. Their estimated number of less than half a million is small by comparison to the more than 3,000,000 farm operators and the total of approximately 26,000,000 agribusiness workers.[1] In spite of the fact that these professionals and specialists in agribusiness are not organized and are geographically dispersed, they exert a power disproportionate to their low numerical strength, due to the knowledge they create and control. The power of these professionals and specialists is neither political nor ideological. They do not constitute a pressure group or a social movement. Their power is functional in nature. They have produced new machinery, technologies, and other innovations which have revolutionized food production, processing, and distribution. Without them there could be no urbanized society. In this sense they are more essential to urbanized society than the farmers themselves.

NATURE OF SPECIALIZATION

Division of labor, specialization, and professionalization reflect the images which men create for their society. As ruralized social organization has declined and urbanized social organization has come to dominance, there has been a concomitant proliferation of statuses and of the knowledge achieved and utilized by men. The value of a complex division of labor for society has been best articulated by Emile Durkheim.[2] Durkheim's thesis is that the division of labor precipitates an interdependent unity of specialists and producers. According to him, the result of such interdependence is the achievement of social solidarity.

The Industrial Revolution of the eighteenth century created many new occupations and demands for a plurality of new skills on the part of workers. The division of labor continued to grow, and by the nineteenth century the organization of professionals and specialists was based upon developments in science and technology.[3] The occupational structure of the era was dominated by such professionals as doctors and engineers who experienced a steady trend toward specialization within their professions and among competing occupations. Responses to specialization varied. Medicine endeavored to centralize its profession; engineering became decentralized. In the fullness of time the differential reaction of these two professions to the shifts of society have become relatively unimportant. At best, each has been able to establish codes of ethics and thereby further its boundary maintenance. When those in new specialty areas could not gain admission into the traditional professions, they followed the only course left to them, namely, the establishment of their own occupational organizations.

Division of labor and specialization are basic in human organization. Professionalization is a specific form of the division of labor that has undergone elaborate development in urbanized society. Yet, a specific profession's roles are never completely assured. A profession which is not sensitive to social change can have its roles contracted. The clergy in the Western world has experienced role contraction for several centuries. The occupation of farming is currently losing many of its former roles due to the recent development of vertical integration and science in agribusiness. The way of life of subsistence agriculture has not been adequate to meet the demands of urbanized social organization. Although there are more than 3,000,000 farmers, most of them have operations which are far too small to enable them to conduct their own scientific research.

The demand of the urbanized society for high-quality standardized products constitutes a powerful social force. The small farm operation cannot meet this demand. Scientific research supported by government and private industry is of such magnitude that professionals and experts come to hold key positions in farming and agribusiness. In a similar way, current experiments with vertical integration and corporate farming grow out of the social environment of mass society and mass marketing. Vertical integration is one mechanism whereby the agricultural industry seeks to respond to society's demand for mass-produced food and fiber. When small independent farmers participate in vertical integration of agriculture, many of their roles are removed. They no longer make all of their own managerial decisions and their production is influenced by the directives of specialists.

Professionals. The word *scientist* did not come into general usage until the 1870's.[4] Early scientists conducted their research and experiments in university laboratories or, if they were men of independent wealth, in their private laboratories. In either event the early scientists were most often concerned with obtaining knowledge for its own sake. Later technicians applied the findings of science to industry. Late in the nineteenth century, scientists were recognized as a distinct occupational category.

The distance from the ivory tower to factories was first spanned by chemists. This was accomplished in Germany. As chemistry developed, it gradually became impossible for brewers, dyers, leather processors, paint manufacturers, and others to provide for their own chemical knowledge. Chemistry grew as a profession, and societies for chemical industry were founded in the 1880's.

In the twentieth century the teaching of science was incorporated into the curriculum of English schools. It soon followed that government departments became dependent upon chemists in guiding farmers.[5] Physics and atomic physics each in turn left the ivory tower to become applied sciencies. With World War II, mass production was introduced; the various forms of engineering subsequently became applied disciplines. Professionals and specialists are still increasing in kind and number. They are born of urbanized social organization.

No exact definition of a profession exists. But the ambitious attempts to achieve professional status on the part of technicians, tradespeople, social workers, and many other occupational groups suggest that this status still has considerable value. The attributes of a profession include: one, a body of knowledge held as a common possession by the professionals; two, a specific educational process based on the body of knowledge, the development of that knowledge, and the transmission of it from one generation to another; three, a standard of qualifications for admission which is determined by training, competence, and the judgment of the existing professional group; four, a specified standard of conduct or code of ethics which provides a guide for the practitioner as he relates himself to clients, colleagues, and the public; five, recognition of status, either formally or informally, by colleagues or by the state; and, six, the organization of the occupational group, enabling it to articulate its concept of social duty, to publish learned journals, and to sponsor meetings.[6]

No clear ideological roles exist for agribusiness professionals or specialists. The dignity of individuals is still respected, and the final responsibility for decision-making remains with the electorate. This, in essence, is the ideology. The fact is, however, that the urbanized social organization of the twentieth century has bred technologies, sciences, and pseudosciences at an accelerated rate.[7] It may be an academic question whether scientists and technicians know more and more about less and less until they are experts about nothing at all, or whether the accumulation of technological and scientific knowledge is synthesized into an integrated understanding. While this question remains unresolved, specialists hold the balance of power of contemporary decision-making. Faith in scientific knowledge persists, and decision makers in government and agriculture continue to formulate plans based on the scientific facts, though these facts are neither accumulated nor thoroughly understood by decision makers. Consequently, they are inevitably dependent upon the reports of scientists and experts.

It is precisely at this point that the new men of power enter agribusiness. Decisions concerning food and fiber production are more and more based upon information provided by these experts. Professionals and specialists can be summoned and dismissed, but they alone provide the necessary information. Therefore, it matters little to the ongoing operation of the society if government can dismiss a given horticulturist, veterinarian, or dietician, since it will be dependent upon another member of that group of specialists for the detailed information needed. In short, specialists hold the information on the basis of which generalists make decisions.

Specialists. Specialists may constitute a subcategory of persons within a profession, or a number of workers pioneering in a new area and who have not yet become organized into an autonomous profession. Professionals and specialists are, therefore, not mutually exclusive types. Professionals have a collective image of themselves which is integrated through their body of knowledge and specific organization. Specialists are characteristically not integrated through their knowledge, work activities, or organizations. Typically, the vanguard of specialists will be insufficient in number to warrant complete organizational activity. The profession of food ionizers, for example, does not yet exist. Scientific specialists, however, are currently engaged in research and study of food preservation through radiation and ionization. Examples of specialists in agribusiness are many, and they can be identified historically as well as contemporaneously.

Food production and processing technology is changing at such a rapid pace that the specialist in agribusiness is of extraordinary importance, even though his numbers are so few and his research areas so unique that a profession in the technical sense is not yet organized around this body of knowledge. Innovation in agribusiness involves a multitude of specialists of highly significant proportions. To confine one's consideration to the established professions would be to overlook a most significant vanguard in changing human relations.

OCCUPATIONS ARE NEITHER URBAN NOR RURAL

Historically, one of the most precise differentiating factors between urban and rural society was occupation.[8] Farming was the classic rural occupation. The old organization of farming involved a great degree of isolation, close communion with nature, excessive physical energy input, and generalized rather than specialized work. Today, as urbanized social organization continues, the criteria by which men formerly differentiated rural from urban occupations are no longer adequate. The general farmer is becoming an anomaly; specialization in such areas as livestock, dairying, poultry, and cotton is much more common. Within the specialty areas of farming, and often within general farming as well, there is systematic planning involving scientific study of plant and animal life cycles, knowledge of mechanization, and a keen understanding of marketing. Business farmers operate by using principles which are similar to those of businessmen in other areas of the urbanized society.

Agricultural science is a misnomer unless it is carefully understood to be a shorthand identification for the application of general scientific knowledge and techniques to a specific subject area. Theories of chemistry and physics are the same whether applied to data and situations pertaining to a metropolitan industry or farming research. Theories of agricultural economics and rural sociology are the same as those of general economics and general sociology.[9] This is true for the long list of sciences which are applied to human enterprises. Principles of the natural, physical, and social world are generic, and not differentiated on the basis of rural or urban location.

Occupations cannot be identified as rural or urban on the basis of the ecological location of the worker. The occupation of veterinary medicine is practiced by persons located in farming as well as in major metropolitan areas. The body of knowledge is applied in large and small animal clinics, to dairy herds, and to domestic pets. Similarly, the nursery operator is neither urban nor rural. Indeed, this is a curious occupation, in which the practitioners work with plant production but often in the modified environment of the greenhouse, completely encircled by the city. Nurserymen and florists are marginal men between occupational orientations in a manner similar to that of social psychologists, chemical engineers, or pharmacists, to name but a few. Agricultural engineering, agricultural journalism, agricultural extension, and home economics are other examples of occupations which are intertwined into the total culture of the society. They bridge the gap between divergent occupational orientations. The very existence of such occupations is an example of the synthesizing and integrating force of urbanized social organization. Cultural universals which guide men in their occupational endeavors are not dichotomized into rural or urban categories; rather they are common to occupations wherever they are located.

Another factor which creates confusion in the attempt to differentiate occupations by rural-urban dimensions is that of employment in industry in metropolitan areas which is rural-oriented and employment in industry in open-country areas which is urban-oriented. Employment in large farm machinery manufacturing enterprises and in the large food and fiber processing enterprises is most often in cities, and frequently in very large cities. This situation is reversed with the decentralization of the nation's industry, which often involves locating new factories and plants in small country towns or in open-country rural areas. Employees in these plants work at unskilled, skilled, and technical-professional occupations which have no direct relation to food and fiber production and processing.[10] There is no sociological basis for observing that city employment in a tractor manufacturing plant is more rural than city employment in a passenger automobile manufacturing concern. Likewise, there is no basis for arguing that employment in an International Business Machine plant located in the open country is rural. On the contrary, both of these situations point up the fact that cultural universals of the work world are part of urbanized society. Work in the employee society is a basic form of activity, neither urban nor rural in nature.

WORK SITUATIONS AND CULTURE

Professionals and specialists in agribusiness form an often silent and invisible category of workers that has an impact on food and fiber production far exceeding its numerical proportion in agribusiness. It is an integral part, perhaps the most important part, of the agribusiness enterprise of the nation. Its work situation is complex, including as principal components: recruitment into the occupation, socialization and training in the skills and knowledge of the occupation, economic remuneration and rewards, work association patterns, client relationships, and professional organization of the occupation.

Recruitment. The recruitment process includes methods of selection of persons admitted to the professional specialist occupations. The recent history of farming has two important occupational characteristics. In the first place, it is among the most hereditary of occupations. A recent study reported that 80 per cent of the beginning farmers had family help.[11] While law and medicine are other examples of highly hereditary occupations, neither of these reaches the magnitude of familial socialization and recruitment that is observed in farming.

The second major and more recent occupational characteristic of farming is its social structure moving people out of the occupation.[12] In terms of the nation's major occupations, this negative recruitment structure is unique. Recruitment is most often thought of only as a process for facilitating entrance into an occupation. In the case of American farming, it has become a process for facilitating movement out of the occupation. Studies of occupational replacement ratios indicate there will be less need for farmers and farm laborers in 1965 than there was in 1955 (see Table XX). A U.S. Department of Agriculture bulletin indicated that only 15 per cent of the farm boys reaching maturity would be able to find occupational positions in agriculture.[13] Replacement ratios are computed on the basis of the number of persons who will retire or otherwise leave their positions in farming, for farms having a gross sale of over $5,000 annually. Farming operations that are not expected to have such a magnitude of gross sales are believed to provide a level of living that would be

TABLE XX. EMPLOYMENT TRENDS: NUMBER NEEDED IN THE LABOR FORCE IN 1965 FOR
EVERY 100 IN 1955

	No. of Workers
Professional and technical workers	137
Managers, officials, and proprietors	122
Clerical and sales workers	127
Skilled craftsmen	124
Semiskilled operatives	122
Service workers	113
Unskilled laborers	97
Farmers	85

Source: Edward V. Pope, *Helping Rural Youth Choose Careers* (U.S.D.A., Miscellaneous Publication No. 771. Oct., 1958) p. 3.

substandard in terms of the general level of the nation's families as well as the ideology of the country.

In contrast to farming, agribusiness provides a multiple number of opportunities. Many of these opportunities are in the professional specialist occupations. The nation's land-grant colleges published an influential recruitment brochure entitled *I've Found My Future in Agriculture*.[14] The message expressed is dramatic and clear. Fifteen thousand college graduates could find employment in agribusiness while the land-grant colleges of agriculture graduated only 7,000 students annually or half of the number needed in 1958. As a recruitment instrument, this brochure was attractively presented, profusely illustrated, and graphically concise. Its intent was clearly to represent a positive, enticing image of careers in agribusiness.

There are many other examples of agribusiness recruitment instruments. A wide range of professional careers is offered in home economics.[15] Careers in forestry are attractively described as professional.[16] Business careers are available with the Rural Electrification Administration.[17] Departments from the institutes of agriculture publish brochures which literally advertise career opportunities in their respective science areas.

In the past the experience of living on a farm has enhanced opportunities for employment in vocational agriculture and in county agent careers. In contrast to the qualifications of farm experience deemed necessary for these positions, some of the recruitment literature now specifically announces that the field is open to persons from both urban and rural backgrounds.[18] Certainly much of the scientific research is of such a basic nature that it provides an intellectual challenge to the curious, regardless of their socialization experiences in rural or urban areas. Examples of this type of research include the use of radiation in the preservation of food,[19] the use of fish as a food for mink,[20] and much of the research in dietetics.[21]

Recruitment into most professional occupations is typically restricted to persons in the young adult years. The social structure out of which this recruitment pattern grows is the belief that maximum intellectual creativity is most often reached in the early years of life.[22] Further, a young age is a practical requirement for candidates to a profession because of the long years of rigorous training which are required to master the skills and body of knowledge. Scientific and professional cognition require long years of training before the neophyte accumulates enough knowledge to be in a position to make original contributions to his field of endeavor.

Professionals in agribusiness are typically male rather than female. Several mores account for this sex differentiation. Farming has been historically a male occupation in the United States. Until the time of recent mechanization and science, it required a maximum amount of heavy physical labor. A nation which has a cultural orientation to women as a fairer and weaker sex, whether this is valid or not, does not encourage females to enter farming. As agriculture now become agribusiness, the tendency still remains to identify the new agribusiness occupations as most appropriate for males. A norm which contributes to greater male participation in the professional agribusiness occupations is the strong rural notion that the woman's place is in the home. Since agribusiness recruits heavily from youth who come from rural backgrounds, it has a greater number of male than female applicants.

The social structure of urbanized society contributes to the recruitment of more rural than nonrural youth into agribusiness. Rural-urban migration continues to involve adjustments to a more heterogeneous environment. As the total society becomes characterized by urbanized social organization, rural-urban differences diminish. There are, however, many survivals of them in the general culture. Consequently—and to the extent that the rural-urban societies are not yet homogeneous—rural youth who migrate to city environments move less in terms of social space when they take up occupations in agribusiness than when they find occupational careers in nonagribusiness activities. Self-identification is achieved more easily in agribusiness for those who have a farm or small-town background. The vocabulary and interests of many people who work in agribusiness contains nuances of a farm-oriented variety which are not found in the large city banking enterprises, industrial enterprises, or law firms. In agribusiness employment the way of dress and the approach to the work situation carries overtones of the earlier rural experience. In general, the style of life and behavior of people in work situations in art museums, for example, are in sharp contrast to those of employees in agricultural extension offices. Consequently, recruits from a farm or small town have fewer new aspects of the culture to learn in a professional agribusiness career than do small-town recruits in a professional nonagribusiness career.

Socialization and training. Among the most important aspects of the very concept of profession are socialization and training. Science and the professions involve a body of knowledge and skills which must be mastered before an applicant can be certified for a position. In the case of agribusiness, education and training constitute the explicit knowledge requirement. Most often, the requirement is a college education involving training and the achievement of high grades in a number of specific courses from chemistry, mathematics, and physics, to economics.

For admission to the more creative fields of professional work, college undergraduate training constitutes a preparatory step required in order to enter a professional or graduate school. The professional or graduate school offers a higher level training, oriented less toward evaluation on the basis of knowledge and skills and more toward evaluation of actual research performance; its aim is to provide the prospective professional with a research situation which will enable him to demonstrate his capacity for original thought and work. Professionally, creative research in agribusiness, as in nonagribusiness fields, involves a minimal amount of structured control in the work situation. The essence of the task is an altruistic commitment to knowledge, learning, the profession, and the career. Proficiency alone is inadequate for the agribusiness profession; commitment, ideology, and character in the work situation are integral criteria for evaluation of trainees.

At the point in which proficiency is demonstrated in the professional education process, the professionals bring important informal socialization mechanisms into action. One of the abiding characteristics of the professional work milieu is the care with which practicing professionals select from a younger generation those who will join their enterprise.[23] Professionals reserve the right ultimately to accept or reject those who will be granted status in their occupation. Socialization is largely an informal process and involves learning a complex behavior. A prospective professional must absorb the proper ideology of the profession, that is, its knowledge, tradition of integrity, system of colleague relationships, and the practical role of the profession's contribution to the larger society.[24]

Remuneration and rewards. Properly earned money is one of the strongest status symbols in American society. Urbanized American society is highly competitive and greatly oriented toward status.[25] But since the 1930's, social structures have been developed for leveling incomes. Originating at approximately the same time, a shift has occurred from a self-employed to an employee society. Along with these changing elements in the social structure, a historic tendency has been set in motion for economic remuneration in agriculture to be slight.

The title *professional* and its accouterments of white collar uniform, research laboratory, office work, secretarial and assistant help constitute other important status symbols in the urbanized society. Another important reward for the professional, particularly to one who is recruited from a traditionalistic rural background, is freedom of expression and creativity in the work situation. An early and abiding abstract sentiment in American society is the high value placed on the freedom of the individual to make his own decisions in his work situations. In the employee society this abstract sentiment is an anomaly. Professionals are among the few employees of the urbanized society who retain a high degree of freedom in decision-making in their work situation. It is the very nature of their creativity that their work situations provide only a minimum structure for direction and a maximum opportunity for innovation. Executives comprise perhaps the only other category of employees in the mass society who experience this measure of freedom in their work situation. This reward aspect of professional life, which in a direct way involves neither status nor money, makes professional agribusiness careers highly attractive to the young person who has been socialized in the small-town and farm environment.

Most agribusiness professionals are salaried employees. Most of them are represented in the so-called new or semiprofessions. Veterinarians are an exception. These are usually fee-taking, self-employed professionals. Most other agribusiness specialists work for the government either at the national, state, or college level. A growing number are employed by private industry, but still as salaried workers.

Economic remuneration in the agribusiness professions is not great, but the meaning of work derives from much more than economics.[26] The rewards of freedom for creativity and the status attribute of professional, combined with the salary, constitute a gratifying position in the work world.

Within the professional world itself, several other rewards accrue to the individual. Professionals in agribusiness characteristically engage in research. Communication avenues have been extensively developed to provide maximum opportunity for reporting research findings to others in the professional world. The very nature of research and the provision for communication of the findings provide an opportunity for recognition by colleagues and, in some cases, by those outside the professional discipline. In the urbanized society, where egotistic and success images prevail, this system for acknowledging outstanding work constitutes an important reward. Over the years the norm has been developed for agribusiness professionals to recognize, in an honorific way, those who have rendered lives of devoted service to their work. The literature is replete with citations such as father of agricultural journalism, father of soil chemistry, and founder of the demonstration method.

Professional colleagueship. Colleague relationships in agribusiness professions are determined largely by the character and organization of employment in federal and state government agencies. Most work activities and research projects entail a degree of approval, and a minimum level of supervision, from superiors. Employment is centralized in a number of research centers and laboratories across the nation. These centers and their supervisory organizations characteristically bring a large number of professionals together within the same specialty areas. Much agribusiness professional life is group activity; most research projects involve a number of people. Often the researchers represent a combination of professional specialties. The extent of this practice is illustrated by the research proposal forms which ask for the name of the director, the location of the project, and cooperating persons and agencies.

Ideally, such colleagueship in research supports the social structure of urbanized social organization. The urbanized cultural universals reflect an integration rather than a differentiation of societal members. Group research involving a multiple number of disciplines breaks down the boundaries between professional areas and serves to contribute to new integration of ideas and specialties. Ideally, group research also contributes a maximum amount of intellectual stimulation. A fraternal form of colleagueship in the rural atmosphere of land-grant colleges often leads to closure of staffs.[27]

Client relationships. A multiple clientele is commonplace among the professionals and specialists. They serve the general public, specific farmers, and farm organizations. They also serve government, in terms of their basic research. The power of older fee-taking professionals typically derives from the organization of their own professional activity. They are seldom in any direct way subservient to a power structure superior to them.[28] Salaried professionals and often the new semiprofessionals may have power over some of their clientele, and typically may be subordinate to others. Their specialty and esoteric knowledge places all of their clientele under obligation to them, at least to the extent that they can demonstrate the importance of their services.

Agribusiness professionals and specialists have a superior, esoteric knowledge over virtually all of the people who benefit from their efforts. They do not characteristically use their knowledge for self-aggrandizement or achievement of higher positions in political structures. Their services are unique, and the best that local people can do if they want a particular type of knowledge or a particular service is to provide a position for such a specialist or an occasion where such a specialist may appear as a consultant. Local people can select the individual specialist who will appear in their midst, but the certification of the specialists is beyond local control. The information and the research activity cannot be made available without the specialist.

On many occasions government stands in the role of client to the technical specialists. This role is a peculiar one, in that the professional as a decision maker and creator of information can best identify vanguard areas into which his discipline should probe. At the same time, he is dependent upon government to appropriate the monies which support his research and activities. In this type of organization he must "sell" government on the validity of his research proposals. Government becomes the client and supporter of the salaried professional's research.

The clientele of agribusiness professionals also includes private organizations and private industry. These professionals can frequently sell their services and knowledge on a consulting basis to industry and organizations. There has been a growing demand in recent years for agribusiness professionals to be employed on a full-time, salaried basis by agribusiness enterprises.

Professional organizations. Veterinary medicine is a highly organized profession. The American Veterinary Medical Association is its principal occupational organization. In addition there is a great multiplicity of diverse associations which illustrate the role of veterinary medicine in urbanized society. These associations are concerned with technical knowledge, care of large and small animals, public health, sanitation, the role of female veterinarians, and other subjects. Associations are organized on state, regional, national, and international bases. The following selected list of associations illustrates this urbanized orientation.

SELECTED LIST OF VETERINARY AND RELATED ASSOCIATIONS

American Animal Hospital Association
American Association of Veterinary Bacteriologists
American Association of Veterinary Nutritionists
American Association of Veterinary Parasitologists
American Society of Veterinary Physiologists and Pharmacologists
American Veterinary Exhibitors Association
American Veterinary Medical Association
American Veterinary Radiology Society
American Board of Laboratory Animal Medicine
Association of American Board of Examiners in Veterinary Medicine
Association of Deans of American Colleges of Veterinary Medicine
Conference of Public Health Veterinarians
Conference of Research Workers in Animal Diseases
International Association of Veterinary Food Hygienists
International Standing Committee on Physiology and Pathology of Animal
  Reproduction and Artificial Insemination
National Assembly of Chief Livestock Sanitary Officials
National Association of Federal Veterinarians
Pan American Congress of Veterinary Medicine
Women's Veterinary Medical Association
World Veterinary Association
World Veterinary Poultry Association

Journals in the field of veterinary medicine also reveal the profession's roles in urbanized society. Their roles are regional, professional, commercial, international, governmental and academic in their sources and orientation. The following selected list illustrates this great diversity.

SELECTED LIST OF VETERINARY MEDICINE JOURNALS

National: *Veterinary Medicine, American Journal of Veterinary Research,* and *Journal of the American Veterinary Medical Association.*

Regional: *Auburn Veterinarian, California Veterinarian, Illinois Veterinarian, Iowa Veterinarian, Maryland Veterinarian,* and *Rocky Mountain Veterinarian.*

Foreign: *Australian Veterinary Journal, British Veterinary Journal, Canadian Veterinary Journal, Folia Veterinaria* (Czechoslovakia), *Investigaciones Veterinaries, Anales* (Spain), *Japanese Journal of Veterinary Research, Nordisk Veterinarmedicin* (Norway), *Revista de Medicina Veterinaria* (Argentina), and *South African Veterinary Association Journal.*

Commercial: *Gaines Dog Research Progress, International Veterinary Bulletin* (Cyanamid), *Modern Veterinary Practice, Veterinary Dispatch* (Schering), and *Veterinary Scope* (Upjohn).

Government: *U.S. Army Veterinary Bulletin, U.S. Livestock Sanitary Association,* and *Federal Veterinarian.*

Miscellaneous: *Veterinary Bulletin* (abstract published in England with international coverage), *Veterinary Student, Tuskegee Student Veterinarian, British Small Animal Veterinary Association Proceedings, Index Veterinarius,* and *Journal of Small Animal Practice Proceedings of the Society of Experimental Biology and Medicine.*

In addition to these professional societies and publications, there is a veterinary code of ethics.[29] This code sets forth the profession's responsibility to serve society, its right to choose clients, obligation to improve veterinary knowledge, and interest in safeguarding the public. Indeed, the science of veterinary medicine has all the principal characteristics of a profession.

Most other specialists in agribusiness are not so clearly organized into professions. However, they often have societies and official journals. The accompanying list exemplifies the variety of this type of occupational organization.

PROFESSIONAL DEVELOPMENT AND SOCIETY

The work of many specialists in agribusiness has not yet achieved professionalization; consequently, it is necessary to refer to both professionals and specialists throughout this discussion. Professionalization in agribusiness areas has been deterred for a variety of reasons. Among the deterrents the most important is the fact that many of the research areas identified with agriculture involve a basic body of knowledge, concepts, and methods also utilized in nonagricultural investigation. Many of the so-called agribusiness specialists qualify for membership in the general and national organizations representing their basic science. This is another illustration of the absence of boundary maintenance between rural and urban activities in urbanized society. The scientific type of cognition which

SELECTED LIST OF SPECIALISTS AND OCCUPATIONAL ORGANIZATIONS

American Association of Cereal Chemists	National Association of Artificial Breeders
American Fisheries Society	National Association of County Agriculture Agents
Bio-Dynamic Farming and Gardening Association	National Association of County 4-H Club Agents
Crop Science Society of America	National Association of Television and Radio Farm Directors
Fiber Society	National Farm Home Editors Association
Illuminating Engineering Society	National Home Demonstration Agent Association
International Association of Agricultural Librarians	National Sprayer and Duster Association
Institute of Food Technologists	Newspaper Farm Editors' Association
	Society of Commercial Seed Technologists

Sources *County Agents Directory,* 46th edition (Chicago: C. L. Mast, Jr., and Associates, 1961); *Encyclopedia of American Associations,* 2nd edition (Detroit: Gale Research Co., 1959).

is so widespread in the United States in the twentieth century is a generic type of mental perception, neither specifically urban nor rural.

Many agricultural specialists aspire to professional status. County extension and home agents are attempting to gain academic status in the hierarchy of the state land-grant colleges and universities. In some states, these often minimally (B.A. degree) trained people who typically do no resident teaching and carry on no systematic research have been able to maintain academic rank and title in a resident university. In terms of social organization, the problem is not whether such persons should or should not be awarded the academic title and professional status to which they aspire. Far more important is the fact that agribusiness specialists, like so many specialists in the other areas of the urbanized society, are anxious to achieve professional status.[30] In the reality of social organization a body of workers, regardless of their specialty, do not announce to their clients and to society that they will organize themselves along the characteristic line of professionals and, *ipso facto,* achieve professional status. This would only create a semiprofession by downgrading the qualities of altruism and service and the value of knowledge and skills; ultimately, the respect of the professional world would be subordinated to more acquisitive interests. Professonal status is achieved not only by internal organization of an occupation but also through a system of recognition and rewards granted by society to professionals.

Agribusiness is rapidly developing along the lines of science. There is not yet evidence of a widespread social mandate that agribusiness specialists be awarded professional status. When Western societies in general, and the United States in particular, developed a high respect for individual life and for healthful living, the practice of medicine was transformed from a low position of bloodletting to a high calling and renowned profession. The skill and knowledge needed to practice medicine require long periods of training and socialization. Society placed a high value on human life, and the practice of medicine developed a set of mores and institutions for recruiting individuals into this profession and for rewarding their altruistic practice. In more recent years, with an explosive population growth and increased longevity, which are precipitating problems of overpopulation and gerontology, the profession of medicine is faced with a new challenge.

In a society which places high value on having a population well-fed and adequately clothed and housed, the goals have largely been achieved. Indeed, overproduction of many of the food and fiber products which contribute to these goals is most perplexing. Under such conditions the society's response to efforts toward professionalization of agribusiness specialists will be apathetic. Many of the nascent specialists in agribusiness may organize themselves and complete all the stages of professionalization, without receiving the rewards from the society which are characteristically endowed upon professionals.

CONTRIBUTION OF PROFESSIONAL SPECIALISTS

The contribution of professional specialists in agribusiness is substantial. In the organization of American food and fiber production, virtually all research, scientific, and technological advances in farming since the 1850's have been achieved by the professionals and specialists and not by the owners or operators of farms. In colonial and early national days a considerable number of gentlemen farmers engaged in their own systematic research. The organization of large farming operations which would have permitted continual research by farmers was never established in the United States, and small farms could not adequately carry on their own research programs. Therefore, practically all scientific or technological developments in farming can be attributed to the professionals and specialists.

The areas of agribusiness which include the production of farm equipment and supplies, and the areas that involve processing and marketing, have advanced as a result of systematic work by professionals and specialists. In these latter cases, the work often has been under the direction and jurisdiction of private enterprise rather than directly under the agencies of government. In either event, success in American agricultural production is largely due to the contributions of professionals and specialists.

Although not precisely measurable, the achievements of professionals and specialists are shown by increases in production, new qualities and types of food items produced, and in the release of a large proportion of the agricultural labor force. This has enabled workers to devote their attention to other types of employment not directly related to agribusiness.

SUMMARY

Professionals and specialists represent a new core of agribusiness workers. They are few, but their information and research makes them vastly important beyond their number. These workers have come into being with the wave of urbanized social organization. They are technical experts whose information is essential to the operation of the urbanized society and to the operation of agribusiness as a part of that society.

Occupations in a society characterized by urbanized social organization are neither urban nor rural. Professionals and specialists in the so-called agricultural sciences utilize the same basic knowledge. Scientific farmers who operate large mechanized enterprises, by definition, combine knowledge and skills that have grown out of urbanized social organization.

The work situations of agribusiness professionals and specialists involve recruitment, socialization, remuneration, colleague relationships, client relationships, and professional associations. These career elements are similar to those of other professional occupations. However, processes of recruitment in agriculture are of particular note in that they include negative recruitment or recruitment out of farming rather than into it. A significant proportion of the individuals who leave farming can be recruited into the agribusiness professional and specialist careers.

Growth and development of agribusiness professional and specialist careers are interrelated with major social structures. Although growth has been rapid, its rate has been deterred by lack of boundary maintenance. For example, specialists such as agricultural economists are potential members of two professional associations. They can associate themselves exclusively with other agricultural economists, or with general economists. The growth of these occupations is also limited by the abundance of food and fiber. Society's need for these experts is less critical than it would be if food and fiber were scarce. These occupations continue to develop in the context of urbanized society.

The contribution of agribusiness professionals and specialists to society is beyond statistical measure. Much of the nation's food and fiber abundance can be attributed to their research and communications ability. They have been practical innovators who have worked successfully with farm operators.

NOTES

1. The professionals and specialists are included in this agribusiness total. See also Lee Taylor and Arthur R. Jones, Jr., *Louisiana's Human Resources, Part II: Agribusiness and the Labor Force* (Louisiana Agricultural Experiment Station Bulletin 562, 1963).

2. Emile Durkheim, *Division of Labor in Society* (Glencoe: The Free Press, 1949).

3. Roy Lewis and Angus Maude, *Professional People* (London: Phoenix House, Ltd., 1952), p. 23.

4. *Ibid.,* p. 34.

5. *Ibid.,* p. 35.

6. *Ibid.,* pp. 55-6. See also Edward Gross, "Some Suggestions for the Legitimation of Industrial Studies in Sociology," *Social Forces,* 33 (Mar., 1955), 233-9; Myron Lieberman, *Education as a Profession* (Englewood Cliffs, N.J.: Prentice-Hall, Inc., 1956), pp. 2-6.

7. Lewis and Maude, *op. cit.,* p. 37.

8. Pitirim Sorokin and Carle C. Zimmerman, *Principles of Rural-Urban Sociology* (New York: Henry Holt and Co., 1929).

9. Charles E. Kellogg, "What is Farm Research?" in *Science in Farming: Yearbook of Agriculture, 1943-1947* (Washington: U.S. Government Printing Office, 1947), pp. 17-18.

10. Alvin L. Bertrand and Harold W. Osborne, *Rural Industrialization in a Louisiana Community* (Louisiana Agricultural Experiment Station Bulletin 524, 1959); Therel R. Black *et al., Industrialization of Box Elder County,* (Utah Agricultural Experiment Station Bulletin 420, 1960); John R. Christiansen *et al., Industrialization and Rural Life in Two Central Counties* (Utah Agricultural Experiment Station Bulletin 416, 1960).

11. Franklin J. Reiss, *Getting Started and Established in Farming with and without Family Help* (Illinois Agricultural Experiment Station Circular 822 and North

Central Regional Extension Publication 8, 1960); A. O. Haller, "Planning to Farm: A Social Psychological Interpretation," *Social Forces*, 37 (Mar., 1959), 264–8; Murray A. Straus, "Personal Characteristics and Functional Needs in the Choice of Farming as an Occupation," *Rural Sociology*, 21 (Sept.–Dec., 1956), 257–66; Charles E. Ramsey, *Vocational Intentions of Wisconsin Farm Boys* (Unpublished doctoral dissertation, University of Wisconsin, 1952).

12. Prodipto Roy, *Factors Related to Leaving Farming* (Unpublished scientific paper 1979, Washington Agricultural Experiment Station); Don Kanel, *Opportunities for Beginning Farmers, Are They Limited?* (Nebraska Agricultural Experiment Station Bulletin 452 and North Central Regional Publication 102, 1960); Edward V. Pope, *Helping Rural Youth Choose Careers* (Washington: U.S.D.A., Miscellaneous Publication 771, 1958).

13. Richard G. Ford, *Manpower in the 1960's* (Washington: U.S.D.A., Federal Extension Service, 1960), pp. 12–13.

14. *I've Found My Future in Agriculture* (American Association of Land-Grant Colleges and State Universities, 1958).

15. *Home Economics* (St. Paul: University of Minnesota, School of Home Economics, pamphlet, n.d.).

16. *The Forest Service Engineer: Your Gateway to the Future* (Washington: U.S. Department of Agriculture, Miscellaneous Publication 841, 1961); *Career Opportunities for Veterinarians in the Agriculture Research Service* (Washington: U.S.D.A. Miscellaneous Publication 727, 1961); *Veterinary Medicine As a Career* (Chicago: American Veterinary Medical Association).

17. *Career Opportunities for Seniors Majoring in Business Administration, or Economics in Combination with Some Business Administration Courses* (Washington: Rural Electrification Administration, 1961).

18. *I've Found My Future in Agriculture.*

19. Bruce H. Morgan, "The Role of Ionizing Radiations in the Future Preservation of Foods," in *Cornell University Symposium Papers* (New York Agricultural Experiment Station Bulletin 780, 1957).

20. J. R. Leekley and C. A. Cabell, *Fish Diets for Minks* (Alaska Agricultural Experiment Station Production Research Report 49, 1961).

21. O. J. Kahlenberg and E. M. Funk, *Experiments in Cooking Poultry for Pre-Cooked Poultry Products* (Missouri Agricultural Experiment Station Research Bulletin 748, 1960).

22. Lindsey R. Harmon and Herbert Soldz, *The Science Doctorates of 1958 and 1959* (Washington: National Science Foundation, 1960), p. 14; and Harvey C. Lehman, *Age and Achievement* (Princeton: Princeton University Press, 1953).

23. Theodore Caplow, *The Sociology of Work* (Minneapolis: University of Minnesota Press, 1954).

24. Caplow, *op. cit.*, pp. 100–123.

25. Richard T. LaPiere, *Theory of Social Control* (New York: McGraw-Hill Book Co., Inc., 1954).

26. Nancy C. Morse and Robert S. Weiss, "The Function and Meaning of Work and the Job," *American Sociological Review,* 20 (Apr., 1955), 191–8; Eugene A. Friedman and Robert J. Havighurst, *The Meaning of Work and Retirement* (Chicago: The University of Chicago Press, 1954).

27. C. Arnold Anderson, "Trends in Rural Sociology," in Robert K. Merton *et al., Sociology Today* (New York: Basic Books, Inc., 1959), p. 364.

28. Stephen Potter, *One-Upmanship* (New York: Henry Holt and Co., 1951).

29. *Journal of the American Veterinary Medical Association,* 137 (Oct. 15, 1960), 35.

30. M. Lee Taylor and Roland J. Pellegrin, "Professionalization: Its Functions and Dysfunctions for the Life Insurance Occupation," *Social Forces,* 38 (Dec., 1959), 110–14.

SELECTED READINGS

Caplow, Theodore. *The Sociology of Work.* Minneapolis: University of Minnesota Press, 1954.

The human relations of work are systematically treated and the various elements of the work situation discussed in detail.

Gross, Edward. *Work and Society.* New York: Thomas Y. Crowell Co., 1958.

Three chapters of this book deal specifically with the work organization of farming occupations: "The Farm: The Work Complex," "The Farm: The Work Structure and the Economic Complex," and "The Farm: Status, Career, and the Work Group."

I've Found My Future in Agriculture. American Association of Land-Grant Colleges and State Universities, 1958.

This brochure illustrates the prominent roles of professionals in the food and fiber industry.

Kellogg, Charles E. "What is Farm Research?" in *Science in Farming: Yearbook of Agriculture, 1943–1947.* Washington: U.S. Government Printing Office, 1947, pp. 17–32.

A brief treatment of the organizational nature of research in experiment stations, the U.S.D.A., and trends in agricultural research.

Lewis, Roy and Angus Maude. *Professional People.* London: Phoenix House, Ltd., 1952.

A careful and critical study of the development of professions, with particular emphasis on England.

14 COMMERCIAL AND PART–TIME FARMING

Farming is the traditional rural occupation. Living on the land, most often in a peasant village, frequently has been equated with tilling the soil. Historically, therefore, agriculture has been more a way of life than an occupation. A penetrating analysis of contemporary rural life reveals that in urbanized social organization living on the land and work in farming involve more than tilling the soil. It has become agribusiness, a specialized aspect of the division of labor and a specific, well-articulated occupation.

OCCUPATIONAL CHARACTERISTICS OF FARMING

The major characteristics of farming as an occupation are clear.[1] It is among the most hereditary of occupations. Recruitment into the occupation is structured so as to discourage sons of nonfarmers from entering its ranks. It is predominantly a male occupation. Until the recent rise of science and technology, informal participant socialization rather than formal training characterized the preparation for work. The career has been characterized by lifetime commitment. Throughout the nineteenth century, if one were reared on a farm, he operated it during his productive years (18–60) and finally retired on it in his declining years. Social status was precise. One worked up the agricultural ladder from laborer to renter, to part-owner and, finally, to full owner. Highest status was awarded the full owner.

Agriculture as a way of life is now declining and, in its place, farming is developing as an occupation. Security and retirement are not provided for the occupation of farming as they were for agriculture as a way of life. Hereditary entrance still characterizes recruitment, although training is becoming more formalized. The study of vocational agriculture in high school is virtually essential if one is to be a commercial business farmer. In-service training is widespread through extension and short courses.

Farming remains one of the nation's foremost self-employed occupations. Most farmers operate small businesses. They provide much of their own management and much of their labor, although management is more and more influenced by the national urbanized market and the federal government.

At peak production periods, farming may utilize eight to nine million workers, but most of them are not in the occupation of farming. In 1959 the total distribution of farm workers included approximately 1,448,000 farmers (Economic Classes I–IV), 4,000,000 hired workers, 2,000,000 unpaid family workers, 965,000 subsistence farmers (Economic Classes V–VI), and 882,000 part-time farmers. Among these workers only those in the first category are, occupationally speaking, farmers. Persons in the other farm worker categories are, from time to time, assistants to farmers, although they are not members of the occupation.

In contemporary American society, farming and ranching become specialized occupations in agribusiness and in the larger society's complex division of labor. These occupations are typically practiced in the open-country areas. Aside from their geographical location, commercial farmers are essentially like other businessmen and, as such, are highly integrated into the total urbanized division of labor. As urbanization comes to characterize the nation as a whole, an occupational stratum of businessmen emerges, the characteristics of which are fundamentally the same whether they are located on Manhattan Island or the King Ranch of Texas. Only the content of their business varies to fit local needs. Therefore, as the occupations of farming and ranching become business-oriented, they constitute work specialties that are more integrated with total society than with either a distinct rural or urban society.

There are several types of farmers. Hence, a simple description of the so-called typical farmer is far from adequate. Some of the major differences among farmers are revealed in the classification contained in the Census of Agriculture, which distinguishes between commercial and noncommercial farms [2] (see Table XXI). Farming is the primary occupation

TABLE XXI. CRITERIA FOR THE ECONOMIC CLASSES OF FARMS AND NUMBER OF FARMS IN EACH CLASS, FOR THE CONTERMINOUS UNITED STATES: 1959

Class	Number of Farms, 1959	Criteria		Farms Excluded
		Value of Farm Products Sold	Other	
Class I	101,835	$40,000 and over	None	Abnormal
Class II	210,162	$20,000 to $39,999	None	Abnormal
Class III	482,478	$10,000 to $19,999	None	Abnormal
Class IV	653,150	$ 5,000 to $ 9,999	None	Abnormal
Class V	616,819	$ 2,500 to $ 4,999	None	Abnormal
Class VI	348,473	$50 to $2,499	Farm operator under 65 years of age. Did not work off the farm 100 or more days. Income that he and members of household received from off-the-farm sources was less than total value of farm products sold	Abnormal
Commercial farms, total	2,412,917			
Part-time	881,883	$50 to $2,499	Farm operator under 65 years of age and he either worked off the farm 100 or more days or the income he and members of his household received from off-the-farm sources was greater than the total value of farm products sold	Abnormal
Part-retirement	403,527	$50 to $2,499	Farm operator 65 years old or older	
Abnormal	3,037	Not a criterion	Institutional farms, Indian reservations, experimental farms, grazing associations, etc.	Abnormal
Other farms, total	1,288,447			
United States, total	3,701,364			

Source: U.S. Bureau of the Census. *U.S. Census of Agriculture: 1959*, Vol. II, General Report, Chapter 11 (Washington: U.S. Government Printing Office, 1962), p. 1192.

of most individuals in the commercial category. The noncommercial farmers live on the land, but most of their gainful work time is devoted to nonfarm occupations.

In terms of production and occupational significance, over 90 per cent of the nation's food and fiber (value of farm products sold) comes from the enterprise of less than 1,500,000 farmers (Economic Classes I–IV). Moreover, 101,800 of the nation's largest farm operators (Economic Class I) have a value of products sold equaling 33 per cent of the nation's total—a proportion far exceeding their numerical rank. In addition to the business farmers, there are some 965,000 subsistence farm operators (Economic Classes V and VI). Occupationally, subsistence farmers are marginal men. They are technically in the occupation of farming in that they work off their farms less than 100 days per year and have a nonfarm income less than their farm income. But their contribution to the value of farm products sold is less than 10 per cent. In 1959 there were 1,288,000 noncommercial farmers. These included 881,880 part-time farmers, 403,-500 part-retirement farmers, and 3,000 managers of institutional (abnormal) farms. Collectively their production accounted for only 2 per cent of the nation's food and fiber.

FARM BUSINESSMEN

Now most farming has become a business occupation primarily; it is a way of life only secondarily. It is one of the few remaining occupations, along with executive and professional occupations, which juxtapose work and a way of life. In all three cases the occupational aspects dominate the way of life.

Most American farms are simultaneously family farms and commercial business operations. Whether one accepts by definition 1,447,000 or 2,412,000 family business farms makes little difference at this point. More important is the observation that these farmers are interrelated within governmental structures to a greater extent than are most of the nation's other major occupational types. Farming as an occupation, when traced through its historic growth and development, clearly illustrates the principle of reciprocal interaction between social structures. Independence and freedom in decision-making have been among the strongest norms of the farming occupation. These norms have been so tenaciously upheld that the ideology of the family farm has been elevated to something of a near spiritual level. The primary scapegoat of the smaller family farm has been the large-scale or factory type of farm organization. Yet one important result of the existence of a large number of small occupational farming units was the establishment and growth of a strong, centralized government agency, the U.S. Department of Agriculture, which now largely guides and, in some respects, dominates the occupation of farming in the interest of the total society.

No other major business occupation has held more tenaciously to the idea of small entrepreneurial units. Apart from farming, a few hundred corporate giants dominate the nation's economy. Three-fourths of the nation's small nonfarm businesses employ less than four people each. The small-scale businesses which do exist are controlled by the urbanized society, as is the small family farm.[3] Big corporations are large enough to provide many of their own regulatory agencies and to provide much of their own research. In both of these areas, they are less related to government than to farming. Farming's major research and most of its regulatory directives are centered in the federal government. Today, farm businessmen, in spite of their ideology of independence, are less free in their total occupational work situation than are many nonagricultural businessmen.

The occupation of business farming is more complex than many other types of work. Most family operated farm units are too small for much specialization of work activity. Therefore, the farm operator needs a fairly scientific knowledge of such diverse matters as the life cycles of plants and animals, soil types, electricity and mechanics, bookkeeping, cost accounting, market organization practices, and occupational organization. In short, farming is a generalized occupation in a specialized society.

Among the major characteristics of an urbanized social organization are the complexity of its knowledge and the large number of technical specialists who know more and more about highly specific areas of investigation. Proliferation of culture and knowledge in the urbanized society is of such great magnitude that the typical citizen can never hope to understand all of his society. Much of the integration of contemporary society results from the interdependence of one category of specialists upon another. Given these conditions in which specialization is generated, the generalized occupation of farming is destined to experience an increasing number of problems. The multiple demands which are currently being made on the farmer require an understanding of far greater ranges of specialized knowledge than an individual can encompass at the present time. The farmer cannot at the same time be a specialist in agronomy, horticulture, animal husbandry, cost accounting, and linear programing.

Consequently, the occupational outlook for technical specialists in the agriculture extension program is promising. The social forces of urbanized social organization will support the necessary mechanisms for applying specialized knowledge to the farming enterprise.

Commercial family farm operators. The roles of the commercial business farmer are more and more determined by national marketing and consumption patterns. For example, the American public is consuming a smaller amount of starchy food in the form of bread, flour, potatoes, and rice. It is consuming a greater amount of meat, milk, and fresh vegetables.[4] There have been vast changes in the facilities for transporting food to markets and for the preservation of foods. These changes reduce the historic advantages of farmers who are geographically near the consuming public.[5] Farmers in remote areas may even have the advantages of less congestion and less zoning complexity than farmers located in areas near the city. As the number of the nation's commercial farmers diminishes, larger and more specialized operations are often more remotely located.

Since 1929 there has been a marked increase in specialized production among the nation's business farmers.[6] Reasons for this specialization are complex, but in the main they embody the American drive for efficiency in the form of larger farms which accommodate new and larger machinery. Specialization is also required so that farmers may obtain the capital necessary to produce goods for mass marketing demands. Farms with 50 per cent or more of their total gross sales in one commodity area are classified as specialized. Farms with less than 50 per cent of their sales in a single commodity remain in a residual general farming category.

Livestock farming is the largest single type of specialization (see Table XXII). It is a high-income type of farming, and it is characterized by a disproportionate number of Economic Class I and II farms. The high position of livestock farming is partly explained in terms of the cultural preference for red meat.[7] Many other types of meat are available, some of which are valued in other societies. Lamb, pork, and poultry could all be provided on a wider scale and more economically than beef, in terms of the amount of land area necessary for their production. Therefore, many of the overpopulated societies of the world could not be expected to have the widespread beef consumption characteristic of the United States. In any event, the highly profitable nature of the production of livestock is determined by the national market rather than by the individual farm operator. The greater economic rewards of the livestock

TABLE XXII. DISTRIBUTION OF FARMS BY TYPE OF FARM: 1959

Type of Farm	Number of Farms	Per Cent Distribution
Cash-grain	398,047	16.5
Tobacco	190,057	7.9
Cotton	241,849	10.0
Other field-crop	38,332	1.6
Vegetable	21,912	0.9
Fruit-and-nut	61,419	2.5
Poultry	103,279	4.3
Dairy	428,293	17.7
Livestock other than poultry and dairy and livestock ranches	616,902	25.5
Livestock ranches	67,159	2.8
General	211,613	8.8
Miscellaneous	37,155	1.5

Source: U.S. Bureau of the Census, *U.S. Census of Agriculture, 1959,* Vol. II, General Report, Chapter 12 (Washington: U.S. Government Printing Office, 1962), p. 1257.

farmer function in a way similar to the differential rewards of medical doctors in the past century. Affluent societies disproportionately reward those occupations which meet needs created by highly regarded cultural values.

The commercial family farm is clearly not a self-contained unit. It is only a family farm in that one family may own the land and provide most of the labor. All other aspects of the business operation make it a small but integral part of the national society. Decision-making concerning supplies and markets is influenced by situations external to the family farm's operation.

Large-scale farms. Large-scale (Class I) farms have been the most rapidly growing type in America.[8] Between 1950 and 1954, the number of these farms increased from 103,000 to 134,000, or by 30 per cent. Economic Class II farms increased by 18 per cent during this same five-year period. All other commercial categories of farms declined. The large Class I farms constituted only four per cent of all commercial farms but produced over 25 per cent of the food and fiber. They controlled 22 per cent of the nation's investment in land and farm buildings, and had gross sales of over $25,000 annually. They paid 50 per cent of the hired labor bill, which was over $8,000 per farm in 1954.

Big among farm businesses, these large farms are typically anything but Paul Bunyon operations. There are some very large factory farming corporations, but they are the exception rather than the rule even among Class I farms. The average large-scale farm is a small business when compared with nonagricultural enterprises. Nationally, a business that employs less than a dozen workers, has a payroll under $10,000, and total annual sales under $60,000 would be considered a small business. Most large farms exhibit these small business characteristics.[9]

Specialty farms, one type of large-scale agriculture, produced over half of the sales in fruits, nuts, and vegetables, and provided more than a third of all cattle and calves. Their focus on the production of livestock and specialty products is a reflection of their keen perception of urbanized social organization and market demands.

Plantation organization is one of the principal types of large-scale farming. In America it has stronger historical precedent than its current situation would indicate. A study of forty plantations in the Delta area of Mississippi reported their large-scale organization.[10] The plantations averaged 1,676 acres and ranged from 934 to 3,130 acres. Plantation organization in this area is characterized by large landholdings, systematic supervision of hired workers, and specialization in the production of one major crop, cotton. In recent years, with the advent of the tractor and other mechanization, these cotton plantations have experienced extensive reorganization. Systematic supervision of workers and a high degree of specialized production are still maintained. However, World War II stimulated a rapid shift from the sharecropper, long associated with plantation operations in Southern United States, to the wage laborer. The two major kinds of wage laborers in the Delta are the resident and day-haul workers. Plantation operators are receptive to new technological advances. For example, an average of twelve tractors was reported on each plantation. An average of two cotton-picking machines was reported for each, and deep tillage equipment was reported on most of the plantations.

Chain-farming, or horizontal integration, is another type of large-scale organization. This is the entrepreneurial operation of a multiple number of farms by one owner or manager. The individual farms may be geographically separated, and each local unit may be given a certain measure of autonomy, sometimes its own individual manager.[11]

A Minnesota situation illustrates the chain operation. In this case, one individual owned six farms within a radius of about sixty miles from his place of residence. The six farms had a total of nearly 2,000 acres. An employed manager lived on each of the chain-owned farms. The local managers operated the individual farms in tenant partnership arrangements with the owner. The owner of the farms supervised the total operation by use of his private airplane. During the summer the owner made a weekly aerial tour of each farm to inspect the crops and operations. In addition to using the plane for systematic farming, this flying farmer used it for pleasure and vacations, and was a member of the National Flying Farmers Association of America.[12]

Farm occupational organizations. It is characteristic of well-organized occupational groups in urbanized society to have associations, societies, and other organizations represent their interests and provide places where members can discuss matters of mutual concern. Farming occupations have organizations, but their existence is often overlooked. This is partly a result of the inaccurate notion that eight or nine million farm workers constitute a single occupation. In fact, they are an employment category, like the census categories of operatives or clerical and kindred workers. Farming occupations are limited to those operators in the commercial business enterprises (Classes I through IV). Specialized farming occupations, within this category of 1,446,000, include: livestock (680,000 farms), dairy (428,000 farms), cash-grain (398,000 farms), cotton (241,000 farms), and vegetable-fruit-nut (83,000 farms). There are occupational organizations for most of the various specialized types of farming (see Table XXIII). There are also general farming organizations such as the Farm Bureau, the Farmers' Union, and the Grange.

TABLE XXIII. CHARACTERISTICS OF SELECTED OCCUPATIONAL ORGANIZATIONS AMONG FARMERS, PROFESSORS, AND ENGINEERS

Organizations	Annual Meeting	Number of Members	Date Founded	Publi- cation
Farmers				
Farmers and Manufacturers Beet				
Sugar Assoc.	no	6,505	1932	no
American Angus Assoc.	yes	34,000	1883	yes
Calavo Growers of Calif.	yes	4,707	1927	yes
American Guernsey Cattle Club	yes	4,485	1877	yes
Holstein-Friesian Assoc. of America	yes	49,000	1885	yes

TABLE XXIII
(continued)

Organizations	Annual Meeting	Number of Members	Date Founded	Publi- cation
American National Cattleman's Assoc.	yes	150,000	1898	yes
National Farmers' Union	no	300,000	1902	yes
American Farm Bureau Federation	yes	1,517,812	1919	yes
U.S. Trout Farmers Assoc.	no	100	1953	yes
National Grange	no	825,000	1867	yes
National Livestock Producers Assoc.	yes	550,000	1943	yes
National Turkey Federation	yes	10,000	1939	yes
American Sheep Producers Council	yes	265,000	1955	no
American Soybean Assoc.	no	6,500	1920	yes
Hampshire Swine Registry	yes	21,285	1893	yes
Burley Tobacco Growers Cooperative Assoc.	no	420,000	1921	no
Vegetable Growers Assoc. of America	yes	4,000	1908	no
National Assoc. of Wheat Growers	yes	8	1950	no
Wine Institute	yes	199	1934	no
American Wool Growers Assoc.	yes	20,000	1865	yes
Forest Farmers Assoc. Cooperative	yes	1,600	1941	yes
National Dairy Council	yes	3,000	1915	no
American Assoc. of Nurserymen	yes	1,555	1875	no
National Agricultural Workers Union		4,500		
Professors				
American Society of Agronomy				yes
American Dairy Science Assoc.	yes	2,300	1906	yes
American Farm Economist Assoc.	yes	3,400	1910	yes
American Anthropological Assoc.	yes	3,756	1902	yes
Assoc. of American Geographers	yes	2,000	1904	yes
American Assoc. of University Professors	yes	37,400	1915	yes
American Mathematic Society	yes	5,300	1888	yes
Engineers				
American Society of Civil Engineers	yes	40,522	1852	yes
American Institute of Chemical Engineers	yes	17,479	1908	yes
American Society of Agriculture Engineers	yes	5,000	1907	yes
American Institute of Electrical Engineers	yes	62,000	1884	yes
National Society of Professional Engineers	yes	43,000	1934	yes

Source: *Encyclopedia of American Associations,* 2nd edition (Detroit: Gale Research Co., 1959).

Other major occupations are similarly divided into specialty areas. For example, within the general occupation of engineering there are civil engineers, chemical engineers, electrical engineers, and agricultural engineers. These various engineering specialty areas all have their own occupational organizations (see Table XXIII). In addition to the specialized societies, there are general organizations like the National Society of Professional Engineers.

Similarly, for college professors there are societies related to their specific fields of research and teaching. Examples are the American Anthropological Association, the Association of American Geographers, the American Mathematic Society, and the American Dairy Science Association. The general occupational organization is the American Association of University Professors.

Farming characteristically has organizations of a type parallel to those associated with other occupations. Generally, they have national memberships, meet annually, and support a publication. The exact meaning and value of these occupational organizations has not been assessed for farm or nonfarm groups. Nevertheless, the fact remains that organizational development is one of the differences between occupations and work categories. Many types of farmers are beginning to develop occupational identifications and images similar to those found in other areas of agribusiness.

Organizations such as the National Flying Farmers Association and the many cooperatives have a significant impact on the various farming occupations. They are, however, not occupational organizations, but they are often regulatory in terms of marketing, purchasing supplies and equipment, and general management.

HIRED FARM WORKERS

Most of the workers engaged in farming are the farm operators themselves. Unpaid family workers are generally members of the farmer's own family. To be included in this category, their participation in farm work must involve fifteen or more hours a week. There are approximately 1,000,000 unpaid workers in the winter, and twice that number during the harvest season.[18]

In addition to operators and unpaid family members, farmers employ between 3,000,000 to 4,000,000 workers, about 2,000,000 of whom work 25 days a year or more on the farms. Half of these are regular or full-time farm workers, and half are seasonal or migratory workers. By definition, regular hired workers are those who spend 150 days as farm employees.[14] They are most often sons of neighboring farm families or members of nonfarm families in the same community.[15] Employment of regular, year-round workers is highly structured and generally constitutes no serious problem in the labor force. About three-fourths of them are employed on Class I and II farms in California, Texas, New York, Pennsylvania, Florida, Wisconsin, Georgia, Virginia, and Iowa.[16]

The number of migrant workers remained under 500,000 between 1950 and 1960.[17] Some of the migrants are unattached males, but a great proportion of them travel with their families. About half of the itinerant workers are domestic, and the other half foreign-born. Most of those in the latter category come from Mexico, a lesser proportion from the British West Indies and Puerto Rico.

The status of the migratory workers is, at best, precarious. Their position is that of a minority, for of all farm workers the itinerants represent less than 2 per cent. They are employed on only 2 per cent [18] of the nation's farms, usually in cotton, fruits, vegetables, and sugar beets.

Itinerant farm workers fulfill positions at the lower end of the socioeconomic hierarchy. Large urbanized societies characterized by success orientations necessarily contain a number of positions which will inevitably be fulfilled by persons who are neither prepared nor given the opportunity for achieving high status positions. Migratory laborers are an example of the inevitable failures (as seen from the dominant cultural point of view) of a success-oriented society. They are persons who have not moved from the proverbial rags to riches. They constitute a subject of considerable embarrassment to the middle classes who subscribe to the abstract sentiment that all men are created equal. From such a viewpoint the plight of the migrant worker is something which must be ameliorated. Furthermore, in an affluent society with a brotherhood-of-man orientation, there is a widespread feeling of responsibility on the part of one social class for another.[19] This sentiment suggests the implicit, although often unexamined, assumption that all persons in the society will accept the same established cultural goals as equally valuable. Examination of the social structures of urbanized society indicates that no basis exists for justifying such an assumption. But, in spite of the lack of evidence to support the possibility of eliminating the social failures, in this case migrant farm laborers, the middle classes engage in activities for alleviating the migrants' conditions.

Many communities are organizing specific programs to improve the conditions and level of living of the migrants. Hollandale, Minnesota, has endeavored to provide school opportunities for migrant children; a community in New York has organized 4-H Clubs in migrant camps; San Antonio, Texas, and Fresno, California, have improved the health conditions of migrants, and many other similar programs have been initiated.[20]

Basic shifts in the technological and scientific organization of agriculture appear to be gradually reducing the number of farm migrant workers required.[21] Production of cotton, for example, is rapidly becoming mechanized, and could become more so if it were not for the excessive displacement of seasonal labor which would result.[22] As a consequence, migrant laborers from farms are gradually finding their way into employment in nonagribusiness positions.

Migrant workers originate in the South, where they work in cotton and specialty crop production. But the South is not the only area which uses migrant labor. Texas, California, Michigan, and New York, in rank order, are the greatest users of migrant laborers.[23] In 1957, all but two states used some migrant farm workers. Routes of migrants run typically from Florida up the East Coast to New York, from Texas into the Central and Great Lakes States, from Texas into the Dakotas and Montana, from Texas through the Rocky Mountain States, and up the Pacific Coast States.

UNION ORGANIZATION AMONG FARM WORKERS

Attempts to unionize farm workers have been made since 1879, but most of these efforts have resulted in failure.[24] One notable exception, dating from the 1930's, was that of the AFL Milkers' Unions in San Francisco and Los Angeles.[25] In Hawaii, sugar and pineapple plantation workers have been unionized. On the mainland, AFL efforts to unionize farm labor failed in the late 1940's. Farm labor collective bargaining has taken place at the large Seabrook Farms in New Jersey, and with the Fellesmere Sugar Producers' Association in Florida.[26]

Again, in the 1960's, the AFL-CIO made a bid for farm organization in California. The giant labor organization supported the Agricultural Workers Organizing Committee with plans, personnel, and money. Reasons for organization in California include: about one-fourth of the nation's hired agricultural workers are employed in that state; farmers pay higher wages there than in most other sections of the country; farming is organized in a highly scientific, technical way, so that systematic and intense labor demands are required and arranged for specific days, weeks, and months.[27]

SUBSISTENCE FARMERS

Subsistence farms have been defined as those in Economic Classes IV–VI.* Economists argue that gross sales of these farms provide a low income and inadequate family level of living. Their incomes are below the national average. Operators of subsistence farms are typically so traditionalistic that they have little opportunity for achieving the high levels of living expected in the urbanized society. Some subsistence farms could be improved so as to provide an income commensurate with the national average, but most of them are located in areas where the potentiality for success is limited. Farms in the subsistence classes comprise over 60 per cent of the nation's commercial farms.[28] They constitute the most rapidly declining economic class of farms. Between 1950 and 1954, Class IV farms declined by 8 per cent, Class V farms by more than 15 per cent, and Class VI farms by 34 per cent.[29]

Subsistence farms are most numerous in the South and are frequently associated with cotton and tobacco. They are, however, found in every state of the nation.[30] They account for 30 per cent of all land in farms, 27 per cent of the value of land and buildings in farms, 12 per cent of the expenditure for hired farm labor, and less than 20 per cent of the value of all farm products sold.[31]

The Rural Development Program has investigated low-production farm areas of the nation. Intensive studies have been made of rural families and their resources in low income areas of North-Central and Western Florida, North-Central New Mexico, the Northern Lower Peninsula of Michigan, Clay Hills of Mississippi, Eastern Ozarks of Missouri, Northeastern Texas, and Northeastern Tennessee.[32] About half of the rural families in the areas studied had annual net incomes of less than $2,000, as did only about one-fifth of the nation. Respondents included both rural farm and rural nonfarm families. Many of the rural farm families studied in these areas were commercial farmers; others were

---

* Notice the overlap of Class IV farms in both the subsistence and the occupational categories. This is necessary due to the minimum boundary maintenance associated with the farming occupation and the cultural variation in minimum levels of economic survival.

part-time farmers. Their low incomes were explained by problems of adjustment, limited employment capabilities of the respondents, and a lack of adequate farm resources, which made it impossible for farmers to accept modern methods. Often the farms were too small to be systematic economic units.

Many of the families in these areas are greatly dependent on some income from nonfarm sources. Thousands of families were reported to have quit farming because of their inability to compete in the technical, scientific farming business. Concomitant with the decline of farming in these areas was a high departure rate of young people in the productive ages. Many of those who remained found nonfarm employment. The great proportion of those who remained in farming did so because of age, physical handicaps, or some other attributes which were not conducive to systematic farming occupations. Finally, because of social security benefits, many persons remained in the area in a state of retirement.

Some individuals who remained in the low-income farming areas did so because of individual and personal preference. Movement in the direction of opportunity is widespread in the urbanized, consumption-oriented society. It involves a conception of success and achievement. Such an orientation has a great measure of risk and often of failure. There are individuals in the society who adjust by ritualizing, if not retreating. They do not rebel against the social norms; nevertheless, they accept them only passively.[33] Adjustment patterns of ritualizing and retreating are often observed in the low-income farming areas. The dominant cultural norms of the urbanized society, both in farming and nonfarming occupations, are based on a highly sophisticated perception of success and opportunity, and an extensive understanding of the total way of American life. Many of the persons who are observed to be in the lower socioeconomic classes, whether in subsistence farming areas or in transitional zones in cities, are there implicitly because of the structure of a society which emphasizes success, achievement, and materialistic knowledge. Residents of the transitional and subsistence areas are often those who are incapable of success in competing for the society's greatest rewards, or those who ritualize and retreat from these goals, not perceiving them to be worth-while or acceptable cultural goals for their way of life. And so it is with subsistence farming; some of those in this marginal occupational category are, in the short run, a social problem resulting from the transition of the society from traditionalized agriculture to scientific, technological agribusiness. In a large and dynamic society, involving more than 179,000,000 people

(1960), and in an agribusiness enterprise involving approximately 40,-000,000 people, adjustment to and acceptance of changes in technology and science do not come about evenly or gradually for all persons. Some are able to perceive the situation and to accept it and adjust to it more rapidly than others. Part of those in the subsistence farming areas, as well as those in transitional zones of cities, are there because of the broader nature of social organization and less because of the specific configuration of society of the urbanized type in contemporary America.

Occupationally, subsistence farmers are a marginal type. Their characteristics are those of rejecting rather than accepting, retreating rather than innovating, nonbelonging rather than belonging. There is considerable ground for questioning whether such a worker is sufficiently cognizant of his fellow workers and the conditions of their mutual work experience to be considered an occupation. In some cases these persons are more physically in, than ideologically of, the society. Nevertheless, many of the subsistence farmers do, or desire to, accept the cultural universals of the greater society. Some are in the subsistence category due to poor management calculations rather than to their rejection of the ideology of the society, and thus continue to be counted in the farming occupation.

PART-TIME FARMERS

In 1954, noncommercial farms constituted approximately one-third of the nation's farms. They produce only 2 per cent of all farm products sold, account for only 12 per cent of the value of land and buildings, 4 per cent of the crop land harvested, and only 11 per cent of the nation's farmland. There are over half a million part-time farmers in the nation, or more than four times as many as there are large or Economic Class I farms.

Part-time farming was practiced throughout the long course of history. In earlier times, in Western Europe, the cottage industry combined farming and manufacturing. In the early United States, part-time farming existed, but it was not a widespread phenomenon. Since the 1930's, part-time farmers have increased continually. In 1930, David Rozman published a bulletin in which he developed the notion that there is much value to be obtained by combining urban work and farm work.[34] A similar notion was expressed earlier by Peter Kropotkin.[35]

Between 1930 and 1950, part-time and residential farms increased by about two-thirds; during the same years, commercial farms decreased by approximately 30 per cent.[36] The decrease in commercial farms and the increase in part-time farms are integral manifestations of far-reaching economic and social changes due to mechanization and science in agriculture. Science and technology in agribusiness have been factors pushing many individuals out of full-time farming—some into part-time farming and some into nonagribusiness occupations. On the other hand, technological advances in transportation have encouraged the movement of people out of the central cities and into residential locations in suburbs and rural-urban fringe areas. As a result, many heretofore systematic farming operations have become segmented. These two shifts in technology and population movement together explain much of the increase in part-time and residential farms.

Much research and discussion is devoted to the subject of the part-time farmer. He is, occupationally speaking, not a farmer at all. His farm is primarily a place of residence and not a business. Indeed, his primary place of work is typically nonfarm. Whatever interpretations are made of this aspect of farming as an occupation must be formed in terms of the purely economic factors involved.

The characteristics of part-time farmers have been analyzed, and both extolled and criticized. Often they are enumerated to suggest that the part-time farmer is a man under stress, who must work on weekends and at nights, who is short of time—often working on his farm after the completion of a forty-hour work week elsewhere. He is seen to be a commuter between his farm and some other place of employment. He is a man who has less time for contacts with county agents and other agricultural specialists. He participates less in farm organizations and, often, less in nonfarm organizations. Those he visits are both farm and nonfarm people. And, most often, the part-time farmer is said to have been previously a farmer or one who was born on a farm.

Part-time farming serves a number of functions in the urbanized society. It provides a mechanism for people who want to extricate themselves gradually from full-time farming, or for nonfarm people to engage gradually in full-time farming. It also provides an opportunity for hobby farming. For some it is a matter of security, a way to subsist when other types of employment are inadequate. Part-time farms provide a residential environment away from the congestion of a central city.[37]

For the urbanized society, part-time farming functions as a shock absorber in the process of shifting between farm and nonfarm occupations.

Its prevalence is currently accelerated due to major scientific and technological shifts in agribusiness. It is a manifestation of an affluent society, by which the luxury of arbitrary occupational choice can be sustained. It also reflects the high value placed on individual decision-making, even when it results in the inefficient use of human energy. Part-time farming is simultaneously an advantage and a disadvantage, depending upon the value orientation of its participants and those who study it.

SUMMARY

Farm operators and hired workers constitute one of the major forces in contemporary American farming. By the middle of the twentieth century, the force of their role in the society has been substantially diminished. Historically, there have been times when farm workers have dominated the society or when they have been a major moving force in its organization. In the contemporary situation, the social structure of food and fiber production in the United States is such that one understands the organization of agribusiness only after first examining land settlement patterns, the role of the federal government in agribusiness, the integration of farm production, distribution, and marketing, the contribution of science and technology to agribusiness, and the importance of professionals and specialists in generating new ideas and technological information. Only then can it be understood how the roles of the farm operator and his laboring assistants contribute to the total agribusiness food and fiber enterprise. The occupational role of these operators and workers is unquestionably modified by the demands the total society makes on food and fiber production. The classic family farm itself is necessarily modified so that it can meet the demand of mass standardized marketing and consumption. Technological advances and vertical integration continue as moving forces due primarily not to the will of farm operators and laborers but to basic changes in the structure of food and fiber production.

NOTES

1. Edward Gross, *Work and Society* (New York: Thomas Y. Crowell Co., 1958), pp. 336–68.

2. R. L. Skrabanek, "Commercial Farming in the United States," *Rural Sociology,* 19 (June, 1954), 136–42; Ronald L. Mighell, *American Agriculture: Its Structure and Place in the Economy* (New York: John Wiley and Sons, Inc., 1955); U.S. Bureau of the Census, *U.S. Census of Agriculture: 1954,* Vol. III, Special Reports,

Part IX, Farmers and Farm Production in the United States, Chapter 9 (Washington: U.S. Government Printing Office, 1956).

3. Arnold W. Green, *Sociology* (3rd ed., New York: McGraw-Hill Book Co., Inc., 1960); "The Fortune Directory: The 500 Largest U.S. Industrial Corporations," *Fortune* (July, 1959), 125–44.

4. U.S. Bureau of the Census, *op. cit.,* p. 18.

5. H. M. Ellsworth, *Improving the Marketing of Fresh and Frozen California Strawberries* (Sacramento: California Department of Agriculture, 1959); Paul Casamajor *et al., Timber Marketing and Land Ownership in Mendocino County* (California Agricultural Experiment Station Bulletin 772, 1960); H. M. Ellsworth, *Expanding the Market for Processed Boysenberries* (Sacramento: California Department of Agriculture, 1956). These publications and many others of a similar nature from other states illustrate the cognizant relation of modern farmers to the national market.

6. Ellsworth, *Expanding the Market* . . . , p. 19.

7. H. M. Ellsworth, *Problems and Possibilities of Expanding the Sale and Consumption of Turkeys in California* (Sacramento: California State Department of Agriculture, 1951), p. 5.

8. U.S. Bureau of the Census, *op.cit.,* p. 18. It is impossible to compare 1954 with 1959 type of farm data due to definitional changes.

9. Mighell, *op. cit.,* pp. 61–2.

10. Nelson L. LeRay *et al., Plantation Organization and the Resident Labor Force, Delta Area of Mississippi* (Mississippi Agricultural Experiment Station Bulletin 606, 1960).

11. Mighell, *op. cit.,* p. 103.

12. *Minneapolis Star,* Sept. 17, 1950, Section 2B.

13. *Farm Labor Fact Book* (Washington: U.S. Department of Labor, 1959), pp. 55–67; *Farm Labor* (Washington: U.S.D.A., Agricultural Marketing Service, monthly).

14. *The Hired Farm Working Force of 1960* (Washington: U.S.D.A., Agricultural Information Bulletin 266, 1960).

15. Mighell, *op. cit.,* p. 147.

16. *Farm Labor Fact Book, op. cit.,* p. 70.

17. *Ibid.,* p. 111.

18. Mighell, *op. cit.,* p. 48.

19. William G. Sumner, *What Social Classes Owe to Each Other* (Caldwell, Ida.: Caxton Press, 1954).

20. *When the Migrant Families Come Again: A Guide for Better Community Living* (Washington: Federal Interdepartment Committee on Children and Youth, 1955).

21. Irving F. Davis, Jr. and William H. Metzler, *Sugar Beet Labor in Northern Colorado* (Colorado Agricultural Experiment Station Technical Bulletin 63, 1958), pp. 8 ff.

22. LeRay *et al., op. cit.*

23. Robin Myers, *The Position of Farm Workers in Federal and State Legislation* (New York National Advisory Committee on Farm Labor, 1959).

24. *Ibid.*, p. 24; Stuart Jamison, *Labor Unionism in American Agriculture* (Washington: U.S. Bureau of Labor Statistics, Bulletin 836, 1945).

25. Ernest Feder, "The Milkers' Unions of San Francisco and Los Angeles Milksheds," *Journal of Farm Economics,* 32 (Aug., 1950), 458-77.

26. Vardern Fuller, *Labor Relations in Agriculture* (Berkeley: University of California Press, 1955), pp. 11-13.

27. Grant Cannon, "Farm Labor Organizes: The AFL-CIO Makes Its Bid for Farm Labor in California," *The Farm Quarterly,* 16 (Spring, 1961), 61 ff.

28. U.S. Bureau of the Census, *op. cit.,* p. 11.

29. *Ibid.,* p. 18, Table V.

30. *Ibid.,* p. 12; also see *Opportunities for Economic Development in Low Production Farm Areas* (Washington: U.S.D.A., Agriculture Information Bulletin 234, 1960), p. 3.

31. U.S. Bureau of the Census, *op. cit.,* p. 11, Table I.

32. *Opportunities for Economic Development.*

33. Robert K. Merton, *Social Theory and Social Structure* (Glencoe: The Free Press, 1949).

34. David Rozman, *Part-Time Farming in Massachusetts* (Massachusetts Agricultural Extension Station Bulletin 266, 1930).

35. P. Kropotkin, *Fields, Factories, and Workshops* (New York: G. P. Putnam's Sons, 1913).

36. Mighell, *op. cit.,* p. 109.

37. H. J. Bonser and C. W. Porter, "Part-Time Farming: Boon or Bugaboo?" in *Farm Economics* (Pennsylvania Agricultural Extension Service, Sept. 1, 1960); Christine H. Hillman, *Part-Time Farming: Its Influence on Young Families* (Ohio Agricultural Experiment Station Research Bulletin 775, 1956); George A. Donohue, "Socio-Economic Characteristics of Part-Time and Full-Time Farmers in the Twin Cities Area," *Journal of Farm Economics,* 39 (Nov., 1957), 984-92; George V. Douglas and Arthur B. Mackie, *Some Social and Economic Implications of Part-Time Farming* (Knoxville: Tennessee Valley Authority, Division of Agricultural Relations, Agricultural Economics Branch, Report No. T 57—1 AE, June, 1957); Mighell, *op. cit.,* Chapter 7.

SELECTED READINGS

Gross, Edward. *Work and Society*. New York: Thomas Y. Crowell, 1958.
See especially Chapters 7, 8, and 9, which deal respectively with "The Farm: The Work Complex," "The Work Structure and the Economic Complex," "Status, Career, and the Work Group."

Ellsworth, H. M. *Improving the Marketing of Fresh and Frozen California Strawberries*. Sacramento: California Department of Agriculture, Marketing Survey Report No. 16, 1959.

This publication is an example of the many important and systematic efforts being made to assist farmers and producers in their marketing situations.

LeRay, Nelson L., *et al. Plantation Organization and the Resident Labor Force, Delta Area of Mississippi*. Mississippi Agricultural Experiment Station Bulletin 606, 1960.
An empirical case study of contemporary plantation organization in Mississippi.

Mighell, Ronald L. *American Agriculture: Its Structure and Place in the Economy*. New York: John Wiley, 1955.
Special emphasis is placed on commercial and part-time farming operations.

Skrabanek, R. L. "Commercial Farming in the United States," *Rural Sociology*, 19 (June, 1954), 136–42.
Primarily a description of the place of commercial farming in the social organization of American agriculture.

15 VERTICAL INTEGRATION IN THE FOOD AND FIBER INDUSTRY

Vertical integration has loomed large on the landscape of farming and agribusiness since 1950. It is viewed variously as a hope or threat, opportunity or frustration. Its impact affects all phases of agribusiness, including production, research, banking, cooperatives, processing, and distribution. Vertical integration is the result of changes in the social organization of society. It constitutes a specific element of the social structure and is not an independent idea manufactured by innovative businessmen. Its roles are viewed as advantageous or disadvantageous according to the individual's value judgments of what constitutes a good society. Notwithstanding such judgments, vertical integration already has come into being.

EMERGENCE OF VERTICAL INTEGRATION

The ideas and experiences of vertical integration are not new. America's nonagricultural business enterprises have experienced vertical integration since before the turn of the century, probably as early as the 1880's.[1] In the 1890's, Andrew Carnegie assumed leadership in the development of vertical integration in the iron and steel industry. His plan brought the various enterprises in iron and steel production under centralized management. The central management controlled ore mining, ore transportation by boats on the Great Lakes, ore carriage by the railways, and the manufacture of a variety of steel products.[2] With this precedent of integration

309

in the iron and steel industry, the new form of economic organization that had been only a gradual tendency up to that time was rapidly elevated to a place of marked predominance.

The early development of vertical integration was directly related to the values of efficiency, expansion, increased levels of living, and the mass society. Vertical integration was part of the nation's maturing; it was a trademark of a society clearly organized around basic cultural universals. The United States had originated in a period in which the colonies were scarcely united at all. The early national period, indeed the pre-Civil War period, was more characterized by federation than by social solidarity. Since the Civil War, the combined social forces of the society have moved in the direction of nearly complete integration. The power of the central government was confirmed. Ideologies of success and achievement, such as from office boy to president, farm boy to senator, and rags to riches, were prevalent throughout the land from the largest cities to the backwoods.[3] Migration from farms to cities integrated the people. Advances in technology made possible rapid transportation and communication among all points of the nation. The development and exploitation of the nationwide market overshadowed local markets, largely as an effect of the economic integration of business and industry. Large and small businesses, from steel and oil to breweries, were vertically integrated in rapid succession. These systems of greater and more uniform production first rose to the challenge of filling existing markets. Later, market research and the creation of markets under managerial enterprise were established. In sum, industry was motivated to develop vertical integration in order to exercise more control over both its raw materials and its markets.

While vertical integration and market expansion were an important part of the developments in industry from the 1880's to the present, scientific research and technological advances became important parts of agriculture. Efficiency in agribusiness production flourished and was destined to surpass that in nonagribusiness. Farms grew larger and became more systematic, usually within the context of a changing definition of family farms. Indeed, their growth was in direct opposition to family farms.

The Grange and the Farmer's Alliance in the 1870's and 1880's were precursors of vertical integration in agribusiness and farming. These organizations were oriented to forming state and regional cooperative federations.[4] Early attempts at cooperative marketing were developed in the late nineteenth century. The earliest major advances were made in the first decade of the twentieth century, when the California Fruit Growers Exchange achieved a successful and stable organization, ultimately to be popularly known by the name Sunkist Growers, Incorporated.[5] In 1912 the successful establishment of the California Associated Raisin Company (later renamed the Sun Maid Raisin Growers Association) was established. Its primary purpose was market control, but it soon became involved in processing, merchandising, and other vertically integrating functions.[6]

After World War I, further systematic organization of vertical integration took place. This was the era of the expansion of regional cooperatives—for example, the Dairymen's League and Land O' Lakes Creameries. Paralleling these experiments with cooperative organization in agribusiness was the establishment of the large-scale supermarket type of retail food organization. A prerequisite for the existence of the supermarket was a large-scale supply system for the foods which they were to retail. The small farmer who operated a diversified or general enterprise could not be relied upon to provide an adequate amount of food to be sold in the supermarket. Moreover, the large-scale marketing process, accompanied by extensive marketing research, contributed to consumer demand for standardized, high-quality products. The farmer, therefore, was required to cultivate high-quality produce in mass quantities. The first step meant farms had to become large in acreage and specialized in production. Next, through vertical integration, farm production was brought into direct association with processing, distributing, and retailing agencies. Such demands or opportunities for farmers who had a scientific knowledge of the life cycle of plants and animals and a technological grasp of equipment constituted the social milieu for big agribusiness.

CONCEPT AND NATURE OF INTEGRATION

Vertical and horizontal integration are both identifiable in industry and, to a lesser extent, in agribusiness. Throughout all socioeconomic organization in the United States, vertical integration is more widespread than horizontal integration. Nevertheless, one type is not found to the exclusion of the other.

Horizontal integration. This form of business organization involves the establishment of central managerial control over multiple units of the

same type of enterprise or the same stage in processing of a specific commodity. Horizontal integration is exemplified in the case of a retail business which has a multiple number of local outlets in different geographical
locations. The chain farm is typically a horizontally integrated operation.
Such farming enterprises are characterized by one management which
owns and directs the operations of a multiple number of farms that,
though often not physically connected, engage in the same business.
Farmers' cooperatives usually represent a form of horizontal integration
when they establish multiple branches. They are primarily concerned
with one stage in agribusiness—for example, the purchasing of supplies
and equipment for farmers or the marketing of the farmers' products.[7]
More recently, some of the larger cooperatives are expanding their operations in the direction of vertical integration.

Vertical integration. Vertical integration is the combination of several
stages or steps in the process of supplying, producing, processing, distributing, and marketing a consumption item. Motives for combining these
stages may range from corporate aggrandizement to social efficiency.
These motives are not necessarily mutually exclusive.

Some vertical integration is described as ascending. It begins at the
farm and progressively moves through the various steps of processing
and distribution. Other vertical integration is identified as descending, or
that which originates at the distribution or processing phases and moves
down to encompass the farm or production phase.[8] In either type, vertical
integration can to a great extent bypass much of the historical identity
and meaning of the local family farm. The local farm unit will continue
to have physical existence, but its production will be under a specific
contract and its identity in the total society will be greatly obscured. The
brand name will be known and identified with the product, whether it be
oranges, raisins, eggs, or beef. The general public will not have a clear
conception of the growing of the product as distinct from its processing
and retailing. Vertically integrated operations under one brand name will
bring all of these stages together in the mind of the consumer.

In societies involving both smaller and larger numbers of people, from
Mexico to China, there are examples of great numbers of people who
do not have a mental image of their society as a nation in the world's
community of nations. Homo sapiens born into any society must be socialized to have an image of his nation and its type of social organization.
Urbanized societies generally have promoted societal images, national

loyalty, and ethnocentrism. Among the specific consequences of this type of urbanized social organization is vertical integration. Local small-town businesses are then replaced by mass markets, states' rights gradually give way to a strong central government, localized school curriculums are rapidly superseded by state curriculums, racial cultural islands by demands for ethnic integration, localized sect and small church groups by large church organizations. Similarly, the small farm is gradually being superseded by vertical integration.

The strong family farm ideology most effectively has blocked horizontal integration or the development of factory farms. In the latter part of the nineteenth and first half of the twentieth centuries the small family farm was able to withstand the social forces for consolidation and horizontal integration largely due to the systematic effort of the U.S. Department of Agriculture as a centralized research agency and arbiter, if not designer, of over-all farm organizational policy. It is certainly true that farmers and the U.S.D.A. have collectively been able to achieve successes in food and fiber production of great magnitude. The people in the nation never have been more abundantly fed and clothed. However, social organization is continually evolving in the form of new social structures.

Farming and agribusiness are engaged in a power struggle to determine how much further their role will be reduced from that of autonomous organizations and integrated as one of several aspects of the general national economy. The situation is complex, but the specific form of its resolution poses no basic problem for social organization. The basic issue is the image of farming as a way of life and as an occupation. It is conceivable that total vertical integration of farming and agribusiness into the general industrial and economic structure of the society could reduce the family farm to a position of insignificance. Food and fiber production would continue at a high rate of efficiency. If the structure of farming had developed along lines of horizontal integration, it is possible that factory farms would have been in a position to bargain with industry, distributors, and retailers in such a way as to influence their organization and maintain farming as a separate but reciprocally related business. Most farm operators today are too small to serve effectively as their own individual representatives or negotiators.

Advantages and disadvantages of vertical integration. Vertical integration must be evaluated in terms of the image which is held of farming, agribusiness, national markets, and the ongoing society. When the integrator is not a farm businessman, the advantage to the farmer is a considerable reduction in risk, since the integrator assumes part of the liability for the operation. It is generally possible for integrated operations to qualify for larger capital loans to assist in the improvement of facilities and expansion of operations. Also, in the integrated organization, there are multiple operators and more detailed record keeping, all of which tend to improve credit. Under a system of vertical integration, the young farmer can begin his operation with limited capital. The integrator typically provides technical and economic assistance to the producer. Further, seasonal and operational fluctuations of income and work load are reduced in vertically integrated operations.

A disadvantage to vertical integration for the farmer and producer is the limited opportunity to make high profits. In addition, the farmer may find it necessary to increase the size of his operation in order to take advantage of the new machinery and labor-saving equipment. Furthermore, those individuals who do not participate in integration will, in some cases, have difficulty in marketing their independently produced products. Underlying all of these disadvantages is a reduction of independent entrepreneurial decision-making.[9]

EXAMPLES OF VERTICAL INTEGRATION

The systematic practice of vertical integration has existed in agribusiness since 1950. Previously, precursors of vertical integration in agribusiness were primarily concerned with the processing, distributing, and marketing of products. During this time, vertical integration included the farmer's operation but did not generally involve the final step of contracting with farmers and ranchers. Ascending vertical integration, starting with the farmer or rancher, was equally unique prior to the 1950's.

There were, however, two notable examples of vertical integration in agriculture before that time. On the West Coast there was the long-standing development of integration among citrus growers, from harvesting through packing and marketing activities, in the well-known Sunkist Growers, Incorporated. A consequence of labor-farmer-processor conflicts in the sugar industry in the late 1930's was the practice of integration through contract farming. Government regulations were established to arbitrate the contract negotiations between sugar beet growers and processors. The Sugar Act (1948) provided for government supervision and analysis of the contracts, control of planting, wage standards, and the elimination of child labor.[10]

Cane sugar. The cane sugar industry in Hawaii was vertically integrated by 1950. The organization is a combination of plantation farming and processing through a system of cooperatives. Cane is produced on plantations which participate in the cooperative. Labor is unionized throughout most of the industry. The cane sugar industry in Florida, Louisiana, and Puerto Rico is only partially vertically integrated.

Citrus production. Vertical integration dominates most of the citrus production in California and Arizona. In Florida, nearly half of the citrus production is vertically integrated. Most of the fruit is produced by growers who are members of marketing cooperatives. Their agreements specify that the grower will market his product through the cooperative. More extensive integration is found in some operations in which the contract provides for complete grove care, including fertilizing, irrigation, spraying, cultivation, and harvesting.[11]

Deciduous fruits and tree nuts. Ascending integration of the grower and shipper variety dominates most of the deciduous fruit industry. Cooperatives handle approximately 20 per cent of the total volume of business. While they are not aimed at directly influencing the farm production practices and decisions, some of the cooperatives do offer some auxiliary field service consultation. In the Northwest Pacific Area, cooperatives handle half of the deciduous fruit industry; the Eastern industry is less integrated.

In California the tree nut industry is highly integrated beyond the production operation. The California Almond Growers Exchange and the Diamond Walnut Growers, Incorporated, are the principal marketers of these two types of nuts. They provide the facilities for shelling, processing, and packaging, in addition to maintaining marketing reserve stocks in the principal distribution centers.[12]

Vegetables. The vegetable industry ranks among the most extensively vertically integrated operations. Nearly 90 per cent of the vegetables which are canned and frozen are grown under contracts from processors. Vertical integration in the vegetable industry varies from region to region, with less of it in the South and more in the West. Almost all of the lima beans, sweet corn, and peas in the nation are grown under contract.

There is a wide variation in the terms of the contracts used in the vegetable industry. The simplest contracts specify only that the processor will take the product at a stipulated price. More elaborate contracts specify dates of planting, variety of seed to be used, spraying practices, schedules of prices by grades, sizes and varieties, and dates of payment. In most cases, the industry is further controlled by the processor through his provision of plants and seed. Growers, too, are becoming more organized, and in some areas they have established their own associations in order to strengthen their bargaining positions with processors.

The fresh vegetable market is more than half integrated. Most of this integration is of the grower-shipper variety. The contracts are frequently oral. They guarantee the grower a market and provide the shipper with some degree of influence in production. About 40 per cent of all potato production is integrated in grower and shipper arrangements; another 10 per cent is handled through cooperative arrangements. The potato industry is heavily concentrated in Idaho, New York, Florida, Alabama, Maine, and Oregon. In these areas, it is common for the contracts to specify the variety of plants, fertilizer and insecticides to be applied, time and method of harvest, and price. In most cases, these operations are controlled by fertilizer companies with financial interests which transcend the production area.[13]

Seed production. Vertical integration in seed production is currently accelerated by the advance of scientific agriculture, which, in turn, demands a higher quality seed. In some cases, the seed industry is highly integrated; for example, 90 per cent of the hybrid corn and grain sorghum seed produced in the state of Texas is under contract.[14]

Poultry and eggs. The most rapid development of vertical integration in agribusiness has been in the poultry industry. Broiler production is the most integrated, turkey production is in the process of rapid integration, and egg production is becoming integrated, although at a less rapid pace.

Over 95 per cent of the commercial broiler industry is integrated. Most broiler integration has taken place between the production and marketing stages of the operation. The integrator is generally a feed dealer or feed manufacturer. He supplies all of the required items for the raising of the poultry, while the producer raises the broilers under the stipulated conditions and delivers them to the supplier at the appropriate date. In some other cases, the processors and hatcheries are the major broiler integrators. Integrated broiler production grew out of the Delaware, Maryland, and Virginia area where the "no-loss" contract became used on a large scale in the 1950's.

The principal types of contracts are *open account, no-loss, feed conversion, flat fee,* and *labor contracts.* In the *open account* method, the dealer takes a chattel mortgage on the birds and furnishes the grower with all of the feed and other supplies. The dealer arranges the sale of the birds, receives the payment, and credits the producer's account. The integrator assumes practically none of the risk in this arrangement. The *no-loss* plan is similar to the open account plan, except that the dealer absorbs labor loss or loss of return on his unused equipment. In *feed conversion contracts,* the grower is encouraged by the nature of the contract to practice the best possible management. Dealers retain title to the broilers and supply all production materials. The grower furnishes the labor and equipment, while the dealer is charged with responsibility for loss. Normally, the grower is paid on a fixed schedule based upon his feed conversion ratio. *Flat fee* contracts provide for the dealer's maintenance of broiler ownership, furnishing of all production items, and arrangement of the sales. The producer is paid a flat fee per bird or per pound sold, as remuneration for his labor and his equipment. Finally, the *labor contract* is a modification of the flat fee plan whereby the grower is paid a weekly wage rather than a unit price.[15]

By the late 1950's, vertical integration was increasing in egg production, accounting for approximately 10 per cent of the nation's total. There are three major types of vertical integration in this industry. The first, contract marketing and a quality control program, provides contracts to market eggs on a specified basis in which uniform high quality is emphasized. This type of integration is found in all sections of the nation. The second form of integration is contract production, which is most widely adopted in the South. Again, the emphasis is on high-quality eggs. Feeds are typically supplied by the integrator, while producers furnish the housing facilities as well as their own labor. The eggs produced belong to the program operator. The producers are paid for the number of eggs produced and frequently given a bonus for high and efficient production. The third major form of integration in egg production is the owner-integrated operation. In these cases the producer owns the production and marketing facilities. Large operators of this kind, who have 100,000 or more laying hens, are found in all sections of the country.

Twenty-nine egg producing firms were studied in 1958 in an effort to acquire information about their new processes.[16] Seventeen of these plants were integrated in the contract quality control programs. The volume of egg production handled by them ranged from less than 1,000 to more than 30,000 cases per week. Some of the plants were owned by cooperatives; others were under private ownerships. The primary goal of these organizations was the elimination of the seasonal factor in high-quality egg production. The contract program was developed in such a way as to pay producers a premium of two cents a dozen for adhering to the contract requirements. These requirements included: a low percentage of blood spots; no more than fourteen months' production for pullets; a regulated feeding program; dry-cleaning of dirty eggs; and refrigerated egg rooms.[17] Definitions for quality operations and adherence to the contract were also provided. Further, to eliminate the seasonal factor, the producers were asked to indicate in the contract the number of eggs they expected to produce each month during the year. When the quality eggs they delivered adhered to this planned production within stipulated limits of deviation, producers were given an additional premium of one cent per dozen. Quality control was systematically exercised, and organized around refrigeration, breed of laying hens, maximum age of layers, type of feed, confinement of layers, gathering of eggs, and vaccination for respiratory diseases.

Contracts often specified the size of flocks at no less than 500 hens; the general minimum was 1,000 to 3,000. Contracts were both written and oral, and were automatically renewable at the end of each year unless terminated by written notice. In the contract quality control programs, the integrators did little or no financing for the producers. All integrators had some means of farm inspection, usually performed by field men. Some of these had the additional role of serving as advisor to the producers on production problems. Higher quality egg production has resulted from this form of integration. The elimination of the seasonal factor has not yet been accomplished, although it is less evident than formerly.

Seven vertically integrated contract production egg centers were studied in the Southeast. The number of hens in the programs ranged from 50,000 to 200,000. Quality control methods again involved refrigeration, breeds, age of layers, feed management practices, cleaning of eggs, and delivery practices. Seasonal production patterns were primarily controlled by the time at which pullets were placed with the producers. An established number of birds were replaced each week under this system. The contract generally controlled the size of flocks, most of them between two and

4,000 birds. Housing provisions also varied from terms which were highly specific to practically none at all. The contract allowed the producer to discontinue his operation at any time, although in actual practice it usually lasted at least for the duration of the production period of the hens. Quality control again yielded high results. Top quality classification was given between 85 and 90 per cent of the eggs produced.

Owner-integrated operations controlled a large part of the nation's total egg market. The operations varied considerably. The first operation reported, controlled by a hatchery and feed manufacturer, involved some 100,000 hens at sixteen locations. Two types of hens, used to produce white eggs, were all fed on the same schedule. Eggs were gathered twice a day in plastic filler-flats, and taken directly to the central farm to be washed and placed in refrigeration. Ninety per cent of the eggs were grade A or better. The eggs were put in cartons the next day and sold through a broker.

Another operation was a corporation formed by nonagriculture businessmen who believed that they could obtain a favorable return on their investment. This operation involved the location of 150,000 laying hens on two farms and the raising of layers on a third. Again, specific feeding, egg gathering, cleaning, and packaging operations were used. Ninety per cent of the production was in high-quality eggs and sales were made through a broker.

A third operation was more highly integrated. It had 100,000 laying hens and was expanding its operation for an additional 80,000 birds. One type of bird was used, feed was manufactured by the firm, much of the grain used in the feed was produced on the corporation's own farms, and pullets were raised on their farms. Feeding, collecting, and processing of the eggs were systematically regulated and, in this case, marketing was part of the integration process; thus, brokers were eliminated. The accomplishments of this type of integration included the production of high-quality eggs, controlling of seasonal distribution, and low grading and marketing costs. Cost accounting, record keeping, research, and systematic labor control were all important features in the organization of these egg producing units.

Other aspects of vertical integration in farming include contract beef feeding,[18] swine production,[19] and contract milking parlors.[20] Examples of vertical integration are numerous, and they continue to proliferate. There are increasing variations both within types of commodity production and in the number of commodities brought into vertically integrated operations. Contracts vary considerably from the minimum oral agreement to the highly specified written agreement which contains numerous details concerning the scientific regulation of commodity production. Vertical integration operations also vary in terms of the number of steps in the total process.

Precise normative patterns of this social structure are not yet clearly established, because vertical integration in agribusiness is still new and may be characterized as developmental. Nevertheless, in the study of contracts and the descriptions of the arrangements which are available, it is observed that the term *farmer* is often replaced by the *producer* or *grower*. The implication of this as a folkway, if not a normative pattern, is that in the nature of social organization in agribusiness and the broader economic institutions of the nation, the ill-fated image of the farmer is destined to be superseded by a new image of the systematic operator, namely, the grower or producer.

RELATION OF VERTICAL INTEGRATION TO OTHER SOCIAL STRUCTURES

Farmer cooperatives. Farmer cooperatives constitute a major moving force in agribusiness. As such, they are much concerned with the development of vertical integration. As early as 1924, attention was called to the necessity for integration in cooperative organization.[21] It was contended that the cooperatives must utilize both horizontal and vertical integration in order to meet the challenges of quality control, standardization, processing, and marketing. The members of cooperatives have been aware of these major shifts and challenges in agribusiness organization; however, aside from the Western fruit and vegetable growers' associations, few major innovations in the direction of vertical integration have been generated among them.

In general, cooperatives have been hesitant about vertical integration. Among the reasons for this is the enormous capital investment required to operate many forms of vertical integration. Furthermore, there are certain aspects of integration which are basically contradictory to some of the principles of cooperatives. There are other aspects in which the two types of organization overlap. Both contract farming and cooperatives typically offer farmers the services of technicians to advise them on the processes of their production. But much of the similarity ends there. Cooperatives, unlike contract organizations, are often obligated to accept all quantities of production from their members. The notion of quantity and quality limitation as specified in a contract is contradictory to some concepts of cooperation. The experience of accepting some and rejecting other products brings the cooperative to the brink of disunity.

Various lines of organization are theoretically open to the farmer cooperatives. Cooperatives could organize their role as that of contract inspectors or negotiators between their member farmers and the integrating organizations. It is possible that cooperatives themselves could become the contracting agencies for their members. Both of these roles, however, signify that the cooperatives will play a passive rather than an active part in the new agribusiness organization.

Another alternative is for the co-ops themselves to engage in integration. This would take the form of integrating marketing and purchasing cooperatives, and could be accomplished if the individual cooperatives expanded their own integration processes.[22] The U.S. Department of Agriculture has implicitly suggested that farmer cooperatives provide an alternative form of integration. By using the cooperative as a mechanism for integration, farmers can reduce the number of managerial decisions they must make, while at the same time retaining more of their own decision-making and reserving for themselves a larger share of the financial benefits.[23]

Although co-ops generally are not taking advantage of the opportunities in integration, there are numerous examples of recent moves in this direction. The Central Carolina Farmers' Exchange, organized as a co-op in the 1930's, now has an almost completely integrated broiler operation.[24] Dairy cooperatives are also moving in the direction of vertical integration. They handle about three-fourths of all the whole milk which farmers sell. In addition to their major function of marketing, they manufacture dairy products, including creamery butter, cheddar cheese, cottage cheese, nonfat dry milk powder, dry buttermilk, dry whole milk, condensed skimmed milk, and ice cream.[25] Co-ops are exploring the consequences of vertical integration in a variety of ways.[26] The relation of vertical integration to cooperatives in the social organization of agribusiness is clearly that of challenge and opportunity. Cooperatives are faced with the need for expansion as well as the need for improving their management operation and the demands for innovation in methods of serving their members.

Banking and integration. Bankers and money lenders have encouraged the development of vertical integration in agribusiness, since they view it

as an organization which entails lower risks and more systematic operation. The organization of integration has increased the volume of loan
funds available for agribusiness. It has shifted the flow of credit from the
growers and producers to the dealers and processors, or to the initiators
of the integration. The integrators in turn make loans or otherwise provide a financial structure for organizing the total vertical integration
operation.[27]

Veterinarians and vertical integration. Vertical integration is a challenge
for veterinarians. Its impact is as great as that caused by the displacement
of the horse by the tractor. With increasing numbers of large, integrated
animal industry operations, greater emphasis will have to be placed on
disease prevention and control. Veterinarians will be called upon to contribute to improved livestock management.

Another aspect of vertical integration for veterinarians is the probability that their rugged individualism or fee-taking entrepreneur business
will be reduced. Large integrated operations will employ veterinarians as
specialists. In short, the veterinarian will become but one aspect of an
integrated organization.[28]

Government and vertical integration. Contract farming operations are
vitally influenced by government policy; they, in turn, have a significant
impact on the government. Government's impact on vertical integration
in agribusiness has taken many forms. One of the most clearly developed
relationships is that of the price support. When the integrator is organizing operations in which the commodity has a government price support,
a minimum return is assured regardless of the state of the market. In
effect, under the price support program, many contract arrangements may
offer few attractive features.[29]

Other manifestations of the relation of government and vertical integration are apparent in the diminished number of farmers who are independent businessmen, and in the diminished importance of the political
farm bloc. The growth in farm size and the reduction in the number of
farms have already created complications for politicians who endeavor
to hold the farm bloc together. New political support will be expected
from expanding agribusiness and vertical integration programs. The degree of this support, however, will be questionable because of the ambiv-
alent positions of agribusiness and integration between the nation's general
economic institutions and the historic family farm. As the "way-of-life"

farm operations decline, and as farm businessmen increase and are taken into the scope of the total nation's economic institution, there will be less need for a separate and distinct farm bloc. Nevertheless, it is to be expected that political leaders will expound at great length for some generations to come on the merit of small farms.

A more important implication is the probability that the Department of Agriculture and the Extension Service will develop programs and services to assist growers and producers in evaluating contracts and in bargaining for terms. Increased government regulation of marketing practices will accompany the role of the specialist. If the experience of vertical integration in nonagribusiness enterprise is a reliable indication, it is to be expected that, along with regulation of the marketing situation, there will be increased government support for the smaller and medium size operations.[30]

SUMMARY

Both horizontally and vertically integrative forms of organization are products of urbanized society. These forms exemplify in part the fundamental concepts of division of labor and specialization. Integration has been a well-organized and functioning part of economic institutions since the end of the nineteenth century. Early innovations in the direction of farming may be found in the history of the integrative and cooperative processes. However, as a major social structural form in farming and agribusiness, vertical integration has come into its own only since the middle of the twentieth century. It is still a developing social structure in agribusiness.

Integrative forms of agribusiness organization first achieved major success in the specialty crop production areas of the Far West. The contemporary expression of this form of organization has reached its greatest articulation in the broiler industry. Vertical integration is developing with different rates of speed in the production of eggs, beef, swine, milk, and a variety of smaller industries. As a basic form of social structure in urbanized social organization, it is found throughout much of Western society.

The implications of expanding programs of integration are many. Along with other major shifts in science and technology in agribusiness, vertical integration is another structural element which implicitly supports the move from the notion of agriculture as a way of life to agriculture as a rational economic enterprise in society. It will indirectly, if not directly, bring continued pressure to bear upon the owner and operator of the independent commercial farm. It can already be observed that contracts refer to producers and growers rather than to the age-old term, farmer. This is a simple, and at first apparently meaningless, change in the normative pattern. However, examination of this change in terminology from farmer to grower or producer suggests deeper meanings for the occupation of farming and for the ultimate goal of agribusiness as one stage of a nationally integrated economic operation—from production to processing through consumption of all economic goods in the urbanized society.

The developing structure of vertical integration has profound social implications for the earlier concept of fee simple ownership. The individual ownership of land and buildings is not directly excluded from the new structure. To be sure, individuals will still be property owners, but the social and economic significance of local property units will decrease. Ownership will essentially involve little more than residential locations in which entrepreneurial activities will become greatly caught up in the larger economic complex.

The social processes of competition in the price structure will be modified in vertical integration to a form of negotiation for pricing. There are numerous checks and balances which operate in the social organization of a society. Accordingly, there are alternatives to integration and there are multiple forms and various degrees by which integration can take place. Although vertical integration is still a developing structure in the area of food and fiber production, its impact already has been substantial. That its future development will be significant seems certain, but it is still too early to ascertain the form which vertical integration will take in its mature development.

NOTES

1. Samuel P. Hayes, *The Response to Industrialism, 1885–1914* (Chicago: The University of Chicago Press, 1957); William F. Willoughby, "The Concentration of Industry in the United States," *Yale Review,* 7 (May, 1898), 72–94, and "The Integration of Industry in the United States," *Quarterly Journal of Economics,* 16 (Nov., 1902), 94–115; D. H. MacGregor, *Industrial Combination* (London: G. Bell and Sons, 1906); Laurence K. Frank, "The Significance of Industrial Integration," *Journal of Political Economy,* 33 (Apr., 1925), 179–95.

2. S. R. Dennison, "Vertical Integration and the Iron and Steel Industry," *The Economic Journal,* 49 (June, 1939), 244–57.

3. Frank Gruber, *Horatio Alger, Jr.: A Biography and Bibliography* (West Los Angeles, Cal.: Grover Jones Press, 1961).

4. Joseph G. Knapp, "Cooperative Expansion through Horizontal Integration," *Journal of Farm Economics,* 32 (Nov., 1950), 1031–47.

5. Irwin W. Rust and Kelsey B. Gardner, *Sunkist Growers, Inc.: A California Adventure in Agricultural Cooperation* (Washington: U.S. Department of Agriculture, Farmer Cooperative Service, Circular 27, Dec., 1960).

6. Knapp, *op. cit.,* p. 1037.

7. *Ibid.;* Martin A. Abrahamsen, "Business-Integration: What It Means to Cooperatives" (Lecture given to the Annual Stockholders' Meeting of the New Orleans Bank for Cooperatives, Biloxi, Miss., Mar. 4–5, 1958); R. D. Hewlett, "Agricultural Cooperatives and Integration—Contract Farming," *World Agriculture,* 9 (July, 1960), 24–7; Dale C. Dahl, *Economic and Legal Aspects of Vertical Integration* (South Dakota Agricultural Experiment Station, Agriculture Economics Pamphlet 95, 1958).

8. Joseph G. Knapp, "The Effects of Integration on Marketing Agricultural Products," in *Adjusting Marketing Service Programs to Changing Conditions* (Washington: U.S.D.A., Agriculture Marketing Service, 315, 1958), p. 52.

9. Robert G. Cherry *et al., Vertical Integration in Texas Agriculture* (Texas Agricultural Experiment Station, L–418, n.d.); *Contract Farming and Vertical Integration in Agriculture* (Washington: U.S.D.A., Agriculture Information Bulletin 198, 1958).

10. D. C. Myrick and Roy E. Huffman, *Sugar Beet Production in Montana* (Montana Agricultural Experiment Station Bulletin 525, 1956); Roy M. Gilcreast, *Sugar Beet Production in the Red River Valley* (North Dakota Agricultural Experiment Station Bulletin 363, 1950); R. H. Cottrell, *Sugar Beet Economy* (Caldwell, Ida.: Caxton Press, 1952).

11. Rust and Gardner, *op. cit.;* H. G. Hamilton, "Integration of Marketing and Production Services by the Florida Citrus Association," *Journal of Farm Economics,* 29 (May, 1947), 495–505.

12. *Contract Farming and Vertical Integration in Agriculture,* pp. 9–10; H. C. Kiger, "Good Merchandising Marks: Diamond Walnut Sales," *News for Farmer Cooperatives,* 19 (Sept., 1952), 8–10.

13. H. B. Sorensen *et al., Vertical Integration in Texas Agriculture, Vegetables* (Texas Agricultural Experiment Station, L–437, n.d.); *Contract Farming and Vertical Integration in Agriculture,* p. 10; D. A. Dominick, Jr., *The Fruit and Vegetable Processing Industry in New York* (Cornell New York Agricultural Experiment Station Bulletin 714, 1949); W. F. Mueller and M. R. Collins, "Growers and Processors Integration in Fruit and Vegetable Marketing," *Journal of Farm Economics,* 39 (Dec., 1957), 1471–83.

14. Regan Brown *et al., Vertical Integration in Texas, Seed Production* (Texas Agricultural Experiment Station, L–432, n.d.); L. R. Hawthorne, *Vegetable and Flower Seed Producing* (New York: Blakiston, 1954); H. L. Schudel, *Vegetable*

and Seed Production in Oregon (Oregon Agricultural Experiment Station Bulletin 512, 1952).

15. Harley Bebout *et al., Vertical Integration in Texas Agriculture, Broilers* (Texas Agricultural Experiment Station, L–443, n.d.); *Contract Farming and Vertical Integration in Agriculture*, pp. 17–18.

16. Ralph L. Baker, *Integrating Egg Production and Marketing* (Washington: U.S.D.A., Agriculture Marketing Research Division, Marketing Research Report 332, 1959).

17. *Ibid.,* p. 11.

18. D. Braun, "Contract Beef Feeding," *Farm Journal,* 77 (Dec., 1953), 37 ff; G. A. Carpenter, "Fundamentals of Buying and Selling Livestock by Advanced Contract," *California Cattlemen* (Mar., 1958), 5–6; F. S. Scott, Jr., *Cattle Finishing in Nevada* (Nevada Agricultural Experiment Station Bulletin 193, 1957).

19. G. Gates, "Fox Built Swine Lease Programs . . . ," *Feedstuffs,* 30 (Mar. 29, 1958), 30–32; B. A. Smith, "A Meat Packer's View of Vertical Integration in Swine Production," *Feedstuffs,* 30 (June, 1958), 76, 78–9.

20. Grant Cannon, "Contract Milking," *Farm Quarterly,* 13 (Summer, 1958), 30–33.

21. John D. Black, *Cooperative Central Marketing Organization* (Minnesota Agricultural Experiment Station Bulletin 211, 1924).

22. Hewlett, *op. cit.,* pp. 25–6.

23. *Contract Farming and Vertical Integration in Agriculture*, pp. 6–7.

24. Martin A. Abrahamsen, "Co-op Integration the Carolina Way," *News for Farmer Cooperatives,* 25 (Aug., 1958), 4–5 *et passim.*

25. Anne L. Gessner, "Dairy Cooperatives Report on Integrated Activities," *News for Farmer Cooperatives,* 26 (Sept., 1959), 12–15; S. H. Behan, *Corporate vs. Cooperative Handling of Agriculture Products* (Northeast Dairy Conference Annual Report, 24, 1959), pp. 57–65.

26. C. A. Johnson, "Land O' Lakes Finds Feeder Financing Builds Business," *News for Farmer Cooperatives,* 24 (May, 1958), 10–12; C. Maurice Weting, "Ohio Farmers Take a Look at Vertical Integration," *News for Farmer Cooperatives,* 25 (Dec., 1958), 15 ff; E. F. Koller, "Vertical Integration of Agricultural Co-operatives," *Journal of Farm Economics,* 32 (Nov., 1950), 1048–58.

27. Scoville, *op. cit.,* pp. 223–4; *Contract Farming—Implication to Banking* (New York: Agricultural Commission, American Bankers Association, 1958); N. R. Gish, "Will Contract Farming Help or Hurt Banks?" *Bank News,* 58 (May 15, 1958), 59–60 ff.

28. Sherwood O. Berg, "The Veterinarian and Our Changing Agriculture," *Journal of the American Medical Association,* 135 (Sept. 15, 1959), 302–4

29. Hewlett, *op. cit.,* p. 27.

30. Earl L. Butz, "The Social and Political Implications of Integration," *Eighth National Institute of Animal Agriculture, Proceedings, 1958* (Lafayette, Ind.: Purdue University), pp. 41–50.

SELECTED READINGS

Hayes, Samuel P. *The Response to Industrialism, 1885–1914.* Chicago: The University of Chicago Press, 1957.

A brief but penetrating history of vertical integration, relating it to many historical movements, one of which is the development of the U.S. Department of Agriculture.

Contract Farming and Vertical Integration in Agriculture. Washington: Agricultural Information Bulletin 198, U.S.D.A., 1958.

Defines, explains the meaning of, and gives examples of vertical integration in the various agricultural enterprises.

Cherry, Robert G. *Vertical Integration in Texas Agriculture.* Texas Agricultural Experiment Station, L–418, n.d.

The first in an important series of leaflets which explain the nature and extent of vertical integration in specific agricultural enterprises.

Collins, Norman R. *Grower-Processor Integration: A Study of Vertical Integration Between Growers and Processors of Tomatoes in California.* California Agricultural Experiment Station Bulletin 768, 1959.

Report of an empirical research project concerning vertical integration in the California tomato industry.

Vertical Integration, Proceedings: Eighth National Institute of Animal Agriculture. Lafayette, Ind.: Purdue University, 1958.

Papers reprinted in the proceedings of this conference of particular interest here are: "What Is Integration and Its Current Status?" "Why Is Integration Developing in Agriculture?" "The Social and Political Implications of Integration," and "How Is the Market Made in Integrated Industries?"

IV SOCIAL INSTITUTIONS IN URBANIZED SOCIETY

16 SOCIAL INSTITUTIONS AND URBANIZED SOCIETY

Societies have been organized in different ways around the world, from prehistoric times to the present. Differences among the ways of life of Tierra del Fuegoans, Australian aborigines, Aztec Indians, North Americans, Russians, and Japanese are based upon their respective institutional systems which regulate population size, amount and utilization of land and resources, methods of production and distribution of goods, and the image and meaning of life. In spite of differential social organization from society to society, there are basic characteristics of Homo sapiens which are found in all societies, and certain fundamental forms of human relationships which are associated with the particular form of organization. Procreation is characteristic of all societies; a certain proportion of the newborn survive and grow to maturity; food and shelter are provided, and life is given meaning of some sort.

Normative patterns, which can be analyzed as folkways and mores, guide the relationships of individuals in the reproductive process, the production and distribution of goods, the training of certain individuals in the skills required by the society, and the explanation of the meaning of life for an individual. Within a society, as population size increases and as geographical space is enlarged to meet the needs of an expanding population, greater specialization in the division of labor necessarily occurs in order to fulfill the requirements of diverse social groups. This process of specialization contributes to greater refinement and detail

331

within various social institutions and sometimes to the development of new institutions.

Urbanized societies have developed recently in the West. The urbanization of Western societies often has been bleakly portrayed and negatively criticized. Yet such societal configurations as urbanization are not the result of surreptitious planning on the part of those in power in the countries involved. It has been pointed out that mass societies are neither imposed by force nor affirmed by self-corruption.[1] Quite the contrary, mass urbanized society is the ordering of large numbers of people, most of whom are in secondary communication with one another, by requiring a common loyalty to government, support of common ideas concerning the production and distribution of goods and services, and belief in common ideas of the meaning of life. In short, urbanized social organization represents a solution to problems which grow out of the inability of traditional societies to deal with increasing complexity and specialization in human behavior. Urbanized social organization constitutes one way of serving various social goals and of rendering high levels of human accomplishment. Principal among its advantages is a standardization sufficient to enable the greatest number of people to internalize a maximum amount of the culture of their society and to be useful citizens with a minimum of difficulty.

SOCIAL INSTITUTIONS

Social institutions are a complex of folkways and mores which establish and regulate the modes of interaction among people in the accomplishment of the basic needs generated by their society.[2] The folkways and mores, for example, concerned with the practice of reproduction, when considered in their interactional totality, constitute the social institution of the family. Similarly, the norms which have to do with producing and trading goods and services, considered in their totality, make up the economic institutions of a society. The folkways and mores guiding and directing people in their patterns of leisure, when considered in their totality, constitute a recreational social institution. The institutions of family, economics, and recreation are not descriptions of concrete situations. They are the organization of several patterns of behavior which focus on a specific function or need of a given society at a given time, and which distinguish that form of behavior from other contemporary patterns of behavior in the society.

Individuals participate in several institutions simultaneously. A man typically begins his day behaving within the structure of folkways and mores that concern his relation with a wife, children, and possibly other relatives. These activities are part of the family institution. They express the norms concerning different age and sex categories, inhabiting the same place of residence, taking meals together, and utilizing the house for preparation for departure to other types of social interaction in other places in the society. Leaving the place of residence and the responsibilities for infant care and child training to his wife, the male may work in an office, factory, or field. There he is guided by another complex of folkways and mores concerning the nature of work and the economic production and distribution of goods and services. The tone of voice and vocabulary used by the male when relating to his family are exchanged for new expressions and new vocabulary which are characteristic of the work situation but not of the home. Other norms establish the amount of work, the conditions of work, the amount of time for leisure and for eating, the type of dress, and other matters apropos of the office, factory, or field. Should the family come to visit the male in his work situation, his response and relationship to them will be different from that typically found in their place of residence.

If family members attend a church, they may be identified by several titles: trustee or educational director for the husband; deaconess or ladies' aid president for the wife, and acolyte for the younger child. They are still the same individuals as earlier found sharing a common residential location, but in the religious environment they are directed in their relationships in terms of a still different set of folkways and mores.

During an evening of another day in the week, this same group, the man and his family, might be found at leisure activities in the town square, with the husband as leader of the community band, the wife as auxiliary director for a children's playground area, and the child as a player on the little league baseball team. The folkways and mores which direct their behavior are part of the complex of ideas concerning recreation and leisure.

Social institutions, in reiteration, are sets of folkways and mores which pattern the behavior of individuals interacting and seeking to fulfill their common needs. The folkways and mores which combine to constitute a social institution are relatively stable and demanding of individuals. Although social institutions are continually being modified by the development of new folkways and mores and the passing of earlier ones, their general character is enduring and highly obligatory. Not only does the institution of the family broadly define the responsibilities of husband to wife, wife to husband, of parents to children, and of children to parents, but also of one generation to another.

NUMBER OF SOCIAL INSTITUTIONS

The number of social institutions is in part related to the type of social organization. In urbanized social organization, there are characteristically a greater number of social institutions than in ruralized social organization. Large complex societies have a greater division of labor, a proliferation of needs, and, accordingly, a greater number of institutions than small societies have.

As societies become more advanced, institutions become firmly developed around the practices of procreation, socialization, production and distribution of goods, political order, and religious explanations of the meaning of human existence. These are often called *primary institutions.*[3] As societies become still more advanced, and reach the character of urbanized social organization, the division of labor and the specificity of activities become focused more on new meanings and new goals of the society. In the case of urbanized America and much of Western Europe, an ever-increasing set of folkways and mores are focused upon welfare activities. In several of these urbanized societies, social welfare is rapidly becoming institutionalized. In some urbanized societies, health is developing as a separate institution. In America, recreation is rapidly reaching the status of an institution as a greater number of folkways and mores define participant and spectator roles, indoor and outdoor activities, and generally legitimize leisure. Human relations and the arts are becoming more widespread and more structured. They too are taking on the character of special social institutions. In several respects, behavior associated with science is greatly structured by specific folkways and mores approaching the form of an institution.[4]

As societies become more complex, more elevated above levels of subsistence, a greater number of goals become identifiable. A greater number of people also have more time which can be spent at their discretion in pursuit of various goals. Social space in society has continued to remain limited while the activities which are deemed important by society have been expanded or reduced throughout the long course of human history. Therefore, new institutions grow and become more specific in a society by filling the social space and functions previously held by other institutions. For example, there have been times and places at which the folkways and mores associated with religious rites of passage included much of the so-called medical knowledge of the society, and much of the recreational activity experienced in the various rites that provided for dancing, feasting, and other forms of social gathering. Folkways and mores associated with learning have at times been dominated by the religious structure, as have many of the folkways concerning political organization which, for example, led to the notion of the divine right of kings. The norms of the institution of art in Tibet have been defined by the religious organization of that society.

When the complex of religious folkways and mores was sufficiently broad to include multiple forms of human expression, the social institution of religion filled a great degree of social space. In urbanized society there have been protests that the religious and moral fiber of the population is declining. This is one way of observing that the religious institutions today constitute less social space than during the Middle Ages. If such a situation is studied systematically, and if questions are raised concerning that social space devoted to religious activities throughout history, it will be found that many of the areas of human experience which were once subsumed under the control of religious institutions are now coming to be dominated by other newly developed social institutions. To a very great extent, most of the formal socialization experienced in an urbanized society is well within the domain of the educational institution and is scarcely related to the religious institution. There are still parochial and church-related schools, but even in these cases, many of the norms which guide teachers and pupils, and which structure the image of learning and knowledge, are basic normative patterns not controlled by religious ideologies.

Control of learning has been separated from the religious folkways and mores. The divine right of kings has become a doctrine appropriate for historical analysis. Most of the norms which guide and direct political behavior are in no way constrained by those directing religious behavior. Separation of church and state is one aspect of social organization in urbanized America.

The specialized and scientific study of the human body has become so advanced that the organized church, far from endeavoring to practice medicine, now looks upon the role of the physician as a high calling. But the developing institution of medicine is not yet completely divorced from the religious institution. Churches, for example, still provide considerable support for medical missionaries and hospitals. But aside from a few sects, most of the major church groups of Western religions concede the validity of new normative patterns directing the activities of medical doctors in areas separated from those of religion. These several tendencies for the development of new institutions mean that there have been encroachments on the social space that has been occupied from time to time by the folkways and mores of religious institutions.[5]

The social institution of religion never has been dominant in the United States. Some localities have been inhabited by people with a stronger religious orientation than others, but the ideal of religious freedom, which was a part of the founding of the United States, served to relegate the role of this institution to a position of less than dominant importance. Freedom in individual life and in social organization serves strikingly different functions. For the individual, freedom may mean a minimum of structural control of human life. In social organization, experience of freedom reflects a value system in which an institution is less important as a controlling factor in human behavior. On the other hand, societies are ongoing organizations. Those areas of human relations which are most important to the needs of a society will necessarily exist in a close relationship to, or in reciprocity with, other areas of the society; hence, when normative patterns are most specific, individuals experience a maximum of structural control of life. Consequently, the institution of religion, less dominant in urbanized society, is less binding on human life than it was during the Middle Ages.

However, there is some evidence that the norms which combine to constitute the religious institution in the United States are expanding. More individuals are devoting more of their time to religious affairs.[6] Expanding church memberships, increased church attendance, construction of new church sanctuaries, and increased donations are among the several indexes of expansion of this institution. There is considerable doubt on the part of the clergy as to whether this expanded interest is genuine or spurious, but in any case it suggests that the institution of religion is receiving more widespread attention. Other normative developments include the generally widespread attention given to the rural and urban church, the consolidation of churches, the federation of churches, and other methods increasing efficiency in religious organizations. All of these various developments are, in fact, mechanisms which could lead to the expansion of this institution and its closer interrelationship with other major institutions.

Where there are only a few social institutions in a society their purposes are broad, and where there are many their purposes are highly specific. Regardless of the number of institutions to be identified in a society at a given time, however, only one or a few institutions tend to dominate the others. Religious institutions dominated the tone of life in the Middle Ages in Europe, not only in religious but also in political, economic, and domestic activities. In Tibetan society, religious activities have had a similar position of dominance. In such societies, however, religion did not reach a position of total transcendance in which the other institutions were abolished.

In much of the Western world in the last two centuries, economic and political institutions have become dominant. For example, the folkways and mores of the arts were greatly influenced by the politicomilitary institutions of Germany during the Hitler regime. Artistic expression continued, but the type of painting and sculpture most rewarded by the society was created in such a way as to provide a naturalistic rendering and a glorification of the *Reich*. Modern expressionistic forms of art were considered to be degenerate. Within a few years after the Communist Revolution in Russia, the new political regime began to dominate artistic expression in that country by patronizing those artists who glorified the new state and the daily man in his working situation, as opposed to the constructivism, and suprematism, and other so-called forms of modern expression that were in vogue in 1917 and the years which followed. The institution of art was not abolished, but its form of expression was directly influenced by other institutions of the society.

In urbanized social organization, procreation is the concern of the family. Family organization is monogamous, with one man married to one woman. The norm for biological exogamy is supported by laws in many states which prohibit marriage of brothers and sisters and first cousins. Folkways further direct the choosing of mates and the announcement of the choice through pinnings, engagements, showers, and stag parties. After a public marriage ceremony, there are folkways which direct such experiences as planning the number and spacing of children. Aside from these normative patterns which guide bringing people together for marriage, the institution of the family is largely diffused and interrelated with other institutions. For example, medical institutions structure much of the care of all members of the family. Welfare institutions provide organizations in which members of the family participate from infancy to old age. Educational institutions have appropriated many of the functions of socialization which formerly belonged to the family, and made them specialized activities of the society. Recreational institutions have recently developed in such extensive and complex ways that much of the experience of leisure involves large numbers of people and varieties of facilities which cannot be encompassed by the small family structure.

Many historical characteristics of the family—particularly of the farm family—which included the welfare of the young and aged, the provision of recreation and medical care for its members, are no longer exhibited. Nevertheless, the major function of the family is not disintegrating. Multiple functions of the family are being reduced because of the development of other institutions concerned with special domestic areas, excluding that of procreation. Urbanized social organization in America still provides a family institution which functions to guide and direct procreation. Indeed, the norms that have governed procreation heretofore have resulted in problems of overpopulation for the society.

In urbanized society, norms governing the socialization process have developed concomitantly with greater specialization in the division of labor. With increasing social complexity and a greater range of culture to be assimilated, more systematic mechanisms are required for passing on the culture of a society from one generation to the next. The school therefore has become specifically organized and is continually expanding to dominate more years of the life of individuals. Starting school at age six has been a normative pattern for approximately a century. Now the normative pattern is changing as the formal socialization experience is initiated at an earlier age, usually in the kindergarten, and even more recently, in the nursery school. The development of schools is supported by a belief in the value of organized and directed group experiences for younger children. Pregrade schools have resulted in greater freedom for young mothers to work or engage in other activities.

As normative patterns of educational requirements have expanded, other changes have occurred in the social behavior of those associated with education. The number of hours families can be together has been reduced. More individuals in their teens are required to participate in school until age sixteen. An increasing proportion of the population is extending its participation in education through the years of college and later in graduate school. Normative patterns in education now provide social reinforcement to individuals spending 25 or more years in preparation for their vocations or careers.

Finally, the institution of education has expanded partly because of shifts in the economic institution of the society. In urbanized society, characterized by greater specialization in the division of labor, extended training is required in order to master vocational skills or otherwise to attain qualifications which are prerequisite to occupational entry. Therefore, persons pursuing certain occupational experiences tend to enter the work world at a later age. The resulting normative pattern, on the one hand, provides greater social space for, and frees individuals from, work experience during the earlier years to pursue formal education and, on the other hand, creates pressure for individuals to make certain sacrifices in order to achieve the necessary and prerequisite formal training. Social rewards for higher educational attainment include positions in occupations and professions with more prestige, proportionately greater economic remuneration, and greater personal and work satisfaction.

Reciprocal shifts in the social organization of a society as indicated above illustrate the interrelationships and interdependence of institutions. The economic institution contributes space to education and at the same time requires the training offered by the expanding educational institution. Similarly, as the advanced years of training extend to include the ages of marriage of young couples, a normative pattern has developed strongly favorable to the status of married students. Student marriage illustrates the interrelationship between the family and educational institutions.

The production and distribution of goods and services has been central to social organization in urbanized society. The expansion of economic institutions was an early part of the shift in social organization from a ruralized to an urbanized state. Work and family life have become separated. The family farm has been a stronghold against the final removal of the place of work from the family. In recent years, and in conjunction with the educational institutions, young people from family farms have been taken from their home environment for training in the schools. The folkways and mores of production and distribution have been influenced by mechanization and the development of national markets. Larger farms, mechanized farms, vertical integration, and horizontal integration, as well as government programs, have all taken their toll in the expansion of production and distribution norms which extend into the rural production and distribution system and make it a part of the national system.

In urbanized society, political order is ever more a matter of national concern. County and township governments still exist, but their functions are being diluted.[7] Norms of the political institution are expanding, particularly in rural areas, through the several government agencies, for example, special districts having regulatory authority over local operations and people. These changes in political institutions are largely related to the fact that most rural people are no longer farm people. Rural nonfarm people frequently have political interests which are more related to those of city than farm people.

The institutions of health and welfare are still developing. Their social space is largely created by encroachment on that of the family, particularly by providing homes for the aged and, to a somewhat lesser extent, by offering nursery schools and health benefits to young people. Art and recreational institutions are developing nationally. America has experienced a museum building boom since the mid-twentieth century.[8] There have been record attendances at spectator performances and a marked increase in outdoor recreation.

SOCIAL INSTITUTIONS IN SMALL SOCIETIES

In many preliterate and nonurbanized societies, social organization, while complex, involves much less specialization of activities, goals, and ideologies than is characteristic of urbanized society. There is a more general interweaving of all aspects of social activity and less differentiation of life into a multiple number of highly specific social institutions. In such socially compact societies, economic, religious ritual, and recreational affairs are deeply interrelated, and at best it becomes an academic exercise to disentangle the patterns and to fit folkways and mores into an institutional frame of analysis.[9]

Social institutions in Tikopia. The nature of social institutions in a small society is illustrated in Firth's classic study of the Tikopian Islanders.[10] Tikopia is located approximately 100 miles southeast of the Solomon Islands, and accordingly is quite isolated in the South Pacific. Its contacts with the outside world were little more than annual events. At the time of Firth's original study, this small island had a population of approximately 1,300 people. The society was structurally self-contained. The clans, religious system, and political organization were all free from outside social alignments. The interrelationships between the various structural elements of the Tikopian community were so compact that:

Economic ritual, and recreational affairs, for instance, are often difficult to disentangle within a complex institutional sequence of events, such as an initiation ceremony, a harvest festival, or even a funeral. Community cohesion, though varying according to such structural factors as the system of kinship grouping, rank, and religious ties, is normally strong. But the scope of social differentiation is usually very much greater than in the small community in the West. The total range is not necessarily wider, since many kinds of economic and political specialization are equally barred. But the great variety of structural arrangements, in kinship groupings, age-grading, sex, and seniority emphases, and the formalization of many relationships which in the West are left informal, allows of much subtle difference in the social position of members of the community.[11]

While certain complexities and distinctions are made in Tikopia which are not made in Western societies, the opposite is also true. From the Western point of view, Tikopia is relatively undifferentiated in its institutional organization. Due to the small population and the low level of technological development, extensive markets and diversified occupations are conspicuously absent. Goods are exchanged, and indeed their systems for exchange are often elaborate. Nevertheless, in most cases the systems for exchange fulfill more a social than an economic end. Production specialists and middlemen do not exist. Large profits are not accumulated by those engaged in production activities. There is no capitalist class. In fact, Firth observes that social and economic relationships tend to merge much as they did in the Middle Ages in Europe. As one examines the various other institutions, he can observe that the Tikopian society functions without either great wealth or extensive poverty.

SUMMARY

Social institutions are greater in number and more specific in function in complex urbanized societies, and fewer in number and more general in function in nonurbanized societies. Social institutions refer to a complex of folkways and mores, which guide human interaction, concerned with a specific goal or function defined as important by a specific society. All societies have institutions that direct human relations in terms of the reproductive process and of training people in the skills and knowledge which are needed for mature living in the society. There are folkways and mores which institutionalize the organization of the labor force and the distribution of goods, that deal with the meaning and motivation of life's experience, and which direct people in terms of political order. In the great majority of all societies, urban or rural, large or small, preliterate or industrialized, such institutions are primary and typically can be identified.

As societies become more developed, more complex, and more urbanized, with their elevation above basic levels of subsistence, additional institutions are defined which develop social space by the appropriation and refinement of some of the activities of earlier institutions. Welfare, health, art, recreation, and science are all institutional developments which come to have a more precise place in urbanized society. The areas of direction over human life which have traditionally been in the sphere of the family institution, the religious institution, and the economic institution are being reduced, as social space is made available for nascent secondary institutions.

NOTES

1. Don Martindale, *American Society* (New York: D. Van Nostrand Co., 1960), pp. 256 ff.

2. Robin M. Williams, Jr., *American Society: A Sociological Interpretation* (New York: Alfred A. Knopf, 1952), pp. 28–35; John W. Bennett and Melvin M. Tumin, *Social Life: Structure and Function* (New York: Alfred A. Knopf, 1948), pp. 166–95.

3. Bennett and Tumin, *op. cit.,* p. 168.

4. Robert K. Merton, *Social Theory and Social Structure* (Glencoe, Ill.: The Free Press, 1949), pp. 289–363.

5. Roy Lewis and Angus Maude, *Professional People* (London: Phoenix House, Ltd., 1952), pp. 17–19.

6. "Religion in American Society," *The Annals of the American Academy of Political and Social Science,* 332 (Nov., 1960).

7. Arthur J. Vidich and Joseph Bensman, *Small Town in Mass Society* (New York: Doubleday Anchor Books, 1960), pp. 110–226; Gordon E. Baker, *Rural Versus Urban Political Power* (New York: Random House, 1955).

8. "The Visual Arts Today," *Daedalus* (Winter, 1960); Katharine Kuh, "What Should a Museum Be: Plus and Minus of the Building Boom," *Art in America,* 49, No. 2 (1961), 40–45.

9. Raymond Firth, *Elements of Social Organization* (London: Watts and Co., 1951), pp. 41–79; Robert Redfield, *The Folk Culture of Yucatan* (Chicago: University of Chicago Press, 1941).

10. Raymond Firth, *We, The Tikopia: A Sociological Study of Kinship in Primitive Polynesia* (New York: American Book Co., 1936), and *Social Change in*

Tikopia: Re-Study of a Polynesian Community after a Generation (New York: Macmillan Co., 1959).

11. Firth, *Elements of Social Organization*, pp. 47–8.

SELECTED READINGS

Bennett, John W., and Melvin M. Tumin. *Social Life: Structure and Function.* New York: Alfred A. Knopf, 1948.
   Chapters 12 and 13 are particularly lucid treatments of the functionalist approach to the study of social institutions.

Firth, Raymond. *Elements of Social Organization.* London: Watts and Co., 1951.
   The first chapter is a most articulate statement of social organization with particular reference to small, preliterate societies. The following chapters describe concrete aspects of social organization in preliterate societies.

Martindale, Don. *American Society.* New York: D. Van Nostrand Co., Inc., 1960.
   See especially Part III, "Social Institutions of Mass Society." The author groups social institutions into three categories: socialization, mastery of nature, and social control.

Merton, Robert K. *Social Theory and Social Structure.* Glencoe, Ill.: The Free Press, 1949.
   A collection of essays concerning theory and social structure, illustrating the functional relationships between elements of social institutions.

Vidich, Arthur J., and Joseph Bensman. *Small Town in Mass Society.* New York: Doubleday Anchor Books, 1960.
   The report of participant observers' case study of a small town in New York that offers a clear example of the nature of social institutions in urbanized society.

17 FAMILY LIFE FROM FARMS TO SUBURBIA

Historically, farm families with their high birth rates have been the cradle of the nation. Reproduction in urban families has frequently not been sufficient to replace population loss, and the population of many urban places would have declined had it not been for the migration of farm youth to cities where they lived out their productive years. By the middle of the twentieth century, the cradle of the nation had expanded to include much of suburbia. Four-bedroom houses, family rooms, game rooms, multiple bathrooms, station wagons, large yards, and playgrounds all reflect the high fertility which is characteristic of suburbia.

By 1960 the nation's families totaled 45,100,000. Some 9,900,000 of these families, located in rural nonfarm areas, had an average size household of 3.5 persons. In rural farm areas there were approximately 3,300,000 families, whose average size household was 3.8 persons. In the urban areas there were 31,900,000 families, with an average size household of 3.2 persons. The average size rural farm family was still the nation's largest, but families in suburbs and urban areas so outnumbered farm families that the greatest proportion of births was in the suburbs and urban areas.

Procreation of the species is the fundamental purpose of the family. Many of the secondary functions in one way or another have to do with socialization. In the tradition of early rural America, the family had been the place of childbirth, rearing, training, health care, protection, recreation, religion, and food and fiber production. In short, the family in early

America was the center of social life. The rugged pioneer experience engendered a social milieu in which the institutional space of the family expanded to incorporate a vast domain of human life.

In more recent years, as the nation has become progressively more urbanized, the social space of the family has contracted. Increased division of labor and the complexity of society have taken many areas of human enterprise away from the domain of the colonial and early American family and combined them into new, specialized human relations. The factory, school, church, hospital, and recreation industry all have combined with a new technology for transportation and communication to reduce the social space of the family.

This chapter examines the changing structure of the family, from the colonial condition of ruralized social organization to the contemporary suburban condition of urbanized social organization.

HISTORICAL BACKGROUNDS

American family patterns were primarily derived from those of Europe. In the New World, however, family life was modified not simply transplanted from Europe. Part of this modification was made because of the struggle for human existence in the new, rugged frontier environment. Furthermore, many of the immigrants were dissenters from the major religious and social traditions of their mother countries. For example, dissenting groups, particularly the Puritans, favored the separation of the church and the family.[1]

By the beginning of the twelfth century, or toward the end of the period of dominant ruralized social organization in medieval Europe, the church had exercised extensive authority over marriage and the family. In that age of ecclesiastical rule, marriage was included with the sacraments.[2] Divorce and remarriage were not an approved part of the social structure of the later medieval family. In England, prior to colonial migration to the New World, King Henry had broken with the Church in Rome. In spite of the rift, family patterns were still largely dominated by the earlier religious tradition. In the New World, however, family patterns developed under the influence of religious dissenters in a manner that deviated from earlier religious tradition.

The colonial family. The New World family was eminently rural. It was a family of the frontier. Whether on isolated farms or in wilderness towns, its traditions were of a common type. It is reported that in early Boston, pigs roamed the streets, and the gardens between houses gave them a distinctly rural character.[3] On the frontier, living amid Indian tribes which were often hostile, the family was faced with the problem of survival and was forced to develop into a self-sustaining primary group. The division of labor was well defined. It was man's work to clear the fields and till the soil and woman's work to cook, spin, and sew. When there was an insufficient labor force within the immediate family to accomplish the tasks at hand, work was performed by members of the extended family. An austere relationship between man and nature fostered family solidarity.

Goals of the early families were simple and forthright. The major goals were to provide food, clothing, implements, and shelter. Family welfare was the result of mutual aid between members of the family in times of health and sickness, happiness and sorrow, youth and age. Training and education were of a practical nature, preparing the younger family members at a relatively early age to become responsible participants in the life processes of the frontier. The types of skill and knowledge were plain and simple, concrete rather than abstract. Most learning was achieved by demonstration and in the form of apprenticeship. Much of the religious experience was contained within the family. Churches were not always accessible, ministers were itinerant and had little influence on family life. Companionship and recreation were achieved through family social interaction, often because of the absence of other persons. "Not only were new members born to families," Sirjamaki writes, "but they were reared, educated, and employed within them as well, they were succored by them in their distresses and at the last buried by them also." [4]

Household manufactures. It was part of the plan of the British colonial system that the colonies should produce raw materials and, in turn, procure their processed and manufactured goods from the mother country. Accordingly, in the early days of the colonies, household necessities were purchased from England. However, this system did not function smoothly. The price of goods was high, the supply insufficient, and the irregularity of cargo ships frustrating. Hence, the colonists established a system of household manufacturing, although its legality was doubtful. Colonial household manufacturing included a long list of items, not the least of which were food, clothing, furniture, utensils, and other artifacts.[5] This type of family household manufacturing enterprise was the initial step in the direction of American industrialization. Concomitant with it was the growth of American towns and cities, and the accompanying division of labor. The smallest villages included sawmills, gristmills, flourmills, and other types of specialized production centers.

The American family. The colonial and early American families were formed in a predominantly rural society. The dominance of the rural family, nevertheless, has been exaggerated. Although most people lived on farms in colonial America, towns and cities were a part of the American idea system and its concrete reality, particularly after the Revolution. The development of household manufacturing and its unique division of labor made for early differences between farm and town families. The Revolutionary War was also a major factor in contributing to the differences between rural and urban patterns of the division of labor. Markets were established and commercial farms were developed in contrast to the self-sustaining family farms. This is exemplified by the Clothier General's continual calls for uniforms, blankets, and other supplies for the Revolutionary Armies.[6] In time, family differences in rural and urban America became even more distinct.

The American family in 1790 was characteristically large. Children were an economic asset; they were needed for the backbreaking labor of the subsistence farms or the cottage industry. Historical statistics reveal that the median size of the family in 1790 was 5.4 members.[7] It is believed that a birth rate of approximately 55 per 1,000 population was necessary to sustain the large family size.[8] The combination of large size and the system of bilateral descent gave rise to the extended family. Another characteristic of the early American family was the European and rural tradition of patriarchical dominance. Residence for a newly married couple was neo-local, which was a convenient means for the family to adapt to the rural economy. As a result of dispersed settlement, each family owned and operated land adequate to sustain its own members.

Subsistence farms and business farms continued to multiply, along with the increase in industry and growth of cities. These factors influenced the changing character of the American family between the days of the Revolution and the Civil War. The predominance of the self-sustaining family of ruralized social organization was continually threatened by the increased specialization and division of labor, which were part of the emergent urbanized social organization.

Differences between rural and urban families reached their peak in the nineteenth century. The opposing family ideologies represented a power struggle, the fate of which was determined by the Civil War. Throughout the seventeenth and eighteenth centuries, colonial and American family life was predominantly characterized by ruralized social organization. Throughout the twentieth century, American family life, whether experienced in the central city, the suburban fringe, or the open country, has been dominated by urbanized social organization. The nineteenth century family was characterized by the struggle and vacillation between these two differential ideologies of social organization. Through the contraction and reorganization of its functions, the family has shifted from a self-sufficient to a consumption-oriented, egocentric, status centered way of life. The procreative activity of the family has been sharply reduced, as indicated by the decrease in family size from 5.4 members in 1790 to 3.2 in 1950 and 3.5 in 1960. Provision of food, household manufacturing, and other economic activities have largely been removed from the domain of the family. Formal education has become a widely developed institution, acquiring much of its social space at the expense of the family. Children are taken out of the home for formal training and for a considerable amount of other socialization. Similar to education, activities in the areas of welfare, health, recreation, religion, and politics have developed along separate institutional lines. In each case these changes have resulted in a reduction of the social space which was occupied by the family in colonial and early America.

Families in the central cities were the first to be influenced by these new conditions of institutional expansion and division of labor. One by one, however, school, church, health, welfare, and recreational activities all have been moved into rural America in an organized way. Concomitantly, masses of the American population have moved from farms and central cities to the suburbs and the rural fringe. The movement of the specialized institutions out of urban America into rural America and the movement of the population to suburbia combine to bring about a new unity in family organization.

During the nineteenth century, the student of American social organization analyzed both the rural family and the urban family. By the twentieth century, the folkways, mores, and social norms, which constituted the guidelines for procreation and other family functions in the United States, were different more in degree than in kind, if differences appeared at all.

CURRENT RURAL AND URBAN CHARACTERISTICS

Normative patterns which supported high fertility were part of the rural tradition. Fertility has continued to be higher in rural than in urban areas, but recent evidence indicates that this difference is narrowing.[9] This may be due to the greater use of contraception and family planning, and to the mobility resulting in increased interaction between individuals in open country and cities. Moreover, the differences in rural and urban fertility rates which remain most pronounced are more the result of educational than of ecological factors.

Freedman analyzed the use of contraceptives by couples with "(1) no farm background, (2) some farm background (either wife or husband lived on a farm for some time, usually *while growing up*), and (3) now on a farm." [10] He found that fewer couples from farm than from nonfarm backgrounds used contraceptives. Furthermore, when the farm couples did use contraceptives, they began using them later, had fewer planned births, and had more accidental pregnancies. Family planning by couples with some farm background was intermediate between that of farm and nonfarm families. Control of pregnancy was also more related to the couples' religion (Catholic versus Protestant) than to ecological location. In summary, Freedman writes:

The variations of family limitation practices that do exist in both religious groups in relation to farm background are closely related to, and may be mainly a result of, differences in education. If the educational background is the same, farm couples are about as likely to have used contraception and to have used it effectively as are indigenous urban couples.[11]

Educational differences between farm and city people are gradually diminishing. Consequently, a continuing reduction of differences in rural and urban fertility rates is to be expected.

Freedman also studied fertility differentials in terms of the couples' current place of residence. For this analysis, seven residential categories were established as follows:

METROPOLITAN AREAS	NONMETROPOLITAN AREAS
Twelve largest cities	Small cities (2,500–50,000)
Other large cities (50,000 or more)	Rural nonfarm
Suburbs of twelve largest cities	Farm
Suburbs of other large cities	

It was found that current place of residence and family planning were not closely related. The fertility of couples living on farms was significantly different from those in the six other residential categories, but it has already been observed that this difference was more related to education than to ecology.

Fertility has been related to the level of economic affluence of the family, the occupational status of the male, and the educational attainment of both members of the marriage. In most studies an inverse relationship has been reported between social class indexes and fertility. The differences have been greatest in urban areas, but they have also been significant in rural areas. In post-World War II years, increased fertility has reduced the differential birth rate between social classes. Some demographers have suggested that the class fertility differential may completely disappear [12] as the society continues toward urbanization.

Differences in rural and urban fertility rates have been widely recorded. Students of rural population who have analyzed the historical data have repeatedly and in various ways validated the assertion that rural areas have contributed greatly to the number of children of the nation. For example, Lorimer and Osborn reported that between 1925 and 1930, rural farm women provided a natural increase of 60 per cent per generation.[13] During the same period, rural nonfarm women provided a natural increase of 30 per cent per generation. Women in small cities and towns produced approximately enough children to replace themselves. By contrast, women in urban areas of 25,000 to 250,000 had a reproductive loss of approximately 10 per cent per generation. In the still larger cities, women had a loss of 20 per cent per generation.

Westoff's study of differential fertility ratios reveals that between 1930 and 1950, the number of children under five years of age per 1,000 women in the 20 to 44 age group increased from 436 to 545 for urban women, an 11 per cent increase.[14] For rural farm women the increase was slight—from 865 to 876, or a 1 per cent increase.

A variety of factors historically associated with differential rates of rural and urban fertility continue to operate, although to a lesser degree, up to the present time. Urbanized social organization has come to dominate the families of the nation's larger cities. In contrast to farm families, the large urban families are oriented toward companionship and toward the struggle for status. According to Glick, the relationships between the sexes in the larger cities are characterized by a greater heterogeneity of personality types, contributing an air of romanticism to sex, courtship, and marriage.[15] Excessive romanticism subverts the attention of the sexes from procreation to the hedonistic pleasures which in most cases are not conducive to family permanence and to high fertility. In short, urban family culture has placed a greater emphasis on sensual than on family values.[16]

In contrast to these characteristics of the urban family, rural families most often emphasize the welfare of the primary group over individual interests. Ideologically, rural people have held hard work, possession of land, and family loyalty to be important values.[17] The pleasure-seeking hedonism of the urban family frequently has been disdained in the ideology of farm people.

Reasons for differences in rural and urban fertility rates have been so often specified that they have become commonplace. Unfortunately, the evidence presented to sustain the validity of these reasons has been more suggestive than conclusive. In the demographic study of rural and urban life, it becomes apparent that there has not been a consistent effort to hold constant the differential effects on fertility by occupation, education, and income, in contrast to the ecological location of the married pair. As Freedman points out, it may well be that even those diminishing differences which still obtain in the fertility rates of rural and urban people can be better explained by occupation and education than by rural or urban residence.

Marital status. Most Americans become married at one time or another during their adult lives. Americans typically marry at an early age and live out their lives as members of a married pair. As late as the 1920's it was observed that marriage occurred earlier and more frequently in cities than in farm areas and, conversely, that divorce was less frequent in farm areas than in cities.[18] By the 1950's the statistical refinement of the earlier generalizations showed, in most cases, insignificant rural-urban differences in age of marriage, number of marriages, and rate of divorce. At mid-century the average male entered his first marriage at age 23 and the average female entered her first marriage at age 20 [19] (see Table XXIV). Both the bride and groom of 1950 were a year younger on the average than those of a decade earlier. This change in the interval of only one decade is in sharp contrast to a similar decline of only two years for the males and one-half year for the females in the entire fifty year period from 1890 to 1940.

At the midpoint of the twentieth century, it was found that urban males were more frequently married than rural males—68.6 per cent compared to 64.0 per cent. Urban females were less frequently married

TABLE XXIV. AGE AT FIRST MARRIAGE IN 1950, BY SEX AND RESIDENCE

Residence	Male	Female
Urban	23.1	20.6
Rural nonfarm	22.4	19.3
Rural farm	23.2	19.7
United States	22.9	20.2

Source: Otis D. Duncan and Albert J. Reiss, Jr. *Social Characteristics of Urban and Rural Communities, 1950* (New York: John Wiley and Sons, Inc., 1956), p. 68.

than rural females—63.8 per cent compared to 70.8 per cent. Widowed and divorced persons, both males and females, more frequently were found in urban than in rural areas.[20]

Family life cycle. The life cycle of the farm family often has a different meaning from that of the nonfarm family. The first stage of the farm family lasts until the young married couple's child-bearing experience. During this period the marriage partners are often both working and enjoy some temporary economic well-being as they try to build up their farm or to acquire a farm of their own. The second stage in the cycle, beginning with the birth of children, is a period of economic struggle since there are more dependents and a decrease in resources because of the removal of the mother from the economic market. Later in this stage the children become somewhat of an economic asset in that they assist with the farm work. Historically, in the days of the premechanized and subsistence farm, the latter part of the child-bearing period was of particular advantage to the farm family. At the present time, however, because of both mechanization and the requirement of a longer period of formal education, children spend less time working on the farm. The third stage of the farm family life cycle occurs when the children reach adulthood and depart from the family of orientation to form their own families. Once again the parental pair achieves some degree of affluence, because there are fewer dependents and because the farm operator's business typically reaches its highest point of operational efficiency. This stage is followed by a final one during which the parental pair reaches the declining years. Retirement is gradual for the farmer, while it is more abrupt and final at an arbitrary age for most nonfarm employees.[21]

The stages of the family life cycle and the farming operation cycle are related.[22] The new farmer's early years are characterized by a shortage of both capital and land. The farm and family compete for the limited funds. Later, as children begin to mature, their relatively inexpensive labor is combined with a larger and more efficient farming operation. The farmer's acreage increases to a maximum at about ages 50 to 55, after which the operation gradually decreases as the farmer begins retirement.[23]

The family's formal participation in the social activities of its area has been found to be related to the life cycle.[24] Families in the second stage have the highest average organizational participation but do not belong to the largest number of organizations. Rather, they participate selectively and intensively in a limited number of organizations. The young family-set serves most frequently in the capacity of officers for the organizations to which they belong. Husbands and wives who are owners of their farms participate more frequently in social activities in all stages of their family cycle than do tenants.

Farm and city work schedules. Division of labor in American family life has been widely established and has endured through a long period of history. In the rural tradition it was the duty of men to operate the farm and the duty of women to manage the house and garden. For both, the place of work and residence were in immediate proximity. As the nation has become urbanized, the family has declined as a production unit. Work has become separated from the place of residence.

Accompanying this separation is a considerable realignment of the so-called appropriate duties for men and women in and around the household It has been found that farm wives do more household work than city wives and, conversely, that city husbands participate in more household details than do farm husbands.[25] It was anticipated that farm husbands would participate more in household duties than city husbands due to the fact that their places of work are closer to their residence. In fact, research findings suggest that the opposite is true. Aside from keeping farm accounts and shoveling a path to the barn, it appears that farm husbands participate less than city husbands in household repairs, yard care, grocery shopping, food preparation, and dishwashing. These various household tasks are done more often by the farm wife than the city wife, and, moreover, the farm wife participates more in male tasks. It is concluded that farm wives perform the traditional household duties more frequently than do urban wives; they also, more often than not, invade the sphere of the man's work world.

IDEOLOGIES AND SOCIAL ORGANIZATIONS

Agrarianism as a way of life dominated the colonial and early American family more because of environment than because of ideology. The moral ascendancy of agriculture, according to Griswold, reached an apex, particularly in England and in France, during the second half of the eighteenth century.[26] This high point of the agrarian experience was ephemeral and marked, in fact, an early stage of the Industrial Revolution. The Industrial Revolution was destined to replace agrarianism, but even during the years of agricultural development it made remarkable inroads. In England the members of the nobility vied with one another in enclosing land and developing great agricultural estates. This new farming gentry participated in experimentation, worked for the organization of agricultural societies, and developed husbandry into a big business. No less than King George III operated a model farm at Windsor. It is reported that the King himself was pleased with the nickname "Farmer George." [27]

Across the Channel in France, notions of the high value of agrarian living were fostered by the Physiocrats, who believed that in the essence of human affairs there was a natural order in which agriculture was the only productive occupation.[28] A belief in the high value of agriculture was espoused by leading citizens in colonial America and subsequently influenced the Founding Fathers of the new nation.

From agrarian familism to urbanized family. Against a background of rising European agrarianism, Thomas Jefferson, James Madison, and John Taylor became the spokesmen for an agrarian democracy in the new nation. The European background for agrarianism was, however, used selectively by the American leaders. Jefferson, for example, differed sharply from the Physiocrats in that he considered the small frontier farm family situation to be unquestionably superior to large-scale farming or scientific estates which the Physiocrats called *la grande culture.*[29] Concerning this situation he wrote:

The political economists of Europe have established it as a principle, that every state should endeavor to manufacture for itself; and this principle, like many others, we transfer to America, without calculating the difference of circumstance which should often produce a different result. In Europe the lands are either cultivated, or locked up against the cultivator. Manufacture must, therefore, be resorted to, of necessity, not of choice, to support the surplus of their people.

But we have an immensity of land courting the industry of the husbandman. Is it best then that all our citizens should be employed in its improvement, or that one-half should be called off from that to exercise manufactures and handicraft arts for the other? Those who labour in the earth are the chosen people of God, if He had a chosen people, whose breasts He has made His peculiar deposit for substantial and genuine virtue. It is the focus in which He keeps alive that sacred fire, which otherwise might escape from the face of the earth. Corruption of morals in the mass of cultivators is a phenomenon of which no age nor nation has furnished an example. It is the mark set on those, who, not looking up to heaven, to their own soil and industry, as does the husbandman, for their subsistence, depend for it on casualties and caprice of customers. Dependence begets subservience and venality, suffocates the germ of virtue, and prepares fit tools for the designs of ambition. This, the natural progress and consequence of the arts, has sometimes perhaps been retarded by accidental circumstance, but, generally speaking the proportion which the aggregate of the other classes of citizens bears in any state to that of its husbandmen, is the proportion of its unsound to its healthy parts, and is a good enough barometer whereby to measure its degree of corruption. While we have land to labour then, let us never wish to see our citizens occupied at a workbench, or twirling a distaff. Carpenters, masons, smiths, are wanting in husbandry; but, for the general operations of manufacture, let our workshops remain in Europe. It is better to carry provisions and materials, and with them their manners and principles. The loss by the transportation of commodities across the Atlantic will be made up in happiness and permanence of government. The mobs of great cities add just so much to the support of pure government, as sores do to the strength of the human body. It is the manners and spirit of a people which preserve a republic in vigor. A degeneracy in these is a canker which soon eats to the heart of its laws and constitution.[30]

The essence of the family farm visualized by Jefferson was first its sociological value and second its economic value. The farm was to be large enough to produce sufficient food and fiber to provide for the needs of the family, and in addition there was to be a slight surplus. Yet it was to be small enough to be operated exclusively by the members of the family. It was asserted that a nation of small land units, each owned and operated by an individual family, would be the greatest guarantee of democracy.

The Jeffersonian type family farm of the 1780's had vanished by the mid-twentieth century. Mechanization and commercialization had made such small units impracticable. If a remnant of the rural farm family of the 1780's could be found at all in the second half of the twentieth century, it might well have been exemplified by the situation described as that of the traditional family farmers in Springdale or Plainville, U.S.A.[31]

Traditional farm families have been bypassed by modern society. The existence of such farms is an anachronism on the contemporary social landscape. Their operations are generally not in step with the times; in most cases their equipment is out of date or conspicuously absent. The continued survival of the family farms is evermore tenuous; indeed, they are more often in than of society. Their family life is characterized by closure and little social interaction with the larger community. School and formal training are not emphasized by their families, rather their members consider training by participation methods to be adequate for their youth. Formal education is regarded as a mechanism which takes the progeny away from the traditional farm. When families have more children than can be sustained on the local farm, some are forced to migrate to find employment, most often of an unskilled or semiskilled type, in the larger cities. Their disadvantages in the labor market are many; they are the first victims of unemployment. The consumption patterns of traditional farm families are characteristically restricted. They possess few industrially manufactured goods. Social participation by isolated farm families is limited; in most cases it includes a few friends of long standing and some contact with a church or sect group and possibly with a farm organization.

In contrast, families of rational farmers participate in business operations. Business farmers organize their operations in relation to the market for their commodities. They are concerned with the efficiency of their operation, and they understand where they are making the greatest profit. The family life of business farmers is oriented to the greater society. They are specialists rather than generalists. Their families occupy fully modernized farmsteads. The number and spacing of children of the rationalistic farm business operators are closely related to those of their city cousins.[32]

The extent of the rationalism of these contemporary rural families may be ascertained by a systematic survey of the cost of rearing farm children and the anticipated amount of income for families whose male head has a given level of educational attainment.[33] Use of scientific knowledge to remove child rearing from the family's way of life to systematically planned basis is certainly not typical. There is little evidence to suggest that family living in rural America has reached a high level of systematic planning prior to each conception. Nevertheless, research reports indicating the cost of the child-rearing experience are in and of themselves powerful evidence of the transition of knowledge systems from the traditional to the urbanized. The out-of-pocket cost in the 1950's for rearing an Oklahoma farm boy and farm girl through the first eighteen years was $11,600 and $11,300, respectively.[34] In the same study it was reported that the cost of childbirth was about $250. The cost of food for the male child was approximately $5,000 and for the female child just more than $4,600. Clothing for the girl was more costly than for the boy, but the difference was not great—$910 and $890, respectively. Other items through medical cost and miscellany were tabulated. The importance of the details lies in the fact that this information can be combined with other aspects of rationalistic family planning.

Materialism and family economics. The crass materialism of American families has attracted the attention of students of social organization and critics of American social life. Numerous studies have been conducted to compare the relative attainment of material wealth on the part of rural and urban families. In the late 1930's, a study of 1,000 rural and 1,000 urban Illinois families revealed differential home ownership—63 per cent in the rural areas and 54 per cent in urban areas; vacuum cleaners owned by nearly 40 per cent of the rural families and over 65 per cent of the urban ones; radios owned by nearly 60 per cent of the rural families compared to well over 90 per cent of the urban families, and pianos in the possession of 35 per cent of the rural families compared to nearly 70 per cent of the urban families.[35]

In addition to differential ownership of creature comforts, Leevy found that in the pre-World War II years the differential use of bakery products was 62 per cent by rural families compared to 93 per cent by urban ones; food canning was participated in by over 60 per cent of the rural compared to 13 per cent of the urban families; taking meals at restaurants was characteristic of 13 per cent of the rural compared to over 46 per cent of the urban families; production of some garden vegetables was engaged in by over 86 per cent of the rural contrasted with only 4 per cent of the urban families, and the making of some of the family clothing was an experience of some 34 per cent of the rural compared to only 16 per cent of the urban families. In the 1950's, Blood found that in urban Detroit and in southeastern rural Michigan, nearly 80 per cent of the farm families still produced most or all of their bakery goods compared to only 55 per cent of the city families; summer vegetables were produced by some 87 per cent of the farm families contrasted with 9 per cent of the city ones; canning and frozen preservation of foods was provided by some 74 per cent of the farm families and 7 per cent of the city families; and dressmaking was engaged in by 15 per cent of the farm families compared to 7 per cent of the urban ones.[36]

Regardless of the meaning of materialism among American families, the various empirical researches implicitly and often explicitly reveal that rural as well as urban families strive for items of material comfort. The differences which obtain are due more to an ability to acquire items than to an ideological acceptance or rejection of creature comforts.

SUMMARY

The American family institution historically has been dominated by ruralized social organization but is now marked by urbanized social organization. The ruralized family was most characteristic of the eighteenth century, the urbanized family of the twentieth century. During each of these two broad time periods, American family life maintained a unity of character. The nineteenth century was primarily a period of transition, during which two rather distinct types of family institutions—rural and urban—were most apparent.

Urbanized social organization is continuing to expand its influence over American family life. Families are still very important on farms and in small towns; however, the cultural universals of family life are structurally the same throughout the national society.

When viewed in historical perspective, the so-called rural and urban family institutions were necessarily transitional. Hence, rural and urban family differences are disappearing.

The social space of the family is in the process of contraction. In the eighteenth century, when the society was characterized by ruralized social organization, the domain of the family expanded beyond the functions of procreation to those of education, welfare, and recreation. By the twentieth century, with the advent of urbanized social organization, many of the latter functions of the family have been removed.

NOTES

1. John Sirjamaki, *The American Family in the Twentieth Century* (Cambridge: Harvard University Press, 1953), pp. 11–27.

2. Arthur W. Calhoun, *A Social History of the American Family,* Vol. I (Cleveland: Arthur H. Clark Co., 1917), pp. 22 ff.

3. Carl Bridenbaugh, *Cities in the Wilderness* (New York: Ronald Press, 1938); Arthur M. Schlesinger, *The Rise of the City* (New York: Macmillan Co., 1933).

4. Sirjamaki, *op. cit.*, p. 30.

5. R. M. Tryon, *Household Manufacturers in the United States, 1640 to 1860* (Chicago: The University of Chicago Press, 1917); Siegfried Giedion, *Mechanization Takes Command* (New York: Oxford University Press, 1948).

6. Tryon, *op. cit.*, pp. 112 ff.

7. *Historical Statistics of the United States, 1789 to 1945* (Washington: Bureau of the Census, 1949), p. 29.

8. Frank Lorimer *et al.*, *Foundation of American Population Policy* (New York: Harper and Brothers, 1940), p. 12.

9. Wilson H. Grabill *et al.*, *The Fertility of American Women* (New York: John Wiley and Sons, Inc., 1958); Clyde V. Kiser, "Changes in Fertility by Socioeconomic Status during 1940–1950," *Milbank Memorial Fund Quarterly*, 33 (Oct., 1955), 394–429; Charles F. Westoff, "Differential Fertility in the United States, 1900 to 1952," *American Sociological Review*, 19 (Oct., 1954), 549–61.

10. Ronald Freedman *et al.*, *Family Planning, Sterility, and Population Growth* (New York: McGraw-Hill Book Co., Inc., 1959), pp. 143 ff.

11. *Ibid.*, p. 144.

12. Dennis H. Wrong, "Trends in Class Fertility in Western Nations," *Canadian Journal of Economics and Political Science*, 24 (May, 1958), 216–29; Westoff, *op. cit.*, pp. 549–61; William Peterson, *Population* (New York: Macmillan Co., 1961), pp. 218–22.

13. Frank Lorimer and Frederick Osborn, *Dynamics of Population* (New York: Macmillan Co., 1934), p. 341.

14. Westoff, *loc. cit.*

15. Paul C. Glick, "The Life Cycle of the Family," *Marriage and Family Living*, 17 (Feb., 1955), 3–9.

16. Peterson, *op. cit.*, pp. 217–32.

17. John Morris Gillette, *Rural Sociology* (New York: Macmillan Co., 1923); Arthur J. Vidich and Joseph Bensman, *Small Town in Mass Society* (New York: Doubleday Anchor Books, 1960), pp. 30–107; James W. Gladden and John R. Christiansen, "Emergence of Urban Values in Mining Families in Eastern Kentucky," *Rural Sociology*, 21 (June, 1956), 135–9; Eugene A. Wilkening, "Techniques of Assessing Farm Family Values," *Rural Sociology*, 19 (Mar., 1954), 39–49.

18. Gillette, *op. cit.*, p. 369.

19. Glick, *op. cit.*, p. 3.

20. Charles P. Loomis and J. Allan Beegle, *Rural Sociology* (Englewood Cliffs, N.J.: Prentice-Hall, Inc., 1957), p. 76.

21. W. A. Anderson, *Rural Social Participation and the Family Life Cycle*, Parts I and II (Cornell: New York Agricultural Experiment Station Memoir 314, 1953).

22. Earl O. Heady *et al.*, *Interdependence Between the Farm Business and the Farm Household with Implications on Economic Efficiency* (Ames: Iowa Agricultural Experiment Station Research Bulletin 398, 1953).

23. Robert E. Galloway, *Farmer's Plans for Economic Security in Old Age* (Kentucky Agricultural Experiment Station Bulletin 398, 1953).

24. Anderson, *op. cit., Part I.*

25. Robert O. Blood, Jr., and Donald M. Wolf, *Husbands and Wives* (Glencoe, Ill.: The Free Press, 1960), pp. 54–74, see especially Table 17.

26. A. Whitney Griswold, *Farming and Democracy* (New York: Harcourt, Brace and Co., 1948), pp. 18–46.

27. Rowland E. Protherd, *English Farming Past and Present* (London: Longmans, Green and Co., 1912), p. 207.

28. Griswold, *op. cit.*, p. 21.

29. *Ibid.*, p. 29.

30. Paul Leicester Ford (ed.), *The Works of Thomas Jefferson*, Vol. IV (New York: G. P. Putnam's Sons, 1904), pp. 85–6.

31. Vidich and Bensman, *op. cit.*, pp. 67–9; Art Gallaher, Jr., *Plainville Fifteen Years Later* (New York: Columbia University Press, 1961), p. 61.

32. "Growth of American Families," *Population Bulletin*, 16 (June, 1960).

33. James D. Tarver, *The Cost of Rearing Oklahoma Farm Children* (Oklahoma Agricultural Experiment Station Bulletin B–457, 1956); *I've Found My Future in Agriculture* (Association of Colleges and Universities, 1958).

34. Tarver, *op. cit.*, p. 2.

35. J. Roy Leevy, "Contrasts in Urban and Rural Family Life," *American Sociological Review*, 5 (Dec., 1940), 948–53.

36. Blood and Wolf, *op. cit.*, p. 82.

SELECTED READINGS

Anderson, W. A. *Rural Social Participation and the Family Life Cycle*, Part I. Cornell: New York Agricultural Experiment Station Memoir 314, 1953.

A study of social participation of families in northwestern New York, by stages in the family cycle and other general social characteristics.

Blood, Robert O., Jr., and Donald M. Wolf. *Husbands and Wives*. Glencoe, Ill.: The Free Press, 1960.

A contemporary empirical study of selected interactional patterns of husbands and wives in Michigan, in and near the Detroit area. The data were primarily collected by interviews with wives.

Calhoun, Arthur W. *A Social History of the American Family.* Vol. I. Cleveland: Arthur H. Clark Co., 1917.

Examines the family in the colonial period, with individual chapters devoted to the status of children and women. In Volume II are included subjects like the emergence of women into the new industrial order.

Sirjamaki, John. *The American Family in the Twentieth Century.* Cambridge: Harvard University Press, 1953.

A readable and informed account of the evolution and present form of the family in the United States.

Tarver, James D. *The Cost of Rearing Oklahoma Farm Children.* Oklahoma Agricultural Experiment Station Bulletin B–457, 1956.

Report of an empirical study designed to enable parents to calculate the minimum cost of rearing farm children to age eighteen.

Westoff, Charles F. "Differential Fertility in the United States, 1900 to 1952," *American Sociological Review,* 19 (Oct., 1954), pp. 549–61.

The findings of this study indicate that differences between rural and urban fertility rates are being reduced because of the post-World War II baby boom.

18 SCHOOLS FOR THE PREADULT YEARS

The practice of separating rural and urban schools is outmoded. Nevertheless, social interactional experiences vary for children in schools located in large metropolitan areas, suburbs, small towns, and in the isolated open country. These variations in experience result from differences in the meaning of education for both children and adults in these four residential areas. There are patterns of social distance and discrimination which pertain to students and teachers from different social classes and different ecological areas. There are also differences in the adequacy of educational facilities.

The social institution of education in the United States is now dominated by major universal patterns, largely the results of urbanized social organization. State departments of education promulgate the primary organizational outline for all public schools. Even when there are multiple school categories, namely, trade schools, technical schools, kindergartens, elementary, junior high, high schools, junior colleges, senior colleges, and graduate schools, the organization within each category is similar. Teachers are certified by the state. Colleges of education provide a common core of training for classroom teaching. Often the selection of public school textbooks and the distribution of educational funds is largely controlled at the state level. Even private schools have a strong tendency to follow the social organization prescribed by the states for public schools. The states actually exercise few direct sanctions over private schools, but the interaction of students, faculty, and staff, and the exchange of facilities

362

all tend to produce similar organizational patterns in private and public schools. The universal patterns which characterize the various states are showing more uniformity; hence, a national educational system is emerging.

The structural universals of education cannot be differentiated on a rural-urban basis. Within separate localities, application of the universals —the formal organization—through concrete and informal organizational patterns is still made with extensive variations. In this chapter attention is focused, first, on local situations and, second, on the comparison of local situations with the emerging general pattern.

Differential rural-urban attainment. Historically, the level of educational attainment of rural Americans has been lower than that of urban Americans. While differences continue to exist, the gap is diminishing. Rural citizens are completing more years of school than they did formerly (see Table XXV). Today greater proportions of rural people have completed

TABLE XXV. NUMBER OF YEARS OF SCHOOL COMPLETED IN 1940, 1950, AND 1960 BY RURAL CITIZENS 25 YEARS OF AGE AND OVER

Years of School Completed	Per Cent Completion		
	1940	1950	1960
1–4 Years	13.0	11.4	8.5
5–6 Years	13.7	11.3	9.3
7–8 Years	36.7	28.5	28.7
1–3 Years of high school	13.5	15.5	17.7
4 Years of high school	10.3	15.3	21.9
1–3 Years of college	4.5	5.5	6.6
4 Years or more of college	2.8	3.6	4.7

Sources: (1940–50 data) Kreitlow, Burton W. *Rural Education: Community Backgrounds.* New York: Harper and Brothers, 1954, p. 22; *Sixteenth Census of the United States: 1940,* Population, Washington: 1943, pp. 82–6.

(1960 data) U.S. Bureau of the Census. *U.S. Census of Population: 1960,* General Social and Economic Characteristics, U.S. Summary, Final Report PC(1)–1C., Washington.

all grades of elementary school and have graduated from high school or college.

In spite of this increase in the number of school years completed by rural people, there is still a discrepancy between their educational attainment and that of rural nonfarm and urban people (see Table XXVI).

TABLE XXVI. HIGHEST SCHOOL GRADE COMPLETED BY URBAN ADULTS AND RURAL ADULTS,
25 YEARS OF AGE AND OVER, IN 1950 AND 1960 *

Highest School Grade Completed	Urban Adults 1950, 1960	Per Cent Completed	
		Rural Nonfarm Adults 1950, 1960	Rural Farm Adults 1950, 1960
None	2.3, 2.2	2.7, 2.6	3.1, 2.3
1–2	1.9 ⎱ 5.1	2.7 ⎱ 8.3	3.8 ⎱ 9.0
3–4	4.9 ⎰	7.0 ⎰	9.9 ⎰
5–6	8.0, 6.7	10.1, 9.2	12.9, 9.8
7–8	24.6, 22.0	29.4, 27.0	27.3, 33.9
1 year high school	5.9 ⎱	5.9 ⎱	5.5 ⎱
2 years high school	7.0 ⎬ 19.8	6.3 ⎬ 18.5	5.1 ⎬ 15.5
3 years high school	4.6 ⎰	4.4 ⎰	3.3 ⎰
4 years high school	22.6, 25.7	17.2, 22.3	12.6, 20.6
1 year college	2.8 ⎱	2.3 ⎱	1.8 ⎱
2 years college	3.6 ⎬ 9.7	2.7 ⎬ 6.8	1.8 ⎬ 6.1
3 years college	1.6 ⎰	1.2 ⎰	.7 ⎰
4 or more years of college	7.2, 8.9	4.7, 5.3	2.0, 2.8

Sources: (1950 Data) Kreitlow, Burton W. *Rural Education: Community Back-grounds,* New York: Harper and Brothers, 1954, p. 23.

(1960 Data) U.S. Bureau of the Census. *U.S. Census of Population: 1960,* General Social and Economic Characteristics, U.S. Summary, Final Report PC(1)–1C., Washington.

1960 data) U.S. Bureau of the Census. *U.S. Census of Population: 1960,* Genthird years of high school, and first, second, and third years of college.

Of urban, rural nonfarm, and rural farm people, 26, 22, and 21 per cent, respectively had completed four years of high school by 1960. The differences in completion of college were even greater—9, 5, and 3 per cent, respectively.

Duncan and Reiss [1] found that in 1950, for whites in farm areas and urbanized areas of 3,000,000 or more, educational attainment was lower than that for the populations of medium size urban places (see Table XXVII). The highest median years of school (10.9) were completed by people in places of 250,000 to 1,000,000. All places under 2,500 population had a median educational attainment of less than ten years, and the median educational attainment for people in the largest urbanized areas was only 10.3.

Among adults age 25 to 44, high school was completed by more than half of all females of all residence areas except open-country rural. For males, however, high school was the median attainment for those in

TABLE XXVII. MEDIAN YEARS OF SCHOOL COMPLETED BY WHITE PERSONS, 25 YEARS OF AGE AND OVER, BY AGE, SEX, AND SIZE OF PLACE: 1950

Size of Place	Total 25 Years Old and Over	25 to 44 Years Old	
		Male	Female
Urbanized areas:			
3,000,000 or more	10.3	12.1	12.1
1,000,000 to 3,000,000	10.8	12.1	12.1
250,000 to 1,000,000	10.9	12.1	12.2
Under 250,000	10.5	12.0	12.1
Places outside urbanized areas:			
25,000 or more	10.6	12.1	12.1
10,000 to 25,000	10.4	12.0	12.1
2,500 to 10,000	10.0	11.5	12.1
1,000 to 2,500	9.4	11.1	12.0
Under 1,000 (incorporated)	8.9	11.0	12.0
Other rural:			
Nonfarm	8.9	9.3	9.6
Farm	8.5	8.7	9.7

Source: U.S. Bureau of the Census. *1950 Census of Population,* Vol. IV, Special Reports, Part 5, Chapter A, Tables 2 and 2a.

places of 10,000 and over. In short, the number of school years completed is nearly equal for all Americans regardless of the size of city, village, or hamlet in which they reside; but open-country and farm residents still lag conspicuously behind the national average.

HISTORICAL DEVELOPMENTS

Colonial schools. Education was a negligible aspect of colonial society, and its formal organization was precarious. Physical facilities were generally meager, and teachers often had doubtful qualifications. Throughout the colonial period, schools were essentially a matter of private enterprise. Private schoolmasters solicited patronage, so that education was primarily available only for children whose parents could pay for it. Occasionally some rudiments of education were given to poor children with the aid of charitable and religious organizations.[2]

The earliest schools were established in hamlets and villages, and in most cases these ultimately became city schools. Rural schools emerged with the first westward population movements in the seventeenth century. In fact, rural school systems originated with the passage of the 1647 Massachusetts Bay Colony statutes in the Colonial Assembly.[3] This colonial rural school development is discussed in the following excerpt from the Massachusetts Bay Colony records:

It being one chief project of that old deluder, Satan, to keep men from the knowledge of the Scriptures, as, in former times, keeping them in an un- known tongue, so in these later times, by persuading from the use of tongues; so that at last the true sense and meaning of the original might be clouded and corrupted with false glosses of deceivers; and to the end that learning may not be buried in the graves of our fore-fathers, in church and com- monwealth, the Lord assisting our endeavors: It is therefore ordered by this Court and authority thereof that every township within this jurisdiction, after the Lord hath increased them to the number of fifty householders, shall then forthwith appoint one within their town to teach all such children as shall resort to him, to write and read; whose wages shall be paid, either by the parents or masters of such children, or by the inhabitants in general, by way of supply, as the major part of those who order the prudential of the town shall appoint; provided that those who send their children be not oppressed by paying much more than they can have them taught for in the adjoining towns.

And it is further ordered that where any town shall increase to the number of one hundred families or householders, they shall set up a grammar school, the master thereof being able to instruct youths so far as they may be fitted for the university; and if any town neglect the performance hereof, above one year, then every such town shall pay five pound per annum to the next such school, till they shall perform this order.[4]

In spite of such provisional colonial legislation regarding education, governmental participation in colonial education was strikingly limited. Even the academy, which was the dominant system of secondary educa- tion, was a private enterprise in colonial times. The private academy continued to dominate the early national period. It was the general prac- tice of colonial governments to grant charters and occasionally subsidies (chiefly land) to these private schools. There was little or no supervision of early academies and colleges. Certainly no colonial government estab- lished a free public education system throughout its territory.

State education systems. The idea of a state public education system was promulgated at the time of the founding of the nation. The Treaty of Paris (1783) endowed the original colonies with sovereign power. Six years later the new federal government, by the Tenth Amendment to the Constitution, left each state with the right and responsibility to control its own educational system. As early as 1816, state interest in education was apparent in the constitution of the State of Indiana, which specified: "A general system of education, ascending in regular gradation from township (district) schools to a state university wherein tuition shall be gratis and equally open to all." [5] In 1827 the Territorial Legislature of Michigan patterned school organization after the earlier colonial Massachusetts experience, but reduced the number of families for which school support would be required. In sparsely settled Michigan only twenty families were required to support a school. In the Wisconsin Territory of 1836, ten families constituted the minimum. [6]

The origins of public education are clear, but their realization has been slow. Indeed, it was only after the War of 1812 that a national consciousness crystallized. The new nationalism constituted the first valid need for a system of public education. Industrialization also brought a need for public vocational education. Urbanization constituted a still more pressing need for universal public education. Hence, from the early nineteenth century onward, national leaders have been concerned with education. [7] It was sufficient for the colonial and early national society to sustain mechanisms for the education of the few. Its purpose was to train God-fearing citizens with a minimum ability to read and understand the scriptures and, at a more advanced level, to train clergymen. In the simple rural society little more was required; most of the knowledge and skills requisite for human existence could be adequately learned through participation in the home and work environment.

After the Revolution, education proliferated due to an exploding population, increasing secularization, and advancing urban development. There was a short-lived renaissance of classical education; however, this was soon supplanted by an emphasis on practical vocational training. Systems of practical education have predominated to the present day. At the university level, curriculums with the highest prestige are those related to training in skills, namely, medicine, engineering, commerce, law, dentistry, and, in some cases, farming and hotel-keeping. [8]

The practical dimensions of education have been materially advanced by federal support since the establishment of the Federal Office of Education in 1867. This office engages in educational research and administers a federal program of vocational education in cooperation with the states. Other federal agencies, for example, the U.S. Department of Agriculture, participate in education through social mechanisms such as the Agricultural Extension Service.

Local control was a primary characteristic of schools throughout the nineteenth century. Schools were organized in districts, and were largely controlled by locally elected boards. As urbanized social organization came to characterize the nation, local systems of education became inadequate and inefficient. Studies of Elmtown, Jonesville, and Springdale have shown local control of education to be technically inadequate and not useful to all the people.[9]

Cultural universals have developed in the institution of education, particularly at the elementary and secondary levels. For example, local control is disintegrating in favor of central selection of textbooks on a district or state basis. Curriculums are coming to be standardized for entire states by experts. Teachers are trained according to a common college curriculum and certified by the state. The length of the school term, the rate of tax levy, and the minimum building requirements are further examples of the schools' structural elements which have been removed from local authority.

SCHOOL SYSTEMS

Education in urbanized social organization is rapidly developing as a social institution dominated by universally structured patterns. Nevertheless, while the direction of this trend toward a common educational system is clear, some very real differential patterns of organization between schools continue to exist. These differences exist on a more complex basis than a simple rural-urban dichotomy. The biennial survey of education reports some of the differential characteristics for rural, county, suburban, and city school systems.

Rural schools. The typical rural school environment is characterized by a sparse population, isolated farmsteads, and decentralized school organization. The sparse and dispersed population is provided for through the consolidation of schools and by some movement of rural people to villages. Other approaches to the problem of isolated rural schools are suggested by the "rural renaissance" movement and the Western States Small Schools Project.

Consolidation, reorganization, or merger are all mechanisms which bring small groups of rural school children into larger, better equipped schools. The process has been relatively slow, even though it is encouraged by states, because local school boards have exercised considerable power in supporting their independent schools. Local and state officials have come into conflict with one another, and this has hampered school consolidation. Nonetheless, the trend toward consolidation has continued and dramatic results have been recorded in some areas. For example, in Goodhue County, Minnesota, the number of school districts was reduced from 155 to 16 between 1946 and 1958. Only twelve of the sixteen school districts actually operated their own schools in 1958. Only twenty public schools operated in Goodhue County in 1958, compared to 130 in 1946. During the same twelve years the county's total school enrollment increased by 25 per cent.[10] For the nation the number of school districts declined from 104,000 to 50,000 between 1947 and 1957. The number of one-teacher schools in the nation declined from 143,000 (1931–32) to 35,000 (1955–56).[11]

The arguments for school consolidation are typically based on the advantages of cost equalization between poor and affluent districts, more highly qualified teachers, more specialized curriculum and equipment, and group adjustment advantages for students.[12]

The rural renaissance [13] movement has consisted of several plans for centralizing specialized educational facilities in such a way that they can be utilized by multiple numbers of schools. One plan contains a proposal for the construction of schoolrooms in triangular shapes to be arranged circularly around a central room known as the equipment "bank." In this central room advanced audio-visual equipment will be immediately available to supplement the classroom lessons. Another plan calls for itinerant teachers, specialists who will serve a number of schools.

Among the most innovative plans was that of the Midwest Program on Airborne Television Instruction (MPATI). This experimental plan for revitalizing rural education was initiated in 1961. It involved the careful preparation of courses to be recorded on video tape, and later telecast from an airplane flying at a high altitude and circling over the schools where the lesson would be received. The elevation of the transmitter a few miles above the earth made possible a broader range of geographical coverage for the televised classroom instruction. In the 1961 experiment there was an audience of about 5,000,000 in 13,000 schools in six states. Courses were prepared for students in elementary schools, secondary schools, and colleges.[14]

Another plan for rural schools was the Western States Project, a three-year experiment undertaken in 1962 and involving Arizona, Colorado, Nevada, New Mexico, and Utah. The assumption of this project was that rural schools have not operated at maximum effectiveness, and that a new system of organization must be created and all attempts to resemble large schools abandoned.[15]

In spite of these changes and proposed changes, rural schools are still numerous. Most school districts (nine out of ten in 1956) were still outside of municipalities, as well as outside of urbanized county school systems. Three-quarters or over 100,000 of the nation's schools are located in centers of 2,500 population or less. As recently as 1954, rural schools served nearly half (45 per cent) of the nation's public school children. By the mid-1950's rural children still attended nearly 35,000 one-teacher schools. The trend, of course, was toward large centralized schools. Many of the consolidated schools were located in communities of 5,000 or more population. While the goals of these rural schools were essentially similar to those of others, they often operated under the handicaps of ungraded classes, insufficient course offerings, crowded teaching schedules, and inadequate educational equipment. The small high school, by definition one with a graduating class of less than 100, has been described as highly unsatisfactory.[16] In the average community, where one comprehensive high school serves all students, it is suggested that only 25 per cent of the students will be able to profit from such advanced subjects as senior mathematics, physics, and four years of foreign languages. The number of potential students for advanced courses is further reduced because female students generally avoid them. The expense of providing high-level advanced instruction in several special subjects is often prohibitive for such a small number of students.

Suburban schools. A recent biennial survey of schools contained a report of 468 school systems in 419 suburban areas. The median salary for suburban teachers was higher than that for those in the central cities and that for the nation as a whole. Similarly, the suburban financial expenditure per student was greater than that for all other cities of comparable size.

However, all is not well with the suburban schools. There are often difficulties resulting from social distance and conflict between old and new residents in the suburbs. For example, a case study in Connecticut [17] revealed that newcomers to the suburb tended to be disproportionately in the young adult, family forming years. School enrollment increased precipitously because of the great number of these young adult families with their many children. In the Connecticut area it was found that 27.3

per cent of all school children were from the immigrant families. These families paid only 21.9 per cent of the town's property taxes, and thereby shifted a disproportionate burden of the cost of educating the children in the local area to the older residents. The state of Connecticut has long made grants to towns for their school system, but still over 80 per cent of the total school budget comes from local taxes. Situations of this type offer direct challenges to the system of urbanized social organization in searching for a mechanism for more equally distributing the cost of education.

Traditionally, the suburban schools have been oriented to the middle and upper-middle classes. Migrants to suburban areas have generally had more than average affluence. Their movement frequently has been partly motivated by the desire for better schools for their children. This interest has been specifically in the direction of superior secondary preparation for college matriculation. Little emphasis has been placed on vocational training. Courses in stenography, auto mechanics, mechanical drawing, or building trades are conspicuously absent in the curriculum, or offered only as electives.[18] In recent years more working class families have been moving to suburbs, but these families are less interested in having their children attend only college-centered schools. Vocational and technical education would be more suited to the reality of their children's situation. Community colleges have been planned for some areas to supplement the training of high schools with limited vocational offerings.[19]

City schools. Independent school districts in population centers of 2,500 or more totaled 3,647 in 1955–56.[20] These have been decreasing in number due to their absorption into larger districts. Their enrollment increased by some 6.5 per cent between 1953–54 and 1955–56, when they totaled approximately 17,000,000 students.

In contrast to the small rural schools and the comprehensive county and suburban schools, urban schools have been more often specialized. In the nation's larger cities, particularly in the East, there are industrial trade schools, commercial schools, theatrical schools, and academic schools, all in addition to general or comprehensive schools.

VOCATIONAL EDUCATION

Vocational education is an integral part of the American school system for both children and adults. Its primary purpose is to help provide citizens with employment skills; it is not a substitute for traditional educational systems for citizenship, culture, health, and other goals.

Most vocational training is under the control of state boards for vocational education and under the direct supervision of local school districts. Due to the vast national significance of the level of vocational proficiency of the population, the federal government has developed special programs to support such training. The primary federal support has been provided by the Smith-Hughes Act of 1917 and the George-Braden Act of 1946. This legislation made federal funds available for vocational training in agriculture, distributive occupations, home economics, trades and industry, practical nursing, and area vocational educational programs.[21]

Vocational education is a cooperative endeavor of the federal and local governments. The Office of Education administers the program for the federal government. Matching funds are required, or the expenditure by state and local governments of an amount equal to that provided by the federal government. For a state to participate in the utilization of federal appropriations, its board of vocational education must submit a plan for vocational training to be approved by the Federal Commissioner of Education. The plans of the state outline the type of vocational education that will be conducted, as well as setting standards for the qualifications of teachers and supervisors. State programs are under continual modification and expansion. Changes in industrialization, agribusiness, commercial organization, and population dynamics all require flexibility in vocational training. There are new and additional demands for industrial technicians, for skilled and semiskilled workers, generated by the pace of new technology. Demands in education increase as salesmanship, business management, and financing meet the challenges of mass society. Farming is becoming agribusiness, and a host of new occupational skills and opportunities are unfolding for the appropriately trained rural and urban youth. Across the entire front of vocational training there is need for dynamic efforts to prepare the citizenry for the work requirements of the times.

The total enrollment in vocational education programs was nearly 4,000,000 in 1960 (see Fig. 21). This represented almost a 2 per cent increase over the preceding year. The largest number of matriculants, over 1,500,000, were in home economics; then trades and industry with over 900,000; agriculture was in third place with nearly 800,000. Area programs in vocational education, the most recently established, increased enrollment from 48,564 in 1959 to 101,279 in 1960.[22]

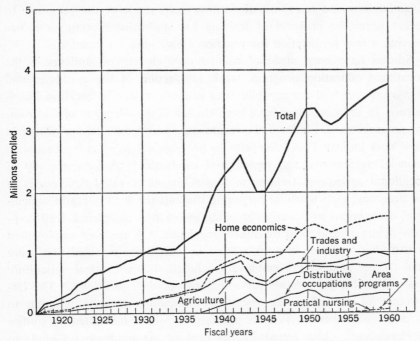

FIGURE 21.   ENROLLMENT IN VOCATIONAL CLASSES BY TYPE
OF PROGRAM

Source: *Digest of Annual Report of State Boards of Vocational Education to the Office of Education* (Washington, D.C.: U.S. Department of Health, Education, and Welfare, Division of Vocational Education, Fiscal Year Ending June 30, 1960)

Vocational agriculture. The origin of agricultural education antedates the founding of the nation, but the early efforts at systematic agricultural training met with very limited success. A youth program in agricultural training was proposed by the Philadelphia Society in 1794.[23] Other efforts were made, but actual programs were few. Following the establishment of the land-grant colleges in 1862, and particularly from the 1890's until passage of the Smith-Hughes Act in 1917, there were increasing demands for all types of agricultural education. By the second half of the twentieth century, vocational agriculture had become a nationwide, federally supported program. However, its role in the urbanized society has not been clear, indeed its position often has been precarious. Farming opportunities have rapidly diminished, and the best exercise of wisdom has been to encourage rural youth to move out of farming rather than into it. The *raison d'être* of vocational agriculture classes has been greatly challenged because of the shift of the occupational structure away from farming.

Examinations and re-examinations have been made of the program. In recent years the prospect of training for agribusiness occupations has become a new justification for vocational agricultural education.

Studies have been made of occupational choices of students in the vocational education program, work satisfaction of the graduates and employers' views of the capabilities of students trained in vocational agriculture. In addition, there have been studies of the adequacy of the training program itself. Findings of a recent survey of vocational agriculture in New York indicated a weakness in the program's training in farm records, financial agreements, and agricultural mechanics.[24] A similar study of vocational agriculture training in Massachusetts revealed deficiencies in the program, particularly in preparing students for such nonfarm agricultural occupations as selective breeding association technician, feed company fieldman, and farm machinery mechanic.[25] A study of employment in two Ohio counties in work related to agriculture revealed that more than 87 per cent of the employers believed that vocational agriculture was a desirable preparation for a majority of their positions.[26] The importance of expanding the vocational agriculture training program to include adequate instruction for nonfarming jobs is illustrated by studies in Nebraska[27] which found 37 per cent of the graduates in nonfarm occupations and in Iowa[28] where 48 per cent were employed in nonfarm jobs. A Missouri study[29] revealed that less than half of that area's vocational agriculture seniors can expect to find farming opportunities. By 1975 the opportunities in farming will be even more sharply reduced.

HUMAN RELATIONS AND DIFFERENTIAL SCHOOL ORGANIZATION

As the nation's schools become integrated into a single social institution in an urbanized society, several distinctive human relations patterns have been observed to have more than an ordinary impact on students in small schools. The most important of these behavorial situations are social distance and prejudice patterns between town and farm students, differential educational and occupational aspirations on the part of farm and nonfarm children, and, finally, differential drop-out patterns by residential areas.

Social distance between rural and urban students. Preference and prejudice patterns were clearly found among rural and urban students in consolidated high schools. A study by Orzack [30] using a sociometric technique of data collection revealed that, with reference to choice of leaders, co-workers, dates, and even enemies, there was a consistently lower degree of preference for rural than urban students. A preference for urban students was expressed by both rural and urban students. Minority group status was extended to students of rural residence, and the lower status was accepted by the rural students. In situations of this type, social consolidation lags behind physical consolidation.

Educational and occupational aspirations. Studies have demonstrated the relationships between socioeconomic status, residence, social class, education, and occupational aspiration. An overview of these findings suggests that rural youth generally have poorer school attendance, lower educational attainment, and fewer vocational skills than do city children. It follows that rural youth are handicapped in the employment market and in opportunities for professional education.

A study of students in a consolidated high school in a rural village and one in a city of 10,000 population, both located in the same affluent rural county in the hinterland of Minneapolis and St. Paul, Minnesota, revealed sharp differences in educational aspirations of students in the two schools.[31] In the rural school there was no statistically significant difference between the occupational choices of town and country students, but there was a tendency for farm boys to aspire to farming. In the urban school a significantly greater proportion of city than country students selected professional and managerial occupations. Also a greater proportion of country than city students in the urban school selected clerical, sales, craft, or operative occupations. In the urban school, neither town nor country students aspired to farming as an occupation.

The findings of the study suggest that physical consolidation of schools, bringing together town and country students, is hardly a guarantee of social and ideological consolidation. Students influence one another by interacting in a common social environment, but occupational choice is more greatly influenced by factors other than school social interaction.

A study of sixteen- and seventeen-year-old youths in three rural Kentucky counties in 1957 revealed differential educational attainment by socioeconomic class.[32] This pattern of differential educational aspiration was supported by the home, school, and community. Higher status children participated more than low status children in school activities, held more student offices, and did less unpaid work. The high status children performed better on mental tests and held higher educational aspirations. Drop-outs were fewer and student-teacher interaction patterns were more satisfactory among the high status than the low status students. This study reveals considerable heterogeneity within the rural community, not unlike that which is often found to exist between rural and urban areas. In the context of urbanized social organization, this suggests the existence of cultural universals. Rural-urban differences accordingly diminish, and the social differentiation which is found is explicable in terms of factors other than residence.

A 1947–48 study of nonfarm senior students in all Wisconsin [33] high schools was designed to test the hypothesis that levels of educational and occupational aspiration of youth are associated with their families' status —when the factor of intelligence is controlled. The findings supported this hypothesis.

Social environment and school attendance. Numerous studies have shown that rural students have a disproportionately higher tendency to drop out of school before high school graduation. Some drop-outs occur before the compulsory attendance age is reached, but most occur immediately after that age. Studies as early as the 1930's in Minnesota [34] reported the reasons for leaving school as "not interested," "needed at home," and "cannot afford to attend." A 1940 study in North Dakota reported that, of a group of 2,171 rural youth ages fifteen to nineteen, 80 per cent were in school. A greater proportion of rural village than rural farm boys attended school, however, 86 per cent and 72 per cent, respectively. Over 70 per cent of the reasons given for dropping out fell into three categories, namely, financial, the need for the youth at home, and the absence of a desire to attend.[35]

In 1946 a comprehensive study was made of student behavior in four Minnesota counties.[36] Among the findings were: in areas with a high proportion of renters there is less education beyond the eighth grade; children from towns aspire to more education than those from farms, and children of the better educated parents aspire more to higher education. All of these factors contributed to a serious differential drop-out rate.

A study of drop-outs in Washington's Whitman County [37] between 1949 and 1954 again revealed the normative pattern. The students were either not interested, preferred work to school, stated that learning in school was difficult, preferred military service, disliked a teacher, or had family problems. Compared to the nation as a whole, Whitman County's drop-out problem was not serious but, nevertheless, the pattern of excuses included the commonplace items. The educational level of parents of drop-outs was considerably lower than that of all adults in the county. Drop-outs came disproportionately from large families and their parents were more often in the labor, service, and craft jobs than in professional and managerial posts.

A comprehensive study of student attendance and drop-out situations was made in eight Louisiana high schools in 1959.[38] Personal interviews were taken with junior and senior students, with youths aged 16 to 19 who had dropped out of school, with parents of both groups of students, and with the teachers and principals. Reasons for dropping out of school were, in order of importance, lack of interest, marriage (almost exclusively given by girls), children needed at home, finances, and health. There was a high degree of consistency in the reasons for leaving school given by students, parents, and teachers. Characteristic of families of the drop-out students in Louisiana, like those generally reported in other areas, included the following: Fathers were more often farmers, more often farm laborers than farm owners, and more often in wage work than in the professions. The educational level of parents of drop-outs was lower, and these parents participated less frequently in school activities. Parents of attending students placed more value on education. Students who traveled longer distances to school had a disproportionately higher rate of drop-outs. Drop-outs had experienced more gainful employment than those who continued to attend school. Grades of the latter group tended to be higher than those of drop-outs. Participation in school activities was higher for those who remained in school than for drop-outs.

The tendency to drop out of school is becoming ever more limited as compulsory education becomes a cultural universal of the educational institution in urbanized society. Attendance is required by law through the upper teen years. Students in certain situations are more prone to drop out, even when the social cost is high. The behavioral pattern of dropping out of school is often generated in the rural farm social environment. However, the educational level and the occupational experiences of the parents of drop-outs appear to be as much a part of the situation as the factor of residence. Indeed, it is the meaning of education in the social experience of those with whom the student has a high frequency of interaction, more than his place of residence, which bears on his continuation of school attendance.

For students whose adjustments to their teen-age environment included dropping out rather than finishing school, there were still more unfortunate experiences. A New York school administrator studied the cases of individual drop-outs and found that they obtained such low-level occupations as dime store clerk, bus boy in a hotel, or laborer in an industrial plant. Remuneration was universally poor, and many young people were reported to have regretted dropping out of school.[39] Interviews with fourteen- to nineteen-year-old youths in Louisville, Kentucky, provide further substantiation of the greater difficulty drop-outs had in procuring a job and in holding it.[40] In 1960, Cooper found that, nationally, students who dropped out of high school found work about as quickly as graduates, but the drop-outs were forced to accept jobs requiring lower skills, and such employment often provided less than a full week's work.[41]

SUMMARY

Differences in the organization of rural and urban schools have rapidly diminished to the middle of the twentieth century. School consolidation has reduced the number of one-room country schools. The dominance of cultural universals for education in urbanized society is leading to statewide standardization of courses of study, teacher training, teacher certification, physical facilities, and attendance laws.

Rural children are now completing more years of formal education than they formerly did and thus bridging the historic gap between them and urban children. Private schools which characterized colonial America are now in a minority; most of the nation's children are educated in public schools. Public schools originated early in the nineteenth century. The various public school systems are still controlled by the states. The Federal Office of Education is primarily a research and administrative agency for some vocational programs.

The challenge of providing education for rural children remains a very real one. Consolidation has been widely adopted as a measure for meeting this challenge, but it is not always adequate. Other rural education programs involve the rotation of specialty teachers from one school to another and the use of televised courses.

Suburban schools still have several advantages over open-country schools. Teachers are paid higher salaries and financial expenditures per student are typically higher in suburbs. Physical facilities are often superior.

Several vocational education programs are specifically oriented to rural youth, among them vocational agriculture and home economics. These programs are cooperatively carried out by the federal and local governments. Vocational agriculture programs have been under special examination, the results of which have led to offering more training for students in careers related to agriculture.

Physical consolidation of rural schools has often not brought immediate social consolidation. Studies have provided evidence of social distance between rural and urban students. Research has also revealed higher educational and occupational aspirations of urban than of rural students. These differential aspiration levels are closely associated with the status of the student's family. Similarly research findings show that rural students drop out of school more frequently than do urban students.

Differences are still observed in the school experience of rural and urban students, but they are diminishing in the face of urbanized social organization.

NOTES

1. Otis D. Duncan and Albert J. Reiss, Jr., *Social Characteristics of Urban and Rural Communities, 1950* (New York: John Wiley and Sons, Inc., 1956).

2. *Education in the United States of America* (Washington: U.S. Department of Health, Education, and Welfare, Special Series No. 3, Revised 1955), p. 1.

3. Burton W. Kreitlow, *Rural Education* (New York: Harper and Brothers, 1954), p. 111.

4. Richard G. Boone, *Education in the United States* (New York: D. Appleton and Company, 1903), pp. 44–5.

5. *Education in the United States of America,* p. 1.

6. Kreitlow, *op. cit.,* pp. 112–13.

7. Ellwood P. Cubberley, *The History of Education* (Boston: Houghton Mifflin Co., 1920), pp. 655 ff.

8. Hugh MacLennan, "The Rout of the Classical Tradition," *Horizon,* 3 (Nov., 1960), 17–24.

9. A. B. Hollingshead, *Elmtown's Youth* (New York: John Wiley and Sons, Inc., 1949); W. Lloyd Warner *et al., Democracy in Jonesville* (New York: Harper and Brothers, 1949); Arthur J. Vidich and Joseph Bensman, *Small Town in Mass Society* (New York: Doubleday Anchor Books, 1960).

10. Lee Taylor *et al.,* "Changing Goodhue County, 1946–1948," *Sociology of Rural Life* (Minnesota Agricultural Experiment Station, 1949), pp. 9–10.

11. *Statistics of Local School Systems: 1955-1956, Rural Counties, Biennial Survey of Education in the United States* (Washington: U.S. Department of Health, Education and Welfare, Office of Education, 1956).

12. Charles P. Loomis and J. Allan Beegle, *Rural Social Systems* (New York: Prentice-Hall, Inc., 1950), pp. 490-91.

13. Edmund A. Ford, *Rural Renaissance: Revitalizing Small Schools* (Washington: U.S. Department of Health, Education, and Welfare, Bulletin No. 11, 1961).

14. *Ibid.,* pp. 15-20.

15. Edmund A. Ford, "The Isolated Small High School," *School Life,* 44 (Oct., 1961), 8-10.

16. James Bryant Conant, *The American High School Today* (New York: McGraw-Hill Book Co., 1959), p. 37.

17. Robert G. Burnight, *Suburban Migration and the Cost of Education* (Connecticut Agricultural Experiment Station, Population Report No. 2, Progress Report No. 15, Sept., 1956).

18. Benjamin Fine, "Educational Problems in the Suburbs," *The New York Times,* Jan. 30, 1957.

19. Conant, *op. cit.,* pp. 13-14 and 91 ff.

20. *Statistics of Local School Systems: 1955-1956,* p. 20.

21. *Digest of Annual Reports of State Boards of Vocational Education to the Office of Education* (Division of Vocational Education, Fiscal Year Ending June 30, 1960, Washington: U. S. Department of Health, Education and Welfare).

22. *Ibid.,* p. 7.

23. Rufus W. Stimson and Frank W. Lathrop, *History of Agricultural Education of Less Than College Grade in the United States* (Washington: U.S. Government Printing Office, 1942), pp. 1-3.

24. Gerald R. Fuller, "The Characteristics of Farming Programs of Junior and Senior Pupils Enrolled in Vocational Agriculture 3 and 4 in New York State for the School Year 1957-1958" (unpublished M.Ed. thesis, Cornell University, Ithaca, N.Y., 1960).

25. Robert C. Jones, "Determining the Training Needs for Selected Agricultural Occupations in Massachusetts and the Role of Vocational Agriculture in Meeting These Needs," (unpublished Ed.D. thesis, Cornell University, Ithaca, N.Y., 1960).

26. John Calvin Billick, "Employment Opportunities in Farm-Related Occupations for Students of Vocational Agriculture in Erie and Huron Counties, Ohio" (unpublished Master's thesis, Ohio State University, 1959); see also Ralph R. Royster, "Analysis of Off-Farm Agricultural Occupations of Boys Having Training in Vocational Agriculture from Selected Counties in Indiana" (unpublished Ed.D. thesis, University of Missouri, Columbia, Mo., 1959).

27. Vernon W. Bachmann, "Factors Influencing Occupational Choices of Vocational Agriculture Graduates of Holdrege High School" (unpublished Master's thesis, University of Nebraska, Lincoln, Neb., 1957).

28. Robert G. Jones, "Influences of High School Vocational Agriculture on the Status of Graduates in Nonfarm Occupations Not Relating to Farming" (unpublished Master's thesis, Iowa State University, Ames, 1959).

29. Earl T. A. Carpenter, "Projection of Farming Opportunities in Missouri to 1975," (unpublished Ed.D. thesis, University of Missouri, Columbia, Mo., 1960).

30. Louis H. Orzack, "Preference and Prejudice Patterns Among Rural and Urban Schoolmates," *Rural Sociology,* 21 (March, 1956), 29–33.

31. M. Lee Taylor and Gordon Bultena, "Occupational Aspiration and Indecisiveness of Students in an Urban and a Rural Consolidated High School," *Proceedings of the Southwestern Sociological Society* (Apr., 1962), 85–94.

32. E. Grant Youmans, *The Educational Attainment and Future Plans of Rural Youths* (Kentucky Agricultural Experiment Station Bulletin 664, 1959).

33. William H. Sewell *et al.,* "Social Status and Educational and Occupational Aspiration," *American Sociological Review,* 22 (Feb., 1957), 67–72.

34. Lowry Nelson *et al., Some Problems of Minnesota Rural Youth* (Minnesota Agriculture Experiment Station Bulletin 358, 1942).

35. Donald G. Hay *et al., Problems of Rural Youth in Selected Areas of North Dakota* (North Dakota Agricultural Experiment Station, 1940, p. 43).

36. Burton W. Kreitlow and William H. Dreier, "Factors Which Influence School Attendance and Anticipated Education of Minnesota Rural Youth," *University of Minnesota Studies in Rural Education* (unpublished ms., Dec., 1946).

37. Carol L. Stone, *High School Drop-Outs in a Rural County: Their Problems and Adjustments* (Washington Agricultural Experiment Station Bulletin 565, 1956).

38. Alvin L. Bertrand and Marion B. Smith, *Environmental Factors and School Attendance* (Louisiana Agricultural Experiment Station Bulletin 533, 1960).

39. Ernst H. Suerken, "When Drop-Outs Go Job Hunting," *Clearing House,* 27 (Jan., 1953), 268–72.

40. Elizabeth S. Johnson, "When Boys and Girls Leave School for Work," *The Child,* 14 (June–July, 1950), 192–4.

41. Sophia Cooper, "High School Graduates and Dropouts in the Labor Market, October, 1960," *Occupational Outlook Quarterly,* 5 (Sept., 1961), 18–24.

SELECTED READINGS

Bertrand, Alvin L. and Marion B. Smith. *Environmental Factors and School Attendance.* Louisiana Agricultural Experiment Station Bulletin 533, 1960.

An interview study of rural youth, juniors and seniors, in eight Louisiana high schools, investigating the drop-out problem in rural schools.

Cubberley, Ellwood P. *The History of Education*. Boston: Houghton Mifflin Co., 1948.
A compact account of education from the ancient and medieval worlds to modern times.

Education in the United States of America. Washington: U.S. Department of Health, Education, and Welfare, Special Series No. 3, 1955.
A brief descriptive statement of all the major American education programs, with sections on vocational education.

Ford, Edmund A. *Rural Renaissance: Revitalizing Small High Schools*. Washington: U.S. Department of Health, Education, and Welfare, Bulletin No. 11, 1961.
Describes some of the most important programs being designed for rural education in the mid-twentieth century.

Kreitlow, Burton W. *Rural Education: Community Backgrounds*. New York: Harper and Brothers, 1954.
The chapters of this book cover such important subjects as "Historical Role of the Rural School," "The Educational Needs of Rural Society," "The Sociology of the Rural Community," "School District Reorganization," "Agricultural Extension Service," and "Rural Library Service."

Lindstrom, D. E. *Development of Rural Community Schools in Illinois*. Illinois Agricultural Experiment Station Bulletin 627, 1958.
A study of the reorganization of school districts in Illinois in the mid-twentieth century.

Orzack, Louis H. "Preference and Prejudice Patterns Among Rural and Urban Schoolmates," *Rural Sociology*, 21 (Mar., 1956), 29–33.
A research report of social distance among school children, based on data from sociometric questionnaires.

Stone, Carol Larson. *High School Drop-Outs in a Rural County: Their Problems and Adjustments*. Washington Agricultural Experiment Station Bulletin 565, 1956.
An example of the type of empirical research being done to understand or reduce the rate of student drop-outs from high schools.

19 LAND–GRANT COLLEGES— ADULT EDUCATION

Adult education has become an integral part of the dynamic urbanized social organization of American society. Historically, the role of education has been the socialization of the youth of a society to become socially responsible and productive citizens. Because of rapid cultural changes in urbanized society, man has a greater need for assimilating new information and understanding, if high levels of living are to be maintained.

To meet these changing conditions, and to supply the people with up-to-date information, both formal and informal educational mechanisms have been established throughout the nation to serve urban and rural people. The land-grant college system constitutes one of the most important adult educational systems in the United States. The cooperative extension service is another. These highly structured programs of adult education are complemented by numerous nonformal, noncredit-bearing, and nonvocational educational programs.[1]

At the outset it must be understood that adult education is not the recognized responsibility of one institution.[2] Its methods and goals are diffuse rather than specific. Schools, libraries, churches, farm organizations, and mass media also contribute to the dissemination of new ideas to the general public.

The American system of education for the masses has been a major contributing factor in the decline of ruralized social organization. The land-grant colleges and universities are, in effect, urbanizing influences.

LAND-GRANT COLLEGES

American land-grant colleges constitute a primary mechanism for achieving personal and rational goals as well as high levels of living. The land-grant colleges mark the fruition of a long, hard-fought battle. Their founding in 1862 was not an occasion recognized as a victory, and at the time, prospects for success were dubious.

School training in the colonial and early national period was, when available at all, provided by private entrepreneurs and thus available only for the few. The curriculum was limited primarily to reading and preparation for the ministry. Later it included law and medicine. Daily vocational skills like farming and homemaking were transmitted from one generation to the next by informal means. However, notions of a division of labor, cities, industry, and scientific agriculture were developed as early as the colonial period, and new types of education were needed for new societal developments to meet the challenge of social change.

Prior to the Civil War, colleges often approximated the academic level of present-day high schools. Students matriculated in their early teens, and were graduated at the same age as that of a freshman in the mid-twentieth century. Research programs for controlling and modifying phenomena in a scientific sense were conspicuously absent. No scientific methodology was included in the science curriculum, and no college had a scientific laboratory.[3]

Pressure was exerted in some quarters for a system of practical education, but it was by no means overwhelming. Many rural people feared education. They suspected, with remarkable insight, that advanced education for rural people would contribute to the decline of the rural way of life. But from this early time the developing tide of urbanism could neither be repelled nor contained. Education moved forward and, with it, so did urbanization.

The first mechanism of practical intellectual enlightenment was the lyceum, a predecessor of the college extension service. The lyceum movement began in 1826 and lasted for several decades.[4] Millions of Americans from farms and small towns attended lectures about a great variety of subjects.

As new states were admitted to the Union, they became the leaders in the movement for democratic and practical higher education. A dozen of the seventeen new states, prior to 1860, established public universities. These faltering attempts at founding state colleges were most vigorous in the South and the West.[5] Success was limited in all cases by a lack of funds, teachers, and students.

Attempts to promote more practical and scientific education were further inspired by the founding of the West Point Academy in 1802. In 1824, Rensselaer founded an institute to promote the application of science to the tasks of daily life. The institute was to train teachers qualified to instruct rural youth in subjects ranging from agriculture, mechanics, and home economics, to philosophy.[6] This was a radical departure from the classics-oriented colleges of the times.

Rensselaer's institute was a forerunner of the land-grant college that followed nearly forty years later. Another predecessor was the Gardner Lyceum (1823) in Maine. This school was the first to be completely concerned with agriculture. In 1792 the Trustees of King's College (now Columbia University) recognized the need for professorships in law, history, chemistry, and agriculture. Funds for the agricultural professorship were granted. In 1835, Harvard College offered practical agriculture instruction. The charter of the University of Michigan (1837) specified instruction in practical farming and agriculture. Agricultural societies proliferated during this period, and they often supported practical education. But in spite of all these efforts, popular support for agricultural education was not forthcoming from the average farmer. Quite the contrary, farmers often opposed efforts toward educational development.[7]

Soon after Morrill was elected to the U.S. House of Representatives (1854), he introduced his first bill proposing the formation of agricultural colleges. The opposition was emphatic. For example, from Minnesota's Senator Rice there was the charge, "We want no fancy farmers; we want no fancy mechanics." [8] There were many other hostile responses to Morrill's proposal, and President Buchanan vetoed the bill in 1859. With Lincoln as the next president, a new Morrill Bill was introduced. It passed both houses of Congress, and was signed into law by the President on July 2, 1862, without fanfare or enthusiasm.[9] It became law more by default than by popular acclaim.

The Morrill Act—1862. The Morrill Act provided 17,430,000 acres of land for the support of colleges. This appropriation of land netted the colleges approximately $7,500,000. By the 1950's the land-grant colleges and universities were still receiving an income of about $1,700,000 from the original Morrill grant.[10] The Morrill Act specified that each state would receive a land appropriation equal to 30,000 acres for each senator and representative. Money derived from the sale of the land was to be invested in safe stocks yielding not less than 5 per cent. This money was to constitute a perpetual fund, the interest of which was to be used to support at least one state college in which agriculture would be a leading subject. Scientific and classical studies were not to be excluded from these schools.[11]

Senator Morrill continued to propose legislation in support of land-grant colleges. For years his proposals were soundly defeated, and frequently the very continuation of the schools was precarious. Near the end of the century their position became stronger. Finally, through encouragement of the colleges' administrators and of a national farm organization, a second Morrill Act was passed in 1890. This act provided an additional endowment and promoted the founding of several Negro Land-Grant Colleges.

Vocational and liberal arts curriculum combined. Discussion has abounded concerning the real intent of Senator Morrill's 1862 proposal for land-grant colleges. The details are unquestionably clouded. But through the maze of apparent contradictions it can be clearly ascertained that Morrill's conception of educational institutions was that they should include both vocational skills and liberal arts. Five years after the passing of the Morrill Act, the senator told the faculty of the Sheffield Scientific School at Yale that his proposal was not for schools of agriculture as such, but for scientific schools as distinct from colleges offering only the classics.[12]

In an address to the Vermont Legislature in 1888, Morrill said:

Only the interest from the land grant fund can be expended, and that must be expended, first—without excluding other scientific and classical studies—for teaching such branches of learning as are related to agriculture and the mechanic arts—the latter as absolutely as the former. Obviously not manual, but intellectual instruction was the paramount object. It was not provided that agricultural labor in the field should be practically taught, any more than that the mechanical trade of a carpenter or blacksmith should be taught.

Secondly, it was a liberal education that was proposed. Classical studies were not to be excluded, and, therefore, must be included. The Act of 1862 proposed a system of broad education by colleges, not limited to a superficial or dwarfed training, such as might be had at an industrial school, nor a mere manual training, such as might be supplied by a foreman of a workshop, or by a foreman of an experimental farm. If any would have only a school with equal scraps of labor and of instruction, or something other than a college, they would not obey the national law. . . .

Whatever else might be done . . . scientific and classical studies, as already stated, were not to be excluded, were, therefore, to be preserved; and this is set forth at the very starting point, but the national bounty act brought to the front "branches of learning related to agriculture and the mechanic arts"— learning in the broad fields of the practical sciences, and none are broader than those related to agriculture. The useful was to have greater prominence in the eyes of students, as it will have in all their after-life, and not stand unequal and shame-faced even in the presence of ancient literature.[13]

On another occasion, Senator Morrill wrote:

I would not diminish by a hair's breadth the prestige or prosperity of our other State institutions of liberal learning. They are in a large sense kinsmen and coworkers in the same field in behalf of humanity, and no one of them could fail to be harmed by the depreciation of any other. . . . By no means was it designed to curtail the usual extent of a collegiate education, but to add thereto such essential and practical sciences as were then almost universally neglected by literary colleges, although indispensable to the advancement of the American people in their industrial and diversified life.[14]

From their inception, the land-grant colleges were destined to be more than schools of agriculture. They propagated a systematic and advanced knowledge which resulted in the decline of ruralized social organization. Congress supported the land-grant colleges because of their potential contribution to the national welfare, not because of agriculture for its own sake. Agriculture was one part of the national welfare.

After floundering into establishment, the land-grant colleges faced their next major challenge in the development of a curriculum. What, specifically, should be taught? There were no well-organized precedents. Michigan offered the best example, which was often followed, but that state, too, was experimenting. It became a tradition for members of the faculties of the new institutions to visit Michigan in order to observe its program.

In these years of struggle to develop a curriculum, there appeared such strange and divergent course offerings as "How to Plow" and "Mental and Moral Philosophy." In 1868–69, the University of Wisconsin's bulletin indicated it was the plan of the university to give a complete course of instruction in the subjects pertaining to agriculture. Graduates were to be thoroughly prepared to operate farms intelligently and profitably.[15] The Kansas State College catalogue in 1875–77 listed such course titles as "The Farm, Nursery, Carpentry, Cabinet Making, Wagon-Making, Painting, Blacksmithing, Dress-Making, Printing, Telegraphy, Scroll-Sawing, Carving, Engraving, and Photography." [16] But, despite the struggle of the faculties, administrators, and trustees of the new colleges, the fact remained that there simply was no body of agricultural, mechanical, and homemaking knowledge developed in the 1860's and 1870's which could be taught. One fact, however, was clear: higher education in agriculture would have to be based on the development of scientific knowledge. Research findings from the agricultural experiment stations contributed the major subject matter for the agricultural colleges after 1887.

By the middle of the twentieth century, the land-grant universities had a full range of course offerings, which ranged from hotel keeping to opera. Among all four-year institutions of higher learning, the land-grant schools enrolled over 20 per cent of the nation's students, conferred over 21 per cent of the bachelor degrees, 25 per cent of the second-level degrees, and 38 per cent of all doctorates. Land-grant universities made more than half of all higher education expenditures for original research.[17] Degrees were conferred in all fields from agriculture through the arts (see Table XXVIII).

Continuation education. Continuation education was first developed in England in the second half of the eighteenth century. The movement spread to the United States, and in the 1890's, schools such as Johns Hopkins, the University of Chicago, and the University of Wisconsin offered continuation courses.[18] These courses are primarily aimed at adult education.

The first major change in social organization which gave real impetus to adult instruction was the return of veterans at the end of World War I. By the 1920's the adult education movement was given another source of support. The Carnegie Corporation, on the basis of recommendations of a representative who toured Europe with the express purpose of observing adult education programs, began supporting many adult education enterprises.

Support for continuation education has come from a wide range of sources, and enrollment has increased accordingly. Table XXIX shows the growth of these programs from 1924 to 1955.[19] The characteristics and interests of students in continuation education have been illustrated by a recent survey of 6,500 participants in the University of California, Los Angeles, program. The survey showed that there were nearly twice as many male as female matriculants, that 60 per cent were 35 years old or under, that half already had a college degree, that a large proportion had positions providing them with high remuneration, and that the overwhelming majority would seek a degree if all requirements could be fulfilled by continuation courses.[20]

TABLE XXVIII. DEGREES CONFERRED BY FIELD, BY LAND-GRANT INSTITUTIONS IN 1958–59

Field of Study	Total		Bachelor		Doctorate	
	Number	Per Cent	Number	Per Cent	Number	Per Cent
Agriculture	4,566	5.31	4,223	5.11	343	10.23
Architecture	798	0.92	797	0.96	1	0.02
Biological sciences	4,123	4.79	3,563	4.31	560	16.71
Business and commerce	10,461	12.61	10,425	12.61	36	1.07
Education	14,354	16.69	13,851	16.76	503	15.01
Engineering	16,263	18.91	15,912	19.25	351	10.47
English and journalism	3,257	3.78	3,174	3.84	83	2.47
Fine and applied arts	2,192	2.54	2,146	2.59	46	1.37
Foreign language and literature	742	0.86	694	0.83	48	1.43
Forestry	991	1.15	985	1.19	6	0.17
Geography	192	0.22	174	0.21	18	0.53
Health services	5,785	6.72	5,700	6.89	85	2.53
Home economics	2,080	2.41	2,063	2.49	17	0.50
Law	1,681	1.95	1,678	2.03	3	0.08
Library science	341	0.39	341	0.41	0	0.00
Mathematical subjects	1,551	1.80	1,444	1.74	107	3.19
Military, naval or air science	386	0.44	386	0.46	0	0.00
Philosophy	215	0.25	203	0.24	12	0.35
Physical sciences	3,797	4.41	3,035	3.67	762	22.73
Psychology	1,391	1.61	1,382	1.67	9	0.26
Religion	21	0.02	21	0.02	0	0.00
Social sciences	8,969	10.43	8,619	10.43	350	10.44
Trade and industrial training	278	0.32	278	0.33	0	0.00
Miscellaneous	1,548	1.80	1,537	1.86	11	0.32
Total	85,982	100.00	82,631	100.00	3,351	100.00

Source: George Lind, *Statistics of Land-Grant Colleges and Universities* (Washington: U.S. Department of Health, Education, and Welfare, Circular 639, 1959), Table 6.

Most colleges and universities now offer some continuation courses primarily oriented to the interests of city residents.[21] Continuation education is essentially an urban counterpart to agricultural extension adult education programs for rural people. By the middle of the twentieth

TABLE XXIX. ESTIMATED PARTICIPATION IN ADULT EDUCATION

	1924	1934	1950	1955
Agricultural extension	5,000,000	6,000,000	7,000,000	8,684,000
Public school adult education programs	1,000,000	1,500,000	3,000,000	3,500,000
University extension and evening college programs	200,000	300,000	500,000	1,500,000
Private correspondence schools	2,000,000	1,000,000	1,000,000	1,000,000
Educational radio and television	500,000	5,000,000	6,000,000	5,000,000‖
Library adult education	200,000	1,000,000	1,500,000	1,961,000
Men's and women's clubs	1,000,000	1,000,000	§	1,525,000
Parent-Teacher Associations	15,000	60,000	§	350,000
Religious institutions	150,000	200,000	§	15,500,000#
Business and industry	100,000	50,000	§	750,000
Labor unions	30,000	15,000	§	850,000
Armed Forces educational programs	*	*	250,000	388,500
Health and welfare agencies	†	†	†	6,500,000
Others ‡	4,681,500	6,156,000	10,000,000	2,000,000
Total	14,881,500	22,311,000	29,250,000	49,508,500

* Not in operation in 1924 and 1934.

† This item included under "Others" by Cartwright and Essert.

‡ Includes alumni education, community organization, organizations of the foreign-born, forums, lyceums and Chautauquas, Negro education, prison education, recreation, settlements, special schools, theaters, unemployed, vocational rehabilitation, and museums.

§ Essert includes these items in "Others."

‖ This decline does not reflect fewer listeners but more rigid criteria as to what is "educational."

This drastic increase is caused both by growth of adult educational activities in churches and synagogues and by improved procedures for reporting enrollments. Adult Sunday school classes are included.

Source: "An Overview and History of the Field," *Adult Education,* 7 (Summer, 1957), 229.

century, the programs of continuation education and agricultural extension have come to overlap considerably.

A county home agent in urban and suburban Ramsey County, where the city of St. Paul, Minnesota, is located, recently reported that the subjects for extension homemaking are not necessarily different for urban than for rural counties.[22] Wisconsin's rural art program and Arizona's art extension program are additional instances of overlapping areas. Both art programs are geared to the interests of predominantly rural people. The former is administered by the Agricultural Extension Service, the latter by General Extension.

AGRICULTURE EXTENSION EDUCATION

The Cooperative Agriculture Extension Service is an adult education program which was originally designed for farm families. Its purpose was to increase the quality and quantity of food and fiber production. This notion of extending the most advanced agricultural information directly to the farmer emerged during the last two decades of the nineteenth century. By the turn of the century, the idea of extension work had taken root and was growing rapidly.[23]

Early college extension efforts were in the form of institutes, correspondence schools, and reading courses in farming. In 1901, Illinois formed an extension staff. Four years later, Ohio State appointed the first permanent extension director. By the termination of the first decade of the twentieth century, 35 institutions were providing extension work.[24] In the first decade of the century, one extension leader outlined the aim of agricultural extension as bringing the work of the agriculture colleges to people unable to attend college. It needed a professional staff of its own, associated with the agricultural colleges' teaching and research programs, but whose chief task would be adult education. The Extension's subject areas would include the economic, governmental, and social problems of farming. It would help rural people in problem areas ranging from taxation to tree pruning.[25] With such a broad assignment, extension work for family and home life was pioneered by Cornell's Martha Van Rensselaer shortly after the turn of the century. Seaman Knapp was a leading figure in extension work in the first decade of the twentieth century. The acceptance of the demonstration method, particularly in the South, is largely due to his efforts.

A dramatic effort was made to establish extension work in 1904 and 1905, when the "Seed Corn Gospel Trains" rolled through the farm areas of Iowa. These trains stopped in communities along the way so leaders could give lectures and distribute charts, specimens, and demonstration books. The Gospel Train's service was at its peak in 1911, when 71 trains traveled in 28 states and reached a total of 995,000 people.[26]

Individual and local efforts were combined in a movement for federal support of extension work. Between 1909 and 1913, some 32 different bills were introduced in Congress. All of these bills failed to pass. Finally, the combined efforts of South Carolina's Lever and Georgia's Smith resulted in the Smith-Lever Act which became law in 1914. This bill was the culmination of many local and regional attempts to promote adult agricultural education. In 1914 adult education was firmly established with federal recognition and support. Although agricultural extension was not created by the Smith-Lever Act, the act centralized the program and gave it a definite, permanent role.

The agricultural extension service was specifically organized to include both farm and home economics programs. Section 2 of the act defined extension work as instruction and practical demonstration in agriculture and home economics for people not in college. The specific extension programs were to be organized in a way mutually agreed upon by the Secretary of Agriculture and the state agricultural colleges.[27] The extension service was organized with a county agent located in practically every county of the nation. Most of the counties also have home agents, and many have 4-H Club agents. These county agents and their assistants work directly with the local people. They collaborate with the state agricultural colleges, where many of the agents are given academic status as professors. They also work directly with the federal government and indirectly with state and local governments.

National Agricultural Extension Center. A notable achievement in agricultural education was the founding of the National Agricultural Extension Center for Advanced Study.[28] The center is located on the campus of the University of Wisconsin. Its objectives include a program for continual examination and evaluation of the place of farming and homemaking in contemporary society, expansion of learning opportunities in administration and personnel management, and development of dynamic approaches to the problems of planning. Graduate courses and seminars have been organized which lead to the Master of Science and Doctor of Philosophy degrees. The program was financially assisted by the Kellogg Foundation and fellowships have been awarded annually to applicants for advanced degrees.

Short courses for farmers and homemakers. Short courses were first organized in the 1880's at the University of Wisconsin. Their rise and decline illustrate changes in social organization. Farm leaders and land-grant college administrators realized, before the end of the nineteenth century, that the great need for bringing new ideas and information to practicing farmers was not being adequately met by four-year college courses. Most farmers' sons and daughters were not in college and many of those who were graduated from the agriculture schools did not return to farming. Short courses were created so that the colleges could offer practical in-service training to farm families.

Throughout the first half of the twentieth century the short courses served a real and vital need. Since World War II, however, the number of short-course programs have declined. By 1959, only fourteen states reported that they had such programs.[29] Other more effective means of extension training, including the use of mass communications, have served systematically to bring more information to farm people. The need once served by the short course is now often more adequately met by other systems of adult education.

These are the major governmental programs for adult education which are associated with the U.S. Department of Agriculture. Examples of the many other adult education agencies and programs that reach rural people are presented in the following sections.

LIBRARIES

Tax-supported libraries in the United States originated in the early years of the nineteenth century. A century later, county libraries designed to serve rural as well as urban people were organized in California, Ohio, Oregon, and Maryland. The "book-wagon" was founded in Maryland in 1905. By 1924 the American Library Association entered adult education in an organized way.[30]

Newly organized libraries, in rural as well as urban America, made a significant impact on adult education. However, the role of libraries, particularly rural ones, has been difficult to carry out. At the beginning of the second half of the twentieth century, adult education through rural libraries was still a largely undeveloped service; only one-third of all rural areas had library service. The greater the rurality of an area, the more inadequate the library service. Library programs were also curtailed due to insufficient funds.[31] In spite of such an unpromising summary, there was evidence that libraries in general, and rural libraries in particular, were being expanded in role and elevated in status.[32]

As library activity increased, three types of libraries became identifiable in terms of their significant contributions to small-town and open-country rural America. These are the county and regional libraries, state agency libraries, and village and city public libraries.[33] County or regional libraries have been organized to serve rural areas under the administration of a consolidated headquarters. These libraries typically have branches, deposits, and bookmobiles. Their structure of organization is consistent with urbanized social organization. In several respects their organization parallels that of consolidated schools, churches, and other services in rural America. State library agencies vary greatly, but they usually provide some book circulation, reference service, and extension activities. They serve as administrative units for federal contributions to local library programs. Village and city libraries provide numerous adult education programs, lectures, records, and movies, in addition to their book holdings.

Federal support for libraries in rural areas. To further promote library development, particularly in rural areas, Congress passed a five-year Library Services Act in 1956. It was later extended to 1966.[34] Appropriations were made available to states proportionate to their rural population. States matched these funds on a scale based on their per capita income. The accomplishments of the program are striking. Thirty-four million people received new or improved library services. Approximately 250 bookmobiles were provided. State appropriations for rural libraries increased by 75 per cent, and local funds increased by 50 per cent.[35] The many successes of this program continue at a rapid pace.

OTHER MECHANISMS FOR ADULT EDUCATION

In addition to colleges, extension courses, and libraries, adult education is fostered as a part of the program of other agencies. Farmers' organizations and cooperatives contribute directly to the dissemination of new ideas. Church programs, professional organizations, and community clubs also further adult education. The International Farm Youth Exchange is a vital educational force in the area of international understanding. Mass media communication are the source of a continuous stream of new ideas.

Farmers' organizations and cooperatives. America has been characterized as a nation of joiners. Voluntary organizations abound, and they permeate both urban and rural areas. In a society that is large geographically and demographically, and which has been oriented toward the doctrine of laissez faire, the voluntary organizations have served a very real purpose as a vital force in the process of idea communication.

Farm leaders believe that one of the primary roles of their organizations is education.[36] Their educational programs were aimed primarily at strengthening the economy, furthering democracy, and promoting international understanding. Nearly three-fourths of the audiences of these educational programs are located in rural areas or towns of less than 2,500 inhabitants. Their educational techniques have been in order of most frequent use, lectures, panels, and small group discussions. Farm organization leaders have estimated that there are over 30,000 local discussion groups in rural America. Their national meetings, in and of themselves, constitute educational experiences. Moreover, they organize institutes, camps, workshops, and leadership training conferences.

Larger cooperatives employ field representatives who are responsible, among other things, for education programs in the local area. This is exemplified by the Consumers Cooperative Association of Kansas City; the Grain Terminal Association of St. Paul, Minnesota; and Midlands Cooperative Wholesale. Midlands has also provided a film lending library for organizations in its region.

Regular publications of farm organizations cover many informational and educational topics. *The Nation's Agriculture, National Grange Monthly,* and the *National Union Farmer* are the major publications of farm organizations. Another important educational publication is *The GTA Digest* (Grain Terminal Association).

International Farm Youth Exchange. Emphasis on international education in rural areas has been dramatically illustrated by the Cooperative Agricultural Extension Service's I.F.Y.E. program (1948). This exchange program enables America's young people to live for a time on farms abroad, and for young farmers from abroad to live on American farms. The program has been well received and has had support both from the federal government and private organizations. I.F.Y.E. delegates are between the ages of twenty and thirty, at least high school graduates, from farm backgrounds, and interested in farming or farm related occupations. Applications are submitted through the county extension agents; and the National 4-H Club Foundation makes the final selections. When I.F.Y.E. delegates return to their home areas, they travel for another year giving lectures, radio, and television talks, and relating their experiences to the people in their home communities.[37]

SUMMARY

Adult education is a primary force in agriculture and the whole of American rural and small-town life. Its formal organization includes the huge land-grant college system, the cooperative agricultural extension service, the network of local libraries, and numerous special programs of a host of voluntary organizations.

The historical development of land-grant schools was due less to the requests of rural people than to the work of national leaders who implicitly supported an urbanized way of life. The very presence of land-grant colleges on the social landscape is inconsistent with ruralized social organization. The agricultural colleges, the agricultural extension service, and related agencies have served and continue to serve the interests of agriculture and agribusiness well—indeed, beyond all expectations. Their service, however, is not to rural people because they are rural or to the farming enterprise as a way of life. These programs, and their personnel are the connecting links which integrate the enterprises of agriculture and urbanization into a common whole—namely, the dynamic American society. Adult education courses continue to function in this manner. Their promotion of farming is in the interest of the entire nation, not only that of farm operators. The very occupation of the business farmer is served most through the continual integration of his enterprise with other business operations in the nation, which are his market as well as his suppliers. Adult education, reaching Americans in rural areas, is one of the great integrating forces of the nation.

NOTES

1. Charles P. Loomis *et al.*, *Rural Social Systems and Adult Education* (East Lansing: Michigan State University Press, 1953), pp. 2–23.

2. Lowry Nelson *et al.*, *Community Structure and Change* (New York: Macmillan Co., 1960), pp. 326–7; cf. also Howard Y. McClusky, "Adult Education and Community Relations," in J. E. Grinnell and Raymond J. Young (eds.), *The School and Community* (New York: The Ronald Press, 1955), Chapter 19.

3. Edward D. Eddy, Jr., *Colleges for Our Land and Time* (New York: Harper and Brothers, 1956), pp. 1–22.

4. *Ibid.*, p. 6.

5. Elmer E. Brown, "The Origin of American State Universities," *University of California Publications in Education*, 3 (Apr. 10, 1903), 31.

6. Charles F. Thwing, *A History of Higher Education in America* (New York: D. Appleton Century Co., 1906), p. 421.

7. Eddy, *op. cit.,* p. 14.

8. *Ibid.,* pp. 31–2.

9. Carl L. Becker, *Cornell University: Founders and the Founding* (Ithaca: Cornell University Press, 1944), pp. 36–7.

10. *Ibid.,* p. 36.

11. Henry S. Commager, (ed.), *Documents of American History* (New York: Appleton-Century-Crofts, Inc., 1948), pp. 412–13.

12. Eddy, *op. cit.,* p. 38.

13. Justin S. Morrill, *State Aid to the U.S. Land-Grant Colleges* (Burlington, Vt.: Free Press Association, 1888).

14. Justin S. Morrill, *The Land-Grant Colleges* (Burlington, Vt.: 1893).

15. Frederick B. Mumford, *The Land-Grant College Movement* (Missouri Agricultural Experiment Station Bulletin 419, 1940), p. 29.

16. Eddy, *op. cit.,* p. 55.

17. George Lind, *Statistics of Land-Grant Colleges and Universities* (Washington: U.S. Department of Health, Education, and Welfare, Circular No. 639, 1959), see especially p. 49.

18. M. E. Sadler, *Continuation Schools in England and Elsewhere* (Manchester, England: Manchester University Press, 1908); George B. Zehmer, "The Development of University Extension Services in the United States," in *Proceedings of the Institute for Administrative Officers of Higher Institutions, 1945,* (Chicago: University of Chicago Press, 1946).

19. Cf. also Mary Ewen Palmer, "Stages of Development in Adult Education," *Adult Education Bulletin,* 11 (June, 1947), 139–42.

20. Lawrence K. McLaughlin, *Student Population in University of California Extension Classes* (unpublished Ph.D. dissertation, Los Angeles: University of California, 1951).

21. Olen E. Leonard and Sheldon G. Lowry, "Continuation Education in Colleges and Universities," in Charles P. Loomis, *Rural Social Systems and Adult Education* (East Lansing: Michigan State College Press, 1953), pp. 233–44.

22. "Life with a County Home Agent," *St. Paul Dispatch* (Apr. 19, 1960).

23. R. K. Bliss *et al.* (eds.), *The Spirit and Philosophy of Extension Work* (Washington: Graduate School, U.S.D.A. and Epsilon Sigma Phi, National Honorary Extension Fraternity, 1952).

24. Eddy, *op. cit.,* p. 130.

25. *Proceedings of the Society for the Promotion of Agriculture Science,* 18 (1904), 60.

26. Eddy, *op. cit.*, p. 132.

27. *Ibid.*, p. 141.

28. "The National Extension Center for Advanced Study," *Adult Education*, 6 (Winter, 1956), 113–16.

29. Lee Taylor, "Farm and Home Week and Rural Arts Programs in the Fifty States and Puerto Rico, 1959" (unpublished survey).

30. Arthur E. Bostwick, *American Public Library* (New York: Appleton, 1926).

31. Ruth Warncke, "Public Libraries," in Loomis *et al., op. cit.*, pp. 172–96.

32. Robert D. Leigh, *The Public Library in the United States* (New York: Columbia University Press, 1950).

33. Helen Ridgway, *County and Regional Libraries* (Chicago: American Library Association, 1949).

34. Hannis S. Smith, *Library Service for Rural People* (Washington: U.S.D.A., Farmer's Bulletin No. 2142, 1959), pp. 11–12.

35. John G. Lorenz and Herbert A. Carl, "The Library Services Act After Four Years," *American Library Association Bulletin*, 55 (June, 1961) 534–40.

36. Wayne C. Roher and Carl C. Taylor, "Adult Education Programs or Activities of the General Farmers' Organizations and Cooperatives," in Loomis *et al., op. cit.*, pp. 100–122.

37. International Farm Youth Exchange (Washington: National 4-H Club Foundation, 1960).

SELECTED READINGS

Bliss, R. K., *et al.* (eds.). *The Spirit and Philosophy of Extension Work.* Washington: Graduate School, U.S.D.A. and Epsilon Sigma Phi, National Honorary Extension Fraternity, 1952.

The extension program is described by subjects such as pioneers, organization and administration, efficiency and educational philosophy.

Eddy, Edward D., Jr. *Colleges for Our Land and Time.* New York: Harper and Brothers, 1956.

The social environment and dynamic social interaction which produced the land-grant colleges are examined in detail. The growth and status of these colleges are the subject of the latter half of this book.

Loomis, Charles P., *et al. Rural Social Systems and Adult Education.* East Lansing, Mich.: Michigan State University Press, 1953.

Chapters are devoted to all the major adult education programs which are wholly or in part oriented to rural people.

Palmer, Mary E. "Stages of Development in Adult Education," *Adult Education Bulletin*, 11 (June, 1947), 139–42.

Summarizes the history of adult education in countries other than the United States.

Parker, William B. *The Life and Public Service of Justin Smith Morrill.* Boston: Houghton Mifflin Co., 1924.

A lucid account of the times associated with the Morrill college idea, with a special chapter on "The Land-Grant College Acts."

Smith, Hannis S. *Library Service for Rural People.* Washington: U.S.D.A. Farmer's Bulletin No. 2142, 1959.

A description of rural library service at the state, county, and local levels.

20 CHURCH ORGANIZATION FROM NATIONAL PARKS TO SUBURBIA

The total number of religious bodies in the United States has exceeded 250 for many years. It has been estimated that less than 50 per cent of the nation's people have been members of religious bodies. Religious statistics in 1958 indicated that church membership has increased to over 60 per cent of the population,[1] the highest in the history of the nation.

The collection of statistics about religion in the United States is difficult because of several features of religious organization. These are the doctrine of separation of church and state, the constitutional guarantee of freedom of worship, and the great diversity of religious bodies. Hence, there are many difficulties involved for the Bureau of the Census in collecting statistical data about religious beliefs and practices. Censuses of Religious Bodies were taken in 1906, 1916, 1926, and 1936. Since 1936 no attempt to gather a government sponsored Census of Religious Bodies has been successful. In 1946 a Census of Religious Bodies was attempted, but the collected data were never published. In 1957 a voluntary sample survey was made by the Bureau of the Census in which respondents were asked, "What is your religion?" Aside from this report, the census enumerators have not asked for information concerning the religion of the nation's population.

In spite of the limited census data concerning American church organization, there exists a relatively large body of verified information concerning church life. This information has been acquired through independent

400

research, committee meetings, conferences, and other programs concerned with describing and analyzing religious organization, planning, and action. Religious social organization in the United States is complex, and the most fruitful understanding of this subject can only be achieved in the light of a historical perspective.

SOCIAL SPACE DOMINATED BY RELIGION

The degree of social space controlled by religion varies from society to society and from one time to another. In ruralized social organization, which is so well illustrated by the middle period of the Middle Ages in central Europe, the social space dominated by religion far surpassed the amount required to realize the basic purpose of the institution of religion. In addition to the church's concern for providing mankind with an explanation of the meaning of existence, the church in the Middle Ages had extended its sway over the spheres of learning, family, politics, and economics. In short, the church dominated the society of that time more than did any other single social institution. Only with the advent of the Renaissance and the Industrial Revolution was it possible for one institution after another to become separated from the control of religion.

Colonial America was founded in a social environment of religious discontent. The ideology of freedom of worship was an index of the limited influence of religion over other social institutions. The extent of religious freedom in the struggling rural colonies was often exaggerated. Several colonies were founded by religious dissenters; however, within their respective territories strict adherence to religious dogma was required. In the early colonial period the Church of England was partially supported by taxes collected in the New England towns.

By the time of the national period, local governments were freed from the responsibility for financially supporting the clergy. On the one hand, the economic independence of the church was consistent with the ideology of religious freedom. On the other hand, the economic independence of the church further contributed to the contraction of the social space occupied by religion in colonial and early America. After the Revolutionary War, economic and political institutions dominated a greater social space than did the social institution of religion.

Piety demanded by the colonial church was reputed to be stern. But, although colorful in the annals of history, this piety was usually accepted by the people only when it served their ends. The sternness of the early church was compatible with the harsh demands made of man in his struggle to carve a nation out of the colonial wilderness. The norms of diligence and hard work espoused by the church were acceptable because they were consistent with other aspects of the total social organization. That these norms may have had meaning in purely religious terms was less important for the study of social organization than that they had meaning in terms of man's relation to his physical environment. Deviations from the stern piety demanded by the church rapidly increased when the amenities of life were elevated above a subsistence level.

Most of the higher education of the early colonial period was devoted to training young men for the clergy. Just prior to the Revolutionary War there was an increase in the number of men training for the professions of law and medicine. After the termination of the war and with the birth of the new nation, training for the service professions of law and medicine was further developed and came to exceed that for the ministry. Throughout the entire nineteenth century the position of the clergy was a precarious one. Frontier life was not conducive to highly organized religion, and trained clergymen were scare. The geographical dispersion of the population was an obstacle to regularity of church attendance. In meeting this challenge, the church showed considerable vigor. Itinerant ministers, now legendary, provided color, drama, and mysticism for scattered rural parishioners. As these circuit riders made their rounds, people came together for marriages, baptisms, and communion, and to hear the Gospel or the threat of damnation. Such gatherings served both religious and social purposes.

TRENDS IN CHURCH MEMBERSHIP AND NUMBER OF CLERGYMEN

A shortage of clergymen in the United States frequently has been reported by many religious bodies. In 1910 the census enumerated 118,000 clergymen and by 1950, 171,000. It is indicated in Table XXX that by 1950 the number of clergymen in the nation had steadily increased, but at a less rapid rate than the population. Between 1950 and 1960 the rate of increase of clergymen and the population was approximately the same. The number of church members per clergyman increased from 326 in 1910 to 507 in 1950. The total population per clergyman for the same time period increased from 779 to 881. Between 1950 and 1960 the population per clergyman decreased to 841. The number of church members is estimated to have been 38,000,000 in 1910, and 86,830,000 in 1950 (see

TABLE XXX. CLERGYMEN IN THE UNITED STATES, 1910–1950

Census Year	Number of Clergymen	Church Members per Clergyman	Total Population per Clergyman
1910	118,000	326	779
1920	127,000	380	832
1930	149,000	394	824
1940	141,000	457	934
1950	171,000	507	881
1960	201,000*	†	841*

Source: *Annals of the American Academy of Political and Social Science*, 332 (Nov., 1960), 147.

* U.S. Bureau of the Census, *U.S. Census of Population: 1960. Detailed Characteristics. United States Summary*. Final Report PC(1)–1D (Washington: U.S. Government Printing Office, 1963).

† Not available in the census.

Table XXXI). By 1958 the total membership of 251 church bodies reached 109,557,741, or 63 per cent of the total population.

Rural-urban distribution of church members. By the middle of the twentieth century, religion, like other major social institutions, was dominated by urbanized social organization. The 1957 Census Bureau's voluntary

TABLE XXXI. TOTAL MEMBERSHIP OF UNITED STATES RELIGIOUS BODIES: 1910–1950

Census Year	Number of Members	Per Cent Total Population of Members
1910	38,497,000*	41.2
1920	48,251,000*	45.6
1930	58,754,000*	47.8
1940	64,502,000	48.9
1950	86,830,000	57.6
1960	112,227,000†	62.7

Source: "Membership of Religious Bodies: 1890–1957," *Historical Statistics of the United States* (Washington: U.S. Bureau of the Census, 1960), p. 228.

* Estimated for these years by straight line interpolation between religious census years.

† *Yearbook of American Churches, 1961* (New York: National Council of the Churches of Christ, 1961).

survey of religious affiliation reported about 119,000,000 church members for the total population aged fourteen and over. Of those who reported religious affiliation, 64 per cent resided in urban areas, 24 per cent in rural nonfarm areas, and 12 per cent in rural farm areas (see Table XXXII).

TABLE XXXII. RURAL-URBAN RESIDENCE OF PERSONS FOURTEEN YEARS OLD AND OVER, BY RELIGION REPORTED, FOR THE UNITED STATES CIVILIAN POPULATION: 1957

Religion	Urban		Rural Nonfarm		Rural Farm	
	Number	Per Cent	Number	Per Cent	Number	Per Cent
Total 14 years old and over	76,298,000	63.9	29,097,000	24.4	13,938,000	11.7
Protestant	44,726,000	56.6	22,633,000	28.7	11,593,000	14.7
White	37,796,000	55.2	20,608,000	30.1	10,071,000	14.7
Nonwhite	6,930,000	66.1	2,025,000	19.3	1,522,000	14.5
Roman Catholic	24,173,000	78.8	4,835,000	15.8	1,661,000	5.4
Jewish	3,718,000	96.1	441,000	3.6	9,000	0.2
Other religion	1,196,000	77.4	230,000	14.9	119,000	7.7
No religion	1,732,000	54.2	1,000,000	31.3	463,000	14.5
Religion not reported	753,000	68.2	258,000	23.4	93,000	8.4

Source: *Current Population Reports, Population Characteristics* (Washington: U.S. Bureau of the Census, Series P-20, No. 79, 1958), p. 7.

A detailed analysis has been made of the rural-urban distribution of religious bodies, based upon data from the National Council of Churches 1956 study of *Churches and Church Membership in the United States*.[2] The findings show that 60.8 per cent of the nation's religious members resided in metropolitan area counties, 33.5 per cent in intermediate counties (neither metropolitan nor entirely rural), and 5.8 per cent in counties where the population was entirely rural. For the total population in the same types of counties the distribution is 56.8, 36.4, and 6.8 per cent, respectively (see Table XXXIII). These summary findings suggest that church members are slightly more often located in metropolitan counties than the population as a whole, but:

. . . it is not at all clear whether church membership of the United States is actually more urbanized than the population in general or whether these figures simply reflect under enumeration of church members in rural tracts and the absence from our statistics of several essentially rural religious bodies.[8]

TABLE XXXIII. DENOMINATIONAL GROUPS BY PERCENTAGE OF REPORTED MEMBERS IN METROPOLITAN AND NONMETROPOLITAN AREAS: 1952

Denominational Group	Metropolitan Counties	Nonmetropolitan Counties	
		Intermediate Counties	Rural Counties
Jewish congregations	97.5	2.5	0
Roman Catholic	74.5	23.0	2.4
Reported members of all Protestant groups	45.6	45.3	9.0
Unitarian and Universalist Churches	74.4	25.6	
Protestant Episcopal	72.8	25.1	2.1
Moravian bodies	70.3	29.7	
Congregational Christian Church	59.9	34.9	5.1
Evangelical and Reformed	59.5	37.0	3.5
Presbyterian bodies	58.1	37.6	4.3
Reformed bodies	54.9	45.1	
Assemblies of God	54.4	45.5	
Adventist bodies	52.1	47.9	
Lutheran bodies	51.1	40.5	8.4
Latter-Day Saints	45.8	44.5	9.8
Friends	44.8	55.2	
Church of the Nazarene	43.8	56.2	
Evangelical United Brethren	42.0	50.6	7.5
Methodist bodies	40.1	49.8	10.1
Mennonite bodies	37.9	62.1	
Disciples of Christ	36.0	53.3	10.7
Brethren Churches	35.7	64.3	
Baptist bodies	34.9	52.2	12.9
Churches of God	34.6	65.4	
Total reported church members	60.8	33.5	5.8
United States population, 1950	56.8	36.4	6.8

Source: *Churches and Church Membership in the United States* (Washington: U.S. Bureau of the Census, Series D, Nos. 3–6, Tables 136 and 139; Series E, No. 1, Table 140).

Ninety-seven per cent of the Jewish congregation members are in metropolitan counties. Nearly three-quarters of the Roman Catholic church members are found in metropolitan counties. Unitarians, Universalists, and Episcopalian have a disproportionate number of members residing in metropolitan counties. Church bodies whose members are disproportionately found in rural areas are Church of God, Baptist, Brethren, Disciples of Christ, and Mennonites. Other predominately rural religious groups are the Lutherans, Latter-Day Saints, Friends, Church of the Nazarene, and Evangelical United Brethren. Between these two types of religious bodies whose members are more often represented by either rural or urban people are the Congregationalists, Evangelical and Reform, Presbyterians, Assembly of God, and Adventists. Church membership has an ecological distribution which approaches the national average for the total population.

Many of the older church bodies, as contrasted with smaller sect groups, have lost membership in rural areas and gained it in urban areas as the nation has experienced a rapid population increase in its urban and suburban areas. In rural areas it appears that the smaller sect groups are growing more rapidly than the older church bodies. The differential growth between the church and sect bodies is integrally related to the type of urbanized social organization which has been advancing for the past several decades.

As churches have become oriented to urbanized social organization, standards have developed for college and seminary trained ministers and new types of specialized personnel, including directors of Christian education, ministers of music, psychological counselors, and welfare workers. Church organization has been expanded to include graded Sunday schools and organizations for men, women, youth, and students. Churches provide meeting facilities for scouting and other activities. They have educational and administrative buildings, as well as kitchen, dining hall, recreation, and lounge facilities—in addition to the traditional sanctuary for worship and for receiving the sacraments.

From one point of view, complex organization is the church's response to urbanized social organization. In order to sustain such a system of organization, the church must have larger congregations. The need for large memberships has prompted church federation, consolidation, and the closing of many small country churches. The more highly educated congregations require the services of college and seminary trained ministers, ministers of music, and directors of Christian education. Highly specialized personnel and complex organizations require a large number of people in proximity to the church. These conditions of church organization are consistent with urbanized society. The rapidly declining one-room country church was consistent with the ruralized social organization of the past.

RURAL CHURCH MOVEMENT

Religion in seventeenth century America was rural. Like other major social institutions in colonial and early national America, church organization manifested few if any real rural-urban differences. During the late eighteenth century and throughout most of the nineteenth century, rural-urban differences became pronounced in the area of religion, as in other major social institutions. From the origins of American society to the present day, ruralized social organization was subjected to many challenges. It faced a continual threat as aspects of industrialization and urbanism became more pervasive. Certain distinct differences appeared between rural and urban church organization in the nineteenth century, which were actually a byproduct of transition in the society rather than a result of differing ideologies of church organization.

The frontier church was a particular form of early rural religion in America. It produced a religious expression based on fear of enemies, starvation, and the elements. These fears led to hyperorthodoxy which resulted in a proliferation of cults and sects. The frontier religion was characterized by anti-intellectualism, emotionalism, and individualism.[4] The rural church was characterized by primary group memberships, familial atmosphere, and deep loyalty on the part of the members, many of whom were related to one another.

Rural churches were many in number and small in size. They were widely divided between church and sect types. Individualistic interpretations of the Bible partially contributed to the appearance of over 250 different religious bodies in the twentieth century. Many of the small rural churches were unable to support full-time ministers. The circuit system, whereby itinerant ministers traveled over the countryside and served a large number of churches, was a common phenomenon. Education of ministers varied, but it was not extensive for most of those who served the small rural churches. It seldom included either college or seminary training. Frontiersmen could not support the aristocratic theologies of Presbyterians and Congregationalists. Rather, their environment nurtured local and fundamentalist groups—in same cases the Baptists, Methodists, and Disciples.[5] These latter denominations were founded on individual responsibility, a democratic gospel of free grace, and a revivalist behavior. Early Baptists in particular opposed a salaried and educated ministry.[6]

The force of the rural church ebbed with the passing of the frontier, in a slow but inevitable fashion. The increasing urbanization of society was imminent. The following is a typical obituary:

Built in 1890's when its township had a population of about 600, the Sedalia (Missouri) Presbyterian Church was abandoned in the 1940's when the township had shrunk to a little over 400 and the countryside was dotted with deserted farmsteads. Since then the church has stood locked and empty upon a windswept hill, saved for the annual "Homecoming." . . . "I knew a peace here I have not known elsewhere," one elderly woman said at the last Sedalia Homecoming—and it is evidence of the church's place in the lives of its former communicants that one hundred and forty of them, some from neighboring states, returned for its annual gathering last September, a full decade after the church's closing.[7]

Town and country church departments. The rural church movement gained momentum after the Civil War. By the 1880's its organization was more precisely articulated, its problems well-defined, and its goals were rapidly being formed.[8] As with so many other aspects of rural organization, however, it was too late to preserve a distinctly rural type of church. The movement was largely the product of conflict, namely, that between urban and rural life. Organized rural church activity has served to strengthen rural-urban differences in the short run, but has not altered the long-run dominance of the urbanized church.

Between the 1880's and the Country Life Commission Report in 1909, discussion was generated concerning the plight of the rural church. Alarm was expressed at the alleged paganism among people in rural areas and the general decay of rural society. In 1910 the Presbyterian Church appointed the first head of a national rural church department. This has been viewed by some as the real inauguration of the rural church movement. From that time to the present, interest in the movement has increased. It has had the advantages of professional leadership and the development of specific programs, organizations, and outlook. Observation of a Rural Life Sunday was first initiated on a national basis in the 1930's. Similarly, the Lord's Acre Plan was given the support of a fully developed organization. Agricultural Missions Incorporated was founded during the 1930's. Other agencies and organizations which first appeared during the first half of the twentieth century included the American Country Life Association in 1919, the Interseminary Commission for Training for the Rural Ministry in New England in 1929, the Federal Council of Churches in 1931, the New England Town and Country Church Commission in 1931, the Christian Rural Fellowships in 1934, and in 1935, the Rural Church Institute, and the first State Christian Rural Fellowship in Iowa.[9]

The rural church movement reached its peak in the 1940's. Professional workers were employed widely. A full-time secretary for town and country church work was appointed in the organization of the National Council of Churches. An annual national convention on the church in town and country was established, along with a journal for communicating news of the movement, which was entitled *Town and Country Church*.

The American countryside was dotted with an excessive number of one-room churches at the time the rural church movement became organized. In several respects the rural church program was to have been their salvage effort. But urbanized social organization already had influenced American church organization. The urban church was characterized by large memberships, a highly trained, salaried ministry, large church sanctuaries, educational buildings, dining halls, recreation facilities, graded Sunday schools, and many specific organizational divisions. Practically none of these organizational programs could be supported in the small one-room country churches. Consolidation, federation, or abandonment loomed like storm clouds over the horizon of the once dramatic frontier rural church. None of the three has, in the course of time, proved acceptable to the several church bodies. The force of reality has been, therefore, all the more oppressive. Changes in rural life in general, and specifically in the location of rural people, have brought about the closing of more than 20,000 rural churches between 1930 and 1955.[10]

CHARACTERISTICS OF THE MINISTRY

Complaints have been made from many sources of an insufficient number of ministers and an even more insufficient number of potential ministerial recruits. Shortage of personnel has been a problem for several other professions in recent years; medical doctors, nurses, and teachers have not been recruited in adequate numbers. Many rural areas have developed specific financial support programs to encourage entrance into these professions. In the area of religion, those denominations which have most elevated their training requirements are the ones that experienced the greatest shortage of ministers. Felton writes:

The complex problems of the modern church require a well-trained ministry. Those denominations which are raising their educational entrance standards are suffering most from the shortage. One church reports that 26 per cent of its pastoral charges are without the ministry of members of conference and are being cared for by 'supplies.' Another large denomination reports that 45 per cent of its parishes are without regularly installed pastors, and 21 per cent are entirely pastorless. Two other large church groups each report over 1,000 vacant pulpits. A shortage of ministers, as well as of doctors and teachers, is felt most keenly in the rural areas.[11]

In 1948, Felton studied 1,978 ministerial students representing 20 major denominations and 57 theological seminaries. Of these ministerial students 34 per cent indicated that they were influenced to enter the ministry by their pastors, 17 per cent were influenced by their mothers, and 11 per cent by their fathers. There was a variety of other influences which represented under 10 per cent of the total.[12] When the ministerial students were asked about the area in which they desired to serve, 52.3 per cent selected towns of 2,500 to 25,000 population (see Table XXXIV). Over 83.5 per cent of the population at the time of this study

TABLE XXXIV. FIELDS OF SERVICE AS TO SIZE OR POPULATION DESIRED BY 88 MINIS-TERIAL STUDENTS, COMPARED WITH THEIR PLACE OF BIRTH, AND WITH THE POPULA-TION OF THE UNITED STATES

Fields	U.S. Population (1940)	Percentage Ministerial Students	
		Place of Birth	Field Desired
Rural (2,500 population and less)	43.5	33.0	28.6
Town (2,501 to 25,000 population)	16.5	31.0	52.3
City (25,001 and over)	40.0	36.0	19.1
	100.0	100.0	100.0

Source: Ralph A. Felton, *New Ministers* (Drew Theological Seminary, N.J., 1949), p. 18.

was centered in the rural community and the large city combined, but only 47.7 per cent of the ministry students desired to serve in the small or large areas. It was also found that rural areas were producing only 33 per cent of the ministerial students, though proportionate to their population their need was for over 43 per cent. Even of those students who were born in rural areas, only 28.6 per cent desired to return to rural locations.

The distribution of types of work desired by 1,400 ministerial students is reported in Table XXXV. Again, the town parish received some 26

TABLE XXXV. TYPE OF WORK DESIRED BY 1,482 MINISTERIAL STUDENTS

Types of Work	Percentage
A town parish	25.7
A rural parish	18.7
A city parish	13.7
Foreign missions	13.6
Teaching	12.1
Home missions	7.1
A suburban parish	6.2
An industrial parish	2.9
	100.0

Source: Ralph A. Felton, *New Ministers* (Drew Theological Seminary, N.J., 1949), p. 19.

per cent of the interest, and the 6 per cent who desired suburban parishes might well be included in that general middle-size city area. The open-country rural parish and large central city parish have far less attraction for ministerial students.

Some important characteristics of rural and small-town clergymen in the state of Missouri are reported by Hepple.[13] The majority of both rural and small-town ministers had lived in rural areas, but 26.2 per cent of the small-town ministers, compared to 16.5 per cent of the rural ministers, had spent the first eighteen years of their lives in villages. Town ministers had entered the clergy at an earlier age than had rural ministers. The "call" to preach was more precisely articulated by rural than urban ministers, even though their entry into the ministry was typically at a more mature age. The amount of formal training received by the small-town ministers was considerably greater than that of the rural ministers. Of the rural ministry, 42 per cent had less than college education, 33 per cent had not studied beyond the college level, and 25 per cent had received seminary training. Nearly half or 48 per cent of the urban ministers had received seminary training.

The practice of serving a multiple number of churches is declining as urbanized social organization increases. The Missouri study reported that 47 per cent of the rural ministers, compared to 76 per cent of the urban ministers, serve but one church. Further, it was found that rural ministers tend to be older than urban ministers and that only 42 per cent of the rural clergy worked full-time, while three-fourths of the urban clergy were classified as giving full-time service.

CHURCH ORGANIZATION

The number and complexity of church organizations are related to the size of the community and the size of the congregation. As congregations increase in number and are located in the larger cities, the labyrinth of specialization includes graded Sunday schools, choirs, men's and women's clubs, youth groups, missionary societies, and frequently scout troops. The most rapidly growing churches are those with the greatest number of organizations and facilities. Churches that do not have running water, central heating, and kitchen facilities generally decrease in membership over a period of time. By contrast, the congregations of churches with two or more such facilities generally increase in size.[14]

Sunday school has become the most common type of organization in the urbanized church.[15] In Pennsylvania it was found that more than 80 per cent of the town churches had regular choirs, but less than 40 per cent in the rural churches had such organizations.[16] Vacation church schools, weekday religious education, and lay leadership training classes were found to be more prevalent in the town than the country churches in Pennsylvania. Over 85 per cent of the open-country churches had no men's organizations, compared to only 35 per cent of the town churches. Women's work was more often organized in both rural and urban churches. Youth groups were not organized in some 40 per cent of the rural churches, and 15 per cent of the urban churches did not have such groups. Midweek services were reported in more than 50 per cent of the open-country churches, but in only 15 per cent of the urban churches.

Suburban churches. Churches have moved with the people, from farms and from cities into suburbs.[17] The supposed expansion of religion as a social institution is most readily apparent in suburbia. There one finds increases in the size of congregations, greater financial contributions to churches, and more new church buildings.[18] Many of the men who have been recruited into the clergy in recent years have been reared in suburban environments, and hence are imbued with suburban values. Finally, the impact of suburbia on churches is felt even in the urban churches, since many of their leaders reside in suburbs and commute to the city churches.

The social organization of both rural and urban churches is in the process of being modified to accommodate dominant suburban values. Put another way, the expression of urbanized social organization has come to characterize American churches everywhere and has brought with it the values of success and bigness, the traits of business, and hyperactivity. Prestige and competition enter into the social organization of the churches. Mobility, a part of urbanized social organization, is commonplace in the suburban church. Indeed, the transference of membership is facilitated by the churches themselves.

The suburban church is family centered. In this way the church has accommodated itself to the high birth rates in its new environment. This accommodation often takes the form of a great number of activities organized for all members of the family.

The religious orientation of the dynamic suburban churches partly expresses a success theme. Many of the new church members come from a nominally religious background and join nominally religious churches. The activism of suburban church culture does not necessarily express a depth of faith.[19]

Park and lakeside churches. Organized religion in rural areas is responding to the new and growing itinerant rural population. One of the manifestations of the churches' response to the vacationing itinerants has been the establishment of a program called "A Christian Ministry in the National Parks." For many years there were individual attempts on the part of some church bodies to provide worship services in open-country recreation areas. The effectiveness of such small programs was continuously subject to question. A well-organized interdenominational program was needed; accordingly, the National Council of Churches established such a program in 1952 under the guidance of an executive director. By the 1960's the Christian Ministry in the National Parks Program was staffed by over 150 student ministers and religious workers representing 23 denominations. The ministry program is organized in 29 national parks. In several parks the program is staffed by full-time ministers and operated on a year-round basis. In most of the parks, however, the program is operated only in the summer with a full schedule of choirs, classes, and services. These programs are organized to provide for both the vacationing itinerants and the resident park employees. It is anticipated that by the mid-1960's the national park ministry program will reach more than a million persons every year.

Most of the people who serve in the national parks ministry program are seminary students, college students, and music students. These students engage in a full-time work program in the parks, in addition to providing religious services.[20]

Ministers are also following the people into other open-country playground areas. This is illustrated by the example of "boat-in" church services on a Virginia lake. In this case the congregation's pews are boats belonging to the worshipers. The pulpit is built on a dock in the shape of a boat's prow. Services like these are attracting hundreds of persons in their vacationing environment.[21] These church programs are vivid examples of the impact of urbanized social organization on the institutions of religion.

SUMMARY

Religion in America is characterized by a plurality of church bodies, most of which represent some form of Christianity. Religious expression in rural America is predominantly Christian, strongly denominational, and often congregational.

The social space dominated by religion never has been extensive in the United States, despite the strong ideology of Puritanism. The frontier church was geographically dispersed, served by itinerant ministers, and colorful in its fundamentalism and mysticism. The proportion of the population reporting church affiliation, however, is larger in the middle of the twentieth century than it has ever been before in the recorded history of the nation. In rural areas, religion is overwhelmingly Protestant.

In the colonial and early national period, religion was rural because the total society was rural. By the nineteenth century, sharp rural-urban differences characterized church organization. A rural church movement that developed in the early part of the twentieth century was aimed at not only preserving but also strengthening the rural church.

While the rural church movement still exists, by the middle of the twentieth century common cultural universals which express urbanized social organization have come to dominate church organization in America. These cultural universals include a professional clergy, large congregations, graded Sunday schools, and a host of other specific organizations within the church.

The church has followed the population movement, from the farm and from the city into the suburbs. Likewise, the contemporary church is following its people into the parks and onto the lakes. The rural church of the twentieth century expresses the urbanized social organization of the nation.

NOTES

1. Benson Y. Landis, "Trends in Church Membership in the United States," *The Annals of the American Academy of Political and Social Science,* 332 (Nov., 1960), 1–8; see also Arthur R. Jones, Jr., "Aspects of the Career Pattern of Clergywomen: A Study in the Sociology of Professions" (unpublished Master's thesis, Louisiana State University, Baton Rouge, 1962).

2. Wilbur Zelinsky, "An Approach to the Religious Geography of the United States: Patterns of Church Membership in 1952," *Annals of the Association of American Geographers,* 51 (June, 1961), 139–93.

3. *Ibid.,* p. 150.

4. Joachim Wach, *Sociology of Religion* (Chicago: University of Chicago Press, 1944), p. 281.

5. Thomas F. Hoult, *The Sociology of Religion* (New York: The Dryden Press, 1958), p. 144.

6. *Loc. cit.*

7. Kenneth S. Davis, "The Challenge of the Country Church," *New York Times Magazine* (May 22, 1955), 26 ff.

8. Mark Rich, *The Rural Church Movement* (Columbia, Mo.: Juniper Knoll Press, 1957).

9. *Ibid.,* p. 215.

10. Davis, *op. cit.,* p. 26–7.

11. Ralph A. Felton, *New Ministers: A Study of 1,978 Ministerial Students to Determine the Factors Which Influence Men to Enter the Ministry* (Madison, N.J.: Drew Theological Seminary, Department of the Rural Church, 1949), p. 5.

12. *Ibid.,* p. 13; cf. Charles W. Glasgow, "Pre-Ministerial Students" (unpublished Master's thesis, Louisiana State University, Baton Rouge, 1963).

13. Lawrence M. Hepple, *The Church in Rural Missouri,* Part V, Rural-Urban Churches Compared (Missouri Agricultural Experiment Station Research Bulletin 633E, 1959).

14. A'Delbert Samson, *Church Groups in Four Agricultural Settings in Montana* (Montana Agricultural Experiment Station Bulletin 538, 1958).

15. Harold F. Kaufman, *Rural Churches in Kentucky, 1947* (Kentucky Agricultural Experiment Station Bulletin 530, 1949).

16. Lauris B. Whitman and William G. Mather, *The Rural Churches of Four Pennsylvania Counties* (Pennsylvania Agricultural Experiment Station Progress Report 76, 1952).

17. Shirley E. Greene, *Ferment on the Fringe* (Philadelphia: Christian Education Press, 1960).

18. Kenneth Miller, *Man and God in the City* (New York: Friendship Press, 1954).

19. Gibson Winter, "The Church in Suburban Captivity," *The Christian Century* (Sept. 28, 1955), 1112–14 and 1134.

20. *A Christian Ministry in the National Parks Offers You Opportunities Unlimited* (New York: National Council of Churches, 1961); "Worship in America's Wonderlands," *Presbyterian Life* (May 1, 1959), 20–22; "Job with a View," *Minneapolis Sunday Tribune* (Sept. 13, 1959), 12–14.

21. Jim Rutherford, "Preaching on the Water," *Presbyterian Survey* (June, 1962), 8–9.

SELECTED READINGS

Felton, Ralph H. *New Ministers.* Madison, N.J.: Department of Rural Church, Drew Theological Seminary, 1949.
　　Research report of a survey indicating the social origin of ministry students.

Hepple, Lawrence M. *The Church in Rural Missouri,* Part IV, Rural-Urban Churches Compared. Missouri Agricultural Experiment Station Research Bulletin 633E, 1959.
　　Part of a series that constitutes a nearly exhaustive description of the rural church in Missouri.

Kaufman, Harold F. *Rural Churches in Kentucky, 1947.* Kentucky Agricultural Experiment Station Bulletin 530, 1949.
　　This research was designed to describe the size and location of churches, the character of ministerial and lay leadership, and the types of services and programs.

Landis, Benson Y. "Trends in Church Membership in the United States," *The Annals of the American Academy of Political and Social Science,* 332 (Nov., 1960), 1–8.
　　A careful review of religious statistics.

Rich, Mark, *The Rural Church Movement.* Columbia, Mo.: Juniper Knoll Press, 1957.
　　Traces the origin, history, growth, and development of the rural church movement.

Samson, A, Delbert. *Church Groups in Four Agricultural Settings in Montana.* Montana Agricultural Experiment Station Bulletin 538, 1958.
　　This report places particular emphasis on church size, organizations, financing, and degree of fundamentalism.

Wach, Joachim, *Sociology of Religion.* Chicago: University of Chicago Press, 1944.
　　A comprehensive review of religion and society in comparative cultures.

Zelinsky, Wilbur. "An Approach to the Religious Geography of the United States: Patterns of Church Membership in 1952," *Annals of the Association of American Geographers,* 51 (June, 1961), 139–93.
　　A comprehensive analysis of the locations of members of various religious bodies, including an important series of maps.

21 LEVELS OF LIVING

Social structures for the production and distribution of goods and services are basic to all human societies. These normative patterns are known collectively as the economic institution of a society. When studied by economists, the productive capacity and monetary relationships of this institution are stressed. The sociological point of view, by contrast, emphasizes the human meaning and value of these relationships and, only secondarily, the monetary factors.

In the organization of human societies there have been both barter and money economies. The former may be considered representative of societies in low stages of development and the latter, of societies in high stages of development. But whether the setting is preliterate or advanced, rural or urban, the sociologists' concern continues to be more the meaning of the relationships than their particular content.

In the United States, the economic institution has shifted quickly from a trade and barter type to an advanced system of monetary and credit organization. In American society the social space devoted to the economic institution is greater than that of most other institutions. Frequently, therefore, the United States is characterized as materialistic. Concepts of advanced or underdeveloped societies are used in countries such as the United States, where the most accepted judgments of human well-being are made on the basis of the number of material objects possessed. In those terms a great accumulation of expensive items of consumption is believed to be an index of advanced economic accomplishment. The implications of such behavioral patterns are indicated in expressions such as *affluent society* and *conspicuous consumption.*

People in rural and urban areas of the United States once viewed economic accomplishment in different terms, but, as the society has become urbanized, conspicuous consumption is found in rural as well as in urban America. Business farmers desire the material conveniences found elsewhere in the nation. The rural nonfarm people desire open space but with all the urban conveniences. Consequently, rural-urban differences in economic achievement, as measured in terms of levels of living, are diminishing.

STANDARDS AND LEVELS OF LIVING

A clear differentiation must be made between levels and standards of living. In popular language, the concept of standard of living is used to the exclusion of level of living. Comparisons in levels of living are often glibly made between the United States, England, France, Germany, and other countries, usually ethnocentrically by individuals who summarize conditions in such a way as to find life in their own country superior to that in others. Aside from these popular uses, it is technically correct to refer first to levels of living. The concept of level of living refers to the actual material attainment of a society at a given time in terms of goods, services, and economic opportunities. The concept of standard of living refers to the goods, services, and opportunities the people of a given society desire to obtain. Standards of living reflect a people's values, and in most cases they are higher than, or in any event different from, the actually attained level of living. In societies characterized by urbanized social organization, levels of living are typically lower than standards of living. There is greater disparity between levels and standards of living in open class societies than in caste societies. Such measures and ideologies of material accomplishment are directly related to the success mechanisms of the open class societies.

The notion of a standard of living as a pattern of accomplishment distinct from a level of living implies the existence of social mechanisms for individual achievements. There must be the opportunity to move from one level to another. This is the experience of achievement or absence of achievement, the experience of success or failure. Under the relatively static conditions of a caste society, levels and standards of living should theoretically coincide. With the process of change from underdeveloped to developed societies, and as individuals obtain enough education to perceive alternative life situations, there is a greater disparity between levels and standards of living. In societies characterized by urbanized social organization, the distance between levels and standards of living is reduced. As great numbers of people in such societies become "haves" in contrast to "have-notes," the disparity between standards and levels of material existence refers more to conspicuous consumption patterns of behavior and less to real differences in the well-being of various groups.

Theoretically, there are other conditions associated with the disparity between levels of living and standards of living. This disparity provides a social environment for individualism and opportunity; however, there is an accompanying structural situation for maladjustment or *anomie* when the disparity becomes too great. In the environments of rural and urban America, the differential levels of living have been marked by high achievement among many urban families and low achievement among many rural families. Consequently, many members of the rural population experience maladjustment or *anomie,* as they seek to obtain a material level of existence equal to that of their urban neighbors or as they learn to adjust to a comparatively deprived situation.[1]

Farm wives have been particularly perturbed by the absence of many household conveniences which are widely used in urban homes.[2] Mass communication systems and mass social interaction extend the knowledge of these various household conveniences throughout the length and breadth of the land. Conflicts arise in farm families over the acquisition of technical machinery for the operation of the farm, the modernization of barns, and the expansion of the farming operation versus the improvement and modernization of the house. Immediately raising the farming operation to a higher technological and scientific competitive level might well increase the household facilities of the family in the long run. The competition for material gadgetry and conveniences, however, constitutes a strong pressure for short-range investments.

RURAL-URBAN DIFFERENCES IN LEVELS AND STANDARDS OF LIVING

Standard-of-living aspirations of rural and urban people are not vastly different. The actual experiences of rural and urban people in the utilization of such services as electricity, and the many accompanying electrical applicanes; telephone, and its many facilities for communication; and transportation in the utilization of both automobiles and trucks—all reveal few significant differences. There are few who reject such materialistic commodities and services in either urban or rural society. The most notorious of those few who do object to these materialistic items are members of subcultural groups, most of whom are rural, whose patterns of behavior and belief systems are not a function of their rural status. An example of a people who reject materialism is provided by the Amish. Except for the members of such subcultural groups, the pursuit of material objects appears to be as ardent among rural as it is among urban populations. When education and age are held constant, it is observed that the younger, better educated, rationalistic farmers are among the first in their areas to take advantage of material items. They are as avaricious in their use of material items as are their urban counterparts.

The quest for material possessions is an interactional, multidimensional behavioral experience. The historic rural values did not include a desire for material possessions but rather personal independence, closely knit family relationships, and pride in creative work. Such values, however, have not been a historic part of urban life. Accessibility to material goods and services has been a feature of cities since their inception, and it constitutes one of the social advantages of nuclear, as opposed to dispersed, residential patterns. Thus, an obsessive desire for—indeed, a value orientation to—the acquisition of material goods and services, has been attributed to urban people. For them the material items, in addition to performing other functions, have served as status symbols. The acquisitive nature of urban societies is not, however, their sole characteristic nor has material austerity been a constant feature of rural life. As material services were brought to the dispersed settlers of rural areas, they were widely accepted rather than rejected. In the nuclear and often congested settlement areas of the larger central cities, residents have sought to combine the values of open-country life with material acquisitiveness. Hence, the early trend to suburbanization, the acquisition of summer homes, the participation in day camping, and the experiences even of part-time farming—all provide examples of values of urban people which transcend those of material advancement.

The rural people's aspirations for the level-of-living services which are a part of urban life are illustrated by such specific programs as the bookmobile and public health service. People in rural areas, which historically have been extolled as conducive to good health, have not rejected but have supported the acquisition of health services. Similarly, the same rural areas in which the sentiment has been bandied about that "too much education will take the farm out of the boy," are the areas where, in the course of time, business farming has brought a value for books and literature. This is illustrated by school consolidation and bookmobile libraries.

Levels of living have historically been different for rural and urban people, and these differences still prevail in several respects. But, as in many other aspects of rural life described elsewhere in this book, the gap between the rural and urban levels of living is diminishing. At present increased efforts are being made to understand the reasons for the existence of the lower level of living of many rural people. After an understanding is reached, action programs may be developed. The goal of these programs is reduction of rural-urban differences by elevating the level of living of rural people. Rural area development programs and rural area administrations are specifically addessed to problems of this type.

Low-income rural areas. In spite of the declining differences between rural and urban levels of living, about one-third of the counties of the nation have low-income farm problems.[3] Most of the low-income farmers are in the small commercial farm categories or are not commercial farmers at all. Their contribution to meeting the nation's food and fiber needs is minimal. Many low-income farmers are more an integral part of a national social problem concerning low-income people than of the national farming enterprise.

The social problem rather than the farming aspect of this situation is seen in the repeated recommendations that low-income farm families need more opportunity for nonfarm employment, more education, and, finally, more capital and vocational training. Out-migration is recommended for a large segment of this population, particularly for the younger people.[4]

Low-income rural people are underemployed. By industrial standards, they utilize only two-thirds of their potential work time. Part-time farming, combined with industrial work, has been proposed as one means to let low-income rural people increase their work experience to full capacity.

REGIONAL VARIATIONS IN RURAL LEVEL OF LIVING

The greatest differences in levels of living are observed within the rural areas themselves, rather than between rural and urban areas.

Farm operator level-of-living index concept. Level-of-living indexes were first published in 1943.[5] However, studies of rural standards and levels of living have been conducted in the U.S. Department of Agriculture since the 1920's. The indexes, by definition,

> . . . are intended to reflect the average level of current consumption or utilization of goods and services . . . not merely a substitute for a measure of income or family-living expenditures. . . . The great variation present among families and individuals in the goods and services entering into their levels of living is averaged out.[6]

Criteria of the level-of-living index include the proportion of farms with electricity, telephones, automobiles, as well as the average value of farm products sold.

Level-of-living indexes.[7] The level-of-living index for the United States was 140 in 1954, as compared to 122 in 1950, and 100 in 1940. The most recent farm operator level-of-living index, of 1954, is higher than that for 1950. The average increase was 15 per cent. While gains were reported for all of the states of the nation, there were variations among states and regions. The Pacific Coast States, the Midwest Corn Belt States, and the Northeastern Seaboard States had the highest level-of-living indexes for farm operators. Only one of these three is a traditionally rural area. Agriculture is important in the other areas, but it is subordinated to nonagricultural enterprises.

In 1954, California, New Jersey, Connecticut, and Iowa were the states with the highest level-of-living indexes for farm operators. In rank order, it may be seen that the first three states are not typically rural. Of the four, only Iowa is a classic rural state. California, New Jersey, and Connecticut have in common a high degree of urbanization. Farm operators in these states, by virtue of their environment as well as their ideology, are more urbanized, scientific, and rationalistic than are the typical farm operators of the nation. Put another way, such reports indicate that, as farm operators come into more frequent social interaction with urban nonfarm people, they manifest more urbanized characteristics.

Counties were also ranked in 1954 according to their rural level-of-living indexes; these ranged from a high of 358 in Kern County, California, to a low of 44 in Lee County, Kentucky. Kern County is adjacent to Los Angeles County and also contains within its own boundary a large urban area. Lee County, by contrast, represents one of the most ruralized areas of the nation. Levels of living, then, are not a simple matter of a rural versus urban economy, because rural counties such as Kern in California have more in common with urban counties than with Lee County in Kentucky.

Level-of-living trends and patterns. Farm utilization and ownership of goods and services, such as electricity, telephones, automobiles, running water, mechanical refrigeration, television, and home freezers, have changed greatly over the past forty years.[8] This is illustrated by the similarity of the level-of-living index trends for all regions except the South. The national rural level-of-living index was 145 in 1956. In the Northeast it was 169, in the West 167, and in the North-Central States 165. The South alone was strikingly low with 119. This regional pattern and the trend since 1930 are indicated in Fig. 22.

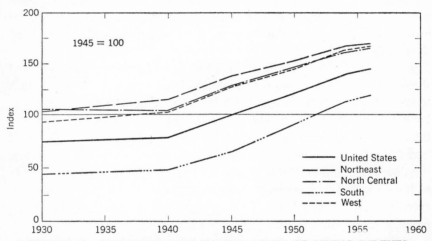

FIGURE 22. FARM OPERATOR FAMILY LEVEL–OF–LIVING INDEXES

Source: Alvin L. Bertrand, *Trends and Patterns in Levels-of-Living of Farm Families in the U.S.* (Washington, D.C.: U.S.D.A., Agricultural Marketing Service, Agricultural Information Bulletin 181, 1958), p. 8.

In 1920, only 7 per cent of the nation's farms reported the use of electricity. In 1956, electricity was utilized by 94 per cent of all farms, 97 per cent of the farms in the West and the North, and 91 per cent of the ones in the South.

The pattern of telephone communication among the nation's farms is far less dramatic than that for electricity. At times, progress in bringing telephones to rural people has been great; in other periods there has been a decline. In 1920, 39 per cent of the nation's farms reported the use of telephones; in 1930, 34 per cent; in 1940, 25 per cent; in 1945, 32 per cent; in 1950, 38 per cent; in 1954, 47 per cent, and in 1956, 52 per cent. Regional variation in telephone availability is far greater than for electricity. Of the Northern farms 73 per cent had telephone service, but of the Southern farms only 30 per cent were so equipped.

Mechanical refrigeration is second only to electricity in the high degree of its utilization. In the first decade of the second half of the twentieth century over 90 per cent of the nation's farms reported the use of mechanical refrigeration. Such refrigeration was available to about 10 per cent less of the Southern than the non-Southern farms, but its use was widespread throughout the nation. Automobiles were also prevalent, reportedly used by residents of more than three-quarters of the nation's farms. Nearly two-thirds of the nation's farms reported the use of running water, representing almost all the Western farms but only half the Southern farms. Television and home freezers were more recent technological arrivals, but about 50 and 40 per cent of the farms, respectively, reported their utilization.[9]

The greatest differences in the level-of-living items for the South and the West were in the proportion of telephones, automobiles, and flush toilets. For each of these the South lagged at least 23 percentage points behind the next highest region (see Fig. 23). The South lagged behind the rest of the nation for each index item reported. Farmers in the West lead the nation in proportion of mechanical refrigerators, home freezers, running water, and flush toilets, and are equal to the North in proportion of homes served by electricity. Compared to the rest of the nation, however, farmers in the North have more telephone service, more automobiles, more power washers, and more television.

When analyses are made within the North, it is observed that Northeast farmers generally have more facilities than those in the North-Central area. Similarly, when the South is divided into South Atlantic, East South-Central, and West South-Central, it is found that farmers in the West South-Central division have the highest level of living in the Southern region. Farmers in the South Atlantic division achieve intermediate levels of living, and those in the East South-Central the lowest level of living.

Variables related to level of living. When owners and part-owners are compared with renters, in terms of possession of level-of-living objects, it is discovered that operators who own their farms frequently possess and

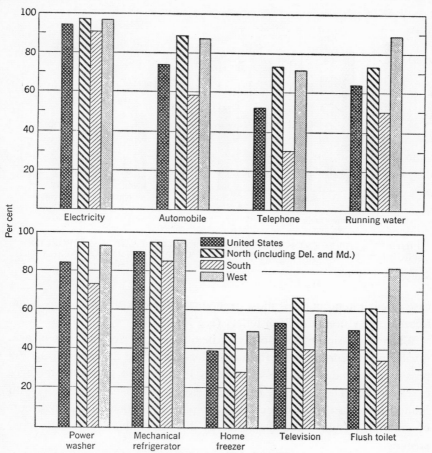

FIGURE 23.   REGIONAL VARIATIONS IN FACILITIES AND EQUIPMENT
REPORTED BY FARM–OPERATOR FAMILIES

Source: *Ibid.,* p. 11.

utilize more level-of-living items than do renters, in every case except that
of ownership of automobiles. Even for this one exception, however, the
difference between the two tenure categories is not great. The total level-
of-living index scores for these two major tenure categories are virtually
the same. This may be partly explained by the tendency for renters to be
on cash crop farms and thereby to receive relatively high values for
the products sold.[10]

The relationship between the education of farm operators and level
of living is traditional. As more education is obtained, the acquisition of
level-of-living index items also increases. The relationship obtains in the

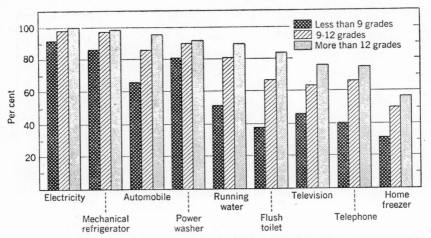

FIGURE 24. PERCENTAGE OF FARM OPERATOR FAMILIES REPORTING
SPECIFIED FACILITIES AND EQUIPMENT BY EDUCATION OF OPERATOR

Source: *Ibid.,* p. 16.

case of each item, but it is most pronounced for new items such as home
freezers, television, and flush toilets (see Fig. 24).

When possession of level-of-living items was analyzed in terms of age,
it was discovered that those farm operators under age 25 and over age 65
possessed the index items less frequently than operators between the ages
of 25 and 65. The two extreme age categories represented operators with
limited incomes. The former can be explained as due to the high cost
of entering farming, and the latter as due to gradual retirement from
farming.

Level of living is directly associated with the income of farm operators.
In 1956, farm operators with an income of $5,000 or more had a level-
of-living index of 167. This was the highest income category analyzed,
and its members had the highest level-of-living index. Conversely, farm
operators with less than $500 income, the lowest category studied, had
a level-of-living index of 119.

Specific case studies of the level-of-living experience of farm operators
typically corroborate the statistical analysis for the nation as a whole.[11]
Farmers in low level-of-living areas typically have less than average education, are characterized by age extremes, often report a disproportionate
burden of poor health, have larger families, and are located on farms with
little or no mechanization. The rural areas with low levels of living are
typically in locations most remote from large central cities. The human

relations in level-of-living situations are integral parts of the total social organization of the nation.

SUMMARY

The meaning of economic institutions in American rural life is reflected in the social structures associated with levels of living. Levels of living in rural areas have historically been lower than those in urban areas, but the gap is narrowing. The standards of living for both rural and urban Americans have been typically higher than the levels of living they achieved. As urbanized social organization has advanced, the meaning of economic acquisitions has come to be the same for all the national population.

At present there are greater differences among the levels of living attained by various regions of rural America than between rural and urban levels. National surveys and case-study research indicate that rural farm opeartors who are located closest to major urban areas typically have the highest level of living of all rural people. Farm operators who are better educated generally have higher levels of living.

The meaning of such level-of-living analysis is clear. The social structure and the social values for economic attainment are characteristically dominated by urbanized social organization throughout the nation. Those few rural areas in which people resist the dominant economic institutions of urbanized social organization are more characteristically subcultural islands than typical rural farm communities. In economic behavior, as in educational, religious, governmental, and other major institutional forms of behavior, historic rural-urban differences are being minimized and supplanted by urbanized cultural universals.

NOTES

1. Daniel E. Alleger, "Anomie: A Basis for Interpreting Attitudes in Low-Income Rural Areas." Paper presented at the 59th Annual Convention of the Association of Southern Agricultural Workers, Jacksonville, Florida, 1962.

2. Christine H. Hillman, *Factors Influencing the Lives of a Group of Young Farm Families* (Ohio Agricultural Experiment Station Research Bulletin 750, 1954).

3. *Development of Agriculture's Human Resources: A Report on Low-Income Farmers* (Washington: U.S. Department of Agriculture, 1955).

4. *Ibid.;* Nelson L. LeRay, *Employment and Underemployment of Rural People: Low-Income Groups in Arkansas, Maryland, and West Virginia* (Washington: Agri-

cultural Research Service, 43–109, U.S.D.A., 1959); Harold F. Kaufman, *Rural Families with Low Incomes: Problems in Adjustment* (Mississippi Agricultural Experiment Station, Sociology and Rural Life Series No. 9, 1957); Ronald Bird *et al.*, *Resources and Levels of Income of Farm and Rural Nonfarm Households* (Missouri Agricultural Experiment Station Research Bulletin 661, 1958).

5. Margaret J. Hagood *et al.*, *Farm-Operator Family Level-of-Living Indexes for Counties of the United States, 1945, 1950, and 1954* (Washington: U.S.D.A. Agricultural Marketing Service, Statistical Bulletin 204, 1957).

6. *Ibid.*, 97–8.

7. *Loc. cit.*

8. Alvin L. Bertrand, *Trends and Patterns in Level of Living of Farm Families in the U.S.* (Washington: Agricultural Marketing Service Information Bulletin 181, U.S.D.A., 1958).

9. Lee Taylor and Glenn Nelson, *Minnesota's People and Farms, 1950–1960* (Minnesota Agricultural Experiment Station, Miscellaneous Report 45, 1961).

10. Bertrand, *op. cit.*, p. 15.

11. Bird, *op. cit.*

SELECTED READINGS

Bertrand, Alvin L. *Trends and Patterns in Levels of Living of Farm Families in the U.S.* Washington: Agricultural Marketing Service Information Bulletin 181, U.S.D.A., 1958.

A report of farm-operator family expenditures, with comparisons between 1920 and 1956 indicating that farm operators have rapidly improved their level of living.

Bird, Ronald, *et al. Resources and Levels of Income of Farm and Rural Nonfarm Households in Eastern Ozarks of Missouri.* Missouri Agricultural Experiment Station Research Bulletin 661, 1958.

An empirical study of low-income farm families, who have constituted a major economic and social problem in Missouri.

Development of Agriculture's Human Resources: A Report on Problems of Low-Income Farmers. Washington: U.S. Department of Agriculture, 1955.

Describes the needs of low-income farm people and focuses special attention on young people.

Hillman, Christine H. *Factors Influencing the Lives of a Group of Young Farm Families.* Ohio Agricultural Experiment Station Research Bulletin 750, 1954.

A study of some of the primary economic and personal problems which influence young farm families, based on interviews with 150 families.

LeRay, Nelson L. *Employment and Underemployment of Rural People.* Washington: Agricultural Research Service 43–109, 1959.

A summary report of studies of low-income rural people in Arkansas, Maryland, and West Virginia.

22 GOVERNMENT, POLITICAL ORGANIZATION, AND IDEOLOGIES

The major characteristics of American rural government may be traced to the European Middle Ages. Many specific elements of government, vital to contemporary urbanized society, grew out of the ruralized society of the ninth and succeeding centuries in England and the Continent. Virtually all people in early America lived under local political and governmental forms often directly influenced by European precedents. Rural-urban differences in local government forms were few, if they existed at all, in early America. As the society became more complex and as urbanization expanded, the forms of local government were modified and new elements introduced. Many such modifications occurred in response to growing differences in rural and urban patterns of life. The strength and tenacity of local rural government patterns can be understood best in a clear historical perspective.

HISTORICAL DEVELOPMENT OF LOCAL GOVERNMENT

England. England contributed more to the basic structure of rural government in America than did any other country. The assimilation of the English social structure in the area of government into American society was essentially as extensive as that in the areas of family, religion, and economics. In the ninth century the various Anglo-Saxon provinces were united into the Kingdom of England. At that time the countryside was divided for governmental purposes into shires, hundreds, and townships.

Shires were the largest governmental areas. Each shire had a semi-annual court composed of representatives from the smaller units of government and from individual land owners. The administration of both civil and criminal justice was the responsibility of this court. Other affairs of business rested with three officials, namely the ealdorman, the shire reeve or sheriff, and the bishop.[1] The early English shire eventually became known as the county.

The hundred was a governmental unit smaller than the shire and usually consisted of several townships. In the hundred, justice was administered monthly by a court constituted of all landlords within its territory. Officials in the hundred were a deputy shire reeve, an elected hundred ealdor, and a committee of twelve senior thegns. The duties of this rural government were similar to those of the larger shire.

The township was the smallest unit of government and in several respects was more a social and economic than a political district. The township was a community of peasants in which local affairs were conducted by an assembly of the inhabitants. Both the township and the shire have endured from the ninth century to the present fundamentally in their original forms. Later, the change of name from shire to county did not signify a fundamental shift in the social structure. The chief officials were the town reeve, a tithingman, a constable, and four other men who represented the township in the court of the shire and the hundred.

Specific offices of the colonial local government, as well as forms of local government, also originated in the ninth and succeeding centuries. The American peace officer, sheriff, a position of fundamental importance in the modern county, originated in the ninth century as the Anglo-Saxon shire reeve.[2] After the Norman conquest in 1066, the power of this local officer expanded until finally he became the King's representative in military affairs. After this, the sheriff gradually lost prestige. The major role of the sheriff in contemporary America has been expropriated by the police in the cities. His role is now reduced in rural areas as a result of the increasing power of the state police.

The constable has an even longer lineage than the sheriff. His position, however, has been marked by a loss of status to the point of near extinction. This office can be traced to the high point of the Eastern Roman or Byzantine Empire, when the position of *comes stabuli,* or count of the stable, was of great significance.

The position of the coroner originates from the 1190's in England when he was a royal officer in a county or municipality. This was the acme in the development of this career. The position is now rapidly succumbing to the authority of the local medical or health officer. The lineage of county treasurers, comptrollers, and commissioners can be traced back to ancient France and, hence, to a Latin foundation. Similarly, the auditor generally has a French heritage. The financial condition of an individual was orally vouched for; hence the word *auditor,* from *audire* (to hear).

Many other lesser officers and minor social structures are rooted in a European past. In the assimilation of these positions and structures in the colonies and the new nation, there were specific changes of content but only minor changes in form.

America. Government in the American colonies was primarily English in origin. The Dutch, French, and Spanish colonials ultimately had very little enduring influence on the original thirteen colonies. In New England the town became the most important unit of local government, although the county existed from the outset. The New England town was a combination of both parish and manor. It was also a community of small land owners, typically members of a common Puritan congregation. Its organizational activities included both sacred and secular interests in the areas of schools, militia, business regulations, land recording, criminal and civil justice, care for the poor, and the assessment and collection of taxes. The democratic town meeting was central to its character. Officers were elected, but they were few in number.

In the Southern and Middle Atlantic colonies, the plantations and hundreds soon grew into vigorous county types of local organization. In 1634, Virginia County was divided into eight shires which ultimately became counties. In 1650 the first county emerged in Maryland. Thus, from the mid-point of the seventeenth century, counties ascended quickly into a position of dominance in all areas except New England.

Between the termination of the Revolution and the end of the eighteenth century, there was a trend in most states to decentralize governmental organization. This required strengthening local governments, which meant a growth in county governments and a dominance of county officials in most of the New England and some of the Middle Atlantic States. In some cases, county officials were elected at local levels, while in others they continued to be appointed at the state level. In either case, the county ruled as a strong local unit of government. As states developed west of the Mississippi River, patterns of local government continued to vary, yet the county remained dominant in each of them. The county's dominance has continued into the twentieth century and it still remains the strongest local unit. In recent decades, however, the force of urbanized mass society has come to circumvent local units, often even those of the county.

Special districts have rapidly achieved a position of vast importance in the government of both rural and urban America. Special district officials are not always elected locally, are not directly subject to the whim or desire of the people, and are subject to the pressure and demand of contractual mass society. The special district, as an aspect of local government, is a recent social invention. Thus, it stands in contrast to the antediluvian nature of the several other forms of local government.

The historic forms of local rural government are coming more and more into conflict with urbanized society. The history of local government in America is an expression of rugged individualism and, historically, has been an integral part of ruralized social organization. Both of these characteristics of social organization, namely, ruralized social organization and rugged individualism, were ideologies of an earlier period. These ideologies are no longer consistent in the order of urbanized society, and the new power structure of government, pressure groups, and special districts often serve as means of bypassing them. Counties have scarcely declined in number, yet their officials are generalists in an age of specialists. They are elected representatives of the people. They may be legitimizers in a local community, but they are always inadequate in urbanized social organization. Generalists as county officers are dependent upon the recommendations of specialists in making decisions and in guiding them in the directions in which decisions should be made. School teachers, welfare directors, and county agents, to name but a few, are specialists who come into a county area and on whom the local officials are dependent. These specialists, by the nature of their positions, maintain an identity with the urbanized society although their work is done in local communities. The qualifications and activities of the specialists are immeasurably beyond the control of the local generalists, the elected officials in the government. Appointment and dismissal of a specialist may be controlled at the local level, but the presence of specialists is made necessary by the nature of the vast urbanized society.[3]

CONTEMPORARY LOCAL GOVERNMENT

The nature and characteristics of a government, according to the census, are: organized entity, governmental character, and substantial autonomy. The manifestations of an organized entity include the possession of corporate powers, the right to sue and be sued, and the power of contract. The organized entity is typically listed as a municipal corporation, public corporation, or bodies corporate and politic. The second characteristic of government specifies officers who are popularly elected or appointed to represent the government. These officials have a high degree of responsibility to their public or constituents. The third characteristic of a government, substantial autonomy, connotes the government's fiscal and administrative independence. This autonomy implies the existence of a right on the part of the government to determine its own budget without review by higher orders. Administrative independence involves the freedom to select and determine the form of political organization.[4]

The number of local governments reported in the 1962 Census of Governments is recorded in Table XXXVI. The number of counties declined between 1952 and 1962 because of state legislation in Connecticut which eliminated the county government. One new county in Wisconsin was created during this decade. The total number of school districts declined greatly, reflecting the continued trend toward school consolidation. The other major change was the precipitous increase in the number

TABLE XXXVI. NUMBER OF GOVERNMENTAL UNITS BY TYPE OF GOVERNMENT, UNITED STATES: 1952–1962

Type of Government	1962	1957*	1952*
Total	91,236	102,392	116,807
U.S. Government	1	1	1
States	50	50	50
Local governments	91,185	102,341	116,756
Counties	3,043	3,050	3,052
Municipalities	17,997	17,215	16,807
Townships	17,144	17,198	17,202
School districts	34,678	50,454	67,355
Special districts	18,323	14,424	12,340

Source: *Government Units in 1962, Preliminary Report Number 7*, Census of Governments, Washington: U.S. Bureau of the Census, GC–P6, Dec. 6, 1962.

* Adjusted to include units in Alaska and Hawaii, which were reported separately prior to adoption of statehood for these areas in 1959.

of special districts, many of which are directly related to the natural resources of rural areas. The principal contemporary governmental units in rural areas are counties, special districts, school districts, municipalities, and townships.

County governments. The county government is the most significant form of political organization in contemporary rural America. Its complex power and duties are divided among an extensive list of individual administrators and a general advisory board whose members are usually known as county commissioners. The major officers of the county government include the clerk, sheriff, prosecutor, and treasurer. A county board usually consists of a small body of members, typically less than half a dozen. They are elected at large from the county or from districts into which the county is divided for that purpose.[5] The county board members are typically generalists rather than specialists. In the majority of rural counties, duties of the supervisors require only part of the incumbents' time. The supervisors' remuneration is equally small, usually a per diem for meeting days plus travel expenses. Members of the board of supervisors are usually prominent farmers, small tradesmen, county bankers, insurance and real estate dealers, physicians, and attorneys.

The power of the county board consists in managing and supervising the affairs of the local government. However, the local government is largely controlled by the county officers and outside experts who make reports to the county officers and the board of supervisors. Usually the board can do little more than appoint and accept resignations of officers and specialists. It can also grant all the necessary money which will promote or frustrate the policies of the officials and specialists, but this falls short of supervision. County boards do have power over the committees which they specifically appoint. The power of the state and of special districts invades the authority of the local county government in many respects; however, important policy questions remain which are primarily determined by the supervisors. Expenditures and contract awards are primarily controlled by the county supervisors. Since the development of the Federal Social Security Program in the 1930's, the county boards' control over social welfare activities has been substantially reduced. The county boards continue to supervise local elections, approve official bonds, and perform a variety of functions of this type.

Most county governments are independently organized, meaning they have little or no responsibility to cities within their boundaries. A few county governments are variously consolidated with city governments located in the county. In addition there are 42 independent cities located outside areas designated as counties. Some counties have no active government, exemplified by Rhode Island. The District of Columbia, Yellowstone National Park, and similar federal areas are without county designation.

Special rural districts. The number of special local district governments has increased in post-World War II years. This type of local government is designed to carry out a limited number of specific functions. The nature of the organization is such that special local districts are sometimes not under the direct control or supervision of local people. To this extent they contradict the ideology of local government and implement the ideology of urbanized social organization.

There are three major types of rural district governments. The first of these categories of government is designed to serve people in nonagricultural rural communities, and they often duplicate the services provided to urban fringe districts. The second category is concerned with rural communities as well as with people engaged in systematic agriculture. The third category is designed primarily to assist farm people in the improvement of agricultural lands.[6]

Special districts have come into existence to serve new societal needs. Their functions include activities such as sewage disposal, police protection, fire protection, library service, irrigation, conservation, and recreation. Several reasons are reported for the development and increase of rural districts. In some cases, city residents have objected to contributing taxes for services in rural areas which are available in cities. In other places, exemplified by the soil conservation districts, there has been promotional activity on the part of the national government. Finally, initiative has been taken on the part of rural inhabitants who have sought independent handling of certain aspects of their social organization.

Soil conservation districts. Soil conservation districts are one of the several outgrowths of the depression years of the 1930's. The erosion of soil and the reduction in general fertility became increasingly apparent over a period of years. The culmination of this concern was reached in 1935, when Congress established the Soil Conservation Service. The development of this agency was, simultaneously, an evolution of a new form of local government. The federal government's concern with soil conservation was broad. There was a keen recognition that systematic soil conservation activities could not be contained within arbitrary political boundaries of county units. Soil types and topography are not necessarily consistent with county political units. Consequently, even though the county is the most prominent existing local government unit, it is not suitable for this new government service.[7]

The new local government unit was implemented in the standard soil conservation district law of 1936. The national government influenced state legislatures to pass enabling acts for the establishment of soil conservation districts in local areas. By the late 1930's, soil conservation districts were established as a form of local government. In 1962, the Census of Governments reported 2,461 governments in the form of soil conservation districts.

The soil conservation district is an unusual governmental unit in rural America. It can come into existence through the initiative of a small number of landowners or land occupiers, with as few as ten to twenty individuals in some cases. These individuals must petition the state soil conservation committee, whose responsibility it is to examine all requests for district formation. The state committee, composed of government officials concerned with various technical aspects of conservation, determines by means of a public hearing the desirability of a proposal, passes on its merits, accepts or rejects the appropriateness of the boundaries and, if the proposal is approved in these aspects, submits it to the local people for vote.[8] The governing body of the district is composed of three elected and two appointed supervisors. The latter are, in most cases, appointed by the state committee.

Another major characteristic of soil conservation districts is that they interlock at many points with other governmental agencies. The Soil Conservation Service has received organizational and financial support from such agencies as the Agricultural Conservation Program and the Production and Marketing Administration.

The strength of the soil conservation program and the Soil Conservation Service can be estimated by several means. This program has made many contributions in reducing the destruction of the soil and water reserves that was so apparent in the 1930's. Most farms and the farmland of the nation are now within soil conservation districts. Acre-by-acre soil surveys have resulted in many benefits to farmers.

Despite its many achievements, this program has certain deficiencies. For example, most districts operate under voluntary or cooperative rather than mandatory power and authority. Originally it was planned that soil conservation districts should not conform to county boundaries. Instead, their boundaries were to be determined by topographical factors and watersheds. This principle, however, has not been effective. About half of the districts now conform to county boundaries, and an increasing proportion of the new districts are being organized within counties.[9] Soil conservation districts, as units of local government, are still new. Judgments concerning their merit must necessarily be tentative.[10]

Irrigation districts. Irrigation farming has become a major aspect of the agricultural enterprise in the Western part of the nation. Farming by artificial provision of water is often too costly to be provided by one individual farm owner or operator. The system of organized provision of water for irrigation, therefore, has been currently provided for by various groups and by government. Government programs which support irrigation are usually known as irrigation districts, water improvement districts, water conservation districts, and reclamation districts.[11] Regardless of their specific form, irrigation organizations constitute another example of specific types of rural district government. They are an integral part of urbanized social organization.* The very existence of special irrigation districts constitutes another index of business-oriented food and fiber production, in contrast to subsistence farming. Irrigation district governments involve a higher order of rationality, scientific inquiry, and application, and of ideologies for maximum attainment in market-oriented production.

The irrigation district idea first achieved the support of state legislation in California in 1887.[12] By the end of the nineteenth century the notion of irrigation districts had gained some general acceptance. Currently, the initiation of such districts comes from landowners, who may or may not be residents of the local area. In many states it is legally required that a majority of the landowners representing a specific proportion of the land acreage be required to support a petition requesting such a district before it is acted upon. It is a typical procedure for such a petition to be presented to the county governing body for a hearing. The state engineer and other specialists contribute technical information concerning proposed

---

* It should be noted that irrigation farming is indeed not new. It was well-known in the ancient societies of the Middle and Near East and continues to be used profitably in many of those areas. Irrigation per se is not an integral part of urbanized social organization, but the particular type of governmental support for this sort of agricultural enterprise is a part of the contemporary social invention of urbanized social organization.

sources and sufficiency of water. Finally, an affirmative vote by a simple majority of landowners is usually sufficient to create an irrigation district. Irrigation districts are allowed maximum independence in their specific planning and financial operation. Directors are elected to act as a governing board, consisting in most cases of three to seven members. It is commonplace for the county treasurer to handle and disburse funds for irrigation districts, but their elected directors are responsible for policy decisions. The key individual in most irrigation districts is the appointed chief engineer, who is usually the general manager. As a technical specialist, this individual is charged by the governing body with the responsibility for the direct supervision of the district.

Special irrigation districts typically lack the power to tax. The power of taxation is one of the major attributes of government, and the absence of it in this case illustrates the uniqueness of the operation. Sources of income are primarily from assessments and bond issues. In spite of the absence of the power of taxation, some of the irrigation districts are large compared with other local government units. For example:

The Imperial Irrigation District of California is among the twelve largest nonschool special districts in the United States. The exclusive supplier of water and power to the Imperial Valley and of power to the Coachella Valley, and the operator of the All-American Canal, the district has more than 1,000 employees and recently had a gross annual revenue of more than $10,000,000 from its irrigation and electric power divisions and its Mexican subsidiary.[13]

Both the national and state governments have made a profound impact on irrigation district activities. The Reclamation Act of 1902 provided the mechanism for the federal government's first major participation in support of irrigation matters. Congress has given the federal government additional legislation in succeeding years in support of irrigation districts.

The specific operation of irrigation districts has been marked by controversy. The decisions of the directors have an immediate and vital significance for the welfare of all participants. The organization of these districts provides the legal structure whereby directors can be removed from their offices. Removal of such directors is not an infrequent occurrence. In short, irrigation districts are significant forms of local government. Unlike many townships whose functions are declining, the operation of irrigation districts is vital. They illustrate the full importance of special districts in local American government.

Another special rural district government is that of the drainage district.

There are approximately 2,200 such districts or more than irrigation and soil conservation districts together. Rural fire protection districts are widespread. More states make this a function of special agents of government than a function of counties or townships. Enabling acts for these districts first came into existence in the late 1920's. By the mid-point of the twentieth century, these districts had rapidly increased to more than 300.[14] Weed eradication districts constitute still another example of new local rural governments. The task of enumerating these new governments is never-ending. Not only is their expansion commensurate with the growth of urbanized social organization, but these types of government are integral parts of the process of urbanization. They are action-oriented. They may not always be democratic in a classic sense, however, they are certainly not antidemocratic. The focus of their organization is more often oriented to the group, the society, and the larger human enterprise, and less to the rugged individualistic welfare of the individual.

Township government. Township governments are of ancient origin. They are fourth in number of local governments, involving 17,144 local units. They are predominantly located in the Northeast and North-Central parts of the nation and in a few places in the state of Washington.

Historically, the organization of the township has been democratic. It has had a closer and more sensitive relationship with the lives and interest of the people than other forms of local government. Ironically, however, this local unit of government has held the ideology of local control so tenaciously that it has failed to keep up with the times. It stands more as a relic exhibiting the tangible consequences of historical change. Except in New England, the township serves no vital functions for the local people which could not be as adequately or more adequately provided by larger units of government. Lancaster writes, "It has been kept alive largely by artificial respiration in its old years and lately by the stubborn inertia of vested interests." [15]

The major functions of township government in most parts of the country are the maintenance of minor roads and weed control. In some cases, the town meeting halls are used as recreation centers and often as places for voting. In practically all other respects the functions of township governments have atrophied.

Municipalities. In 1962, municipalities numbered 17,997 in the United States and were slightly more prevalent than townships. Municipalities are increasing while townships are decreasing. By definition, municipalities are incorporated places operating under laws determined by state legislatures. They are popularly considered to be the cities or urban places of the nation. In these instances they are forms of government *par excellence* which are nonrural. On the other hand, smaller cities far outnumber the large ones. More than half of the nation's municipalities have less than 1,000 people. Accordingly, their populations constitute a large proportion of rural nonfarm people. To this extent, such municipalities are in most cases very real units of local rural government.[16]

School districts. School districts have experienced the most precipitous decline of the various forms of local government. Between 1942 and 1962, the number of such districts declined from 108,000 to 34,678. School districts are often coterminous with towns or with counties. Numerically, they are the most common type of local government.

By the second half of the twentieth century, school districts had few of their former peculiarly rural characteristics. School systems are more and more often organized on a state basis and oriented to training and preparing the nation's youth to be functional and competitive citizens in urbanized social organization. As school consolidation becomes one of the most striking features of the open-country landscape, the rurality of the school district as a unit of local government declines.

MAJOR FUNCTIONS OF LOCAL RURAL GOVERNMENTS

Counties have fulfilled a primary function as local agencies of state and federal governments. County government has had considerable influence in the areas of law enforcement, tax assessment and collection, welfare administration, and the local administration of other state agencies.

Judicial functions of local rural governments can best be illustrated by the special county courts. These courts are usually presided over by an elected judge. In most cases, the judge's authority includes original jurisdiction over civil and criminal matters. The county court judge also has authority to hear appeals from justices of the peace and other minor magistrates. In other cases he is given power over probate matters. County courts, therefore, are often considered to be a midway category between general trial courts at the top and the justice of the peace at the bottom in the hierarchy of local court systems.

Probate courts are common at the county level. Their primary function is to probate wills and supervise the management and settlement of the estates of deceased persons.

Justices of the peace are the lowest level in the judicial hierarchy in rural America. They are usually elected by a popular ballot, but they may be appointed by governors. Their term of office is short, frequently four years or less. Their judicial functions are usually divided into three categories. First, they are concerned with the trial of civil cases where the fixed monetary amount is usually $300 or less. Second, they try minor criminal cases. The sentences imposed by justices of the peace are rigidly set by the constitutional laws and statutes. A third function of the justice of the peace is the holding of preliminary hearings in cases involving serious crimes. These officers of the court are more popularly known as the "marrying justices," a term which conveys their authority in cases of marriage.

Local law enforcement further includes the roles of the sheriff, constable, and coroner. The sheriff is one of the oldest officers of local county government. His duties include maintenance of the peace in his county, serving as an officer of the county court, and serving as keeper of the county jail. In several respects the position of the sheriff appears to be precarious in the struggle for survival. Now more crime takes place in rural areas as the work of criminals is facilitated by mass communication and mass transportation. Concomitant with this development has been the addition of new roles for state police, who now have jurisdiction in many rural areas once the domain of the sheriff. In some states, the state police have the right to enter towns as well as to patrol open-country areas.

The position of constable in a township is similar to that of the sheriff in the county. Constables, usually elected officials, are charged with the responsibility of maintaining peace. As officers of the justice of peace court, constables serve summonses, warrants, and subpoenas. Concerning these responsibilities, Sunderland writes:

Constables suffer from many of the same disqualifications as township justices. Individual constables, other than those serving in cities large enough to sustain a municipal court, do so little business that they acquire only the smallest amount of knowledge or skill as a result of experience. They have no organization, no central office, no system of records, no established procedure, no traditions regarding standards of performance. Their income from official activity is usually so small and irregular that it would rarely attract men of ability. Their large numbers and the restricted extent of their individual activities divide and dissipate public attention. This confers upon them a certain anonymity which tends to withdraw their activities from public criticism.[17]

The position of coroner in the local government often has been filled by individuals with minimum qualifications. In urbanized society the alternative to the position of coroner is often that of the medical examiner. In similar ways, other aspects of the social structure of local rural government are either being modified or are atrophying in the face of broad demands for change.

Rural roads. Mobility is a long-standing characteristic of the behavior of Americans. Roadways were the subject of concern even in the days of the horsedrawn carriage or the "spring-wagon." By the end of the nineteenth century, most rural roadways in the United States were still dirt roads, simply graded and locally controlled. All-weather roads were usually constructed of gravel or crushed stone.[18] The trend toward improved roads began in the early 1800's, but the great change came with the advent of the automobile in the early 1900's. The new emphasis on improved highways was an integral process in the urbanization of society; for example, it was related to the consolidating of school districts and, by midcentury, to the transporting of more than 6,000,000 school children in 100,000 buses to 40,000 schools. In like manner about 40,000 rural mail carriers traveled more than 1,500,000 miles in rural areas to provide regular mail service. Three-fourths of the nation's livestock is now brought to stockyards by truck. Farmers themselves are highly mobile, and it is not uncommon for them to have replaced the weekly wagon trip to the nearest town with daily travel to nearby city shopping centers.

Rural roads are of vast importance to urban residents who use open-country areas for leisure and vacation trips. Better local roads have contributed to the improvement of health facilities for rural people. These roads have made urban medical facilities more accessible to them; further, the improved roads have made it possible to provide local medical public health units for rural areas. The bookmobile, too, extended its services because of improved road conditions.

Historically, local rural roads have been provided by township, county, and other local governments. The precedent for state aid was established in New Jersey in 1891. By 1917, all states had made some provision for financing road construction. The first federal aid to local road construction came in 1916, when the demand to "get the farmer out of the mud" reached a high point of intensity. In the various states, responsibility for road construction and upkeep may be made under state control, county control, township control, special districts, or any combination of these.

Providing rural roads in open-country America is still confounded to a great extent by waste and inefficiency, due to the authority of many units of local government which are too small to provide modern highway systems. In the nineteenth century, many townships and counties were capable of providing for simple dirt roads where maintenance machinery was usually of a horsedrawn type. Modern highway construction, by contrast, requires complex machinery as well as the services of highly trained engineers. Many of the local units of government are too small to employ the engineers and to purchase the needed equipment. At best they are forced to contract for these services, and at worst they are in a poor position to negotiate the most favorable contracts.[19]

By the middle of the twentieth century, a trend toward the centralization of control of local roads was developing. Centralization of control often involved the full transfer of highway functions from some local units of government to larger ones, the transfer of specific road managers from the jurisdiction of one small unit of government to larger ones, or the expansion of state administrative supervision of roads.

Local government support for health programs. Traditionally, it was believed that the health of Americans was better in rural than in urban areas. In the past there were several justifications for this notion, but at the present time health facilities for rural people are often inferior to those for urban people. In many rural areas there are single and multi-county local health units, and in some states, state health districts have been organized. Demands for increased public health responsibilities are growing. In short, as medical technology and urbanized social organization have expanded, the historic local governments are most often inadequate in size and resources to cope with the new developments. Hence, the special district or other kinds of administrative division become operative for local governments which have failed to meet the new demands.

Local governments and public welfare in rural America. From colonial times to the present, local government has played a significant role in American public welfare. In the nineteenth and early twentieth century, the county farm and the almshouse were familiar features on the landscapes of local areas. By contrast, care for criminals, infants, and defective persons has traditionally been a responsibility assumed by larger units of government, usually state or federal. After the depression years of the 1930's, however, the federal government in particular, and the state governments in several cases, came to dominate or substantially share in the support of the needy. By the middle of the twentieth century, the responsibility of local governments had shifted from almsgiving to primarily administering public assistance programs.[20]

School goals and local governments. State governments determine the unit of local authority that will control schools. In Delaware there is a statewide unit system. Fifteen other states use the county as the predominant system of school administration, nine use the township, and 23 employ school district systems. In most states, however, the systems of local control of schools are not mutually exclusive, and, therefore, multiple types of local control are found in the same state. Approximately half of the nation's school children still attend elementary and secondary schools in rural areas. The role of local governments in the provision of schools is, therefore, very important. Schools are the largest single capital investment of local governments.

The above, then, constitute the major functions of local governments. Few generalizations are warranted concerning them. The very essence of local control and democratic ideology allows and encourages extreme variation in the organization and function of local governments. Many additional functions are provided by local governments on a limited basis and in highly specific areas. New governmental functions are often integral parts of urbanized society and largely bypass local geographical areas. Such new units of government reflect the fact of contemporary social organization rather than the ideology of the land. The great majority of citizens are sufficiently mobile to bypass many local governments. That is, not only do local governments overlap in function, but also the daily life of the people requires interaction among multiple local government units. Both factors reduce the effectiveness of local governments for a mobile population.

POLITICAL ORGANIZATION

The county government is an important unit in political organization throughout most of rural America. In most areas the county is an arena for the election of its own officers. County officers are generally elected as part of the general state and national balloting. Even party lines play a role in county elections. In some states the county is also a unit of representation in the state legislature. Consequently, the county is the scene of many campaign activities for local, state, and federal delegates. It is often a proving ground for political ascendancy.[21]

By the middle of the twentieth century, party organization became circumscribed by state law and by party rules. There are several political structures contained in most county organizations. Typically, there is a committee for each area from which officers are elected as well as a committeeman for each voting district or precinct. In the state there are usually a central committee, congressional district committees, legislative district committees, county committees, and township committees.

The county committee ranks above the precinct committee in the organizational hierarchy and is one of the most active agencies in the political system. It is composed of precinct committeemen whose terms are generally from two to four years. The primary function of the county committee is the organization of the local campaign.[22]

The task of local voters is complicated in rural America by excessively long ballots. Rural political organization is eminently democratic in ideology, but local elections are often combined with state and federal elections, making the long list of candidates so cumbersome that it bewilders voters.

FARM PEOPLE AND POLITICS

The rural vote in America has long been a phantom threat and a subject of controversy. The decline of farm people has been so extensive in recent decades that, far from being a major group, farmers have become a fractional minority.[23] This precipitous decline of farmers suggests to some that the time is near when the farm vote will be too small to warrant concern. This may be a myopic judgment, however, in light of power politics. Systematic pressure from the farm bloc has been more effective than a large mass vote in times past.

Perhaps more significant than the decline in the number of farm people is their general absorption into urbanized social organization. The attitudes toward politics of progressive business farmers are often not perceptibly different from those of other major categories of citizens. Consequently, the most bitter opponents of much city legislation are certain city legislators who represent different interests and legislators from suburban areas.[24]

In general, the rural-urban differences in political attitudes are becoming less pronounced. As farms become mechanized and as rural farm and rural nonfarm people become absorbed into the general population, the cultural universals of the nation are more similarly interpreted. Differential rural-urban tolerance, according to the findings of a study by Stouffer,[25] is greatly influenced by the educational level of the respondent, although place of residence is still significant. As the level of education of rural people increases, rural-urban tolerance increases.

There is considerable evidence that legislative bodies in America have been greatly controlled by rural representatives and that rural people have had a disproportionate amount of representation in legislatures.[26] These inequities continue to be real in some cases, but it must be observed that the general urbanization of the nation is so advanced that it reduces the relevance of this factor. The one-time rural legislator is less an instrument of farm pressure and more an individual who represents the majority of open-country people. His constituents are rural nonfarm people. Hadwiger writes:

Farm forces in the Congress are divided, as the Farm Bureau is in fact divided, basically because of changes in the farm labor forces which have divided farmers themselves. Rural people and rural areas are losing their homogeneity. At the same time they are becoming a less significant feature in the political landscape. There is no longer any basis for describing the Congress as the representative of rural America. This is because of conflicting economic interests as well as the division among farm groups. It is because of the demise of the single-interest, one party district and the loss of exclusive advantage from seniority, and it is because the decline in the number of farmers within the total population is being followed inexorably by reduced numerical representation of rural areas within the Congress.[27]

IDEOLOGIES

Ideologies of government and of power structures have changed greatly in the past century and a half in the United States. The changes came about primarily because of an expanding geographical area and an ever growing population. The problems and challenges of organizing a society of over 179,000,000 people in 1960 are necessarily different from those of organizing a society of less than 4,000,000 at the time the nation was founded. The earlier ideologies of a forceful democracy remain as abstract sentiments. In the fact of daily social life, urbanized society at best requires that people elect representatives rather than represent themselves. This is not a negation of democracy; it is a modification aimed at making representative government more acceptable. Hence, one of the most rapidly growing forms of local government is that of the special district. Again, in ideology, its purpose is to strengthen and modify democracy and to make it continually more acceptable and functional in urbanized society. Large-scale organization, nevertheless, is the cradle of all large and mass societies. Political allegiance of masses of people to a large central government continues to require some sacrifice of the individual and some giving up of local decision-making, i.e., the recognition of the transcendence of the interest of the nation over the interest of the individual. It is this conflict between individual interest and the interest of the nation that must be observed in a study of the changes taking place in local rural governments.

Problems and prospects. Local governments are often characterized as too profuse, too small, too overlapping, and too inefficient. Consolidation is a recommendation that has come to be standard for rural life in urbanized society. There are patterns of school consolidation, church consolidation, increasing farm size (which most often means consolidaiton), and vertical and horizontal integration (both forms of consolidation). Consolidation is consistent with the shift in ideology focusing less on individuals and more on the greater society.

The consolidation of counties has been urged for decades by political scientists. In a few counties, in which major cities are located, consolidation has been achieved. This is exemplified by San Francisco, Denver, Baltimore, and St. Louis. Partial city-county consolidations are exemplified by Boston, New Orleans, New York City, and Baton Rouge. There is no record of rural county consolidation.[28]

The call for the abolition of townships has been repeated so often that it has become axiomatic. Authors of such requests view townships as units of government whose functions overlap with other units. Thus, the township is seen to be wasteful and too costly for the taxpayer's money and time and found to offer few benefits in return. Defense of the township is maintained on the basis that it constitutes a unit of government which is closest to the people. In this respect, it is a reality of democracy.

Urban affairs department proposals. Proposals for the creation of a department of urban affairs or a department of urbaculture are other examples of the changing ideologies. These proposals imply that a dichotomy obtains between rural and urban affairs. The proposal for a governmental unit to deal with human relations in a specific geographical area is largely inconsistent with the concept of urbanized social organization. Not only would such a government further the distinction between rural and urban life, but it would contribute to the even more precarious distinctions between urban and suburban and between urban and rural-urban fringe.[29]

SUMMARY

The primary experience of governmental organization in open-country rural America in the post-World War II years has been the emergent representation of both farm and nonfarm people. Rural government elements have had a vast range of variations. By the middle of the twentieth century, they have in several respects reverted to a condition similar to that of their origin. When the United States was a colonial society characterized by ruralized social organization, the rural or local governments were the governments of all the people, because all the people were fundamentally rural. In the nineteenth century, the rural-urban dichotomy was fully realized. At that time, rural and urban governmental activities were clearly separate and distinct. By the middle of the twentieth century, however, most of the content and configuration of social life in the United States has shifted from ruralized to urbanized social organization. As the society becomes more urbanized, the people must respond to the same cultural values. The functions of local government are no exception. Activities such as soil conservation, irrigation and weed control are primarily related to rural areas, while slum clearance, utility provision and parking facilities, are fundamentally related to urban areas. But even these well-chosen examples do not in fact imply a rural-urban dichotomy. Often the concern with weed control, soil conservation, and irrigation are prompted as much by rural nonfarm residents, suburbanites, or rural fringe people as by farm owners and operators themselves. Similarly, the problems of urban renewal and parking facilities are often initiated by, or in the interest of, the suburban residents who migrate regularly to and from the central cities and who, therefore, have an interest in such services and facilities.

The traditional forms of local government in the United States, namely, townships and counties, originated in Europe, specifically in England. They have endured to the present in so much the same form that they are often dysfuntional in an urbanized society. Due to their flexibility, many of their functions are being absorbed by special districts which hold less allegiance to the local governments and are more in alignment with the state and federal governments.

The shifts in balance between the traditional local government and the ever increasing special districts constitute a social organizational condition which illustrates the nature of change in political ideologies. These shifts point to a synthesis of the ideology of local control and the immediate need for urbanized cultural universals.

NOTES

1. Clyde F. Snider, *Local Government in Rural America* (New York: Appleton-Century-Crofts, Inc., 1957), pp. 3–10.

2. Harold F. Alderfer, *American Local Government and Administration* (New York: Macmillan Co., 1956), pp. 51–92.

3. Arthur J. Vidich and Joseph Bensman, *Small Town and Mass Society* (New York: Doubleday Anchor Books, 1960), see especially pp. 110–230; Robert Goldschmidt, *As You Sow* (New York: Harcourt, Brace and Co., 1947); Art Gallaher, Jr., *Plainville Fifteen Years Later* (New York: Columbia University Press, 1961).

4. *Governmental Units in 1962, Preliminary Report Number 6* (Washington: U.S. Bureau of the Census, Census of Governments, GC–P6, Dec. 6, 1962).

5. Lane W. Lancaster, *Government in Rural America* (New York: D. Van Nostrand Co., Inc., 1957), pp. 54–61.

6. John C. Bollens, *Special District Governments in the United States* (Berkeley: University of California Press, 1957), pp. 139–78.

7. *Soils and Men, Yearbook of Agriculture, 1938* (Washington: U.S. Department of Agriculture, 1938), p. 300.

8. Bollens, *op. cit.,* p. 160.

9. Charles M. Hardin, *The Politics of Agriculture* (Glencoe: The Free Press, 1952), p. 71.

10. W. Robert Parks, *Soil Conservation Districts in Action* (Ames: Iowa State College Press, 1952).

11. Bollens, *op. cit.,* pp. 141–2; U.S. Census of Agriculture: 1950, Vol. 3, *Irrigation of Agricultural Lands* (Washington: U.S. Bureau of the Census, Agriculture Division, 1952), p. 3.

12. Wells A. Hutchins, *Irrigation Districts: Their Organization, Operation and Financing* (Washington: U.S. Department of Agriculture, Technical Bulletin No. 254, 1931), pp. 70–71.

13. Bollens, *op. cit.*, pp. 150–51.

14. *Ibid.*, p. 173.

15. Lancaster, *op. cit.*, p. 62.

16. Alderfer, *op. cit.*, p. 5.

17. Edson R. Sunderland, "A Study of Justices of the Peace and Other Minor Courts —Requisites for an Adequate State-Wide Minor Court System," *Fifteenth Annual Report of the Judicial Council of Michigan*, Part 2 (Lansing, Michigan, 1945), p. 112.

18. *Highways in the United States* (Washington: Bureau of Public Roads, Government Printing Office, 1951).

19. Clyde F. Snider, "The Twilight of the Township," *National Municipal Review*, 41 (Sept., 1952), 390–96.

20. Snider, *op. cit.*, p. 407.

21. Charles E. Merriam and Harold F. Gosnell, *The American Party System*, fourth edition (New York: Macmillan and Co., 1949), pp. 192–3.

22. Leon Weaver, "Some Soundings in the Party System: Rural Precinct Committee Men," *American Political Science Review*, 34 (Feb., 1940), 76–84.

23. Don F. Hadwiger, "Political Aspects of Changes in Farm Labor Force" in *Labor Mobility and Population in Agriculture* (Ames: Iowa State University Press, 1961).

24. David R. Derge, "Metropolitan and Outstate Alignments in Illinois and Missouri Legislative Delegations," *American Political Science Review*, 52 (Dec., 1958), 1051–65.

25. Samuel A. Stouffer, *Communism, Conformity, and Civil Liberties* (New York: Doubleday and Co., Inc., 1955), pp. 109–30.

26. Gordon E. Baker, *Rural Versus Urban Political Power* (New York: Doubleday and Co., Inc., 1955).

27. Hadwiger, *op. cit.*, p. 66.

28. Snider, *op. cit.*, pp. 533–5.

29. Robert H. Connery and Richard H. Leach, *The Federal Government and Metropolitan Areas* (Cambridge: Harvard University Press, 1960), pp. 164–93.

SELECTED READINGS

Alderfer, Harold F. *American Local Government and Administration*. New York: Macmillan Co., 1956.

A comprehensive description of the entire range of local governments in the United States.

Baker, Gordon E. *Rural Versus Urban Political Power*. New York: Doubleday and Co., Inc., 1955.

This brief monograph traces the rural heritage and theory of equal representation, and describes the rural-urban imbalance in state legislatures.

Bollens, John C. *Special District Governments in the United States*. Berkeley: University of California Press, 1957.

Chapter Five traces the general development of rural districts, with special attention to such important districts as irrigation, conservation, drainage, and fire protection.

Lancaster, Lane W. *Government in Rural America*. New York: D. Van Nostrand Co., Inc., 1957.

A general description of local government in America, with special emphasis on the increased role of state and federal governments.

Parks, W. Robert. *Soil Conservation Districts in Action*. Ames: Iowa State College Press, 1952.

A detailed study of the soil conservation district as a unique administrative device—its origin, role, and prospects for the future.

Snider, Clyde F. *Local Government in Rural America*. New York: Appleton-Century-Crofts, Inc., 1957.

A substantial general study of American rural governments.

23 HEALTH AND WELFARE PROVISIONS AND IDEOLOGIES

Health has been a long-standing major social value in the United States. It is a principal dimension of the American concept of democracy, which includes the belief that human life is valuable and that all citizens should enjoy well-being. The universal value placed upon health is based upon humanitarianism. Few societies have exceeded the United States in the high value placed on health.

In an urbanized society, health is a sign of status as well as a physical value. Visiting one's physician, dentist, or optometrist is often ritualized and a matter of prestige as well as a matter of immediate need. Another secular feature is that membership in voluntary health organizations is often viewed as an effort to secure economic rather than sickness protection.

The high value placed on health and medicine is one index of the advanced condition of urbanized social organization. In urbanized society a premium is placed on scientific knowledge and values. It is everywhere apparent that the high priests of the body far exceed the high priests of the intellect or the soul in prestige and remunerative rewards in contemporary America. Medical personnel are city-oriented and city-generated. The greatest medical centers and the complex of medical facilities are, by definition, urban phenomena.

The values placed upon health and medicine do not exist in a vacuum but are integrated with a whole set of other values. From one point of view it may be said that the reward to society for the conquest of infec-

452

tious diseases is the proliferation of chronic disorders that bring great economic devastation. Societies characterized by urbanized social organization have an increasing incidence of mental illness. However, it must be acknowledged that the higher incidence of chronic disease and mental and gerontological disorders are partly a function of more extensive diagnoses and reporting procedures. One also observes that the excessive attention devoted to medicine, more than any other factor, has contributed to the condition and problem of gerontology.

A study of health and welfare in urbanized social organization is most enlightening to the student of society. These institutions exemplify the paradox of a people who, on the one hand, receive better medical care and experience longer and healthier lives than ever before, but who are, on the other hand, challenged by the growing problems of gerontology.

HISTORICAL DEVELOPMENTS OF HEALTH PROVISIONS

Since the termination of home remedy medicines in the time of ruralized social organization, American health care—both rural and urban—has been primarily organized as a function of private enterprise. Government has had some interest in health care, but until early in the twentieth century its provisions were dwarfed by those of private enterprise.

As early as 1797, local health boards were reported in Massachusetts.[1] Such boards developed rapidly during the nineteenth century until virtually all towns and villages had some health provisions. Rural areas were served through township and county health organizations. The organization and authority of these early health boards were often more nominal than real, their function little more than establishment of quarantines in the face of threats of communicable diseases. Their personnel were most often appointed on a part-time basis. Frequently they were laymen rather than professional physicians.[2]

In 1912 the first rural county health department was established on a full-time basis in Robeson County, South Carolina.[3] From this beginning, county health departments have expanded their domain to encompass the services of full-time medical directors, as well as nurses, sanitation engineers, and appropriate clerical personnel, in each local area.

Scientific knowledge in the area of health and medicine has resulted in an increase in the cost of medical care to a magnitude far beyond the resources of many townships and counties. Thus, there has been a movement for the development of multicounty health departments, or a cooperative organization of city and county health departments, and county and township health departments. By the 1950's, 34 states had permitted the establishment of multicounty health units, and another fifteen states had authorized the establishment of multicity and county departments or other cooperative arrangements.[4]

HEALTH AND RURALIZED SOCIAL ORGANIZATION

Mutual aid among friends, relatives, and neighbors has been extolled as the classic and appropriate way to provide for rural health needs.[5] Moreover, the natural rural environment has been praised for its healthful advantages. Death rates generally have been lower in rural than in urban America, but this difference has virtually vanished. As early as 1907 it was observed that:

Of all persons, the farmer should be best provided with healthy surroundings. He has room, sunlight, clean air, exercise, normal sleep,—blessings so indigenous that he does not know their value; he does not realize the necessity of giving attention to sanitary surroundings. There are no energetic boards of health to look over his premises. He is so separated that the neighbors do not complain. He has taken health for granted. His exercise is likely to be only work, and it may not develop his physique or contribute to the promotion of health. The number of crooked and bent persons on the farm is very great. The city man is likely to have a better carriage. Probably no persons are in greater need of physical training and setting-up than the farmer, to correct efforts of his daily occupation and to keep the body resistant and resilient.[6]

Conditions of health in early rural areas were left to the forces of nature more often than to the manipulations of men operating and inquiring within the frame of reference of science. Concern with sanitation, for example, was usually conspicuous by its absence. Typhoid was originally a rural disease and was ultimately combated by the systematic control of rural privies and other sources of pollution. Early rural schools were charged with the responsibility of inculcating the local people with a systematic understanding of the nature and propagation of diseases.

These conditions illustrate the very essence of a nascent urbanized social organization, in which systematic surveys and analyses of conditions have served to promote understanding among the people. The conditions attacked by programs growing out of urbanized social organization were:

So long as farmers empty slop and sewage about wells which contain their drinking water, dig wells in barnyards to be used alike by man and beast, maintain outdoor closets so vile and filthy as to stifle those using them, leave dead animals to rot unburied near dwellings, encourage conditions which breed germ transmitting flies by the millions, defy laws of air space and ventilation in homes and school buildings alike, there is ample confirmation of the assertion that our rural schools should give instruction in these subjects.[7]

Even in their inception, health norms in the ruralized social organization of the United States were changing. The scientific investigation of man's physical condition and the sanitary conditions of his environment were already germane to the society before the national period. The ideological virtues of healthful living in rural America made for colorful oratory, but scientific medical facilities were desirable from the outset.

HEALTH AND URBANIZED SOCIAL ORGANIZATION

Health care in urbanized society has a number of dimensions. These include rigorously trained and highly specialized medical personnel, the ready availability of medication, and physical facilities including hospitals, clinics, and rest homes. Also included are socialization programs in the public schools to inculcate people with an understanding of the importance of medical care. These dimensions of health care cannot be realized for rural people by traditional mutual aid practices. Rural people face acceptance of the urbanized cultural universals, or being viewed as a social problem by the greater society.

The items of health care most frequently utilized by farm operators are reported in Fig. 25. In order of decreasing importance, they include the procurement of nonprescribed medications, use of physicians, use of prescribed drugs, dental care, health insurance, eye care, hospitals, and surgeons. There is considerable regional variation in the utilization of these health services. Farm operators in the West report most frequently the use of prescribed drugs, dental care, eye care, hospital utilization, and surgical utilization in that order. Farm operators in the North are most often reported as users of physicians and health insurance. The various health services are used slightly less frequently in the South than in the other regions.

Farm operators in 1955 reported expenses for health care to be the fifth most costly item in their family living. In rank order, health care was exceeded by outlays for housing, food, clothing, and transportation. Items which cost less than health care included recreation, gifts and contributions, personal insurance, personal care, tobacco and alcoholic bever-

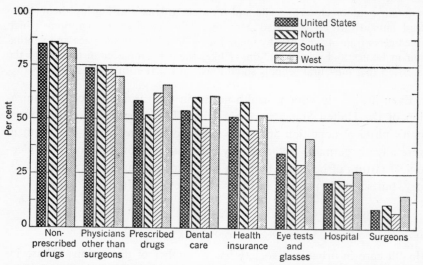

FIGURE 25. ITEMS OF HEALTH CARE MOST FREQUENTLY REPORTED
BY FARM–OPERATOR FAMILIES IN 1955

Source: Alvin L. Bertrand and Donald G. Hay, *Farmers' Expenditures for Health Care
in 1955* (Washington, D. C.: U.S.D.A., Agricultural Information Bulletin 191, 1958), p. 4.

ages, reading, and education.[8] The average cost of a farm family's
expenditures for health care in 1955 was some $240. The distribution of
this health care expenditure is illustrated in Fig. 26. Cost of the services
of physicians and surgeons constituted the greatest single item, 25 per
cent. Medications in the form of drugs and vitamins cost 18 per cent of
the total, health insurance another 18 per cent, hospital expenditures 13
per cent, dental care 11 per cent, eye care 5 per cent, and all other medical
expenditures 10 per cent.

Differential expenditure patterns are reported for farm families, by
socioeconomic characteristics. For example families on the larger commercial farms spend more money for health care. Those farm families in
the age category 35 to 54 years have the highest expenditure for health
care. As the level of living for farm families increases, the expenditures for
health care rise.[9] The health care cost of farm operator families, by
regions, is reported in Fig. 27. The trend is for the highest expenditures to
be found in the West, the lowest in the Southeast, and the middle-range
expenditures in Central and Northeastern states.

Medical personnel and facilities. Medical practitioners and facilities for
medical care are typically less prevalent in rural than in urban areas.

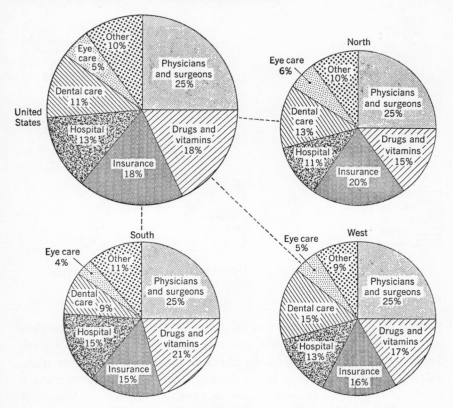

FIGURE 26. HOW FARM–OPERATOR FAMILIES SPENT THEIR
HEALTH DOLLARS IN 1955 (DIRECT EXPENDITURES ONLY)

Source: *Ibid.*, p. 7.

Rural people have a smaller number of doctors, dentists, nurses, and
hospital beds than urban people have. For example, in 1940 there was
one doctor for every 831 persons in the nation, but in rural areas, one for
every 1,700 people.[10] Similarly, in the metropolitan areas there was one
dentist for about every 1,300 people, while in rural areas one for every
4,000 persons. Less than 20 per cent of the nation's graduate trained
nurses were located in rural communities.[11] In 1960 there was one medical or other health worker for every 130 persons in the nation, but one
for 270 persons in rural farm areas.

A case study of the number and distribution of medical personnel in
Missouri revealed a decline in the number of physicians proportionate to
the population, and a shift in the location of physicians from rural to
urban areas.[12] In 1912, Missouri reported one physician for every 550

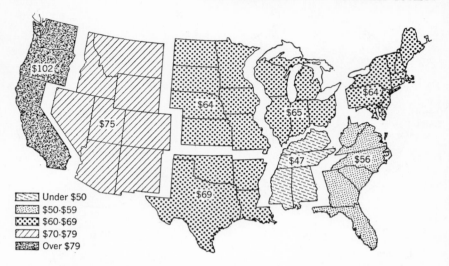

FIGURE 27.   WHAT HEALTH CARE COST EACH FARM–OPERATOR
FAMILY IN 1955

Source: *Ibid.*, p. 7.

persons. By 1950, there was one for each 779 persons. The smaller proportion of medical doctors was concentrated in the state's four metropolitan areas where there was one physician for every 544 persons. Outside these four metropolitan areas, there was only one medical doctor for
every 1,405 persons. Medical doctors had not typically moved their practice from smaller to larger centers but, as losses occurred through death
and retirement, there were few young men who established practices in
the smaller areas. Medical doctors chose to locate their offices in the
larger centers near major hospital facilities.

Changes in the distribution of medical doctors have been studied in
Oklahoma.[13] It was found that the total number of medical doctors has
declined. In 1909 there were 2,703, and in 1950 there were only 2,164.
There were 587 people per physician in 1909, but more than 1,000 in
1950. By 1950, Oklahoma's doctors tended to abandon the small towns
for the larger cities. In 1950, only 298 Oklahoma towns had doctors,
while there were another 235 towns without doctors. Over 600 places still
existed which had had a physician some time prior to 1950. The major
factors which were found to be associated with physicians' moving from
small towns to larger cities were changes in medical facilities, population
losses in small towns, loss of many traditional service functions by small
towns and villages, and preference of doctors to practice in towns similar

to those in which they were reared (most medical students had come from larger cities).

Rural public health departments have expanded their operations in such a way as to improve facilities for rural areas. Their services, however, remain inadequate. Rural communities have made considerable efforts to encourage young medical practitioners to practice there. Some communities contribute to the initial capital outlay for young practitioners. Others have engaged in fund raising to provide office facilities, clinic facilities, and a variety of other amenities to encourage young physicians to establish themselves in their area.[14] In New England, some towns offer direct cash subsidies to attract physicians. Their purpose is to guarantee a minimum annual income for the physician.[15] The arguments against rural location most often offered by young physicians are that they may wish to specialize, possible professional isolation, insufficient opportunity to consult with colleagues, and lack of opportunity to keep abreast of current developments in medicine.[16]

Health insurance programs. The history of public and private responsibility in the area of medical care began in England and was part of that great reservoir of culture which was ultimately transplanted to the New World. The Elizabethan Poor Laws of 1601 and the North American Social Security Act of 1935 can be cited as starting points for government participation.[17] By the 1960's in the United States, approximately 20 per cent of health expenditures were absorbed by the government, 20 per cent provided through voluntary health insurance, and 60 per cent paid directly by the general public.[18] Facilities such as tuberculosis sanitariums are almost exclusively provided by governments.

Voluntary health insurance programs have expanded rapidly. It was found in a 1953 survey that over 87 million people, or 57 per cent of the national population, subscribed to some form of hospital insurance. Seventy-four million or 48 per cent of the population had surgical and other medical insurance.[19] Rural-urban variations in enrollment in voluntary health insurance programs were great. Of the urban families, 70 per cent had some type of insurance, compared to only 45 per cent of rural farm families. Of the urban families, 63 per cent carried some form of hospital insurance, compared to only 38 per cent of rural farm families. Anderson explains part of this difference through the greater opportunity for group membership in urban types of employment, as contrasted with the individualizing and isolating situation of the self-employed farmer.

Voluntary hospital insurance programs had their origin in the United States in the eighteenth century. Their first major growth, however, came in the depression years of the 1930's. At that time the Blue Cross plans were established and commercial insurance companies expanded.[20] There are more than 700 commercial insurance companies in the United States that provide some form of health protection. There are more than 70 Blue Cross plans in the United States, each with its own separate region, separate rates, and specific benefits. Their territories are mutually exclusive, and the organizations do not compete with one another. Their coverage ranges from individual counties to entire states. They are supervised by a board of directors and operate as nonprofit organizations. Typically, they are supervised in their operation by some state agency. The attitude of the public has continually become more favorable to health insurance programs.[21]

Public welfare has been provided from the earliest times in America. Ideologically, its position has been second-rate; indeed, most often negative and degrading. At best, the need for public welfare was looked upon as a sign of poverty, and poverty was regarded as disgraceful. The social stigma applied to public welfare is apparent in such terms as "Pauper Laws," "Public Assistance Codes," "Needy Persons," "Poor Relief," "Overseers of the Poor," "Poor House," and "County Home."

Welfare organization is complex and directly related to the economic well-being of the society. For example, it is reported that certain Indian tribes in the United States, at the time of the arrival of white men, were so poor in material goods that they were unable to afford the luxury of sustaining their aged beyond that point in life where they were capable of producing for themselves. Accordingly, the aged were abandoned to die. This was not inhumane but most humane in such societies. In sharp contrast, the American society of the twentieth century has achieved an abundance of material production and combined this accomplishment with a strong value placed upon human life. Few crimes are more abhorrent to the American than euthanasia or "mercy-killing." The urbanized society has developed a cultural system which sustains the life of people into the upper years, far beyond their period of biological and social usefulness. Senility is still far from a state of grace but difficult to avoid in the so-called advanced societies of the Western world. It is a paradoxical price of progress in medicine and economic materialism. In essence, humanitarianism of urbanized social organization has created a Homo sapiens zoo and is filling it with an ever increasing number of specimens of "Homo senilitas." For those who fail to study the chronicles of history, welfare for the aged and the infirm is viewed as a mark of progress. Gerontological homes are a status symbol for the affluent and successful. For the student of history, their form is different from the poor house, the almshouse, and the earlier varieties of public assistance, although their meaning has remained constant throughout history.

WELFARE AND RESPONSIBILITY AMONG SOCIAL CLASSES

In the ruralized society of colonial and early America, rugged individualism prevailed. Part of the price of organizing large masses of people is the forfeiture of much of this individualism. The broad national unity has sustained notions of prestige, success, and egoism, while initiative and competition continue to be rewarded. Individuals who achieve dramatic success are culture heroes. Such a system of social organization which produces many successful persons also produces many more who are failures. The failures and near-failures or the less successful are not forgotten. They are often viewed as a blemish on the social landscape.

Among the urbanized societies of the world, where statistics are widely gathered and comparatively analyzed, success is more than a matter of individual achievement; it is a matter of group achievement or national pride. Hence one of the greatest frustrations of Western societies is to have visiting dignitaries from another society produce statistics to support an argument that health, housing, transportation, and welfare provisions are better in some other country. Such a criticism supported by comparative statistical analysis usually prompts action programs. These programs, in effect, mean that one social class or category of people in the society will assume considerable responsibility for those in another social class or category. Hence, there are numerous action programs in the United States aimed at upgrading the conditions of low-income farm people.

The responsibility of social classes to each other may be less a matter of respect and opportunity and more a matter of national prestige. Much of the concept of developed and underdeveloped countries, of "have" and "have-not" countries, of industrial and nonindustrial nations, in fact constitute differential statements concerning the welfare of men. The considerations of human welfare appear basic, but their content may vary from humanism to prestige in comparative statistics. Provisions for welfare may range from abandonment of the indigent among preliterates to the extension of life into senility among advanced societies.

WELFARE IN RURALIZED SOCIAL ORGANIZATION

Rural people receive less welfare than urban people. It has been pointed out to confirm this rural-urban difference that pauperism and poverty were more extensive in cities than in the country. Persons dependent upon public relief have been found more often in cities than in the country.[22]

Two types of relief systems have been used to provide for dependent persons. One is to place them in institutions and thereby separate them from their families. This system is illustrated by the use of the county farm or the almshouse. The second system is to provide relief directly to family units. This latter type is often referred to as outdoor assistance, the former as indoor assistance. A stigma has been attached to the almshouse, poor house, poor farm, infirmary, poor asylum—all names for the same institution. In recent years there has been some trend toward removing the stigma which applies to them. One measure was the renaming of these indoor assistance units as county homes, rest homes, or sunset homes. Such nomenclature is assumed to be less offensive.[23]

In most cases, almshouses are operated by county governments. In the states of Delaware, New Mexico, Maryland, Michigan, Rhode Island, West Virginia, and Wyoming there are substantial state programs which supplement or supersede the county type of almshouse. In New England the so-called county almshouses are operated by the towns. The physical facilities of the almshouses have been poor and inadequate. Frequently the provisions have been equal in amount for men and women, regardless of the fact that the male population in such institutions is usually greater than the female population. Lighting and ventilation have been inadequate. Special facilities for health care are generally nonexistent. Medical service is usually provided on a very limited basis by county physicians. In conjunction with the almshouse there has been the county farm on which there is in some cases excess production for market sales. The superintendent of this almshouse is typically appointed by the county board of supervisors. Traditionally, this individual has been a local farmer, and his wife has served as the matron, neither usually trained in social welfare. The population of the county almshouse has traditionally been heterogeneous to the point of making systematic provision for the inmates nearly impossible. These populations have included both old and young, able-bodied and sick, the mentally normal and the mentally disturbed, along with a variety of other unique cases. But most of the inmates were the infirm, afflicted, feeble-minded, and those suffering many other deficiencies.

The development of the social security program has contributed greatly to the reduction of inmates in county almshouses and, in some cases, to the closing of such institutions. The decline, however, has not been as precipitous as was anticipated, due primarily to the large numbers of inmates in almshouses who suffered from chronic diseases and who needed continuous nursing service.[24]

Conditions in the county almshouses have improved greatly, but they are still often unsatisfactory in the judgments of modern social welfare workers. The general improvement has been due to an effort to reduce heterogeneity in the population by the removal of children to special children's homes, the removal of the insane and feeble-minded to institutions organized specifically for their care, and, finally, the retaining of the almshouse principally as a home for the aged. There have been considerable advances in improving the physical facilities of these local institutions. Some of the newer institutions are organized in terms of a cottage system.

The county nursing home is coming to be more widely used, and in many cases it replaces the almshouse. It was given great impetus in 1950, when the Social Security Act was amended to provide federal grants for aid to the permanently and totally disabled. States having the largest number of nursing homes are California, Illinois, Michigan, New York, and Wisconsin.[25] County nursing homes are licensed and supervised, but their facilities and provisions are far from standard. Their development is still too recent to have allowed for stable normative patterns.

WELFARE IN URBANIZED SOCIAL ORGANIZATION

The most dramatic instrument of social welfare in urbanized society was the Social Security Act of 1935. This act gave governmental sanction to the provision of welfare services, making them an integral part of the society. The precursors of the program were many. However, it largely grew out of the traumatic depression experience of the 1930's. In effect, it put aside as outdated the earlier doctrines of individualism and private welfare provision. The new doctrine was that government should assume at least a minimum of responsibility for all people in the areas of welfare provision. The premise was that individuals and families were unable to provide systematically for themselves without group support.[26] The original act in 1935 provided multiple services, but the principal aid was old-age insurance for industrial workers. It was expanded in 1939 to provide benefits for dependents and survivors of the insured workers. In 1950 the program was broadened again to include some farm workers and domestic employees and many nonfarm self-employed persons. Again, in 1954 the program's coverage was extended to self-employed farmers and more hired farm workers.[27] In more recent years there have been continued amendments to expand the program, some of which include cash and share farm renters.

The old-age survivors and disability insurance is fundamentally a program of family group insurance, organized and operated by government. Workers pay premiums, as it were, during their productive years. In return, protection is provided for disability. This is of vital importance for the young farm families. To older farmers the retirement benefit comes to be of primary importance in their declining years. The program is now compulsory for farmers and farm landlords, and for hired farm workers whose earnings are sufficiently great to meet the requirements of the law. The four major types of benefits which are provided by old-age survivor and disability insurance include monthly retirement payments, survivor payments to dependents, disability payments, and lump sum payments in the case of the death of the insured.

Since 1955, farm operators who make a profit of $400 or more in a single year are covered by Social Security and accordingly required to pay Social Security tax. Farm landlords who "participate materially" in the production of crops and livestock, or the management of farms, are covered by and required to participate in the program. Hired farm and farm household workers are covered by Social Security if they receive cash payment of $100 in a calendar year, even if the work is not regular. To be eligible, however, the hired worker must have the minimum of $100 from one employer rather than from multiple employers. The impact of the 1954–56 amendments to the Social Security Act, which extended coverage to any category of farm work, is not yet fully known. Major social structural considerations include the possibility that farmers may retire earlier, that they may sell their farms earlier, and that such a provision may influence the value of farm lands.

A study of farm retirement in Minnesota revealed that the normative age for leaving farm work was between 62 and 70. Ill health was most frequently reported as the reason for retirement, and increasing age second-most frequently. Retired farmers generally supported themselves on rent from their farms, small chicken farming operations, or income from the sale of their farms. Half of the Minnesota farmers studied had either sold or rented their farms. In most cases, the sale or renting of the farm was to one of their own children. Only about 12 per cent of the retired farmers were unable to finance their own retirement and, hence, were forced to rely on pensions or relatives. During less prosperous years, however, it may well be anticipated that the number of farmers able to provide their own full retirement might have been fewer.[28]

Adjustment to retirement was studied in six rural counties in New York State in the early 1950's. The primary aim of the investigation was to evaluate the widely held assumption that aging in rural areas was less traumatic and problematic than in urban areas. Accordingly, the sample included both farm and nonfarm people, retired and nonretired respondents. It was found that rural as well as urban groups sustained economic decline as a part of their retirement. Over half of the retired persons were forced to curtail their expenditures and to make other adjustments related to less income. Social Security played an important part in the retirement program of the nonfarm individuals. The farmers, by contrast, were occupationally active for a longer period of time than the nonfarmers. Desire for more leisure time was offered as a reason for retirement more frequently by nonfarm than farm respondents. Indeed, the farmers were more reluctant to retire and often viewed retirement as in basic conflict with their strong value orientation toward being useful in life. Nevertheless, in spite of this conflict in ideologies it was found that farmers ultimately adjusted more amiably to retirement than did nonfarmers. A plausible explanation for the better retirement adjustment of the farmer may be found in the normative structure of retirement in rural areas. This includes a gradual reduction of the number of hours worked per week, continual work beyond the years of normal retirement, and the better financial situation of farmers as compared to nonfarmers.[29]

SUMMARY

Health has been a long-standing value in American society. As urbanized social organization has advanced, scientific medical technology and facilities have been desired by both rural and urban people. Health boards have been established in rural as well as urban areas. The cost of providing modern medical facilities is great, and many local townships and county governments have had to organize cooperative health units to meet their needs.

Health care items most frequently used by rural people are nonprescribed drugs, physicians, prescribed drugs, dental care, and health insurance. Health care costs in 1955 were highest for farm operator families in the Pacific Coast States, Mountain States, and Southwest States, and lowest in the South-Central States.

Medical personnel are disproportionately found in the larger population centers. This concentration of medical doctors is related to factors ranging from accessibility of hospital facilities to their personal desires to live in a larger place. To attract physicians, many rural areas are now offering clinics, office space, and other inducements.

Welfare has had a negative image. The county almshouse and poor farm had a social stigma attached to them. The number of these institutions has greatly decreased since the passage of the Social Security Act in 1935. As urbanized social organization has come to dominate rural areas, social security protection has been extended to include farm operators and other rural people. Their acceptance of the program has been more enthusiastic than was anticipated.

Health and welfare provisions are an integral part of the total society, and their application is rapidly becoming universal for both rural and urban areas.

NOTES

1. Wilson G. Smillie, *Public Health Administration in the United States,* third edition (New York: The Macmillan Co., 1947).

2. Allen W. Freeman (ed.), *A Study of Rural Public Health Service* (New York: Commonwealth Fund, 1933).

3. Haven Emerson and Martha Luginbuhl, *Local Health Units for the Nation* (New York: Commonwealth Fund, 1945), p. 12.

4. Clyde F. Snider, *Local Government in Rural America* (New York: Appleton-Century-Crofts, Inc., 1957), p. 387; Clifford H. Greve, "Provisions of State Laws Governing Local Health Departments," *Public Health Reports,* 68 (Jan., 1953), 31–42.

5. J. H. Kolb and Edmund de S. Brunner, *A Study of Rural Sociology* (New York: Houghton Mifflin Co., 1935), pp. 540–71.

6. Liberty H. Bailey, *Cyclopedia of American Agriculture* (New York: The Macmillan Co., 1909), Editorial Note to Vol. I, Chapter 8.

7. John M. Gillette, *Constructive Rural Sociology* (New York: The Macmillan Co., 1913), p. 238.

8. Alvin L. Bertrand and Donald G. Hay, *Farmers' Expenditures for Health Care in 1955* (Washington: Agriculture Information Bulletin No. 191, Agricultural Marketing Service, U.S.D.A., 1958), p. 10.

9. *Ibid.*, p. 1.

10. Snider, *op. cit.*, p. 383.

11. Frederic D. Mott and Milton I. Roomer, *Rural Health and Medical Care* (New York: McGraw-Hill Co., Inc., 1948), pp. 151–92.

12. Edward Hassinger and Robert L. McNamara, *What's Happening to Rural Doctors and Health Facilities?* (Missouri Agricultural Experiment Station Bulletin 735, 1959).

13. John C. Belcher, *The Changing Distribution of Medical Doctors in Oklahoma* (Oklahoma Agricultural Experiment Station Bulletin B-459, 1955).

14. Clyde Hofstetter, "How Some Towns Get Doctors," *Town Journal*, 62 (Aug., 1955), 22–3.

15. Menton I. Roemer, "Rural Programs of Medical Care," *Annals of the American Academy of Political and Social Science*, 263 (Jan., 1951), 160–68; Mack I. Shanholtz, "Supplying Rural Virginia with Doctors," *State Government*, 28 (May, 1955), 105–6 and 117–18; Julia C. McCoy, "Mississippi's Medical Education Loan Program," *State Government*, 26 (Apr., 1953), 113–15 and 125.

16. Snider, *op. cit.*, p. 384.

17. Odin W. Anderson, "Private and Public Action in Meeting Health Needs," *Annals of the American Academy of Political and Social Science*, 337 (Sept., 1961), 57–69.

18. *Loc. cit.*

19. Odin W. Anderson, *National Family Survey of Medical Costs and Voluntary Health Insurance* (New York: Health Information Foundation, 1954).

20. Frank Van Dyke and Ray E. Trussell, "Voluntary Hospital Insurance as a Mechanism for Meeting Health Needs," *Annals of the American Academy of Political and Social Science*, 337 (Sept., 1961), 70–80; *Sourcebook of Health Insurance Data* (New York: Health Insurance Institute, 1960), p. 12.

21. D. G. Hay and C. H. Hamilton, *Acceptance of Voluntary Health Insurance in Four Rural Communities of Haywood County, North Carolina, 1953* (North Carolina Agricultural Experiment Station, Progress Report Rs-24, Department of Rural Sociology, 1954).

22. John M. Gillette, *Rural Sociology* (New York: The Macmillan Co., 1923), p. 106.

23. Clyde F. Snider, "The Fading Almshouse," *National Municipal Review,* 45 (Feb., 1956), 60–65.

24. "Effect of Social Security Program on Almshouses," *Monthly Labor Review,* 47 (Sept., 1938), 518–24; T. C. Philblad, "A Study of Missouri Alms Houses," *Southwestern Social Science Quarterly,* 19 (Sept., 1938), 201–10; Loula Dunn, "Status of County Almshouses in Alabama," *Public Welfare News,* 6 (Mar., 1938), 2–4; Violet M. Fischer, "Kansas County Homes after the Social Security Act," *Social Service Review,* 17 (Dec., 1943), 442–65; Raymond M. Hilliard, "The Emerging Function of Public Institutions in our Social Security Structure," *ibid.,* 20 (Dec., 1946), 479–93; Ellen C. Hotter, "State Responsibilities for the Care of the Chronically Ill," *State Government,* 19 (Feb., 1946), 39–42.

25. Snider, *op. cit.,* p. 423.

26. Anderson, "Private and Public Action in Meeting Health Needs," pp. 59–60.

27. Everett E. Peterson and Elton B. Hill, *Farm Families and Social Security* (North Central Regional Extension Publication No. 5, 1956).

28. Lowry Nelson, *Farm Retirement in Minnesota* (Minnesota Agricultural Experiment Station Bulletin 394, 1947).

29. Philip Taietz *et al., Adjustment to Retirement in Rural New York* (Cornell New York Agricultural Experiment Station Bulletin 919, 1956); see also Walter C. McKain, Jr., and Elmer D. Baldwin, *Old Age and Retirement in Rural Connecticut* (Connecticut Agricultural Experiment Station Bulletin 278, 1951); William H. Sewell *et al., Farmers' Conception and Plans for Economic Security in Old Age* (Wisconsin Agricultural Experiment Station Research Bulletin 182, 1953); T. Lynn Smith, "The Aged in Rural Society," in *The Aged and Society* (Chicago: Industrial Relations Research Association, 1950).

SELECTED READINGS

Anderson, Odin W. *National Family Survey of Medical Costs and Voluntary Health Insurance.* New York: Health Information Foundation, 1954.

Report of a survey of a national sample of families concerning their voluntary health insurance, with special emphasis on rural and urban areas.

Belcher, John C. *The Changing Distribution of Medical Doctors in Oklahoma.* Oklahoma Agricultural Experiment Station Bulletin B-459, 1955.

This analysis of trends in the distribution of medical practitioners in Oklahoma is primarily based on data from the *American Medical Directory.* It records the declining number of physicians in small towns.

Bertrand, Alvin L., and Donald G. Hay. *Farmers' Expenditures for Health Care in 1955.* Washington: Agricultural Information Bulletin No. 191, Agricultural Marketing Service, U.S.D.A., 1958.

Provides comprehensive information concerning health and medical care expenditures of farm families.

Friedson, Eliot, and Jacob J. Feldman. *Public Attitudes Toward Health Insurance.* New York: Health Information Foundation, 1958.

An important finding of this report, based on a cross-section of the American population, is that insurance was viewed more as economic protection than as health protection by a large segment of the population.

Hassinger, Edward, and Robert L. McNamara. *What's Happening to Rural Doctors and Health Facilities?* Missouri Agricultural Experiment Station Bulletin 735, 1959.

Again indicates the decline in doctors and medical facilities in rural areas.

Snider, Clyde F. "The Fading Almshouse," *National Municipal Review,* 45 (Feb., 1956), 60–65.

A brief article on the decline and change in function of the almshouse.

Taietz, Philip, *et al. Adjustment to Retirement in Rural New York.* Cornell: New York Agricultural Experiment Station Bulletin 919, 1956.

Research findings concerning the nature and meaning of retirement among people in six rural New York counties.

24 PARTICIPATION IN THE ARTS

Some form of art expression is found in all societies.[1] People in even the poorest, most primitive, or newest frontier societies do not devote all of their energy to the acquisition of food and shelter. Some attention is devoted to things of an aesthetic nature, even if this takes the form only of ornamenting functional objects or of chanting verse or song to the rhythm of work.

In spite of the widespread participation in art forms, it does not appear that art institutions have ever dominated human society. Often the folkways, mores, and structural patterns related to the arts are of such secondary concern in the total society that this form of human expression is not recognized as an institution. In fact, it is not uncommon for participation in the arts to form a subarea of various other institutions, for example, of religion, education, recreation, or politics.

Such general absence of structural norms in guiding art creativity and participation was evident in the United States. From colonial times through the nineteenth century, the arts have been secondary to economic and political institutions and to other areas of human organization considered more important in the pragmatic society.[2] Because of a minimum structuring of art norms, artists and the general public both have had a certain amount of freedom.[3] Practicing artists were given few guidelines to suggest the type of expression which would communicate to large numbers of people in society. Artists have been free to express themselves as they desired. But the creative arts are social and used by vast numbers of people when they are understood. When the forms of artistic expression are not understood and fail to communicate, they are of little value to society.[4] In some extreme cases, such as that of Dada, they may not be viewed as art at all.[5] Freedom of expression not accompanied by normative guidelines that reveal social functions often leads to anomie and frustration on the part of artists.[6]

SOCIAL STRUCTURE AND THE ARTS

The structure of art varies from one society to another. In some cases, women have been the creative artists, virtuosos in their work, while men seemed to achieve little aesthetic creativity. In other societies, men have been the artists. Among the California Indians, basket making was the principal art and defined as an occupational role appropriate only for women.[7] Also along the West Coast there were tribes of Indians who expressed their aesthetic creativity in woodworking, constructing such objects as boxes, kettles, buckets, cradles, totem poles, and houses. The division of labor defined such activity as appropriate for males. Decorative art applied to functional wooden objects was done by men, and creative activities of women were conspicuously lacking.

In seventeenth century Japan, a new social class characterized by moderate affluence emerged, the product of a long period of class struggle. This new class of merchants achieved a level of education and announced their status by their attendance of the Kabuki theatre, their familiarity with literature, and their enjoyment of the *Ukiyo-ye* school of art (original color prints). The subject of the *Ukiyo-ye* school was directed toward the developing market of the parvenu class. The style was popular, gay, and colorful. The form of expression was greatly innovative but well understood by its potential audience.[8]

In Tibetan society the normative patterns of art are structured within the Lamaist religious organization. Most Tibetan artists are monks who create works of art specifically for the religious order. The sacred text establishes the requirements for painters and furnishes the ideals of being holy, learned, charitable, and not too circumspect. These conditions for artistic expression, which are virtually absolute, preclude styles and periods of individuality which are found in European art.[9]

Social structures which encourage art collecting are of increasing importance in contemporary American society. People collect art for a variety of reasons. Social prestige is recognized as one of the rewards of collecting works of art, as collecting has become a mechanism for social mobility. Another purpose of art collecting is interior decoration. This is illustrated by the matron who wants two paintings of a stipulated size, compatible with the amount of wall space in her living room, framed in a wood to match other furnishings, and of a color to carry out the accents of the room. Further, there are collectors who are interested in the investment values of art. These individuals study the art market and the careers of young, developing artists to purchase compositions at minimal cost before the artist's reputation is established. Such collectors seek an opportunity to sell their purchases at a later date for several times the original cost. There are also those who collect for the deeper pleasures of intimately living with works of art.[10]

Collector clubs have been established at art museums. Their role is to encourage collecting, provide advice, and generally facilitate the acquisition of art. Art collecting has become a widespread practice, but structural guidelines have not been firmly established for this form of social participation. In times past, men of great wealth collected art avariciously and often were more possessed than possessors.[11] They were guided in their enterprise by the judgments of time. Others before them had collected the same items. One of the folkways of art collecting was the validation awarded a composition when it had the pedigree of having been in the collection of several famous men. The judgment of the most recent collector was less at stake, because previous collectors had in effect confirmed the validity and high quality of the work.

Most of the art of earlier centuries by now has found its way to relatively permanent places in art museums or art centers. The little which does remain available generally commands such a high price that most middle class citizens are scarcely potential collectors. On the other hand, art which is being created contemporaneously with the collector is more available and at a lower cost. Characteristically, such art has not been in the collection of others nor has it withstood the judgment of time. Therefore, it places the contemporary collector in the frustrating situation of having to expose his naked judgment in an otherwise mass society.[12]

The structure for collecting art is still elementary and developmental. The role of art in contemporary society is still indefinite. Hence, it remains unclear whether a particular form of expression—for example, figurative, impressionistic, cubist, constructivist, primitive, or realistic— will have a wider acceptability or market among the collecting population than some other form. When the *Ukiyo-ye* school of art developed in

Japan, the function of the art was relatively precisely defined. In this way, the ability of the artist to create a maximum number of readily acceptable compositions was facilitated.

HISTORIC DEVELOPMENT OF THE ARTS IN THE UNITED STATES

Development of the arts in the United States was guided by a rich European heritage, just as were other major areas of social life in the new nation. The decline of the ruralized social organization of the earlier Middle Ages was sharply contrasted in Europe with the advancement of the arts in the Renaissance, from which period so many of the works of the great masters came. Religious art, literature, and music of the late Middle Ages were gradually superseded by secular art expression. It was during this time of the advancement of the arts that colonial America was founded.

In the New World, however, the progress of the arts was seriously impeded for two major reasons. In the first place a new civilization was born in a land that was unknown to Europeans. Ideals of materialistic achievement were germane to agriculture and later to industrial organization. Consequently, the arts were subordinated to economic activity. This constituted a serious deterrent to artistic development. The second major complication in the development of art norms resulted from the negative attitude of many religious groups to artistic expression. This attitude was often expressed by extolling the value of simplicity of life rather than by formally attacking the arts.[13] Neither the economic nor the religious institutions conspired to do away with art. They only kept the development of art in this country to something considerably less than that of Renaissance Europe.

In America during the eighteenth century and the first half of the nineteenth, most art expression was associated with local craft and took the form of decoration of utilitarian items of life. The early patterns of art are variously called primitive, folk, or rural.[14] This early art form, according to Drepperd, was not a systematic movement or school. Most often it was the simple indigenous expression of a schoolboy, farm hand, blacksmith, sea captain, or some other rank and file citizen expressing an aesthetic idea in a crude way in the absence of systematic social structures in art.[15] It was a pioneer and amateur expression, generated in a society in which the social structures for other major institutions were primary ones to which the arts were subordinated.

Early American art was never a folk art in the European sense. Folk art in Europe was systematically expressed in a characteristic idiom, not as a stage in the history of the developmental processes of art. In America the artistic expression of the settlers was not systematic, nor was it that of a school structured by folkways and mores. Rather, it was a part of the general changing social milieu which was ultimately to contribute to urbanized social organization and the contemporary art schools. From 1650 to 1850, American art and craft expression was neither orthodox nor traditional. Many of the early Americans were escaping a folk tradition in Europe and, while certain motifs from the parent countries were utilized, there was no effort to reconstruct them in their totality or to respect the earlier tradition. Often reward was given for innovation and change.[16]

Throughout the first half of the nineteenth century, America was growing and expanding in population. There was a continual migration westward. With the need for furnishing millions of new homes, arts and crafts from furniture building, glass blowing, silvermaking to painting were widely developed as prosperous businesses. The cost of importing such objects was generally prohibitive. Consequently, the home market was expanded to fill the demands. Advertising art was widely used between 1800 and 1850 to accompany the development of transportation, manufacturing, and commercial activities. Paintings of the Hudson, Ohio, and Mississippi Rivers, of boats, canals, and summer resorts were not a primitive school of expression, but commercial art.[17]

Portrait painting became an important activity for the early limners. Artists discovered in the new nation a greater demand for portraits of Washington than for portraits of King George III in England.[18]

The structuring of the arts by educational tools and techniques was soon initiated. Henry Beachem's book, *Graphics: The Most Ancient and Excellent Art of Limning,* published in London in 1612, was probably the first instructional book to reach the American colonies. Pattern books used by women in making embroidery were brought by the earliest colonists. Such books are exemplified by *A Schole-house for the Needel* (London, 1624 and 1632) and *The Needles' Excellency* (London, 1634, 1636 and 1640).[19]

During the first half of the nineteenth century, instruction in the arts was sought by many Americans. Some books were published in America and others imported from Europe to meet this need for instruction. Dance, music, painting, drawing, and writing masters; teachers of stenciling, sign painting, decorating, singing, and acting migrated from area to area with considerable assurance of being able to conduct classes wherever they went.[20]

Art schools came to play prominent roles in New England and the Middle Atlantic States by the end of the eighteenth and the early nineteenth centuries. In the South, New Orleans was one of the leading centers for art activities prior to the Civil War.[21] Other art activities were found in Wisconsin as early as 1661. There was an art auction in Indiana in 1808, and one in San Francisco in 1859.

Theatrical developments have been a vital part of American history. The first play, "Ye Bare and Ye Cubb," was produced in 1665 by amateur players in Virginia. There was great objection to this production, and the players were prosecuted but acquitted.[22] Nevertheless, the shows went on, and the first American theater was constructed in Williamsburg in 1716. By the middle of the eighteenth century an American acting company was organized in Philadelphia. Related developments brought a company of players from England in 1752 and a permanent theater to Philadelphia in 1766. After the Revolution there were notable advances in the theater.

In the second half of the nineteenth century, and particularly after the Civil War, the character of the arts became generally more structured and grandiose. There were new advances in literature and the theme often centered on the West. By the 1880's, participation in the visual arts was sophisticated; collecting was avaricious and in European taste.[23] The New York Philharmonic Symphony Society, America's first professional orchestra, was organized in 1842. This was a forerunner of a profusion of symphony orchestras including the New York Symphony Society (1878) the Boston Symphony Orchestra (1881), the Chicago Symphony Orchestra (1891), and the Cincinnati Symphony Orchestra (1895).[24] Many other important symphony orchestras were established in the first quarter of the twentieth century; indeed, by this time the organized social institutions were deeply involved in art participation. The establishment of human relations in the arts as an integral part of urbanized society was facilitated by the absence of a clear and precisely developed rural art.

ART PARTICIPATION BY TOWN AND COUNTRY PEOPLE

Farm and nonfarm people both participate in some form of aesthetic expression. As urbanized society has grown out of ruralized society, there has been some basis for differentiating folk art from the so-called professional art, and associating the former with agrarian peasant peoples and the latter with urban industrial peoples. A widespread folk expression never developed in the arts of the United States. As the society has become urbanized, the number of professional artists has increased considerably, along with an increase of structural elements which guide both their training and creativity and the public in the utilization and understanding of their work. Parallel to this development, and at the same time forming a part of the general structure of art in society, there are numerous normative patterns which guide and promote the interests of amateur artists. Amateur art expression is a mechanism for extending appreciation of art. In terms of the ecological residence of most artists and the subject of their compositions, the professionals can most often be identified as urban. An urban-rural distinction here is not, however, precise. Its greatest utility is for the study and analysis of the developing art institution.

Professional artists are found in rural and urban areas, have come from both areas, and create compositions which reflect the idiom of both areas. In contrast, amateur artists can hardly be associated with an ecological area. Amateur art colonies have in their memberships both small-town and big-city people. In urbanized culture, with its vastly integrated systems of communication, amateur artists, regardless of their location, have a relatively sophisticated knowledge of the mainstreams of art. They frequently create compositions reflecting human conditions in areas remote from their location, as well as experiences in their immediate environment.

There has been much art expression which to some extent reflects a rural idiom: Beethoven's "Pastorale," Grofé's "Grand Canyon Suite," Grainger's "Country Gardens," Rodgers and Hammerstein's "Oklahoma!," Samuel F. Smith's "America," and Katherine Lee Bates's "America the Beautiful." At the other extreme, compositions which reflect urbanization themes are: the electronically [25] composed "Poème électronique" by Edgard Varèse, "Cough Music" by Richard Maxfield, the "Commuters' Special" by Beatrice P. Krone, and "Rolling Down the Highway" by Irving Wolfe.[26]

The extent of professional and amateur participation in the arts by people residing in urban and rural areas is not known. There are several specific social mechanisms which are designed to promote participation in the arts among people in small-town and rural areas. Twelve states, in addition to Puerto Rico, have specific programs for art participation by rural people. Several of the states include music and dramatics as well as painting and crafts.[27] Some states have employed specialized personnel through the Agricultural Institute and Agricultural Extension Service to promote the arts among rural people. In addition to this type of governmental support, there are many county and state fair art exhibitions. The structure of the fairs and their art shows is such that they tend to be relatively more rural than urban. These programs themselves are structures within the greater art institution of the urbanized nation. They implicitly, if not explicitly, provide a communication between amateur and professional participants in the art world.

Rural art in Minnesota: a case study. A profile of rural artists in Minnesota was constructed in 1959 by studying those amateurs who participated in the Institute of Agriculture's Annual Farm and Home Week Art Show.[28] The artists were predominately female (73 per cent). Over half of the male respondents (57 per cent) were in white collar occupations, 27 per cent professionals—most often in public school teaching. Sixty per cent of the females were housewives. The median number of school years completed by rural artists was twelve, compared to nine for the state and nation. The median income for those under age 65 was over $5,000. Over 72 per cent of these rural artists had received some training in art, ranging from almost none to some attendance at special art classes or art schools, college art training, high school art training, and a variety of correspondence courses. Most of the rural artists had some communication with the greater art community through visits to art museums and galleries. Forty per cent reportd visiting an art gallery or museum every other month, and only 6 per cent indicated they never visited art museums. Art magazines were less widely read by the amateur artists; only 15 per cent reported reading them. Over three-fourths of the artists believed most of their work should be classified as realistic, yet there was considerable interest in expressionistic, impressionistic, primitive, abstract, cubist, and surrealistic forms of art. The so-called "isms" of art were typically known to the rural artist and occasionally imitated.

Other organized participation in arts by rural people.[29] Participation in art by rural people in Wisconsin has reached a high point of organizational development. Art expression in pioneer Wisconsin was meager and limited. In recent years, rural Wisconsin residents have demonstrated an intensive interest in art. There has been a formal response to this interest in the provision of structural mechanisms to encourage and promote arts among the open-country and small-town people. The University of Wisconsin College of Agriculture in the 1930's recognized the desirability of extending its educational program beyond the usual courses. Efforts were made to extend the institute's educational program into literature, art, music, philosophy and history, to improve the character of rural living. One of the specific steps was the appointing of John Steuart Curry as artist in residence in 1936. He was provided a studio on the agricultural campus and contributed to the university's program of implementing the general appreciation of art.[30] The rural arts program in Wisconsin was further implemented by the appointment of a full-time extension specialist in art education who, with his staff, organizes and carries out art workshop programs throughout the various regions of the state, organizes local and regional art exhibitions, and contributes to the organization of an annual statewide rural art show. The rural art extension specialists have produced radio programs and a variety of other programs in response to particular local interests and needs.[31]

The Kansas State College art faculty for several years has maintained a program of bringing art appreciation and studio instruction to people in rural and urban areas throughout the state. The program is twofold, involving both appreciation and how-to-do-it courses.[32] It has become vital in a state in which only two cities have supported art museums. The program is, in effect, an agent of change, since its purpose is to broaden the horizons of people in rural communities beyond making a living or housekeeping. A large number of local art classes and some district art exhibitions by amateur artists have been organized. Another dimension is the picture-of-the-month program, in which local public libraries or schools receive paintings, borrowed from the university's permanent collection, which circulate on a round-robin schedule from one exhibition location to another. Paintings are shipped in specially prepared cases which form part of the frame when the front cover is removed. These pictures are accompanied by a descriptive catalogue.

The University of Arizona has inaugurated a program of taking the museum to the people of the Southwest.[33] The director of the University of Arizona Art Gallery and his staff carry on a program in the residence museum. In addition, they organize regular tours by which they bring original works of art to people throughout the states of Arizona, New Mexico, Utah, and in some cases to Mexico. Twenty tours a year are made to the rural areas by a station wagon loaded with original works of art. The art is exhibited in libraries or similar sites where previously scheduled classes meet for art appreciation lectures on the compositions. Lectures are organized in a series so that there is an opportunity to establish rapport with the participants, discover their state of knowledge and interest in the arts, and then, from time to time, continue to help them in expanding their interest and knowledge.

In South Dakota the organization of rural interests in the arts have been most advanced in the theater movement. Arvold founded the Little Country Theater movement in South Dakota early in the twentieth century.[34] The purpose of the Little Country Theater was to promote the production of plays by community people which they could stage in a country church basement, a rural school, or the sitting room of a farm home. This theater movement grew and stimulated a folklike theater interest among the rural people of the state. Performances proliferated and attendances have been over 10,000 at many of the plays and pageants. The theater has made pilgrimages across the state, which have been received with great success as rural people manifested their interest in live theater.[35]

In North Dakota an art program has been developing even in the face of an opposition which still grows out of its comparatively pioneer conditions.[36] Moreover, those who have manifested some interest in the arts have been largely discouraged by the lack of opportunities or faced with the necessity to migrate out of the state in pursuit of art. By the middle of the twentieth century, the state was experiencing new expressions of interest in art as a hobby, recreation, and means of relaxation. Magazines and newspapers in the area contained stories of art activities. The university's classes in painting and sculpture were filled to capacity, with groups of various ages from university students to grandparents. At the end of each school year, students organized an exhibition of art which they created as members of classes in the department. An annual art week exhibition is sponsored in Bismarck, where the attendance runs into the thousands. Fargo has had a Fine Arts Club. Art classes have been held in a number of other towns throughout the state. In rural North Dakota it is probable that by the middle of the century there were over a thousand individuals engaged in art activities.

Other manifestations of participation in the arts by open-country and small-town people have been observed from time to time. For example, a Beaux Arts Ball, modeled on the Paris event, has become the highlight of the social season in the corn country town of Davenport, Iowa. It is an extravagant social occasion on which bankers, merchants, farmers,

and persons of many other occupations enjoy a communitywide cele-
bration. Farmers are known to complete their evening chores as early as
possible in order to attend this annual costume ball.[37]

Others have reported the use of art as a means of financial adjustment
to retirement.[38] At the annual conference of the Institute of Gerontology
at the State University of Iowa in 1958, a farm woman stated her intention to use the money from the sale of her oil paintings as a supplement
to her retirement income. For many years she had participated in water-
color painting as a hobby, but in later life, due to complications of ar-
thritis, she had shifted to the painting of oils. As an amateur landscape
painter, she provided oil paintings largely on request. She exhibited at
fairs and local art shows, as well as providing a roadside display at her
farm produce stand.

PUBLICATIONS AND RURAL ART

There are a variety of publications associated with participation in the
rural arts. These include instructional bulletins, examples of which are
Creative Drawing [39] and *How To Mat and Frame Pictures*.[40] There are
numerous historical and quasihistorical reports on developments of arts
in small community areas, examples of which are *Theatrical Entertainments in Rural Missouri*,[41] *Rural Artists of Wisconsin*,[42] *Art in Red
Wing*,[43] and catalogues of the many rural art exhibitions. Finally, there are
various magazines or newsletters published by organizations of rural
artists, an example of which is the *Minnesota Rural Artists Association
Newsletter*.

SUMMARY

Aesthetic expressions have been continuous from colonial time to the
present in the United States. In the early period of colonial rural America,
the normative patterns of behavior of the arts had a minimum of structural guidance; indeed, they were not elevated to a position of institutional organization. Much of the early art expression was by rural people
and concerned rural living conditions; frequently, it expressed a rural
idiom. Historical evidence suggests, however, that the early art expression
was not a folk art in the sense of systematic type expression. In contrast,
it was typically the unstructured and impromptu expression of the people
to decorate the utensils used in daily living. During the nineteenth cen-

tury, participation in the arts was more structured and gradually became an integral part of urbanized social organization. By the later nineteenth and early twentieth century, two major forms of participation were established—the professional and the amateur.

Amateur participation in the arts has been more typical of people living in open-country and small-town areas. Colleges and institutes of agriculture, along with other organizations, have developed specific mechanisms to stimulate and promote participation in the arts.

NOTES

1. Franz Boas, *Primitive Art* (New York: Dover Publications, Inc., 1957).

2. Frederick P. Keppel and R. L. Duffus, *The Arts in American Life* (New York: McGraw-Hill Book Co., Inc., 1933); Melvin E. Haggerty, *Art, a Way of Life* (Minneapolis: The University of Minnesota Press, 1935); Elizabeth McCausland (ed.), *Work for Artists: What? Where? How?* (New York: American Artist Group, 1947).

3. Ernest P. Mundt, *Art, Form, and Civilization* (Berkeley: University of California Press, 1952).

4. William G. Haag, "The Arts That Survive," *Delta,* 11 (1957), 71-6.

5. Roy G. Francis and M. Lee Taylor, "Social Scientists Look at the Humanities," *Indian Journal of Social Research* (in press).

6. Mundt, *op. cit.*

7. Boas, *op. cit.,* pp. 18 ff.

8. J. Hillier, *Japanese Masters of Color Print: A Great Heritage of Oriental Art* (New York: Phaidon Publishers, Inc., 1954).

9. Jisl Lumir, *Tibetan Art* (London: Spring Books, 1960).

10. John I. H. Baur, "A B C for Collectors of American Contemporary Art," *Art in America,* 46 (Summer, 1950), 45-8.

11. Aline B. Saarinen, *The Proud Possessors: The Lives, Times and Tastes of Some Adventurous American Art Collectors* (New York: Random House, 1958).

12. M. Lee Taylor and Roy G. Francis, "Human Relations and the Visual Arts," *Indian Journal of Social Research,* 2 (July, 1961), 69-74.

13. Russell L. Lynes, *The Taste Makers* (New York: Harper and Brothers, 1955); Edward D. Andrews, "The Shaker Manner of Building," *Art in America,* 48 (No. 3, 1960), 38-45.

14. Carl W. Drepperd, *American Pioneer Arts and Artists* (Springfield, Mass.: The Pond-Ekberg Company, 1942); Nina F. Little, *The Abby Aldrich Rockefeller Folk Art Collection* (Boston: Little, Brown and Company, 1957); John T. Howard and

George K. Bellows, *A Short History of Music in America* (New York: Thomas Y. Crowell Co., 1957); Pitirim A. Sorokin, Carle C. Zimmerman, and Charles J. Galpin, *A Systematic Source Book in Rural Sociology* (Minneapolis: The University of Minnesota Press, 1931), II, Chapter 15.

15. Drepperd, *op. cit.*, pp. 2–3.

16. *Ibid.*, p. 143.

17. *Ibid.*, p. 8.

18. *Ibid.*, p. 15.

19. *Ibid.*, p. 13.

20. *Ibid.*, p. 6 *et seq.*

21. *Ibid.*, pp. 39–48.

22. Don Martindale, *American Society* (New York: P. Van Nostrand Co., Inc., 1960), p. 517.

23. Saarinen, *op. cit.*

24. John H. Mueller, *The American Symphony Orchestra: A Social History of Musical Taste* (Bloomington: Indiana University Press, 1951).

25. Spencer Klaw, "The Cultural Innovators," *Fortune*, 61 (Feb., 1960), 147 ff.

26. Irving Wolfe *et al.*, *Voices of America* (Chicago: Follett Publishing Co., 1958).

27. See mimeographed report by M. Lee Taylor, Jan. 25, 1960, University of Minnesota, Agricultural Experiment Station.

28. M. Lee Taylor and Gordon Bultena, "Minnesota's Rural Artists: Participants in the Farm and Home Week Art Show," *Sociology of Rural Life* (Minnesota Agricultural Experiment Station, Scientific Journal Series, No. 4208, 1959). See also A. Russell Barton, *Rural Art Shows: A Ten Year Review* (St. Paul: University of Minnesota, 1962).

29. Marjorie Patten, *The Arts Workshop of Rural America* (New York: Columbia University Press, 1937).

30. *John Steuart Curry: Artist of Rural Life* (University of Wisconsin, College of Agriculture, 1937).

31. John Rector Barton, *Rural Artists of Wisconsin* (Madison: University of Wisconsin Press, 1948).

32. Roman J. Verhallen, "We Bring Art to Kansas," *Bulletin of the National University Extension Association, Spectator*, 24 (Dec., 1958–Jan., 1959), 3 ff.

33. Adrienne Richard: "An Extramural Museum," *Art in America*, 48 (Summer, 1960), 89.

34. Alfred G. Arvold, *The Soul and the Soil* (New York: National Recreation Association, 1916).

35. A. G. Arvold, *The Little Country Theater* (Fargo, N. D.: A. G. Arvold, 1945).

36. Paul E. Barr, *North Dakota Artists* (Grand Forks: University of North Dakota Press, Library Studies No. 1, 1954).

37. "A Left Bank Shindig in Iowa," *Life* (Dec. 1, 1958), 145–6.

38. "Will Use Artistic Talent to Finance Retirement," *Adding Life to Years: Bulletin of the Institute of Gerontology,* 5 (Dec., 1958), State University of Iowa, Iowa City, Ia.

39. E. J. Tomasch, *Creative Drawing* (Kansas Engineering Experiment Station Bulletin, No. 87, 1960).

40. Ruth Davis, *How To Mat and Frame Pictures* (Wisconsin Agricultural Extension Service Circular 461, 1953).

41. Elbert R. Bowen, *Theatrical Entertainments in Rural Missouri* (Columbia: University of Missouri Press, 1959).

42. Barton, *op. cit.*

43. Laurence E. Schmeckebier, *Art in Red Wing* (Minneapolis: University of Minnesota Press, 1946).

SELECTED READINGS

Davis, Ruth. *How To Mat and Frame Pictures.* Wisconsin Agricultural Extension Service Circular 461, 1953.
   An instructional extension bulletin with illustrations and explanations concerning the normative patterns for displaying art.

Drepperd, Carl W. *American Pioneer Arts and Artists.* Springfield, Mass.: The Pond-Ekberg Co., 1942.
   A careful study of art activities in the early history of America, with special attention to instructional books, art teachers, genre painting, portraits, and folk art.

Patten, Marjorie. *The Arts Workshop of Rural America.* New York: Columbia University Press, 1937.
   A capable descriptive treatment of the various arts, including drama, theater, opera, music, hobbies, and crafts.

Schmeckebier, Laurence E. *Art in Red Wing.* Minneapolis: University of Minnesota Press, 1946.
   This monograph examines the use of art in a small community as it is found in home, church, and school architecture, in a library, theater, and window displays.

Sorokin, Pitirim A., Carle C. Zimmerman, and Charles J. Galpin. *A Systematic Source Book in Rural Sociology,* Vol. II. Minneapolis: University of Minnesota Press, 1931.
   Chapter 15 treats the subject of art and develops the thesis that rural and urban art are separate types.

Taylor, M. Lee, and Gordon Bultena. "Minnesota's Rural Artists," *Sociology of Rural Life.* Minnesota Agricultural Experiment Station, Scientific Journal Series No. 4208, 1959.

Report of an empirical investigation of the social characteristics of rural artists in Minnesota.

Taylor, M. Lee. "Participation in the Art World by Town and Country People," *Journal of Home Economics,* 52 (June, 1960), 421-4.

In this article, rural and amateur artists are viewed as a social structural foundation upon which to build art as a social institution.

Taylor, M. Lee, and Roy G. Francis. "Human Relataions and the Visual Arts," *Indian Journal of Social Research,* 2 (July, 1961), 69-74.

Outlines some of the major considerations which must go into research on the human relations of art.

AUTHOR INDEX

SUBJECT INDEX

Agribusiness: basic dimensions of, 211; concept of, 209; nature of, 210; organization of, 213; origin of, 205; vertical integration in, 219

Agribusiness, government's role in, 218; antitrust legislation, 219; policies, 217; research authority, 247; *see also* Agricultural development and stabilization agencies

Agribusiness labor force, 211

Agribusiness research, 218, 234; animal, 238; food, 244; government authority in, 247; new products, 244; plants, 241; private, 246; science in, 271; soil, 242

Agricultural development and stabilization agencies, 196; Commodity Exchange Authority, 197; Farmer's Home Administration, 199; Federal Crop Insurance Corporation, 198; Federal Extension Service, 197; Foreign Agricultural Service, 197

Agricultural engineers, 256

Agricultural Experiment Stations, 186; prior to federal support, 192

Agricultural Extension Service, 186

Agricultural journalism, 230, 232

Agricultural marketing, 262

Agricultural research service: advisory committees, 191; research policy, 190; research project systems, 191

Agricultural societies, 227

Agriculture: historical relationships with industry, 111; history of scientific applications in, 223

Art: collecting, 472; folk, 474; participation in by town and country people, 475; publications, 480; rural, 473; rural-urban shows, 477; and social structure, 471; supported by agricultural colleges, 478; theater movement, 475, 479

Automation, 260–61

Census of Agriculture, 214

Church: consolidation, 409; Federal Council of Churches, 408; frontier, 407; lakeside, 413–14; membership trends, 402; National Council of Churches, 404; in National Parks, 413; organization, 412; rural movement, 407; rural-urban distribution of members, 403; suburban, 412; town and country departments, 408

Clergy: characteristics of, 409; ministerial students, 410; multiple pastorate, 411; number in U. S. 1910–1950, 402

489